Imagining Transmedia

Imagining Transmedia

edited by Ed Finn, Bob Beard, Joey Eschrich, and Ruth Wylie

The MIT Press
Cambridge, Massachusetts
London, England

The MIT Press would like to thank the anonymous peer reviewers who provided comments on drafts of this book. The generous work of academic experts is essential for establishing the authority and quality of our publications. We acknowledge with gratitude the contributions of these otherwise uncredited readers.

This book was set in Stone Serif and Stone Sans by Westchester Publishing Services. Printed and bound in the United States of America.

Library of Congress Cataloging-in-Publication Data

Names: Finn, Ed, 1980– editor.
Title: Imagining transmedia / edited by Ed Finn, [and 3 others].
Description: Cambridge, Massachusetts : The MIT Press, 2024. | Includes
    bibliographical references and index.
Identifiers: LCCN 2023021142 (print) | LCCN 2023021143 (ebook) |
    ISBN 9780262547437 (paperback) | ISBN 9780262377515 (epub) |
    ISBN 9780262377508 (pdf)
Subjects: LCSH: Mass media—Technological innovations. | Digital media. |
    Intermediality. | Convergence (Telecommunication) | LCGFT: Essays.
Classification: LCC P96.T42 I43 2024 (print) | LCC P96.T42 (ebook) |
    DDC 302.23—dc23/eng/20231019
LC record available at https://lccn.loc.gov/2023021142
LC ebook record available at https://lccn.loc.gov/2023021143

10 9 8 7 6 5 4 3 2 1

Contents

Foreword: What We Mean by "Transmedia"

Henry Jenkins

Imagining Transmedia is an ambitious project involving interdisciplinary bridge-building between academic research and industry practice. Not surprisingly, much ink is spilled here on definitional questions, as participants explain how and why they use the term "transmedia." Readers should pay close attention to how each writer defines transmedia's boundaries or maps its relationship to other related terms (such as "cross-media," "cross-platform," "intertextuality," "multimodality," and "paratexts"). "Transmedia" literally means "across media," and it denotes a structured relationship of texts and practices that cut across multiple media. Elsewhere, Benjamin W. L. Derhy Kurtz and Mélanie Bourdaa (2017) use the term "transtexts" to refer to both commercial and fan works that interact together within a transmedia system, while others argue that there is no such thing as a "transmedia text" since the texts gain meaning only relationally. From that perspective, "transmedia" refers to a production strategy or an interpretive practice.

Given how expansive some theories of media are, we should not be surprised that writers differ over what constitutes a medium (McLuhan, 1964; Peters, 2015). "Transmedia" is less a noun than an adjective: it needs to modify something. In my own recent work (Jenkins, 2017), I talk about "storytelling," "learning," and "activism" as often overlapping logics describing the general aims of a particular transmedia project. How could we have a stable or even coherent definition of "transmedia," given the fact that we are discussing emerging and evolving practices within a media landscape that is itself always being reconfigured? These ambiguities have surrounded the concept from the start.

I should know. I am often called the "father of transmedia." I duck this label. I did not coin the term (Marsha Kinder may have, in 1993). I did not produce the first transmedia properties. And I was not the first to describe the new storytelling practices enabled by the convergence of media industries or new technology. Janet Murray (1997) cited the encyclopedic dimensions of digital narratives; Will Brooker (2001) discussed narrative "overflow"; Mimi Ito (2005) described the "hypersocial" dimensions of the Japanese "media mix"; Frank Rose (2008) spoke about "the art of immersion"; and P. David Marshall (2002) documented "intertextual commodities"—all alternative ways of framing aspects of transmedia entertainment and branding. I entered an existing conversation, discussed a known phenomenon, and applied an existing term, and somehow it stuck.

Consider Marsha Kinder's use of "transmedia intertextuality" in her 1993 book *Playing with Power in Movies, Television, and Video Games: From Muppet Babies to Teenage Ninja Turtles.* She describes children's media properties as constituting an entertainment supersystem:

> A supersystem is a network of intertextuality structured around a figure or group of figures from pop culture . . . In order to be a supersystem, the network must cut across several modes of image production; must appeal to diverse generations, classes, and ethnic subcultures, who in turn are targeted with diverse strategies; must foster "collectability" through a proliferation of related products; and must undergo a sudden increase in commodification, the success of which reflexively becomes a "media event" that dramatically accelerates the growth curve of the system's commercial success. (122–123)

Rereading Kinder's book today, what's striking is the relative absence of "storytelling" or "worldbuilding," concepts that are central to contemporary transmedia studies. Her focus was on how transmedia characters assume new roles, adapt to new markets, address diverse audiences, and appear in shifting configurations.

My 2006 book *Convergence Culture: Where Old and New Media Collide* reworked Kinder's definition in some important ways: "Transmedia storytelling represents a process where integral elements of a fiction get dispersed systematically across multiple delivery channels for the purpose of creating a unified and coordinated entertainment experience. Ideally, each medium makes its own unique contribution to the unfolding of the story." Discussing The Matrix rather than a children's media franchise, I explored how the practices that Kinder associated with entertainment supersystems were deployed for adults. Where Kinder saw consumers, I saw participants, whose activity minimally involved tracking down and consolidating information found dispersed across multiple media or platforms and might more broadly involve various creative projects where audience members remade, reimagined, and redistributed that content. Pushing beyond critiques of media concentration, I recognized the creative value of transmedia practices in the service of storytelling and entertainment. A core tension in transmedia entertainment is that it is simultaneously a marketing strategy motivated by configurations of corporate ownership and a creative strategy growing out of the ambitions of media-makers to tell more complex stories on a larger canvas.

Convergence Culture made the case for a comparative media studies approach to studying the increased entanglements of media industries, technologies, and audiences in a world where new media platforms were enabling audiences to act upon mass media content in a more participatory and public manner. I stressed dispersal as a central dynamic of how modern media operated—every story, image, sound, and relationship would ultimately play itself out across every available platform; audiences wanted the content they wanted, when and where they wanted it, and were prepared to spread content illegally if it was not available legally. Content—often defined as "that which is contained"—doesn't really capture this situation. Transmedia assets are anything but contained in contemporary culture. All media produced today follows a transmedia logic, loosely speaking, but I used "transmedia" to narrowly refer to an intentional, coordinated strategy for spreading story elements across multiple media platforms.

Convergence Culture juxtaposed The Matrix as a mass-media franchise with a range of other then-emerging examples, including Haxan Films' promotion of *The Blair Witch Project*, the CW's "Dawson's Desktop" project, and *The Beast*, an alternate reality game linked to the release of the film *A.I. Artificial Intelligence*. Here, the juxtaposition of cases via sidebars substituted for developing a more coherent picture of the boundaries of transmedia storytelling. Transmedia might describe examples that are more or less structured in terms of the flow of narrative information, more or less centralized in their production practices, more or less bounded in terms of what constitutes an element within the system, more or less participatory in terms of the behavior expected from the audience, more or less hierarchical in terms of whose contributions to the story are canonical, and more or less redundant in terms of how much overlap or repetition exists across different instances.

We can understand these distinctions more clearly if we consider the example of Marvel. In the early 1960s, Marvel deployed "radical intertextuality" across their superhero comic books: characters crossed boundaries between individual titles and interacted; publisher-wide events periodically intersected every comic book series that Marvel produced. Here were many of the worldbuilding properties associated with transmedia practices, but they did not yet involve movement across multiple media. With the launch of the Marvel Cinematic Universe (MCU), the company's intertextual practices were applied to a large-scale project involving dozens of feature films, some introducing individual characters, some bringing them together, all shaping our collective response to these characters and situations. Marvel's entertainment supersystem now unfolded across multiple media, though only limited efforts were made to coordinate across them: shared characters but contradictory representations. Today, the launch of Disney+ as a distribution channel and Disney's consolidation of transmedia rights has enabled a new strategy to introduce developments through television series, such as *Wandavision* or *Loki*, that have repercussions within the cinematic universe. Only now do Marvel's production practices fully meet my original transmedia definition, though much can be learned about transmedia logics by looking at Marvel's evolving strategies.

One lesson that we can take from Marvel has to do with its mechanisms for educating and orienting its fans: step by gradual step, they introduced new characters, expanded the spaces where stories could take place, developed universe-expanding conflicts, and added new media to the mix. With each step along the way, they developed content that was accessible to new viewers but rewarded the mastery of hard-core fans. As they have brought more assets under their control, they have expanded into other media, incorporating them into their canon only after they have educated the audience for what comes next. The new Disney+ shows are designed to introduce new villains and explain the logic of the multiverse before it is introduced into the more costly big-screen extensions. Educators might well study the process of exposition, elaboration, and extension that has ensured the accessibility and thus success of what otherwise might be an unwieldy fictional realm. And we should acknowledge that some critics of the genre are fundamentally illiterate in terms of the skills needed to appreciate and understand a contemporary superhero franchise, further suggesting the way learning occurs within the MCU.

In Hollywood franchises, top priority is given to the "mothership" (the feature film, the television series, or perhaps the video game—wherever peak capital outlay and major profits are centered), and all other media instances are called "promotional" or "ancillary." Independent artists, working with limited budgets and thus incurring lower costs, mostly release digitally distributed media texts, which provide greater equivalence among all the pieces within a particular project. This distinction between indie media on the East Coast and Hollywood franchising on the West Coast, introduced by Brian Clark (2011), has led me to consider other media ecologies that are generating transmedia stories. The Wachowskis' decision to stage The Matrix saga across multiple media was informed by Japan's much older media mix strategies that reflected the different structures of media production, intellectual property ownership, and fan practices in Tokyo. Countries with public-service media structures (such as the European Union) or those where state subsidies have driven the adoption of transmedia strategies (such as Canada and Brazil) stress education, diversity, or cultural enrichment goals rather than entertainment and promotion.

The transmedia concept was embraced by other groups for their own reasons. Reflecting this book's focus, I am going to focus on transmedia learning and transmedia activism/organizing.

In a 2006 white paper for the MacArthur Foundation, *Confronting the Challenges of Participatory Culture*, my coauthors and I identified "transmedia navigation"—"the ability to follow the flow of stories and information across multiple modalities" (4)—as a primary new literacy that young people needed to acquire in order to meaningfully participate in the new media landscape. Here, we drew on the more expansive concept of media convergence rather than a narrower definition. All future research would require students to trace and assess information across multiple platforms.

My use of the term "multiple modalities" connected transmedia practice with discussions among learning scientists, inspired by the work of Gunther Kress (2003), regarding the ways that textbooks deployed multiple modes of representation, including maps, graphs, charts, photographs, cartoons, and boxed texts. Each mode has its own affordances, its own strategies for producing and organizing knowledge. Kress argues that this tendency toward multimodality changes how we teach because students must learn to make meaningful choices among different possible modes of expression and determine which is most effective in reaching their audience and communicating their message. Kress advocates "design literacy," or what others called "multiliteracies" (New London Group, 2000), as the basic expressive competency of the modern era. Others linked transmedia practices with Howard Gardner's concept of "multiple intelligences" (1983), the idea that different children lean on different cognitive and sense mechanisms as they process new information. Spreading information across multiple media might increase opportunities for students with learning biases to master the material.

In *T Is for Transmedia*, Becky Herr-Stephenson, Meryl Alper, and Erin Reilly (2013) stressed the learning activities—informal or formal—that take place around a transmedia franchise: "The multi-modal, multi-sited nature of many transmedia productions challenge children to use varied textual, visual, and media literacy skills to decode and remix media elements. In these ways, the active, ongoing, creative engagement with complex stories required of participants in a transmedia play experience stands in contrast to the routine, decontextualized learning that, unfortunately, all too often characterizes children's experiences in school" (10).

Transmedia models were quickly incorporated into a larger movement toward games-based learning, informed by concepts such as James Paul Gee's suggestion that educational design more generally should be drawing on principles of good game design (Gee, 2003) and examples such as Sasha Barab's *Frankenstein* project (Barab et al., 2010), Laura Fleming's *Inanimate Alice* (2013), or Jean Begeal and Lance Weiler's *Robot Heart Stories* (Jenkins, 2012). Fleming (2013), a school library literacy specialist, was among the first to write about "transmedia learning," defined as "the application of storytelling techniques combined with the use of multiple platforms to create an immersive learning landscape which enables multivarious entry and exit points for learning and teaching. . . . [resulting in] a landscape for learning that has few, if any, boundaries" (371). Fleming continues, "With philosophical underpinnings in constructivist and connectivist theories, a transmedia pedagogy uses technology in an integrated way that allows learners and content to flow seamlessly across media platforms. . . . Transmedia techniques, when responsibly and effectively applied in an educational context, immerse students in their own learning and, as a happy corollary, advance media literacy education for all" (371). Here, transmedia is understood as something that requires active processing—something we do, rather than something that we consume.

Transmedia learning advocates also saw transmedia worldbuilding as an entry into systems thinking (Pendleton-Jullian and Seely Brown, 2018). The production designer and educator Alex McDowell offered this definition: "World building is a design/storytelling practice that combines rigorous scientific inquiry with humanistic values to create the entire context—the world—that surrounds a problem or question. This deeply contextualized exploration allows us to reach unforeseen, fresh, deeply satisfying and tangible solutions that can be tested and made manifest in both virtual and real worlds" (Jenkins, 2015). McDowell's claims for the multidisciplinary nature of worldbuilding paralleled claims made for games as a learning environment by the game designer Will Wright almost a decade earlier: "The best games will probably be very interdisciplinary and cross all these boundaries. The chemistry teacher will like a little segment of it or the history teacher will like a little segment, and the kid going through there will be motivated by the different aspects. It's very hard to package a really compelling experience into one disciplinary boundary" (Jenkins, 2006). Combine these various claims, and it is easy to see how transmedia learning was situated at a vital intersection between significant pedagogical trends—multimodality, multiliteracies, multiple intelligences, constructivism, games-based learning, simulation and visualization, systems and design-thinking—which have shaped educational debates in the early twenty-first century.

Something similar has been taking place around the concept of transmedia activism. The documentary producer Lina Srivastava was among the first to advocate transmedia activism—"the coordinated co-creation of narrative and cultural expression by various constituencies who distribute that narrative in various forms through multiple platforms, the result of which is to build an ecosystem of content and networks that engage in community-centered social action" (Jenkins, 2016). Not unlike McDowell, she felt that transmedia models offered great tools for depicting systems rather than being restricted to individual perspectives in telling the story. Srivastava was one of a number of collaborators who developed Priya Shakti, a transmedia awareness campaign in India that called attention to sexual violence against women. The campaign included the use of comics, street art, and augmented reality apps, among other tools. Dan Goldman (personal conversation), the comics artist on the team, suggests that some of Priya Shakti's strategies, particularly the cutting-edge use of augmented reality, were less effective at reaching the low-income and lower-caste audience toward which the campaign was directed, even if they generated much media coverage and interest from the donors. He now argues for transmedia activists to break more fully with entertainment-based models and ground themselves in the concept of appropriate technologies, choosing tools that are small-scale, affordable by locals, decentralized, labor-intensive, energy-efficient, environmentally sound, and locally autonomous.

Writing about the immigrant rights movement, Sasha Costanza-Chock (2014) argues that transmedia approaches encourage more participatory and less hierarchical forms of politics. These approaches are often described as "leaderless," though they might also be called "leaderful" since leadership is dispersed and all members help to articulate the movement's core message through whatever media skills and access they can tap. Costanza-Chock describes "transmedia organizing" as "how savvy community organizers engage their movement's social base in participatory media-making practices. Organizers can push participatory media into wider circulation across platforms, creating public narratives that reach and involve diverse audiences. When people are invited to contribute to a broader narrative, it strengthens their identification with the movement, and over the long run increases the likelihood of successful outcomes" (47).

In our own research on participatory politics (Jenkins et al., 2016), we have found that young activists think almost instinctively in transmedia terms, recognizing the flow of stories, sounds, and images across media platforms as part of life in the twenty-first century. Rather than maintaining centralized control, they urge movement participants to produce media that tells their own stories and contributes to larger political narratives—for example, young Dreamers producing YouTube videos where they come out as undocumented within their own communities of interest. Young activists also stress their limited opportunity to tell their own stories through mass media, and thus the need to deploy whatever grassroots tools will give them access. They spread their message "by any media necessary," an approach that stresses more open-ended, less tightly structured, and more participatory forms of transmedia practice. Emilia Yang, one of my PhD students, has coproduced a collective memory project, AMA y No Olvida (https://www.museodelamemorianicaragua.org), in her native Nicaragua, where victims of governmental terror and trauma collaborate to tell their stories and commemorate lost family members across platforms. Such communication is precarious under autocratic regimes, always subject to potential censorship or repercussions, but also mobile, able to crop up somewhere else, as needed, to evade state constraints.

Our current focus on civic imagination (Jenkins et al., 2020) explores ways that young activists increasingly frame political change in a vernacular drawn from popular culture. Figures such as superheroes, zombies, or wizards, often from transmedia franchises, are immediately recognized by their peers and can create awareness around topics that might be less accessible when put in more conventional political language. Our research team also uses worldbuilding to conduct civic imagination workshops with groups ranging from mosques to labor halls, from preschoolers to senior citizens. These workshops encourage participants to imagine the ideal world of 2060, to construct narratives of change that might make a better future possible, to remix inspirational stories, and to share memories through showcasing beloved objects, among other practices (Peters-Lazaro and Shresthova, 2020). Embracing a "by any media necessary" approach, we encourage participants to use whatever media resources are at hand to depict imagined social change.

This turn toward transmedia as a political tool has significant ethical implications. One challenge grows out of more centralized and commercial models. Insofar as concentrated media ownership limits who gets to tell their stories, the focus of more resources on a narrower range of big blockbusters and transmedia franchises has a corrupting effect on the popular imagination. Disney now has a near-monopoly on the foundational stories for children and youth. Such megacorporations amplify and accelerate the spread of their stories across the planet. So, what ethical standards do these transmedia producers apply in deciding which stories to tell and how?

Other challenges may surface around more independent media production. I've already cited Dan Goldman's questions about the use of appropriate technologies and the co-creation of content with the communities addressed by awareness campaigns. The game designer and theorist Mary Flanagan (2013) has raised questions about the unintended consequences that arise when people choose to play out their fantasies in public spaces where others are conducting their lives, especially in a context of gross class inequalities (e.g., hipster gamers intersecting with the housing insecure) or inappropriate behaviors (e.g., the disruption of graveyards or Holocaust sites by people playing *Pokémon Go*).

A third challenge reflects more participatory models of transmedia production. Consider, for example, the destructive impact of the QAnon movement on American political culture. The HBO documentary *Q: Into the Storm* offers a rich account of the mechanisms by which this conspiracy theory has spread across the culture, starting with an inner circle of posters who self-identified as "Q" and conducted information drops onto fringe discussion boards. Another level of interpreters, using YouTube, podcasts, and blogs, deciphered Q's cryptic messages, making significant contributions to the community's lore and spreading its themes. The news media picked up on local participants displaying Q-related artifacts (such as protest signs); political leaders such as US president Donald Trump retweeted QAnon messages; and, ultimately, participants acted upon this disinformation and misinformation, sometimes with horrific effects (ranging from local shootings to the US Capitol insurrection). The mechanisms that mobilized QAnon followers resemble those deployed in alternate reality games, but they also follow those that Costanza-Chock associated with transmedia organizing. These mechanisms displace the role of gatekeepers, for better or for worse, resulting in the mutual production and dispersal of conspiracy thinking and greater skepticism toward efforts to debunk them. "Q" (whoever they may be) provided the raw materials of the movement, but it is through its interpreters, followers, and other participants that QAnon made its impact.

Imagining Transmedia's contributors situate themselves in relation to these and other alternative definitions. They deploy transmedia principles toward diverse ends, toward diverse audiences, and in diverse disciplinary domains. Some produce transmedia, some study it, and most do a bit of both. As you read these accounts, pay attention to what the writers mean by "transmedia" and why they are tapping its affordances. Definitions are still hotly debated, even though most have embraced a more fluid and expansive vocabulary. I hope that, by tracing some of what has come before, readers can better appreciate where we are at in understanding and deploying transmedia as a resource for building a better world for all of us.

References

Barab, Sasha A., Tyler Dodge, Adam Ingram-Goble, Patrick Pettyjohn, Kylie Peppler, Charlene Volk, and Maria Solomou. 2010. "Pedagogical Dramas and Transformational Play: Narratively Rich Games for Learning." *Mind, Culture, and Activity* 17, no. 3: 235–264.

Brooker, Will. 2001. "Living on *Dawson's Creek*: Teen Viewers, Cultural Convergence, and Television Overflow." *International Journal of Cultural Studies* 4, no. 4: 456–472.

Clark, Brian, 2011. "Reclaiming Transmedia Storyteller." Facebook, May 2, 2011, http://www.facebook.com/note.php?note_id=10150246236508993.

Costanza-Chock, Sasha. 2014. *Out of the Shadows, Into the Street: Transmedia Organizing and the Immigrant Rights Movement*. Cambridge, MA: MIT Press.

Derhy Kurtz, Benjamin W. L., and Mélanie Bourdaa, eds. 2017. *The Rise of Transtexts: Challenges and Opportunities*. London: Routledge.

Flanagan, Mary. 2013. *Critical Play: Radical Game Design*. Cambridge, MA: MIT Press.

Fleming, Laura. 2013. "Expanding Learning Opportunities with Transmedia Practices: *Inanimate Alice* as an Exemplar." *Journal of Media Literacy Education* 4, no. 2 (2013): 370–377.

Gardner, Howard. 1983. *Frames of Mind: The Theory of Multiple Intelligences*. New York: Basic Books.

Gee, James Paul. 2003. *What Video Games Can Teach Us about Literacy and Learning*. New York: Palgrave-McMillan.

Herr-Stephenson, Becky, and Meryl Alpert, with Erin Reilly. 2013. *T Is for Transmedia: Learning through Transmedia Play*. New York: Joan Ganz Cooney Center/Annenberg Innovation Lab.

Ito, Mimi. 2005. "Technologies of Childhood Imagination: Yugioh, Media Mixes and Everyday Cultural Production." In *Structures of Participation in Digital Culture*, edited by Joe Karaganis and Natalie Jeremijenko, 44–67. Durham, NC: Duke University Press.

Jenkins, Henry. 2006a. *Convergence Culture: Where Old and New Media Collide*. New York: New York University Press.

Jenkins, Henry. 2006b. "From Serious Games to Serious Gaming," *Confessions of an Aca-Fan*, November 9, 2006. https://henryjenkins.org/blog/2006/11/from_serious_games_to_serious.html.

Jenkins, Henry. 2012. "On Transmedia and Education: A Conversation with Robot Heart Stories' Jen Begeul and Inanimate Alice's Laura Fleming," *Confessions of an Aca-Fan*, January 27, 2012. http://henryjenkins.org/blog/2012/01/on_transmedia_and_education.html.

Jenkins, Henry. 2015. "World-Building as a New Media Literacy: A Conversation between Alex McDowell and Henry Jenkins." *Journal of Media Literacy* 62, no. 1–2: 11–18.

Jenkins, Henry. 2016. "Telling Stories: Lina Srivastava Talks about Transmedia Activism." *Confessions of an Aca-Fan*, January 19, 2016. http://henryjenkins.org/blog/2016/01/telling-stories-lina-srivastava-talks-about-transmedia-activism-part-one.html.

Jenkins, Henry 2017. "Transmedia Logics and Locations." In *The Rise of Transtexts: Challenges and Opportunities*, edited by Benjamin W. L. Derhy Kurtz and Melanie Bourdaa, 220–240. London: Routledge.

Jenkins, Henry, with Katie Clinton, Ravi Purushotma, Alice J. Robison, and Margaret Weigel. 2006. *Confronting the Challenges of Participatory Culture: Media Education for the 21st Century*. Chicago: MacArthur Foundation.

Jenkins, Henry, Sangita Shresthova, Liana Gamber-Thompson, Neta Kligler-Vilinchek, and Arely Zimmerman. 2016. *By Any Media Necessary: The New Youth Activism*. New York: New York University Press.

Jenkins, Henry, Gabriel Peters-Lozaro, and Sangita Shresthova, eds. 2020. *Popular Culture and the Civic Imagination: Case Studies of Creative Social Change*. New York: New York University Press.

Kinder, Marsha. 1993. *Playing with Power in Movies, Television, and Video Games: From Muppet Babies to Teenage Mutant Ninja Turtles*. Berkeley: University of California Press.

Kress, Gunther. 2003. *Literacy in the New Media Age*. New York: Routledge.

Laurel, Brenda. 2001. *Utopian Entrepreneur*. Cambridge, MA: MIT Press.

Marshall, P. David. 2002. "The New Intertexual Commodity." In *The New Media Book*, edited by Dan Harries, 69–82. London: British Film Institute.

McLuhan, Marshall. 1964. *Understanding Media: The Extensions of Man*. New York: McGraw-Hill.

Murray, Janet. 1997. *Hamlet on the Holodeck: The Future of Narrative in Cyberspace*. Cambridge, MA: Free Press.

New London Group. 2000. "A Pedagogy of Multiliteracies: Designing Social Futures." In *Multiliteracies: Literacy Learning and the Design of Social Futures*, edited by Bill Cope and Mary Kalantzis, 9–38. London: Routledge.

Pendleton-Jullian, Ann, and John Seely Brown. 2018. "Worldbuilding." In *Design Unbound: Designing for Emergence in a White Water World, Volume 2: Ecologies of Change*. Cambridge, MA: MIT Press.

Peters, John Durham. 2015. *The Marvelous Clouds: Toward a Philosophy of Elemental Media*. Chicago: University of Chicago Press.

Peters-Lozaro, Gabriel, and Sangita Shresthova. 2020. *Practicing Futures: A Civic Imagination Action Handbook*. New York: Peter Lang.

Rose, Frank. 2008. *The Art of Immersion: How the Digital Generation Is Remaking Hollywood, Madison Avenue and How We Tell Stories*. New York: W.W. Norton and Company.

Introduction to *Imagining Transmedia*

Ed Finn, Bob Beard, Joey Eschrich, and Ruth Wylie

What Is Transmedia?

Depending on how you count, "transmedia" is entering its third, or fourth, or fifth decade as a critical term. As some authors in this collection argue, the practices may extend back much further, to Shakespeare and the Globe Theatre, or perhaps all the way to prehistory and the original storytellers weaving reality and narrative together around the campfire. Its scholarly roots date back to early work on propaganda and mass communication, during and after World War II, from writers as diverse as Hannah Arendt (1951) and Vannevar Bush (1946), Marshall McLuhan's writings on media theory in the 1960s (cf. 1964), and the emergence of new media theory in the 1990s and 2000s popularized by Janet Murray (1998), Lev Manovich (2001), N. Katherine Hayles (cf. 2008), and many others. Today, transmedia occupies a busy intellectual intersection between literary and textual studies, epistemology, archival research, public history, communications, and perhaps a dozen other fields—an idea with a large and boisterous intellectual family. As a critical concept in its own right, transmedia grew to prominence in the 2000s as a way to grapple with an increasingly saturated, polysemous media environment, where audiences became collaborators and more stories began to spill across the boundaries of medium, platform, community, and that contested borderland between fiction and reality.

This book takes aim not at the critical landscape of transmedia theory but at the phenomenon itself, asking what relevance transmedia has today when almost every cultural act involves transmedial creation, collaboration, and transmission. We approach transmedia as a set of practices of textual production, community orchestration, and narrative design—as well as practices of interpretation, collective meaning-making, and collaborative learning—rather than as a strictly bounded category of texts (Dena, 2009; Costanza-Chock, 2014; Kurtz and Bourdaa, 2016). These acts take place in both corporate and community venues, engaging many modes of story-telling and diverse politics of identity, participation, and collective action (Wolf, 2014; Hassler-Forest, 2016; Guynes and Hassler-Forest, 2017; Kinder and MacPherson, 2021). Transmedia practices long predate the emergence of the critical term, and they build on rich traditions of storytelling across media and time (Scolari, Bertetti, and Freeman, 2014).

The multiplicity and complexity of our shared stories have expanded tremendously over these same decades. The culture of media has evolved in step with our changing technologies of connection and interaction, from smartphones and algorithmic filters to ubiquitous computing and the growing tranche of personal information that each of us deposits online (whether intentionally or not). Today's media ecosystem is dominated by multitudes of niche networks and programming, the expansion of major brands and intellectual properties to emerging platforms, and burgeoning experiments in mixed reality everywhere, from theme parks to car dealer-ships to backyard Pokémon hunts (Giddings, 2017; Evans, 2011). The land-scape is so crowded and confusing that perhaps the real question is: what *isn't* transmedia?

Despite this veneer of utter novelty in the digital age, however, these practices that link disparate texts, diverse groups of people, and variegated modes of engagement, encoding, and decoding grow from, and build upon, a foundation of popular practice, textual production and reception, and scholarly inquiry across disciplinary lines. Scholars like Kittler (1990) and Hayles (2008) bring transmedial perspectives to predigital forms of author-ship and information storage, while historians like Robert Darnton and Daniel Roche illuminate the essential role of media ecologies in shaping world-historical events like the French Revolution (Darnton and Roche, 1989). The fields of public history and digital humanities have also engaged substantially in this notion of transmedia practice, inviting broad public participation in projects to document, curate, and annotate materials as diverse as fragments from a medieval Egyptian synagogue or the impact of railroads on the American West (Scribes of the Cairo Geniza, 2017; White, 2012). While contemporary digital tools have empowered new kinds of pub-lic engagement and collaboration, projects like this also highlight how richly mediated human history has been for centuries, even when the particulars and practices of our ancestors are difficult to interpret retrospectively.

In the academy, "transmedia" became a keyword in a number of related fields, including media studies, cultural studies, literature, public history, informal learning, communications, and journalism. Each of these schools of thought puts transmedia to its own uses, as a mechanism for consumerism or collective action, avant-garde expression or corporate hegemony, novel identity formations or the iteration of long-established imagined communities. This was brought home to the editors of this volume when Ed Finn was asked to organize a panel on transmedia for the National Science Foundation (NSF)'s biannual meeting for the Advances in Informal STEM Learning conference. The participants in that session spanned executives at major public television studios, science communicators, literary scholars, and learning scientists, and they brought intellectual frames that ranged from marketing to acoustic ecology to our discussion about the practice and value of transmedia today.

As that cross-section of public humanities, informal learning, and commercial media suggests, the stakes of this question extend beyond the academy. In the commercial realm, transmedia narrative tactics that seemed complicated and expensive in the 1990s, achievable only by global corporations like Microsoft or Disney, are now simply expected: fictional characters have social media accounts and every new intellectual property (IP) seems to come with limited-run podcasts, companion comic books, and apps that reveal additional lore and narrative context. Creators work in a world where such transmedia practices are everyday aspects of marketing, and any successful project needs to deploy its narrative hooks across multiple media and platforms to be legible in this environment. In part, this is because so much of our cultural infrastructure has been rebuilt in digital media: maps, phone books, and newspaper ads have been subsumed into the folds of behemoths like Google, Apple, and Facebook, such that even basic facts about what exists in the world are immediately filtered through the transmedia lens of, say, a map application that pops up star ratings, user comments, and location-based ads.

It turns out that the arrival of virtual and augmented reality is finally being achieved not so much to create new experiences of fictional universes but rather to project digital capitalism into our living rooms. The power to command attention and encourage audiences to buy into particular corporate-dominated media ecosystems is increasingly wielded by a small number of hyperempowered global conglomerates, projecting a narrow worldview determined by disproportionately White, cisgender, heterosexual, male economic elites.

At the same time—to some extent as a result of the totalizing hegemony of tech-led "platform capitalism" (Srnicek, 2016)—the tools for transmedia production and consumption have never been so accessible and affordable, although many people across nations and regions still lack access to digital tools (van Dijk, 2020). The case studies in this book demonstrate how civic-minded and grassroots efforts to harness the power of transmedia storytelling, from health care and K–12 classrooms to tabletop role-playing game (TTRPG) communities and independent theater troupes, are flourishing in the interstices between our stultifying experiences with algorithmic governance and the seemingly endless combinatorial outputs of big-media universes, from Star Wars and Marvel to Harry Potter and the Disney princesses.

This book does not present one answer to the question "What is transmedia?" but it does have a point of view. First, as a critical term, "transmedia" is still valuable because it describes a form of mediation that now encompasses more or less every cultural expression that engages the digital. As the transmedia practitioner Andrea Phillips wrote in 2016, "The genie is out of the bottle." Transmedia is no longer visible as a distinct genre or area of artistic practice because its techniques now inform projects in many fields, from virtual reality (VR) and augmented reality to immersive theater and social media. Responding to Phillips, the communications scholar and transmedia practitioner Ramona Pringle (2016) argues, "Where transmedia was once an option, now it is a necessity. A way of life."

Second, transmedia is an important frame for describing a school of practice, a set of techniques and tactics for worldbuilding, engagement, and epistemological framing that have become so pervasive as to be invisible. As our media have evolved, we have evolved too, adapting knowledge from predigital cultural traditions to play out our lives across multiple platforms and channels where we are producing or performing cultural work as often as we are consuming it. The boundaries of professional, personal, fan, and community identities blur and recombine in ways that fundamentally shape our expectations of how stories and audiences ought to behave. Our own evolution as participants in these forms involves fashioning and performing new kinds of identities, as well as forming new communities and coalitions. Transmedia is second nature to us as both consumers and collaborators in the coproduction of contemporary culture.

As we have learned to construct ourselves as transmedia entities, we have also learned to construct our world. Social media have become news outlets not just in a programmatic or business sense, but in an epistemological and even ontological one: the feeds are *what happens* now. Coups d'etat, war crimes, quarantines, stock-market runs, and high-stakes politics play out on Facebook, Twitter, and TikTok. Something over half of the human population uses the internet, but all of us are transmedia figments tallied and narrativized in the databases and models of governments and corporations.

Because transmedia is *what happens* in so much of our collective culture, we face a crisis of narrative epistemology. The dark arts of transmedia underwrite disinformation and psychological warfare campaigns designed to destabilize democracy, sow doubt, promote cynicism, and buoy the shortsighted ambitions of autocrats and demagogues. Social media can have profound impacts on individual mental health and shared conceptions of governance, justice, and democracy. Sustained exposure to the warping effect of these damaging epistemologies has profound consequences, from teenage trauma to middle-aged insurrection (Wells, Horwitz, and Seetharaman, 2021; Alava et al., 2017). Toxic media cultures continue to metastasize across national, cultural, and moral boundaries, and we often seem to lack not only effective responses but even the vocabulary to describe what is happening to our collective discourse.

These negative influences have many origins and goals, but they share a common set of tactics. We need to keep transmedia firmly in sight as a set of practices that are being deployed for, by, and against us all the time. How do we foster literacy and agency in this environment? How can we develop a collective narrative immune system to combat the dangerous viruses circulating in our collective digital consciousness? These are central challenges for the next few decades, which will require a clear, compelling, and widely accepted grasp of the existential threats before us, especially assaults on democracy, the climate crisis, and economic inequality.

More ambitiously, framing transmedia in this way necessitates a cross-cutting literacy built on a different epistemology: one that posits media texts as intrinsically intersectional, protean, and liminal as they hover between fiction and reality, product and collaborative performance. We should understand transmedia as an ecological framework for approaching and interpreting not just entertainment media, but all of our digitally inflected cultural interactions with texts, interfaces, and communities. There is no way to live in an environment without being part of a larger system of interactions, energy exchanges, and feedback loops, and every action has significance to many layers of the ecological network. Living as we do in the forest of media, we cannot help but see every animal play its part, "perform" its function, in both the scientific and theatrical senses of that word. This perspective on the inherent vitality and inescapability of transmedia is a provocation, a question that this book poses through the multiplicity of ways in which our authors describe transmedia narratives flourishing across various media and contexts.

This collection works toward provisional answers, as well as articulations of this new understanding, by building up from the particular. In bringing theorists and practitioners together, we have sought to focus the book on how transmedia works today, and what the stakes are, across a variety of domains ranging from entertainment media and education to journalism and medicine. A surprising realization stemming from that NSF panel was how little traffic there is between different streams of transmedia practice; the shared spaces for dialogue, resource-sharing, and ethical deliberation that we might expect do not yet exist. So a second key goal of this project has been to foster conversations among scholars, educators, scientists, producers, artists, and others who grapple with transmedia as both a theoretical lens for their work and as a set of practical tools for simply getting the work done.

We began those conversations by hosting two workshops supported by the NSF (grant No. 1516684) in 2020 and 2021, where we asked a diverse group of scholars, producers, and artists to collaboratively discuss and define the vitality and relevance of transmedia today. In these workshops, our authors spent hours in large-group discussions, small-group working sessions, and our own multiply mediated hum of synchronous Zoom chats and collaborative Google Docs. We shared perspectives on efforts to define and operationalize transmedia, and on the art of crafting enriching, rewarding transmedia experiences for patients, students, news consumers, sports fans, local pubgoers, and other communities both locally bounded and globally distributed. The pairings of chapters that structure this book were born in the workshop, as our editorial team listened carefully and began surfacing connections between seemingly disparate transmedia interventions and insights. Our goal was to draw together a community of practice engaged in dialogues about the art and philosophy of transmedia, in a cultural moment when it seems so pervasive as to render us blind to its affordances and enchantments, as well as its foibles and abuses. In that sense, this book represents an attempt to capture the energy of those initial conversations and social encounters, a collective excitement about how transmedia tactics can draw together far-flung geographies and modes of work.

The essays coming out of those sessions to form this book span pedagogy, practical industry perspectives, case studies, lessons learned, and critical extrapolations, drawing together many decades of combined experience—along with some fresh perspectives from emerging thinkers and creators—to imagine what transmedia means now, and what we should be doing with it. We also asked our pairs of authors to engage in more informal conversations that cut across disciplines and methodologies and delve into lived experiences of transmedia in thought and action. These interstitial conversations, which we call "crosstalks," are woven throughout the chapters that follow, along with brief editorial notes that precede each chapter, teasing out additional connections beyond those pairings and across the entirety of the text.

The chapters in this volume sensitize us to the power relations inherent in all manner of transmedia activities; if we view transmedia as a practice, a *doing*, that cues us to interrogate the cultural and economic logics behind the experiences in which we find ourselves caught up. While some experiences seek to solidify and shore up existing power structures—enlisting us as "prosumers" (du Plessis, 2019) generating free promotional content for corporate media universes or brands, inviting us into seditious viral pro-authoritarian conspiracy theories, or extracting health data without any tangible therapeutic benefit—many of the chapters describe experiences designed to support positive change, solidarity, local civic pride, learning, and community building. As the authors in this volume detail, the larger flows of capital and technology access that undergird transmedia production are inescapable, but equally important are the fluid, evolving relationships that form between transmedia creators and audiences, which often involve collaboration, critique, careful listening and adaptation, and moments of true co-creation, where unexpected joy, imagination, and possibility can be located. This volume exemplifies how transmedia storytelling can be a space to challenge existing imbalances in power, renegotiate roles, and present alternate ways of being that cut against prevailing systems of economic domination, colonialism, heterosexism, ableism, and more.

We hope that this collection contributes to broader discussions of transmedia across its range of academic homes, but also provides some practical inspiration for those within and outside the academy who must contend with the fact that all of our work, too, has become transmediated. How many of our most important intellectual conversations now play out across a blend of social media, video conferences, digital sidebars and chat windows, collaborative cloud-based documents, and informal comments on the official "work" outputs, be they journal articles, films, websites, or blog posts? How often do we, as white-collar knowledge workers, creatives, content producers, and critics (or choose your own ideologically loaded terminology to describe what exactly we are all doing with our screens every day), work not just to perform the work but to perform ourselves, our roles and missions in these precarious times? This, too, is transmedia, and the diverse authors and practices included here offer some models for just how it is done.

About This Book

We have organized this book to juxtapose a variety of critical and practical approaches, weaving together very different accounts of how to design, teach, produce, share, and interpret transmedia.

The first section begins with an examination of transmedia practices through personal journeys and professional affiliations with massive, familiar commercial properties as well as smaller, more intimate and community-driven projects. In chapter 1, transmedia creative, author, and educator Maureen McHugh Yeager frames the commercial history of the industry as an evolution in forms of communal storytelling. Executive producer and strategist Caitlin Burns follows in chapter 2 with a methodology for describing and assessing how commercial transmedia projects gain support, measure success, and build lasting engagement with their audiences. In chapter 3, media scholar Paweł Frelik brings a very different viewpoint to these foundational questions, arguing that transmedia is a critical methodology, a set of linked questions and areas of intellectual focus, rather than an academic discipline that can easily be disentangled from much older discourses like adaptation, paratext, and remediation. In chapter 4, author and filmmaker Dilman Dila draws on both commercial and narratological perspectives in a more personal vein, defining transmedia through the biographical frame of his own upbringing as a storyteller and story sharer. Transmedia creative Yomi Ayeni continues this biographical thread in chapter 5, meditating on transmedia as a vehicle for new modes of communal experience and social cohesion, even around challenging topics like racism and colonialism. In chapter 6, members of the Theater Mitu collective describe the process of creating *UTOPIAN HOTLINE*, a project in which building a community shapes decisions about design and media forms, inviting audience members to become active participants and co-creators through experiences digital and physical, synchronous and asynchronous.

Our second section explores the implementation of transmedia techniques for new methods of teaching and learning. Camillia Matuk writes in chapter 7 about how science, technology, engineering, and math (STEM) education itself might be considered a transmedia exercise, building on her experiences using speculative design as a way to inspire adolescent engagement with STEM topics. In chapter 8, Francis Quek, Sharon Chu, and Niloofar Zarei push this envelope further, arguing that the cognitive imagination processes that support storytelling are also a form of transmedia, and reporting results from a set of experiments with children in collaborative storytelling across different media. Understanding transmedia as not just a pedagogical but an epistemological frame also informs Lee Emrich's case study in chapter 9, about a university course that interpreted the entire oeuvre of Shakespeare and Shakespeare studies as a multicentury, collective transmedia phenomenon. Then, in chapter 10, Jennifer Palilonis explores how to teach these processes in a hands-on journalism course, describing a project-based learning experience where students created a transmedia narrative with a community partner organization. The constructive epistemology of scientific knowledge takes center stage in Katherine Buse and Ranjodh Singh Dhaliwal's essay, chapter 11, which reflects on the complex history of *Foldit*, a protein-simulation citizen-science game, and their own participation as authors of a new narrative layer for the *Foldit* platform. Chapter 12, the final chapter in this section, describes the findings of the editors' own research on scientific creativity and responsibility in our *Frankenstein200* project, which sought to build STEM engagement and science self-efficacy through transmedia narrative, museum partnerships, and hands-on interactives.

In the third section of the book, we look to the future of transmedia: the ways in which this process or toolkit of meaning-making continues to have a significant impact on how we live and find meaning in our lives. In chapter 13, Kirsten Ostherr takes notions of efficacy and transmedia narrative in a powerfully intimate direction in her study of medical transmedia, the set of practices through which patients contend with illness and medical experiences on their own terms. In chapter 14, Zoyander Street describes their work creating art installations that communicate the experiences of transgender people in ways that avoid reinscribing notions of otherness and normativity, but instead use transmedia logics to unsettle dominant narratives about identity and relationality. Terra Gasque, in chapter 15, similarly approaches transmedia as charged with liberatory potential, examining how tabletop role-playing can provide design principles to restore the democratic, collaborative energy that permeates transmedia storyworlds, but is often squelched by corporate IP owners. Finally, envisaging a future in which civic life is rife with transmedia experiences, Ioana Mischie in chapter 16 uses *Tangible Utopias*, a VR experience built through a process of intergenerational collaboration that crosses the digital and physical, to argue for *omni-transmedia*, a paradigm that builds pathways from digital experiences and communities to real-world social transformation.

The volume concludes with a coda in which our authors offer a constellation of brief insights for readers who are looking to apply transmedia methods to their own work. We posed two future-oriented questions to them, addressing both the ethics of transmedia and the potential of this bundle of practices to advance positive change in the world:

- What are the most important considerations or unexpected ethical challenges for transmedia projects in the future?
- It's perhaps easier to think of worst-case scenarios in this industry, but can you envision a future project that uses the logics of transmedia for social good?

References

Alava, Séraphin, Divina Frau-Meigs, and Ghayda Hassan, with Hasna Hussein and Yuanyuan Wei. 2017. *Youth and Violent Extremism on Social Media: Mapping the Research*. Paris: United Nations Educational, Scientific and Cultural Organization (UNESCO). https://unesdoc.unesco.org/ark:/48223/pf0000260382.

Arendt, Hannah. 1951. *The Origins of Totalitarianism*. New York: Schocken Books.

Bush, Vannevar. 1946. *Endless Horizons*. Washington, DC: Public Affairs Press.

Costanza-Chock, Sasha. 2014. *Out of the Shadows, Into the Streets! Transmedia Organizing and the Immigrant Rights Movement*. Cambridge, MA: MIT Press.

Darnton, Robert, and Daniel Roche, eds. 1989. *Revolution in Print: The Press in France, 1775–1800*. Berkeley: University of California Press.

Dena, Christy. 2009. "Transmedia Practice: Theorising the Practice of Expressing a Fictional World across Distinct Media Environments." PhD dissertation, University of Sydney. https://ciret-transdisciplinarity.org/biblio/biblio_pdf/Christy_DeanTransm.pdf.

du Plessis, Charmaine. 2019. "Prosumer Engagement through Story-Making in Transmedia Branding." *International Journal of Cultural Studies* 22, no. 1: 175–192.

Evans, Elizabeth. 2011. *Transmedia Television Audiences, New Media, and Daily Life*. New York: Routledge.

Giddings, Seth. 2017. "*Pokémon GO* as Distributed Imagination." *Mobile Media & Communication* 5, no. 1: 59–62.

Guynes, Sean, and Dan Hassler-Forest, eds. 2017. *Star Wars and the History of Transmedia Storytelling*. Amsterdam: Amsterdam University Press.

Hassler-Forest, Dan. 2016. *Science Fiction, Fantasy, and Politics: Transmedia World-Building beyond Capitalism*. New York: Rowman & Littlefield.

Hayles, N. Katherine. 2008. *Electronic Literature: New Horizons for the Literary*. South Bend, IN: University of Notre Dame Press.

Kinder, Marsha, and Tara McPherson, eds. 2021. *Transmedia Frictions: The Digital, the Arts, and the Humanities*. Berkeley: University of California Press.

Kittler, Friedrich. 1990. *Discourse Networks, 1800/1900*. Translated by Michael Metteer, with Chris Cullins. Stanford, CA: Stanford University Press.

Kurtz, Benjamin W. L. Derhy, and Mélanie Bourdaa, eds. 2016. *The Rise of Transtexts: Challenges and Opportunities*. New York: Routledge.

Manovich, Lev. 2001. *The Language of New Media*. Cambridge, MA: MIT Press.

McLuhan, Marshall. 1964. *Understanding Media: The Extensions of Man*. New York: McGraw-Hill.

Murray, Janet. 1998. *Hamlet on the Holodeck: The Future of Narrative in Cyberspace*. Cambridge, MA: MIT Press.

Phillips, Andrea. 2016. "What's Happened to Transmedia?" *Immerse*, November 15, 2016. https://immerse.news/whats-happened-to-transmedia-855f180980e3#.ryt 6bo729.

Pringle, Ramona. 2016. "The Storyteller, the Fixer." *Immerse*, November 15, 2016. https://immerse.news/the-storyteller-the-fixer-866fe492fa49.

Scolari, Carlos, Paolo Bertetti, and Matthew Freeman, eds. 2014. *Transmedia Archaeology: Storytelling in the Borderlines of Science Fiction, Comics and Pulp Magazines*. New York: Palgrave Macmillan.

Scribes of the Cairo Geniza. 2017. Zooniverse. https://www.scribesofthecairogeniza .org.

Srnicek, Nick. 2016. *Platform Capitalism*. Malden, MA: Polity Press.

van Dijk, Jan. 2020. *The Digital Divide*. Malden, MA: Polity Press.

Wells, Georgia, Jeff Horwitz, and Deepa Seetharaman. 2021. "Facebook Knows Instagram Is Toxic for Teen Girls, Company Documents Show." *Wall Street Journal*, September 14, 2021. https://www.wsj.com/articles/facebook-knows-instagram-is-toxic -for-teen-girls-company-documents-show-11631620739.

White, Richard. 2012. *Railroaded: The Transcontinentals and the Making of Modern America*. New York: W. W. Norton.

Wolf, Mark J. P. 2014. *LEGO Studies: Examining the Building Blocks of a Transmedial Phenomenon*. New York: Routledge.

I Approaches to Transmedia

1 Transmedia, Tech, and Culture

Maureen McHugh Yeager

Maureen McHugh Yeager's introductory chapter sets the tone for the rest of this volume, examining transmedia storytelling and the advent of alternate reality games (ARGs) as both an experimental medium and a natural evolution of humanity's desire to connect, communicate, and confederate via storytelling. An early architect of ARGs, McHugh Yeager draws on her own firsthand experiences and recollections from her co-creators to share the excitement, confusion, and surprises of creating new communities and grammars of action in the nascent days of mass computer-mediated communication. Later in this book, in chapter 2, Caitlin Burns demonstrates how these outputs were formalized and institutionalized by mass media conglomerates, with a focus on metrics and assessing success, while McHugh Yeager focuses on the broader cultural impact of this medium, arguing that the transmedia literacies developed by a generation of ardent ARG players and casual observers have transcended their corporate-owned sandboxes, informing grassroots, participant-driven storyworlds like those described by Dilman Dila, Yomi Ayeni, and Kayla Asbell et al. (chapters 4, 5, and 6, respectively). These same processes of transmedia production and reception, established by ARGs, undergird the educational experiences detailed in later chapters by Camillia Matuk, Lee Emrich, Jennifer Palilonis, and Ruth Wylie et al. (chapters 7, 9, 10, and 12, respectively). McHugh Yeager also considers how the tools that she and her colleagues helped develop can be used to engender new social movements, pointing to QAnon as a dark application of transmedia logics and human tendencies, while chapters 14 and 16 by Zoyander Street and Ioana Mischie, respectively, examine more prosocial uses of their audiences' time and energy.

In 1999, Microsoft bought the game designer Jordan Weisman's company FASA Interactive. Microsoft had just paid an enormous amount of money for the game rights to a movie called *A.I. Artificial Intelligence* (hereafter *A.I.*). Stanley Kubrick had been developing the film for years; it was picked up by Steven Spielberg in 1995 and eventually released in 2001. A movie by Spielberg about robots—how could it not make money?

There is some speculation that no one actually read the script.

A.I. is a retelling of *Pinocchio*, about a robot boy who wants to be loved like a real boy. It is not an action-adventure yarn, but rather an examination of family, love, humanity, and the future.

Microsoft had a problem. Some of the most popular video games in the year 2000, when the *A.I.* adaptation had been slated to be released, included the "hack-and-slash" action role-playing game *Diablo II*; *Deus Ex*, a cyberpunk role-playing stealth/shooter; and *The Legend of Zelda: Majora's Mask*, the latest in the legendary fantasy action-adventure series. In this games market, there wasn't exactly a clear path to making money off a non-action remake of *Pinocchio*. They needed Weisman to figure out if there was something they could do with these rights. He'd started in tabletop games, creating, among other things, a cyberpunk role-playing game called *Shadowrun* that still has a following, and he had also worked on the futuristic robot battler *MechWarrior*, as well as virtual reality (VR) games in the 1990s.

Weisman, an innovative thinker, was the right person to tap to figure out a good way to monetize this odd movie. His suggestion was to create a kind of *A.I.* universe: a whole world where the film's story was only part of it.

Sean Stewart, the narrative designer for Weisman's project, explained, "No one ever walked out of *Schindler's List* saying 'gotta play the game.' But if you create the Second World War, *Schindler's List* sits in it, but so does a tactical game and so does a strategy game and so does the first-person shooter game. The games never got made or shipped, but the container part did happen" (personal correspondence, 2020). Weisman's team could extend and expand on the setting of *A.I.* to create a world in which a multitude of experiences could be situated. The "container" to which Stewart referred was a story set in and exploring that world—a story that was revealed on the internet. And while this story went on to become one of the first experiences that people recognized as being transmedia, neither Weisman nor Elan Lee, then a game designer at Microsoft and a key collaborator on the project, realized that they were inventing a new medium.

Toward a Definition of Transmedia

I worked for a decade as a writer on transmedia projects with Elan Lee and Sean Stewart (including *I Love Bees* for the Halo franchise and *Year Zero* for Nine Inch Nails), and then as a partner and narrative designer for No

Mimes Media, making interactive experiences. I teach narrative design for interactivity at the University of Southern California. Transmedia is a concept that defies precise definition even now, but it does have a core set of characteristics, some of which I'll define in this chapter.

The definition of transmedia is so elusive that it can feel like the old story of the blind men describing an elephant. It's flat—no, it's like a snake—no, it's like a tree. . . . As an art form, transmedia falls into camps. Transmedia projects were funded primarily by intellectual property (IP) holders: sometimes as an extension of a film, game, or creative project, and sometimes as marketing. Often, they are crafted by contracted third-party independents like 42 Entertainment or Starlight Runner. For some practitioners, transmedia is the constellation of stories (books, comic books, movies, and television), objects (toys, clothing, jewelry, and any other merchandise), and works associated with an IP like a video game or a film, sometimes created in concert with the creative team that inaugurated the IP (e.g., George Lucas

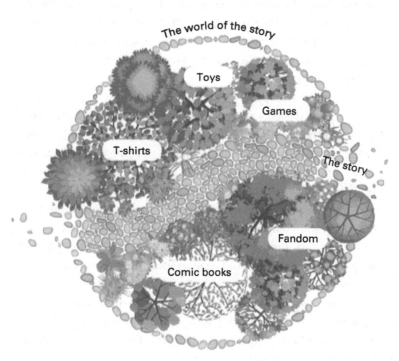

Figure 1.1
Visualizing a transmedia storyworld. Image by Nina Miller.

for Star Wars or Trent Reznor for Nine Inch Nails), plus experience and narrative designers. A story forms the spine of the experience, and there may be lunch boxes, T-shirts, trailers, Pez dispensers, even fan-created works.

In this definition, for example, the television show *Stranger Things* could provide the main storyline. A *Stranger Things* Licensed Pop-Culture Gender-Neutral Long-Sleeve Tee for Kids is transmedia. Each piece is a stand-alone, complete in itself. The main movie, comic book, or television series can be enjoyed in and of itself, and the other objects and stories arrayed around it each work on their own. But taken together, they tell multiple stories or represent objects that populate the story universe.

Another version of transmedia, the one that Weisman was busy designing in 2000, takes a single story and distributes it across multiple platforms. *A.I.* was a movie, but the experience that he created encompassed multiple websites, emails, audio logs, puzzles, and live events, which together told the story. In terms of interactive media, a film or a book is a "lean back" experience, one that happens without your input. The experience that Weisman created, officially untitled but nicknamed *The Beast*,[1] required its players to find websites, call phone numbers, solve puzzles, and even, at times, "hack" (by examining code and brute-forcing passwords) as part of the game. It was a "lean forward" experience.

It's a different way to experience a story. In the early 2000s, fewer people were online; when I started writing for these experiences, I had a flip phone that didn't even have texting capabilities. Google was in its early stages—no one googled anything. People had external navigation aids (ours was a Garmin GPS; others stuck with paper maps) rather than using an app on a smartphone for directions.

As more and more of us experience the world augmented by our smartphones, tablets, and computers, our sense of distance, of what it means to "know" somebody, fundamentally changes. Our reality is mediated by technology. What we read, see, and hear on the computer can feel as real as what we experience anywhere else.

Joe DiNunzio of 42 Entertainment, where Weisman, Stewart, Lee, and I worked designing and implementing some of these experiences, called what they were making a "search opera." The players called it an alternate reality game, or ARG for short, and the name stuck.

Weisman's experience for *A.I.* started with a website where a woman talked about the suspicious death of a close family friend. She shared a strange image that she'd received as a digital message from someone who only identified themselves as "Sencha," a kind of green tea. Players examined the image and realized that it was a puzzle. When they solved it, the puzzle pointed them to another website. Yet another puzzle allowed them to "hack" the website—players who solved the puzzle could use the solution as the password to unlock a coroner's report—revealing that the family friend had been murdered. In game design, something that a player has to do to advance in the game is called a "gate." The puzzles acted as gates; solving them allowed the player to advance, revealing more of the story.

Using puzzles wasn't particularly innovative. For example, the tremendously popular 1993 computer game *Myst* used puzzles as gates. What was different about this experience was that it lived on the internet; the gates led to websites, or sometimes real-world sites or videos.

What was unusual about *The Beast* was that it had no edges. Works of art usually have boundaries. A book is enclosed in covers or comes in readable files, and I can be confident that the totality of the story is contained in the book. A movie usually starts with the opening and the title, ends with the credits, and is one continuous thing. A painting is usually enclosed within a frame. One of the radical things that Weisman did was to use the whole world as the canvas.

Weisman was fascinated by an urban legend/conspiracy theory that Paul McCartney had been killed in a car accident in 1966 and replaced by a lookalike. The theory swept through college campuses in 1969. A caller to the Detroit radio station WKNR told a DJ about the conspiracy, and they discussed it for the next hour. The term "going viral" wasn't used in 1969, but that's what the "Paul is dead" theory did. Within a few days, it was on radio stations in New York, and it continued to be transferred via word of mouth among Beatles fans (Winick, 2018).

Weisman was interested in the way that people spread the story. With the internet, a newspaper article could be published in Istanbul in the morning and be read by a teenager in Iowa in the afternoon. The team at Microsoft, including Elan Lee and Sean Stewart, created a story and shattered it across the internet. The project was a gamble: Would audiences respond? Could you create what in effect was a viral property—one spread, like an internet meme, by the audience? No one knew.

Where Does Art Come From?

To design art forms like video games and ARGs, designers need to think about what a technology allows. These affordances are constantly expanding as technology develops.

New art forms arise out of new technologies, and art is in constant tension with innovation. The invention of the camera created photography, which initiated a crisis in painting and illustration. Before photography, drawing and painting were ways to record the world visually. Of course, not all painting was about accurate representation, but there weren't many ways to know what a place looked like. If you were British and you wanted to know what Japan looked like, someone had to draw or paint it.

Photography recorded details in a way that felt "real." Suddenly, if you wanted to know what Japan looked like, someone could take a photograph. Painting can compete with photography—there are schools of realism and hyperrealism—but a photograph is a fast, easy, and (as we're mostly conditioned to believe) accurate rendition of what something looks like. Photography allowed citizens of the nineteenth century to "see" the Civil War like never before. As camera technology improved, becoming more popular, affordable, and accessible, a greater number of people adopted this new art form, collecting images and using them to document both their history and daily lives.

Photographs of the Civil War by Matthew Brady and his associates felt authentic to audiences at the time—never mind that Brady was a Northerner who had been given permission by President Abraham Lincoln to document the war. Never mind that he once moved a body to imply that rather than being an infantryman, the subject of the photo was a lone rebel sharpshooter who was fatally injured in his sniper's nest and lay down and died (Library of Congress, n.d.). The naive audience saw the photos as true and had no frame of reference for things like bias, or staging a narrative, just as naive audiences on the internet today often don't recognize Photoshopped images or "deepfakes" as manipulated.

Over the next century and a half, technology changed the way that we communicated. Recorded sound meant that everyone could hear a speech or a song, and the radio meant that everyone could hear the *Hindenburg* disaster live in their home. Movies combined sound and image. Phones erased the distance between people.

Not all communication technologies give rise to new art forms; there is no mass-market art of the telegraph. Initially, there was no reason to think that there would be a mass-market art form for the computer. Computers were computational devices for doing calculations quickly. Today, it's easy to conflate personal computers (including smartphones and tablets) with the internet that connects and delivers content to and among them, but they are really two different technologies with distinctive affordances. And it was the affordances of the computer that gave rise to a new mass-market art form: video games.

It's hard to sufficiently emphasize the difference between computer games and previous forms like movies, radio, and books. There have always been games, but mass-market art forms—movies, books, theater, concerts, operas—are rarely interactive.[2] Movies are "lean back" experiences. The audience is passive, and the movie rolls on at twenty-four frames per second. Audiences might shout back at the characters, but the characters never respond.

Video games bring the audience into the game. In game design, the actual interactions are called "mechanics." "Shoot" is a mechanic. "Jump" and "run" are mechanics, as is driving a car. If you press one or more keys or buttons and a predictable thing occurs, that's a mechanic, even if it's just clicking on something to zoom in and see it better.

Current mechanics are crude analogs of actions—swinging a sword or shooting a pistol doesn't work in real life the way it does in video games, and dialogue trees—those lists of things that a player can choose to have their character say in the course of conversations with other characters—rarely include the kinds of things that an actual person would ask or say in the situation; rather, they are tailored toward moving the player to the next interaction. They don't feel like natural conversations because they are constructed as role-playing and narrative choices rather than acts of communication. But it's telling that interaction is so fundamental that video game players will learn complex and sophisticated sets of interactive skills to play a game like *Dark Souls* (2011), a brutally difficult and narratively oblique dark fantasy role-playing action game.

In *Dark Souls*, which has spawned a whole genre of "Souls-like" games, the player meets an interaction—a simulated combat encounter—and more or less inevitably, their character dies. Upon dying, they lose all the resources they have accumulated (though they do have a chance to retrieve them later) and must start over from a checkpoint, losing many minutes of progress. They must start over, again and again, replaying each encounter to learn the sequence of artificial actions that allow them to successfully complete it: a heavy swing of a sword here, a dodge or parry there, evading a punishing enemy attack here. When they finally learn the pattern well enough to succeed, they move on to another new area of the game or a new series of enemies, and they must fail and retry all over again. This requires incredible repetition, and one of the game's rewards is the gradual, grinding mastery of its mechanics. The game has a compelling story, but it's fragmentary and elusive, and fairly scanty. The majority of the experience is about acquiring a very specific set of skills and honing them over time, while the narrative is meant to evoke tone more than tell a cohesive story. The bar for story engagement in interactive experiences like *Dark Souls* is a lot lower than it is for movies, for instance, because doing is more compelling than merely watching.

The other important characteristic of computers as a platform for art is that computers have evolved to encompass other mass media. The computer is different from most other art forms because it's multiplatform. A book is a printed object; it doesn't play music. You can show the printed word in a movie ("A long time ago in a galaxy far, far away . . ."), but there's a reason that audiences don't sit in a movie theater and read a movie for an hour and half. Movies use visuals and sound to tell a story. But on my laptop, I can watch a movie, read the *New York Times*, and play a song on Spotify. Computers mimic, absorb, and/or re-present other media platforms. Video games range in style and structure from text adventures and "visual novels" that are primarily read, to highly interactive, mechanically "crunchy" or "grindy" experiences like *Dark Souls*, to nearly cinematic experiences like the *Uncharted* series, featuring thrilling high-definition videos, full musical scores, and vivid, memorable characters. Video games often include brief movie-style sequences without interaction, called "cut scenes," that carry the story. Designers have learned that players are often impatient with cut scenes, so they often include a mechanic that allows the players to simply skip them to return to the interactive aspects of the game. Some players enjoy the narrative, but others feel that it interrupts the experience. For many players, again, doing is more compelling than telling.

While some books have images in them, this conflation of platforms is not a primary characteristic of earlier art forms. It is a central characteristic of computers—they are *platform-agnostic*.

How is the internet different from a computer as a platform for art?

Like computers, the internet is platform-agnostic. Newspapers and magazines sit next to Netflix and *The Sims 4*, and all of them exist on your computer. The first designers of transmedia used the multiplatform nature of the internet and the interactivity of gaming as a new way to tell stories.

But the internet does something that a personal computer does not. It connects people. Jordan Weisman caught a glimmer of this when Microsoft asked him to design something for the film *A.I.* But no one yet foresaw the way the internet was fundamentally different.

When they were designing *The Beast*, the designers consciously leaned into the multiplatform and interactive aspects of the online experience— the *affordances* of the space. They took it even further. Clues to unlock the story were embedded in ads in major newspapers. There were live meet-ups with actors playing members of competing factions. The game existed in the world, and the way to begin was by going through a *rabbit hole*.

The rabbit hole (a reference to Alice falling into Wonderland) is something that cues the audience that there is a story to be discovered. Rabbit holes are usually intentional, carefully thought-out clues placed where the public will find them, like movie posters or even television ads. But not always. The 1999 microbudget indie horror-movie sensation *The Blair Witch Project* is a kind of transmedia experience, although it was not designed to be. *Blair Witch* is a "found footage" movie that tells the story of three young people who disappeared in Maryland's Black Hills. The handheld-camera "found footage" that makes up the film reveals that they were killed by the mythological Blair Witch. This, of course, was all fiction. A year before the film's release, the makers of *Blair Witch* (Michael Monello, Robin Cowie, Bob Eick, Kevin J. Foxe, and Gregg Hale) created a website to advertise their movie, and as part of the website, they included an online forum where people could post comments and talk with one another. The site was "in the world"; like the movie, which was staged as a pseudodocumentary, it was set up as if the three young people portrayed in the movie had actually disappeared.

The idea of websites for films was quite new, and naive audiences took the website at face value. It felt real. It felt authentic. They started posting about hauntings in other places. The website became part of the experience of the movie. You could watch the movie without ever visiting the website, but if you did visit, the experience of both added up to a richer, more complex story. If you had posted hauntings, then you, like the three characters in the movie, were participating in the experience. Michael Monello says that the movie was originally supposed to have a more conventional beginning and end, with the found footage framed by traditionally shot footage. The filmmakers came to believe that both the found footage (which was filmed by the actors using handheld cameras) and the website eliminated the need for the more conventionally filmed portions of the story. The story took place on the web and in the film, and the incredible success of the film's marketing exerted an effect on the film itself. That was a fundamental change.

Jordan Weisman wasn't thinking about *Blair Witch* when he and Elan Lee were hammering out the design for their "search opera" at Microsoft. But they, like Monello and company, found that the audience would take their content and own it, reinterpreting and remaking it in ways that were rarely possible before the internet.

Community

These were the puzzles that would take a day, these were puzzles that would take a week, and these puzzles they'd probably never figure out until we broke down and gave them the answers. So, we built a three-month schedule around this. And finally, we released. [Pause] The Cloudmakers solved all of these puzzles on the first day.

—Elan Lee, speaking at the Game Developers Conference (GDC), 2002

Jordan Weisman wasn't thinking about community. He was thinking about the connectedness of the web, that newspaper article in Istanbul in the morning and the kid in Iowa reading it in the afternoon. About the "Paul is dead" conspiracy, and how that spread from radio station to radio station and by word of mouth across college campuses. He was thinking about how fast that could be shared over the web.

Community threw a surprising curve into the design. In *The Beast*, players solved puzzles to uncover clues that led to more content, more clues—most of them hosted on a constellation of seemingly unconnected websites. At first, though, no one found the websites at all, or even knew there was a story to find. An online group at Ain't It Cool News (AICN), a website where film buffs gathered, noticed a credit in the promotional poster for the film *A.I.* Along with the usual credits—Warner Brothers, Amblin Entertainment,

Steven Spielberg as director, and others—was a credit for "Jeanine Salla—Sentient Machine Therapist." Credits in Hollywood are codified, reviewed, and arbitrated. There are standards in the movie business about who gets credited how and where, and "Sentient Machine Therapist" was not a credit anyone had ever seen before. This was before Google's total dominance of online searches, so the community at AICN used a search engine called AltaVista and found a website that claimed to be from the future.

There was a link on that site to sign up for emails, and the people who signed up began to receive messages from one of the characters in the story. That is to say, audiences looked at the game and it felt as if the game looked back at them. It was a rabbit hole into a new kind of story.

This excitement was exactly what Weisman and Lee had hoped for.

They planned that the first week, the puzzles would be difficult. In week two, more websites would go up with other difficult clues and the existing puzzles would be replaced or made easier, and then in week three, the puzzles would be made very easy. In subsequent weeks, they expected that as new content went up, earlier content would continue to be made easier—over the couple of months that the story was being published and updated, some people would be solving things and getting ahead while others wouldn't progress, and therefore they wouldn't see all of the content until later. Weisman and Lee thought of the players as individuals of differing investment and skill levels, experiencing the story asynchronously. People who were good at puzzles would roll through the story week by week, and the rest of the audience would trail behind.

This is not what happened.

A bunch of people from the AICN community formed a group on the (now-defunct) Yahoo Groups platform called Cloudmakers, and instead of playing solo and solving puzzles themselves, members pooled their efforts. It turns out that when a game mechanic includes using search engines to find things like websites, that naturally leads to using search engines to find out if anyone else has seen this and what they think is going on. Puzzles that Lee and Weisman didn't expect anyone to find for weeks were solved the first day.

If an ARG finds an audience, it follows that a community gathers to discuss it and, in a sense, co-creates the experience out of the raw material that the designers have put out on the web. The audience assembles the story, decodes it together, and tells it to one another.

Every week, the game would update twice, once on Tuesday and once on Saturday. At noon (PST) in the US, websites would change, adding more information. An email would go out from "Jeanine Salla" to people who had signed up. The audience would convene on the forums and instantly (possibly ravenously) catalog the new information and updates, searching for puzzles and new clues. The experience became an increasingly difficult race to create puzzles and content that would satisfy the relentless demand of the hive mind, the networked collective bent on cracking the puzzles and revealing the story. Behind the scenes, Weisman's team of game designers, writers, and artists found themselves struggling to keep up.

During *The Beast* experience, what transmedia storytelling had going for it was that it wasn't like anything anyone had ever seen before, and people liked to talk to each other about it.

Art exists in a balance between novelty and convention. Think of television procedurals like *NCIS* or *Law and Order*, which are structurally not experimental. They're predictable, and their pleasure comes from their familiarity. If the medical show *House* is on TV as you pass through the room, and Dr. House is sitting in his office, tossing a ball in the air and quietly thinking, it's about fifteen minutes before the end of the show. There's a formula: two unsuccessful attempts to cure the disease of the week, and then the third time, a lightning bolt of unexpected insight, followed by the real cure.

The pleasure of procedurals is your knowledge of the form. It's the pleasure of a sonnet. The story has to be novel enough (in the case of *House*, the strangeness of the disease and the interactions between the main character and everyone else were interesting and constantly evolving) to entertain. It doesn't matter that people rarely died on the show. The pleasure lies not in anticipating *what* will happen, but in anticipating *how* it will happen.

Stick too closely to the form and the work feels cliché, positively boring. Go too far from the form and it's experimental, potentially off-putting. Without expectations, the audience flounders, and most people become frustrated. The more familiar the form, the more comfortable people are; the more experimental, the more unmoored people feel—and usually, the smaller the audience. It's not an exact science, of course. Experimental work like the blockbuster augmented reality game *Pokémon Go* can be both profitable and successful, and most games on the video game website Steam are conventional genre fare, but most of them have little or no audience. Nevertheless, this balancing act between novelty and convention is a design consideration.

Inventing a new art form necessarily means throwing the audience into the experimental, and one of the big struggles in ARGs was getting people to understand just what this new form was. As it turned out, the answer to that was community. The Cloudmakers didn't just solve every puzzle on the first day; through their enthusiastic, concerted interaction with the game, they became the center of the experience.

The community explained to each other what was going on. They tracked their progress, creating walkthroughs and guides. They established and moderated forums. In ARGs, the makers throw pieces of the story everywhere. The community collects those pieces, puts them together, and tells each other the story.

One puzzle in *The Beast* involved a website where, if someone had computer speakers turned on and was paying attention, they would notice that the site played a sound—a dripping tap. It wasn't loud, or something that most players would notice. But someone who paid attention noticed that the sound wasn't regular—it had a pattern. The pattern was Morse code, and the dripping sound was a puzzle.

As a puzzle in a game that was necessary to figure out in order to finish a level, it was so easy to miss and so hard to solve that it should have been a disaster. Playing a blockbuster action game like *Grand Theft Auto* or *Call of Duty*, how many people are going to stop to decode the faint sound of a faucet dripping in Morse code? But a community experience means not everyone has to notice; if one person figures it out, then it's decoded for the whole community.[3]

The audience didn't merely notice the puzzles that were there; they latched onto things that the designers hadn't intended. A bit of website graffiti—a comment hidden in the source code of a website—was signed "The Red King." It was just a throwaway, a hacker tag, but the audience wanted to know more about the character, so the Red King was created and, in subsequent updates, became part of the story.

One of the unexpected things that happened with ARGs was that the audience was eager to affect the narrative. They wanted to transform the story, to touch it back, to make it about themselves.

This is a characteristic of the internet—it's very visible in fandoms. One of the largest sites for fan fiction is Archive of Our Own (Ao3), a website run by the nonprofit Organization for Transformative Works. It's a place where fan writers can post original works of fiction about their favorite celebrities, books, and shows, so long as they do not charge for them. As of May 25, 2021, Ao3 hosted 158,687 works about the Korean boy band BTS and 315,895 works about the Harry Potter universe. These works range from stories that happen between scenes in canonical Harry Potter books and movies, to works that revise the story to put Harry in a romantic relationship with another character, to stories where Harry Potter characters are living in the distant future, or enrolled in a normal Earthly high school (called AUs, for "alternative universe" works). This work of transformation and personalization is profoundly powerful for fandoms. It was something that Weisman and his team didn't foresee.

ARGs asked the audience to follow, and in a limited way, interact with the experience. But they didn't allow transformation—except perhaps inadvertently, as with the Red King. (This is not uncommon in television shows, where a character who is only expected for a one-shot or a couple of episodes becomes popular and is integrated into the series.) When the experience ended and the creators and designers came forward to talk to their audience, one of the common questions was, "What did we make you change?" That is, "How did we transform this story? How did it become ours?"

This desire to transform leads to a problem with transmedia. The hive mind sounds inclusive, but the experience of it can be very exclusive. The communities that formed around ARGs consistently had people engaged at different levels. Based on observation of the number of hits on ARG experiences versus active player engagement, we formulated the 90:9:1 Rule: for every 100 people in the community, 90 lurk, 9 participate in chat and discussion, and 1 is very active in the game—solving puzzles, guiding newcomers, telling the story, and speculating on what it means. The 90 players are not interacting with the story much; they're watching others. But they're still an extended part of the hive mind, and if something comes up where they feel they have special knowledge, they might become part of the middle group—the 9. But for the majority of the ARG audience, they don't feel as if they are participating. For them, the experience isn't interactive. Instead, it can feel confusing.

Narrative on the Internet

ARGs were an attempt to make a mass-market narrative art form for the internet. The decision was conscious. So why aren't there more people joining communities and experiencing stories through the internet?

In one sense, ARGs failed. Although millions of users would "touch" an ARG like *The Beast* or *Year Zero*, most people didn't keep looking. In ARG design, it's a truism that every time there is a shift in platform—a transmedia jump, if you will, from a website to a video to an audio file to a physical poster or location—the experience loses people. The number of people who did more than check out a website and read a couple of posts in the forum was relatively small. People didn't understand what the websites were and didn't know how to experience the stories. It's a dirty secret of video gaming that most players don't finish long, sprawling games. They play until they get bored or stuck. Most people who clicked on the rabbit hole or a link didn't play through the entire ARG, either.

Following an ARG had a steep initial learning curve. If a player found the experience after it had already been running a couple of weeks, they would have to hunt down a forum of material to catch up on what had already happened; the experiences unfold in real time, like a TV series without reruns.

ARGs attracted a certain kind of audience; early experiences were intense, demanding a significant commitment of time and energy and appealing to a niche group. They were expensive to make, requiring art teams, producers, website and experience designers, and writers. They rarely engaged enough people to be anything more than an expensive promotion with a fairly low return on investment. Spending a million dollars to entertain ten thousand people is not a good financial idea. There were some large, high-profile ARGs in the 2000s, like *The Lost Experience*, linked to the television series *Lost*, and *Why So Serious?* for the movie *The Dark Knight*. But the form never took off in the way its creators had hoped. Without sponsors, they were too expensive to make, and without a large enough audience, there were no sponsors. They are finding a new niche, often local, like the *Reality Ends Here* ARG at the University of Southern California, an experience for freshmen that provides a framework for them to meet one another and explore the campus. But they have not, as yet, turned out to be the mass-market narrative form of the internet.

Does transmedia really represent a viable art form on the internet? Or are transmedia experiences simply too expensive and demanding on their audiences to be workable?

One sign that transmedia remains a viable form of storytelling is the way that culture has invented it yet again. As an article about the *I Love Bees* ARG pointed out, the ways that communities arose and organized themselves naturally felt like a real, lasting popular phenomenon. It felt as natural as historical popular reactions to media, like Beatlemania in the 1960s. Rather than being centrally orchestrated, it was catalyzed, as mass movements are, by people banding together:

> [*I Love Bees*] displayed all the characteristics of a mass movement, propelled into existence in a matter of weeks simply by collective enthusiasm guided by a few cyberspace "avatars" . . . (Lott, 2008)

Movements arise on the internet, and although people who are part of those movements often adopt tactics to consciously increase reach—or, as with ARGs, create guides and FAQs to help orient newcomers—they are not necessarily IPs, ideas owned by people who control publication and collect profit from the central or canon property. No one owns these multiplatform experiences. Rather, they are artifacts of the affordances of the internet itself. A clear example is another mass movement: QAnon.

The internet generates communities—fractured, siloed, but in surprising numbers. These communities find homes on discussion-driven websites like the old AICN, Reddit, and 4chan. The characteristics of ARGs—that they are multiplatform and interactive, and that they develop communities—are key characteristics of the internet as a communications medium. And the form of the ARG is visible in other mass-market experiences. Humans tell stories, and when they tell stories on the internet, the result often looks like an ARG. Take the designer, author, and games-industry executive Adrian Hon's analysis of the devastatingly popular QAnon conspiracy theory, for example:

> QAnon is not an ARG. It's a dangerous conspiracy theory, and there are lots of ways of understanding conspiracy theories without ARGs. But QAnon pushes the same buttons that ARGs do, whether by intention or by coincidence. In both cases, "do your research" leads curious onlookers to a cornucopia of brain-tingling information.
>
> In other words, maybe QAnon is . . . fun? (Hon, 2020)

ARG audiences were naive because as the form was being pioneered, experiencing the world with the internet was new. Because the border between what is in the story and what is not was, and remains, so permeable, they will often identify things as "in-world" that weren't created by the team. Humans are very good at detecting patterns. So good, in fact, that people often detect patterns that aren't there, a phenomenon called *apophenia*. Imagine flipping a coin six times. The first five times, the coin comes up heads. What are the chances that the coin will come up heads on the sixth try? Fifty-fifty. It's true—the odds of a coin flip coming up heads six times in a row is just 1.56 percent, but that doesn't affect the odds of that sixth coin flip being fifty-fifty. Despite the math, we remain drawn to the mythos of the hot streak, a discernible pattern amid the chaos of lived experience.

The thrill of being an insider, of knowing about a thing that is important to you and a select community, is probably hardwired into humans. The internet, once envisioned as a plurality, an open, democratic space with a flat hierarchy for disseminating and debating ideas, has splintered into echo chambers. People follow people who have the same interests and beliefs. Tight-knit communities form around media (fandoms) and political movements.

QAnon, a conspiracy theory and digital community, was started on the internet by someone (or a group of people) who identified themselves only as "Q" and who claimed to be a high-ranking member of the US military and defense establishment. And 4chan, a web platform hosting forums where posters are anonymous, was, among many other things, a mecca for groups that felt marginalized, including men's rights groups, 9/11 conspiracy theorists, and White supremacists. QAnon attracted people who felt that their freedom was at risk and that media and social elites were turning the US into a socialist country.

On 4chan, and later on a similarly structured site, 8chan, "Q drops" were ambiguous posts that hinted at deeper knowledge of then–US president Donald Trump's clandestine political activities and plans, especially in relation to supposed (which is to say, fictional) misdeeds committed by powerful political figures in the US political system—especially, but not exclusively, members of the Democratic Party (Bessi and Quattrociocchi, 2015) (figure 1.2).

ARGs classically started with a rabbit hole, a series of clues, and a mystery that led to a website. QAnon started with a rabbit hole: posts on 4chan that eventually migrated to 8chan, then to its successor site, 8kun, and then to Twitter and Facebook and beyond. In a typical Q drop, there would

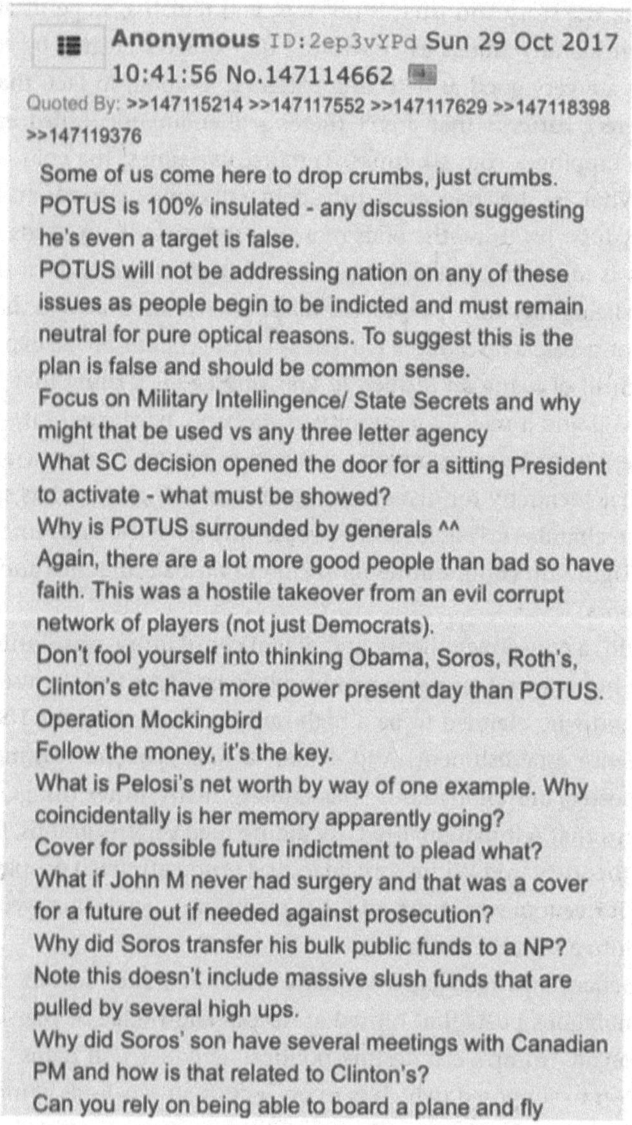

Anonymous ID:2ep3vYPd Sun 29 Oct 2017 10:41:56 No.147114662

Quoted By: >>147115214 >>147117552 >>147117629 >>147118398 >>147119376

Some of us come here to drop crumbs, just crumbs.
POTUS is 100% insulated - any discussion suggesting he's even a target is false.
POTUS will not be addressing nation on any of these issues as people begin to be indicted and must remain neutral for pure optical reasons. To suggest this is the plan is false and should be common sense.
Focus on Military Intellingence/ State Secrets and why might that be used vs any three letter agency
What SC decision opened the door for a sitting President to activate - what must be showed?
Why is POTUS surrounded by generals ^^
Again, there are a lot more good people than bad so have faith. This was a hostile takeover from an evil corrupt network of players (not just Democrats).
Don't fool yourself into thinking Obama, Soros, Roth's, Clinton's etc have more power present day than POTUS.
Operation Mockingbird
Follow the money, it's the key.
What is Pelosi's net worth by way of one example. Why coincidentally is her memory apparently going?
Cover for possible future indictment to plead what?
What if John M never had surgery and that was a cover for a future out if needed against prosecution?
Why did Soros transfer his bulk public funds to a NP?
Note this doesn't include massive slush funds that are pulled by several high ups.
Why did Soros' son have several meetings with Canadian PM and how is that related to Clinton's?
Can you rely on being able to board a plane and fly

Figure 1.2
An example of a QAnon "Q Drop" from October 2017.

be a variety of murky calls to action for readers and elliptical directives like "Follow the money." Although short on substance, they were evocative and mysterious. They felt as if they were revealing something. They hinted at a mystery and invited readers to unravel it, to speculate and build on one another's ideas.

Following the initial ARG rabbit hole usually leads to a community space where background information and story elements are revealed. The rabbit hole on 4chan was the series of posts from Q. Three 4chan users—a woman named Tracy Diaz and two 4chan moderators—created YouTube videos, a "subreddit" message board on the platform Reddit, and requested and received donations through Patreon and PayPal, based on the cryptic posts of "Q" (Zadrozny and Collins, 2018).

In an ARG, participants play "roles" in which they are completely themselves, with their own lives, their own jobs or schoolwork, except that they pretend that the ARG is real. In *The Beast*, they were themselves except for one significant wrinkle: they were receiving emails from and emailing back to Leia Salla, a character from the ARG.

In the ARG *Why So Serious?* which told the story of the events between the movies *Batman Begins* and *The Dark Knight*, they are themselves, but living in Gotham City and participating in the city's election for district attorney, with the character Harvey Dent as a candidate. People who "registered to vote" through the ARG received physical voter registration cards in the mail, complete with fictional Gotham City addresses. So participants were themselves, except that they adopted the role of denizens of Gotham City.

QAnon followers are themselves, with their own jobs and their own lives, who either believe or engage with a reality in which an elite international ring of pedophiles run the world. As the internet provides a larger and larger share of our lived experiences, the conspiracy theories of the internet threaten to feel like, and even become, a reality. QAnon shares many of the characteristics of *The Beast*: people find cryptic clues, engage in analysis with other like-minded people, and are slowly immersed in a world where the internet lays a filter of meaning over the things that they see in their everyday lives.

Community, plus the psychological mechanics of confirmation bias, the tendency for humans to interpret information in ways that support their own preexisting beliefs, are what drive QAnon.

The same pattern shows up in fandoms organized around popular fictional universes, like Star Wars or the Marvel Cinematic Universe (MCU).

They create their own stories and fan videos. They make art. Those representations transform the existing IP.

In the last few years, many of those fan communities have become divisive, and sections of them have become conspiracy-driven, much like QAnon.

Star Wars fans are enraged over the direction of the franchise's recent feature films. Historically, when fans didn't like things, they wrote and posted screeds about the movies, and even occasionally organized petitions to get a beloved show back on the air. Over the past few years, there has been a trend for fans to look "behind the scenes," scrutinizing details of production that traditionally have gone uncovered by entertainment media. Fans analyze studio news, public appearances, and press releases, and in much the same way that QAnon followers do, they construct theories.

A vocal portion of the Star Wars community believed that Kathleen Kennedy, president of LucasFilm, would be fired for the poor performance of movies like *The Last Jedi* (2017) and *Solo* (2018). When Kennedy didn't get fired in 2018, they pushed back the date when she would be, like members of an apocalyptic cult. Years later, community members continue to look for patterns and construct ornate narratives of behind-the-scenes drama and maneuvering. Unlike being a member of an apocalyptic cult and selling all your possessions or being a vaccine denier, the belief that Kathleen Kennedy is going to be fired is not particularly harmful, but its persistence points to the way that the internet provides powerful affordances to support this confluence of constructed reality and confirmation bias.

Because the internet and many of its grammars for interaction are still new as media forms, many people do not have filters and expectations to guide their understanding. In some sense, QAnon is echoing the days of yellow journalism, of 1898's "Remember the *Maine*" incident, where William Randolph Hearst's newspapers claimed that a boiler explosion on a US ship docked in Cuba was actually an attack engineered by Spain.

In the decades following the worst abuses of yellow journalism, standards developed around newspapers, their veracity, and their sources. The legal and social conventions here are complex; there are protected sources and revealed sources, and there are hierarchies of reliability—that is, no one expects the *Weekly World News* to have high standards of journalism, but they do expect information printed in "newspapers of record" like the *New York Times* and the *Washington Post* to be fact-checked and verified. The internet allowed the rise of citizen journalism and for a panoply of views outside the mainstream to challenge and undermine the perspectives, framings, and reportage of more established media institutions. Darnella Frazier's cell phone recording of the murder of George Floyd at the hands of Minneapolis police officers was an act of citizen journalism with far-reaching repercussions for racial justice, policing, and other social issues (Nieto del Rio, 2021). But just as photography felt organically "true" to early and naive audiences—and in some ways, despite our knowledge of photo manipulation and deepfakes (Smith and Manstead, 2020), it still does today—many people have no internal sense of the veracity and verifiability of news that they find online. Bad actors and structural biases for profitability and sharing (as on Reddit and Facebook, where the platforms are built to make sharing videos and articles easy, regardless of their veracity) drive what is read online (Stuhr, 2020). Meanwhile, QAnon rewards people who believe in it with a sense of special knowledge, of community, and with proof that they are right.

An ARG is a consciously constructed piece of art; although the audience for it may not behave in ways that the designers expected, at the end of the day, the narrative is controlled. QAnon is primed by posts from "Q," but unlike an ARG, where the designer controls the narrative, QAnon is constantly creating multiple narratives. Audiences are naturally transformative and will add, revise, and reinterpret the information that they encounter on the internet. Since "Q" is anonymous, anyone can be "Q," and any attempt to reveal the identity of "Q" can be spun by the audience as "fake news." QAnon believers find clues and confirmation of their beliefs in informational noise that is far outside the bounds of "Q drops." For example, in an October 2017 press conference, President Trump made an inclusive gesture to people arrayed in a semicircle around him. After the first "Q drop" message, as *Atlantic* editor Adrienne LaFrance explained in an interview with NPR:

> This YouTube video of this event has become something of folklore for QAnon followers because, you know, the president does gesture frequently with his hands. But if you're a conspiracy theorist who is picking apart every last thing that he does, a sort of gesture to an assembled crowd could, in their minds, look like a secret gesture of the letter Q. And that's what a lot of QAnon folks have claimed. (LaFrance, 2020)

The way that QAnon is thriving, despite its formlessness and a continuous stream of evidence demonstrating that the narrative at its heart is not true, is evidence that there is something about this form of transmedia storytelling—borderless, interactive, multiplatform, community-based—that is a natural way for people to behave on the internet at this time.

So, does that mean that ARGs are an early version of a viable art form? There are parallels with the history of film and movies. Early films shot by the Lumière brothers and others were short, around fifty seconds initially, because of the length of film required and other technological limitations (Kuhn and Westwell, 2020). They were popular and wonderful, but they were not seen as art—not like poetry or orchestral music. It took more than fifteen years to develop a longer film that could unfold a story in multiple parts. Perhaps the ARG is, like cinema at the end of the 1800s, still finding its form.

The ARG is an early form of internet narrative art, and most designers tend to repeat the successes and failures of the first recognized ARGs. The experiences use puzzles as gates. They are borderless, and they don't acknowledge the existence of the designers. If the ARG is to become a form that could reach and engage a mass audience, it will need to evolve as it hasn't yet done. ARGs may in fact have inherent features that preclude success on a massive scale—because the community is a group of individuals coming into the experience at different times and with different expectations, there is a lot of repetition in their communications, cross-information, and ill-conceived or hasty posts, so wading through the postings can be boring and frustrating. There is a high barrier to entry and the form makes particular and stringent demands of its audience. ARGs failed because they couldn't find a way to appeal to a large enough audience to create a viable monetization model. But the appetite for borderless, interactive, community-driven experiences where the audience can actively transform the presentation of the content—interpreting the fragments of story they find, sharing it with others, assembling a coherent narrative out of the fragments, often while attempting to filter errors and misinformation, adding their own images and text—seems to be a mode of experience that arises fairly organically from the affordances of the internet. As fandoms and QAnon are showing, in the absence of artists and designers, communities of users craving these modes of sociality and engagement will create these experiences on their own.

Technology is changing very fast, and in confusing ways that strike at our ability to discern reality from fabrication, illusion, and distortion. Take deepfakes—videos that are made using machine learning to create convincing simulacra of real people, which are difficult to recognize as constructions. In one case featured by national media, an alleged deepfake video of a teenage cheerleader using a vape pen, ostensibly created by the mother of a rival cheerleader vying for a spot on the same competitive team, turned out to not be a deepfake at all—but the local sheriff, like most of us, didn't understand enough about the technology to understand how unlikely it was that the accused parent could have created it (Korducki, 2021). The technology is evolving rapidly, and it's possible that convincing deepfakes will soon become easy enough to create that social platforms will be full of them. The unknown unknowns mean that a sudden leap in technology could lead to narrative possibilities that aren't available. The evolution of cultural understanding of the internet, as well as the cultural norms surrounding it, like the evolution of ethics and standards in newspapers and televised journalism, could mean that audiences have different cultural expectations of what they consume.

But there is something, at least at this moment in the confluence of technology and society, that suggests that transmedia, in some version, arises easily. Discovering and analyzing pieces of information, developing theories and narrative around those pieces, and sharing them with others are real and persistent experiences on the web and in web communities.

Can this style of borderless, co-created, interactive storytelling be designed for an audience that transcends a diehard niche? Or is the purest form of transmedia merely seeded, like QAnon, with scant foundational information and "designed" by the audience in collaboration with the seeders?

Transmedia is an art form, either designed or emerging organically from the community-forging and transformative possibilities that the internet affords, which insinuates itself into the online lives of the audience in a way that is particularly pleasurable. ARGs failed to make the transition from niche entertainment to mass market, but the affordances that gave rise to ARGs—the technological ability to interact, to create communities, and to generate multiplatform experiences and movements—suggest that transmedia principles are emergent, and they will be part of culture in complex ways across multiple disciplines. Transmedia is here, in our lives, our stories, and our politics.

Notes

1. The nickname *The Beast* was an internal invention. At one point, an asset list—a list of required images, text, and website addresses that made up the experience—had 666 items on it. The actual experience was not initially named. See Handy 2005.

2. There has always been interactive art—the happenings of the 1960s and 1970s and performance art, for example—but they have not been mass-market experiences.

3. An extreme example of this is from the *Year Zero* ARG, linked to the Nine Inch Nails album of the same name. The ARG started before the album was released, while the band was still touring for its previous album, *White Teeth*. In Spain, the designers arranged for a thumb drive to be left in a men's bathroom with an unreleased song from *Year Zero*. It seems unlikely that someone would find a thumb drive in a men's room in a coliseum in Spain and stick it in their computer, much less upload the song to the internet. Not only did that happen in less than twenty-four hours, but someone ran the file through a visual sound wave generator to reveal an image encoded in the sound of a hand reaching down—and uploaded that, too.

References

Bessi, Alessandro, and Walter Quattrociocchi. 2015. "Disintermediation: Digital Wildfires in the Age of Misinformation." *Australian Quarterly* 86, no. 4: 34–39.

Handy, Alex. 2005. "The Buzzmakers." *East Bay Express*, May 18, 2005. https://web
.archive.org/web/20070407060201/http:/www.eastbayexpress.com/2005-05-18
/news/the-buzzmakers.

Hon, Adrian. 2020. "What ARGs Can Teach Us about QAnon." *MSSV*, August 2, 2020. https://mssv.net/2020/08/02/what-args-can-teach-us-about-qanon.

Korducki, Kelli María. 2021. "The World Thought This Cheer Mom Created a Deepfake to Harass Her Daughter's Rival—But the Real Story Is Way More Confusing (and Bizarre)." *Cosmopolitan*, September 21, 2021. https://www.cosmopolitan.com/lifestyle
/a37377027/deep-fake-cheer-scandal.

Kuhn, Annette, and Guy Westwell. 2020. "Actualities (*Actualités*)." In *A Dictionary of Film Studies*, 2nd ed. Oxford Reference. Oxford: Oxford University Press. https://
www.oxfordreference.com/view/10.1093/acref/9780198832096.001.0001/acref
-9780198832096-e-0006.

LaFrance, Adrienne. 2020. "Journalist Enters the World of QAnon: 'It's Almost Like a Bad Spy Novel.'" Interview by Dave Davies. *Fresh Air*, NPR, August 20, 2020. https://
www.npr.org/2020/08/20/904237192/journalist-enters-the-world-of-qanon-it-s
-almost-like-a-bad-spy-novel.

Lee, Elan. 2002. "This Is Not a Game." Lecture at the Game Developers Conference (GDC). McEnery Convention Center, San Jose, CA, March 22, 2002.

Library of Congress. n.d. "The Case of the Moved Body." Part of the Civil War Glass Negatives and Related Prints Collection. Accessed May 24, 2021. https://www.loc
.gov/collections/civil-war-glass-negatives/articles-and-essays/does-the-camera-ever
-lie/the-case-of-the-moved-body.

Lott, Tim. 2008. "The Internet Is Proving That 200 Heads Are Better Than One." *Sunday Telegraph*, March 30, 2008, 42.

Nieto del Rio, Giulia McDonnell. 2021. "Darnella Frazier, the Teenager Who Recorded George Floyd's Murder, Speaks Out." *New York Times*, May 25, 2021. https://www.nytimes.com/2021/05/25/us/darnella-frazier.html.

Smith, Hannah, and Katherine Mansted. 2020. "Weaponised Deep Fakes." In *Weaponised Deep Fakes: National Security and Democracy*, 11–14. Canberra, Australia: Australian Strategic Policy Institute. http://www.jstor.org/stable/resrep25129.7.

Stuhr, John J. 2020. "Truth, Truths, and Pluralism." *Journal of Speculative Philosophy* 34, no. 4: 526–544. https://doi.org/10.5325/jspecphil.34.4.0526.

Winick, Stephen D. 2018. "Rumors of Our Deaths: Fake News, Folk News, and Far Away Moses." *Journal of American Folklore* 131, no. 522: 388–397. https://doi.org/10.5406/jamerfolk.131.522.0388.

Zadrozny, Brandy, and Ben Collins. 2018. "How Three Conspiracy Theorists Took 'Q' and Sparked Qanon." *NBC News*, August 14, 2018. https://www.nbcnews.com/tech/tech-news/how-three-conspiracy-theorists-took-q-sparked-qanon-n900531.

2 Who, Where, and How: Building Successful Transmedia Campaigns across Industries

Caitlin Burns

Following Maureen McHugh Yeager's account of early experiments in transmedia in chapter 1, this chapter provides an insider's view of how these practices have since been codified by the entertainment industry to drive corporate strategy in the age of megafranchises and consolidated storyworlds. While the rest of this volume is less concerned with commercial applications of transmedia, this chapter illustrates the myriad tactical choices made by transmedia producers to artfully craft and precisely deliver experiences that drive audience engagement while fortifying the infrastructure that makes these experiences possible—decisions about content, interaction, and structure that are at the heart of each case study covered in the rest of the volume. Examining the key performance indicators (KPIs) behind various types of transmedia projects and distribution platforms, Burns provides a scaffolding for production and assessment. The chapter considers how successful transmedia experiences are born of a networked model of creative development, a process that considers the ever-evolving needs and whims of the audience (for whom the experience is ultimately crafted), while attending to often-conflicting mandates of platform owners, financiers, and organizational partners whose loose confederation must be maintained and reaffirmed for a project to launch, grow, and thrive. In chapter 10, on constructing a transmedia experience around boys' and men's volleyball, Jennifer Palilonis explicitly examines this alignment between narrative worldbuilding and the practical systems thinking that supports it, judging the efficacy of a set of interventions and texts against the KPIs of social media metrics. Meanwhile, Kirsten Ostherr argues for a corrective to the impersonal quantitative measurement of nuanced human emotion in chapter 13, about transmedia logics in health care. In both of these examples, as well as elsewhere in this volume, Burns's thesis rings true: contextual awareness of how value is defined and measured by both audiences and stakeholders must be carefully considered before embarking on this type of work.

Introduction: Key Performance Indicators and Where to Find Them

Early in my professional career, I was thrust into the maelstrom of Hollywood film franchise development as a transmedia producer. It was a new title at the time, and my job involved organizing storytelling across platforms so that each game, book, web series, or other creation could both stand alone as a fun experience and connect to a bigger storyworld—without repeating the same story over and over. The goal of this work—with over thirty groups of storytellers making experiences on different platforms—was to put the storyworld of an intellectual property (IP) first. Executives had the radical idea that if the story is good wherever an audience member engages with it, the audience will like it more and it will make more money.

As a green, young producer suddenly finding myself in rooms with prestigious studio executives, this was a daunting task. Luckily, the idea that making connected experiences would drive audiences across platforms worked! Surprisingly (but maybe less so in retrospect), creating a big storyworld together led to fruitful and enjoyable collaborations, as consumer-products groups, game divisions, publishing groups, and visionary filmmakers joined forces to create decade-spanning story arcs. Projects like Disney's *Pirates of the Caribbean*, *Descendants*, and *Tron: Legacy*, Microsoft's *Halo*, and Nickelodeon's *Teenage Mutant Ninja Turtles* all used transmedia techniques and production methodologies to build global success stories.

I've since had the opportunity to create my own independent transmedia projects, like *McCarren Park*, a microbudget project that spanned two years of online content, live events, and a feature-length film distributed by bar crawl in Brooklyn, New York. I've worked with major nongovernmental organizations (NGOs) on projects like *UNICEF Kid Power*, data scientists on multiplatform visualization experiences, and even in commercial space tourism, trying to make astronaut training available to anyone on Earth. What all these transmedia projects have in common is that none of them would have been possible without a group of people working together, pooling their resources and reaching out to audiences.

Creating a successful transmedia project requires a team. This is true whether the project is an independent piece of work being developed in the creator's spare time with a few volunteers or a global multiplatform campaign engaging thousands of creators and reaching hundreds of millions of audience members. That team of stakeholders is called a *community of interest*. This group of creative, production, distribution, and financing allies together contribute the resources needed to bring a transmedia project to life.

Each member of a community of interest—whether an individual or a company—will have their own skills, needs, goals, and resources. Each one will want the project to be successful, but success will mean different things to everyone involved. As a transmedia practitioner, understanding and balancing the goals of a community of interest is the path to finding the financing, resources, and audiences that your project needs to thrive.

All transmedia projects require time, creative minds, artistic vision, collaboration, money, and production resources, in some combination. Even with the most brilliant artistic concept, if a team lacks one of those other requirements, they have to expand their project's structure. This usually means bringing in a new member of the community of interest—an individual or a company—and adapting the project structure to accommodate their needs. Need someone to organize the production process? Find a producer. Need to compensate writers or developers for their time? Find a financier. Want to reach a wider audience? Find a distributor for a major production asset like a film, podcast series, or TV show, and work with it to feature a portion of the transmedia project.

There is an art and a science to creating successful and popular transmedia experiences, both built on the interlocking goals of their community of interest, the skills and creativity of the artists involved, and the behaviors of the audience members.

What Gets Potential Allies into a Transmedia Project's Community of Interest?

Understanding everyone's goals and making sure that they get what they need from the production is critical for a producer, creator, or practitioner. If creators and their project can show how they will answer the core needs of production partners, and showcase that in a way that others in that field will also see clearly, it becomes straightforward to find the partners that best fit your project's creative goals. Imagine that you've got a great animated series for kids featuring a series of charming warrior animals. You might want to reach out to a toy company that makes action figures. If your content is a documentary about a social issue, you might look to foundations or institutions that are looking for ways to raise awareness of that issue.

Each project's community of interest is different, brought together by shared creative and commercial goals. These communities of interest are diverse and often lead to innovation and breakthroughs via creative collaboration. Each transmedia project also represents a fascinating challenge as shared goals, and the specific goals of each community member, must be assessed, integrated, measured, and analyzed.

This chapter will discuss the reasons that major industry partners decide to ally themselves with transmedia projects, committing large budgets and distribution platforms that can get their work seen by millions of audience members. Understanding why potential industry partners make the decisions they do can help transmedia creators build communities of interest to craft creatively and financially successful productions.

How Do Creators Assess the Goals of Their Potential Major Platform Partners?

Every potential partner is different, and the relationships that lead to successful productions are usually built when producers connect with individual champions for a transmedia project who are situated within larger organizations. To find those champions, it helps to understand the background of the target industry.

Each major content type in the entertainment industry has its own history, decision-making style, production needs, and prior experience with transmedia techniques. While they all want to reach and engage with audiences, the methods that they utilize vary broadly and will determine where transmedia productions are created or managed in their organizations, how they are funded, and what their team's goals are.

Partners in a community of interest will judge a transmedia project by the rubric of their traditional, single-platform projects first. They will be able to experiment and expand their thinking *only* when a concept can enhance or amplify their single-platform goals. How will the extended platforms drive audiences to a season (or multiple seasons) of a podcast or television show? If there's no reason to believe that the partner will be successful in its core business, why would it support the other platforms?

The great news for practitioners is that interwoven narratives and experiences *do* amplify those goals, and creators can make strong arguments for their expansive productions—if they're able to demonstrate a clear understanding of those single-platform goals first.

In practice, potential industry allies will define success with different *key performance indicators (KPIs)*: the specific metrics used by creators and companies to gauge performance on each platform.

What Are the Common Goals of All Commercial Creative Industries?

Every successful multiplatform or transmedia campaign figures out how to combine the goals of its community of interest and balance four major goals that all projects have in common:

- Creative execution
- Outreach and engagement
- Sustainability
- Longevity

Creative Execution

Every project must meet a different set of needs in order to bring its artistic vision to life: this constitutes the *arts* part of "creative arts." Whether their producers classify the work as fine art, low art, or a purely commercial product, all artistic projects aim to elicit an emotional response in audience members to evoke a specific behavioral outcome. These outcomes vary, so the assessment of the success or failure of a creative execution is often subjective.

The themes of a narrative may aim to establish long-lasting relationships with characters that appeal to positive human virtues. Other campaigns may seek to educate, or to sell toothpaste. Still others are optimized to inspire political activism or apathy. Experienced creative teams will build various narrative and experiential solutions based on the artistic parameters set by the goals of the community of interest.

In some projects, the creative goal may be to encourage empathy, present an alternative life experience, or technically explore a new animation style. While the Assassin's Creed franchise (a blend of deeply researched historical adventure and science fiction) centers on tremendously successful video games that have expanded, with broad critical success, into transmedia extensions in social and mobile games, its 2016 feature film is largely unremembered. While many mobile, online, and social games based on the storyworld were able to find commercial and audience success, when creative execution is overtaken by other goals or when projects merely rehash thoroughly trodden narrative ground, transmedia extensions can falter. Many elements led to a lackluster feature-film extension of Assassin's Creed, but compressing a storyline that fans of the game had already experienced over the course of twenty to forty hours into a ninety-minute span—rather than exploring a new facet of the storyworld better suited to the film medium—was a major factor. Fans of the franchise felt that the film was made for audiences that weren't them, and wider audiences perceived the film as geared for the gaming audience. As a counterpoint, *Halo 4: Forward Unto Dawn*, *Halo: Reach*, and *Halo: Nightfall* all explored stories that related to game releases in the venerable Halo sci-fi space opera series, but they presented genuinely new storylines and perspectives, and therefore they attracted critical praise and high audience numbers.

Other game franchises, like Microsoft's futuristic military property Gears of War, expand their storyworld through transmedia novel extensions. The Gears novels provide insight into the emotional lives of the macho military main characters, adding depth to the storyworld while topping the sales charts. Gears of War's novels developed older female characters who later made their way into the console games after proving their popularity with fans via the books. While the series's video games hit big with men aged eighteen to twenty-four, the novels reached outside the core demographic and became bestsellers for men and women aged eighteen to forty-five. This new audience converted to new game players across genders and age demographics, and even led to the integration of characters who were more reflective of that broad audience base—notably Bernadette "Bernie" Mataki, a marine in her fifties featured first in Gears of War novels written by Karen Traviss, who then made her first game appearance in *Gears of War 3*.

In an IP universe like Hasbro's Transformers, a character rubric that allows creators to iterate an infinite number of new characters for future toys led to the creation of a Cybertonian astrology chart. Based on Western European astrology, this tool allowed the new characters' personalities to be based on star positions around the Transformers' home planet, Cybertron, while connecting to existing characters, lore, physical characteristics, and archetypes. While the goals that tool supports are not purely creative, they were extremely useful for future creators of games, comics, animated series, and more.

Experienced transmedia creators devise where these KPI parameters exist and share them with their creative collaborators. For example, a creator might say, "We expect to get X number of impressions on this content based on similar projects" or "This is a great opportunity to tie in with a sponsor you may already have on board—we can determine how long each player spends in this online game and show your sponsor engagement data, based on content with their product placement."

Many creators have an intuitive sense for additional parameters that they'll need to include in their artistic vision: where to invite audiences to new platforms in an experience, what element feels like a distant mountain for a future story, or identifying an Easter egg for a storyline in another experience. On the practical side, these KPIs show creators how their work engages their audiences across platforms. KPIs like overall impressions will show creators who and where their audience is, when they're engaging, and which platforms have more engagement than others. These parameters and creative techniques can help creators show how their artistic vision connects with their partners' goals. These indicators will also be the barometer of the health of, and interest in, a transmedia world overall and guide decisions about where a creator should apply more resources and which extensions failed to grab enough audience attention.

Establishing a moving, successfully crafted experience is the key to connecting with audiences on one platform or multiple platforms. *The success of a creative execution is measured in the reaction of audiences.*

Outreach and Engagement

1. It is universally acknowledged that an audience with discretionary income must be looking for a commercial storyworld. The underlying truth is that every media project wants an audience and must invest significant time, resources, and energy to find, develop, and sustain one.

2. Whether a project is built to span continents and decades, aiming for billions of viewers to become the next Star Wars, or to create a deep, intimate, exclusive experience that a select few will talk about for the rest of their lives, like the Wu-Tang Clan's album *Once Upon a Time in Shaolin*, that project has to invite its audience to engage with it.

For transmedia projects, finding and expanding an audience are essential parts of how the success of that project will be measured. In fact, that's the entire point of transmedia technique—that a production can draw an audience across multiple platforms to achieve a larger creative goal. The outreach goals of each project add to the artistic parameters used in the project's creative execution, and when creativity is applied to outreach goals, unique and exciting experiences are often created.

To reach audiences, productions must first understand who their potential audiences are. In some cases, partners in a project's community of interest may already have research departments or platform-specific data on who they can reach directly. A great virtue of transmedia production techniques is that unique content can be targeted to specific, niche audiences, with content directly tailored to their interests, while other platform extensions can reach more broadly across demographics. A single transmedia franchise can contain children's books for kids ages eight to fourteen, games rated for mature audiences, and one-event-only experiential activations at SXSW or San Diego Comic-Con without breaking the continuity of its storylines or offending fans.

Outreach is not only conducted before a project is released, but as an ongoing process of evaluating both projected and actual audience behaviors and refining projects in response to audience feedback. *The success of outreach is measured in how many audience members engage with a project's content: number of viewers, tickets sold, and time spent engaging with content, among other factors.*

Sustainability

Sustainability is often dismissed as a critical element when discussing art, but the ability to finance, produce, distribute, and maintain a piece of creative work is the parameter that most often determines the success or failure of a production. If the project does not have the financial resources to sustain itself, it won't realize its goals.

Commercial artists are intimately aware of the critical dynamic between budgeting, financing, and successful projects. Most ambitious or notable fine artists have also had to carefully balance and budget volunteer and donation-based resources in order to realize their visions—as well as to avoid legal and tax trouble.

More than any other constraint, planning how to apply financial resources to creative execution and outreach determines the scope and scale of the artistic experience. It's no wonder that artists often bristle at the perceived constraints of budget-conscious executives and producers stomping all over their vision.

Finding financial support for projects often means including specific parameters in your community of interest. Some commercial partnerships feel like obvious fits because they've proven themselves. After passing on a toy partnership with Star Wars in 1977, Mattel commissioned a new IP that they could support and ended up creating the sword-and-sorcery inspired Masters of the Universe line, featuring the iconic He-Man, in partnership with Filmation. This animated series rapidly developed a life of its own, sprawling across TV, home video, games, and comic books, as well as the popular spin-off She-Ra. This initial financial investment meant that so long as the franchise kept selling toys, they could explore complex and sometimes controversial themes: feminism and gender roles in *She-Ra: Princess of Power* (1985), and later, issues of identity and LGBTQIA+ attraction in the breakout reboot from Netflix, *She-Ra and the Princess of Power* (2018). All the stakeholders were able to reach their goals creatively and financially, and *Masters of the Universe* is still a profitable franchise forty years later.

A toy company investing in a children's animated series may seem like an obvious fit among partners in a community of interest. The first potential financial partners in any community of interest are usually the ones who seem most obvious. A transmedia creator seeking financial partners must take a few steps back and identify those potential fits for the type of project that they are creating and how these puzzle pieces of complementary goals might go together.

Sustainability is about applying financing and practical resources throughout the production ecosystem to ensure that all the goals of creative execution, outreach, and longevity are achieved. *The success of sustainability is measured by the revenue that a project gains versus the amount of resources invested to achieve specific project goals.*

Longevity

Archiving and recapitulating transmedia campaigns for future audiences have long been pain points for practitioners. While passive content in traditional platforms like feature films continues to be available for decades after release, the often-exceptional interactive works that initially built their fan bases are rarely preserved. Transmedia extensions are rarely viewed by major industry partners as deserving of additional investment beyond artists' portfolios or a digital agency's case-study reel—unless their creators have a strong plan in place for longevity. How long a project persists in the market is a function of how much outreach and budget are required to sustain the creative experiences.

Short-term projects where conception, production, and goals are meant to be met over the course of weeks tend to have higher budgets but lower longevity, disappearing from the public consciousness almost as soon as they arrive. These short-term projects are characterized by large external investments that support experiences, usually platform experiences that do not need to be self-sustaining in revenue. They are often aimed at shifting specific audience attention or behavior goals of promotion or activism. An example might be an advertising campaign like Microsoft's *Camp Know Where* for *Stranger Things*, which was designed to run for a single summer; all of the experience's content was taken down after Halloween 2020.

Long-term projects like film franchises involve multiple layers of multiplatform experiences that are planned strategically over the course of years. By design, these storyworlds seek to capture audience attention for years or even decades, connecting audiences with narratives and characters. Some content in these projects is built to be easily archived and adapted for ongoing viewing, while associated experiences are built for shorter-term goals to engage audiences with direct outreach, or in reaction to experiential trends.

The television series *Orphan Black*, a science fiction thriller about human cloning, built a cult following that sustained a five-season run on broadcast television. While the seasons were later syndicated and reaired on streaming platforms, a robust fan community continued to discover and fall in love with the show. These fans were also active creators of fan fiction (also known as *fic*, or *fanfic*). Data from fic platforms and portals like Wattpad showed that people were reading, writing, and commenting on these fan-created stories, indicating healthy demand for new content about *Orphan Black*'s characters. While the fan base wasn't strong enough to launch a new television series, it was large enough to bring Serial Box Publishing, a company that distributes novels through weekly chapters, to create new novelizations in the storyworld years after the series finale, leading to critical and audience acclaim. *The success of longevity is measured by how long a project can connect with old and new audiences to achieve its core creative and thematic goals.*

Does an Audience Really Want This?

While creative execution, outreach, sustainability, and longevity all pertain to the goals that go into the creation of a production, there is one metric that will make or break a project: *For a media production of any kind to succeed, it must be something that an audience will find desirable.*

If a creator cannot demonstrate a clear, obvious, and reasonable argument as to why people will want to engage with their idea, then audiences will not connect with it. If a creator or producer is approaching partners and doesn't know anything about who this project is for and what it wants to achieve, there's no reason for them to invest their time, creative energy, or money.

The audience is the most important participant in a transmedia production's community of interest. All of the other metrics are aimed at how to best support interactions between the audience and a creative work:

M1. **Creative execution**: Creating engaging experiences for audiences to interact with that they will enjoy.

M2. **Outreach**: Inviting the audience in and letting them know this experience is desirable.

M3. **Sustainability**: Making sure that the audience has experiences to engage with that can be financially self-sustaining or profitable.

M4. **Longevity**: Ensuring that the experiences are available to future audiences to discover, engage with, and enjoy.

In the following sections, I will go deeper into how each industry field engages with its audiences. Every member of a project's community of interest, and all the artistic parameters that a creative team uses to frame its work, depend on audience members engaging with the work.

To examine the interplay between creative execution, outreach, sustainability, and longevity, and to understand how these goals operate as KPIs in different industries, the following sections evaluate key decision-making factors for four industry partner types for transmedia content: film, television, streaming media, and AAA games (a term denoting video games with large marketing and development budgets).

Table 2.1.
Goal emphasis by industry

Industry	Outreach	Creative Execution	Sustainability	Longevity
Film	High	Medium	High	High
TV	Medium	Medium	High	High
Streaming	Low	High	Medium	High
AAA games	Low	High	Medium	Medium

The key differences between a game created to complement a film franchise and an advertising pop-up experience for a television series become clear when you look at the goals that initiate the decision-making, which usually emerge from a central industrial leader at the core of a production.

Film: Building Storyworlds to Span Decades

Industry	Outreach	Creative Execution	Sustainability	Longevity
Film	High	Medium	High	High

Feature-length films are big-budget investments. High-budget films cost hundreds of millions of dollars, while a midrange project may cost between $35 million and $75 million to produce. Low-budget features are classified as having budgets under $10 million, which still exceeds the capital raised by the vast majority of the world's start-up businesses. With such large financial investments, this industry is risk-averse and wants to invest those big budgets in projects with a high likelihood to return their investment.

This risk aversion led to the rise of the Intellectual Property Franchise: multifilm storyworlds that often start with existing fan bases and build larger and larger audiences over time. For major studios, creating "evergreen properties"—storyworlds that can launch new titles for decades—became a critical factor in investment in the first two decades of the twenty-first century. Usually comprising three or more iterations or sequels, the name recognition and connected storylines of these franchises can be relied on to draw audiences to new titles and allow for the growth of fan bases that can be tapped as audiences for transmedia extensions, licensed products, and word-of-mouth promotion.

How Film-Based Groups Determine Success

Creative Execution

The global film franchises of the twentieth century—properties like Star Wars, Back to the Future, and the James Bond movies—have created lasting commercial success. In the twenty-first century, studios rushed to purchase or license works with franchise potential: they understood that building new storylines from storyworlds that were already familiar to audiences, and which could grow sustainably over time, would increase longevity, reduce risks in sustainability, and simplify outreach.

Franchise transmedia development is characterized by the development of storyworlds across multiple platforms, with a focus on high-budget platforms like films and video games. In this development model, IP owners and managers rely on transmedia techniques to tell stories that may roll out over the course of decades, employing complex storyworld building to architect story arcs and parameters that will be used by thousands of creators to generate hundreds of stand-alone experiences.

While franchise transmedia has many standout examples, the Marvel Cinematic Universe (MCU) has become the gold standard for film-based franchise storyworlds. At the turn of the twenty-first century, studios believed that audiences would become bored with a storyworld after a three-film trilogy. The Star Wars franchise tested this supposition with its release of Episodes 1, 2, and 3, and audiences showed up—but the MCU was a more ambitious plan altogether. Based on the success of persistent story arcs proven to build audiences in comic books for decades, the MCU wove together major story arcs or "phases" of three- to five-character-led films, culminating in a team-up film. They then repeated the formula in subsequent story arcs following the success of the first phase, which culminated with *The Avengers* in 2012. The Marvel Comics audience had been an increasingly aging, White, male demographic; the MCU films transformed it into a global, diverse, millions-strong fan base that shows up at the box office in larger numbers for each new release. The success of this cinematic universe has also reinvigorated interest in Marvel's comic books and launched dozens of associated games, novels, and consumer products.

Outreach and Engagement

In the vast majority of cases, the film industry has invested in the exploration of transmedia extensions in storyworlds through marketing departments. These groups have more short-term audience engagement goals and see transmedia experiences as avenues to engage audiences with new stories or support fans with more of what they already love. Some of the twenty-first century's most notable transmedia campaigns and alternate-reality games were marketing efforts for feature film franchises, including *Why So Serious?* for Warner Bros.' *The Dark Knight* and *Flynn Lives* for Disney's *Tron: Legacy*. While some of these transmedia campaigns seed content for fans years before a film's release, the investment in these productions tends to be limited to the prerelease period, ending once a film has been released for rental and ownership.

The primary goal for studios and distributors when investing in marketing-based transmedia is developing audience members into fans. By investing in the early life cycle of a storyworld, inviting audience members to explore and engage, they spark the imaginations of audience members. The audience members that want to spend more time in that world are provided the means to deepen their fandom and are thus more likely to spend time (and money) in extensions on other platforms in the future—and to evangelize the storyworld to others.

Sustainability

While it's easy to look at big-budget film franchises and imagine that they have limitless money to sustain each storyworld, this assumption is false. While feature-film budgets balloon thanks to visual effects and star salaries, data-conscious budgeting is critical in the film industry—especially for transmedia and licensed extensions, where budgets are smaller and the goal is to promote the long-term life cycles of films themselves. For new franchises, a test-and-learn process wherein multiple experiences are piloted to targeted audiences is common, with successful, self-sustaining productions being expanded only if they prove profitable. While the Hunger Games films initially relied on fans of the novels to drive promotion, it amplified its investments in expanded social media, gaming, and consumer-products extensions once the first film was a proven box-office hit.

A key factor underpinning sustainability is the disposition of IP. The first question that a film partner will ask about a project they're interested in is: is this the creator's story to tell?

The *IP owner* is the originator of a creative work (either the original author, the company that developed it, or heirs of the original author). IP owners have the legal right to make whatever story or experience they like and to license their storyworld: that is, to give legal permission to other creators to make specific experiences.

Many studios and production companies license IP as *IP holders*, an arrangement wherein an IP owner has sold to other groups the permission to create experiences in that storyworld. The IP holder also has the rights to grant *internal licenses* to creative groups within their company, or *external licenses* to other companies to create work within the IP during the term of the license (e.g., mobile games, cruise-ship experiences, or books). To retain licenses of IP—even for things that have not seen great success in the market—a license holder will often have to create a new public production of that work every seven years, or else the rights will revert to the original owner (US Department of Justice and Federal Trade Commission, 2017).

Film groups have a vested interest in investments that they can grow, and even A-list talent has to show that a new IP is a viable investment. It took twenty years for James Cameron to produce the film *Avatar*, a storyworld that he invented when he was driving trucks on sets in the early 1990s (Keegan, 2017). It wasn't as simple as just selling a script—Cameron set out to create a filmic storyworld that could also tell its story through games, books, theme-park experiences, and more. The reality of producing such a sprawling vision, even for a legendary A-list director, is complex, requiring billions of dollars in investment from partners and studios, as well as legions of creators to bring the vision to life.

Longevity

While feature films have long life spans as rentals and on streaming platforms, their transmedia extensions tend to disappear within a year of their release. This is because licensed projects' success is measured quarterly and annually based on short-term promotional or revenue goals. The rollout of films and their promotion follow a "windowed" model, designed to optimize a film's revenue-generating potential at release.

Distribution Windows

For film studios and distributors, decision-making metrics focus on how to maximize their financial returns in a series of "windows" spaced out over the weeks and months of a film's initial release:

- Domestic box office theaters
- International box office theaters
- Hotel and airline on-board viewing licenses
- At-home entertainment purchases
- Rental purchases
- Ownership purchases
- Premium network and streaming network licensing
- Broadcast TV, cable network syndication

For decades, these windows represented a pattern that allowed films to reap revenue in a consistent chronological sequence, but in the 2010s, this model began to break down. By 2020, the disruption of the COVID-19 pandemic shifted these windows permanently, driving studios and distributors to break with the brick-and-mortar and on-board viewing windows and bring first-run releases directly to audiences at home. Nonetheless, these windows, as well as the multistage model that they represent, are still critical considerations for studios that wish to optimize revenue generation for their films.

While franchises like the MCU and Star Wars allow for longer-term metrics to be analyzed, the vast majority of transmedia extensions—games, books, online and physical experiences—are built for specific promotional purposes, without long-term archiving in mind. For the film industry, the film is forever, while a partner will be looking for fresh experiences across platforms to promote a new title within a storyworld for each new film's release.

Major Film Key Performance Indicators

1. Domestic US box office receipts
2. International box office receipts
3. Distribution license sale or presale
4. Cable, premium, or streaming network licensing or presale
5. Home entertainment sales (physical or digital)

6. Consumer product sales

7. Game, publishing, and other licenses

8. Rental sales

9. Earned media (word of mouth, buzz)

10. Fan base activity

11. Social media activity

Television: Serialized Content and Sustained Real-Time Engagement

Industry	Outreach	Creative Execution	Sustainability	Longevity
TV	Medium	Medium	High	High

In the transmedia or entertainment industry context, the term "television partners" refers to broadcasters, production companies, and networks that showcase serialized content, traditionally on a week-to-week rollout schedule. While some of these companies create IP that they own, many do not, thanks in part to the deregulation of the broadcast industry in the 1990s.

These groups have been around for almost a century, and for the vast majority of that time, they were supported entirely by on-air advertising. There are two axioms that shape the decisions of ad-based television networks about what transmedia extensions they greenlight:

- Will audiences be more likely to tune in to content that showcases advertisements based on this content?
- Will advertisers support this content?

For television partners that own IP or act as IP holders, the goal is, as with film franchises, to develop fan bases over time. Most television shows require two seasons of content before they can say that they've found their full audience base. Even so, the need to demonstrate strong audiences in early episodes is critical to keep a show on the air long enough to reach that larger potential audience. Many shows are cancelled within six episodes of initial airing because they do not demonstrate sufficient initial audience interest.

With the advent of television shows' syndication to streaming services, the potential long-term audiences for shows have expanded. While *The*

Walking Dead first premiered for US audiences in 2010 on the AMC cable network, domestic and international audiences are discovering it for the first time through streaming and looking for ways to engage in the storyworld, breathing new life into older game releases. In 2021, fan clubs for shows like *Dawson's Creek* (1998–2003) are bringing new superfans to shows that first ran when the fans were babies or even not yet born. As the long-term audience has expanded, so has the opportunity for transmedia extensions to draw in viewers or enhance the experience of a television show over time.

For television partners that are only broadcasting content, they may or may not have license to create transmedia extensions. When they do, those transmedia campaigns' goals tend to focus on launching a new show or season, supporting week-to-week tune-in, and/or showcasing popular shows at events like San Diego Comic-Con or SXSW with content that can go viral, earning media attention or supporting a show's pursuit of major awards.

How Television-Based Groups Determine Success

Creative Execution

Transmedia extensions for shows tend to be short-term experiential promotions, or narratives that can stand alone outside the real-world air dates of a season of episodes, serving to extend storyworlds. Licensed novels, like those created for the ABC series *Castle* (mystery novels ostensibly written by the show's lead character, a novelist who works with a detective to solve crimes), are remembered fondly, while being sufficiently self-contained that someone who discovered the show years after its initial airing could still enjoy them. Meanwhile, more ephemeral and less modular extensions, like the well-received Twitter account for the title character, Richard Castle, are rarely remembered. Mobile games that allow players worldwide to explore different areas of storyworlds, like the mobile game for Disney's Descendants, are developed with a careful eye to budget and audience outreach, expanding their scope only if they prove to be self-sustaining.

Like film franchises, television series are long-term projects, aiming to span years or even decades if they're successful. For most television series, transmedia campaigns are launched to help introduce new shows, invite audiences into their world, and test and learn what audiences will want within that world. Creatively, transmedia expansions for television series tend to take place in real time in the interstitial period between new episodes airing.

The Descendants franchise is a fascinating hybrid of film and television considerations and a standout example of transmedia storytelling. Featuring the children of legendary Disney heroes and villains in a magical, singing, dancing high school, the franchise's driving platform is live-action films presented on the Disney Channel. For the Disney Channel, it is also an opportunity to expand its core audience, and to appeal to older audiences with transmedia story extensions.

Aiming to reach older audiences—specifically "new adult" readers of young adult fiction, ages thirteen to thirty-four—they created a trilogy of novels featuring storylines that were more mature than the on-air content. To connect with emerging fans, the property commissioned an in-world social media publication, *Auradon Buzz*, that updated in real time based on events in the novelization, leading up to the premiere of the first Descendants film. The social content continued to update based on events of *Descendants: Wicked World*, an animated series skewed toward younger audiences. These three major narrative drivers were able to tell a broader and more complete story than the films themselves, and audiences responded by role-playing as denizens of the fictional world in the comments section of *Auradon Buzz* and celebrating every time a new Easter egg was revealed across the platform extensions. Most of these platforms yielded well-deserved success, which validated the hypothesis that this storyworld would be a hit—and led to the greenlighting of a full novel trilogy, expanded storylines in on-air animation, and the engagement of high-level live-action talent in additional story extensions aimed at social media.

Outreach and Engagement

A critical consideration for transmedia extensions is *earned media*: how much attention a piece of promotional content can attract from press outlets. Networks' ability to fund and continue to air shows depends on demonstrating to advertisers the value of the time slots that they are purchasing—measured in viewers, press, and prestige. Because most transmedia extensions for television serve a promotional purpose, networks rarely invest significant budget on promoting their promotions, even if they generate revenue. Eye-catching installations, shareability on social media, and the ability to generate press are strong motivators for television industry groups to invest in transmedia extensions. Campfire's *Game of Thrones* food trucks, *Breaking Bad*'s "Better Call Saul" billboards, and *The Man in the High Castle*'s *Resistance Radio* album are examples of buzzworthy experiences that gave audiences a thrill while attracting millions of impressions through press coverage.

The SyFy Channel bucked the promotion-only transmedia investment style by devising a concept entirely integrated with *Defiance*, its postapocalyptic sci-fi Western series created in partnership with Trion Worlds. Learning from the popularity of licensed multiplayer gaming drawn from the Battlestar Galactica universe, and from their attempt at a connected game and original movie with *Red Faction: Origins*, created in partnership with the game studio THQ, SyFy created a truly connected television experience. Between episodes of *Defiance*, players of the massively multiplayer online game (MMO) were invited to complete challenges relating to the events of the series, pushing further into the universe and inviting audiences deeper into the storyworld. While the show ended its run after three seasons, the MMO persists and maintains an active user base nearly a decade later.

Sustainability

Overall investment in shows in the US is at or above $5 million per episode for a major cable network, not including the associated administrative and marketing costs (Ryan and Littleton, 2017). Even for a short-run series, those numbers add up fast. The financial model of televised series relies on constant fundraising approaches to advertisers, and decisions are made mostly with quarterly and annual budgets in mind. For transmedia extensions, budgets are mostly drawn from marketing to help develop and showcase the audience numbers that will eventually yield lucrative syndication licenses to rerun shows on cable networks or streaming services.

Beyond syndication, a major sustainability question is: can the series be translated to an international market as a format? Pioneered in reality television, a television show format refers to a piece of original IP that can be adapted or reshot for the needs of another country's broadcast market. Shows like *Survivor*, *MasterChef*, and *The Voice* are all multibillion-dollar formats with dozens of localized spin-offs. Successful narrative television shows also follow this model, either spinning off local versions of shows, like *24: India*, with new characters, or reshooting the entire narrative run of shows with local actors as in *Metástasis* (*Breaking Bad* in Colombia) or *Jane the Virgin* and *Queen of the South*, both successful shows in the US that were adapted from telenovela formats from Colombia and Mexico.

The ongoing value of international and streaming licensing for IP owned by networks has begun to shift priority toward stand-alone, revenue-generating, multiplatform experiences, like licensed casual games that can be distributed globally, but those extensions still carry promotional goals to spread awareness and engagement with on-air series.

Longevity

As syndication to streaming networks has increased, networks find that their shows develop international audiences on schedules totally disconnected from traditional Fall and Winter seasons. Even shows that are years past their initial release are finding new fans thanks to streaming services—and those fans want more content. For networks that own all or part of the shows on their network, this means they have a vested interest in keeping those shows running, building those audiences, and benefiting from platform extensions that may be sponsored or generate revenue.

The SyFy Channel is an example of a network that rarely owns the IP of the shows that it airs, and it has a reputation for canceling fan-favorite shows like *Firefly* and *The Expanse*. Other networks, like AMC, own all or part of the IP for series that they air and have an ongoing interest in the success of shows like *Breaking Bad* and *The Walking Dead*, even holding licenses to develop multiplatform extensions. Goals and metrics for IPs are evaluated annually as well as quarterly, but the goals for transmedia extensions (as with film-focused properties) are reviewed based on quarterly performance and rarely aggregated into the bigger picture.

Networks like AMC have been steadily building their stable of owned IP, expanding their ownership stakes in The Walking Dead IP by owning portions of storyworld expansions like the spin-off series *Fear the Walking Dead* and *The Walking Dead: World Beyond*, as well as licensed games. For other projects where AMC has a major stake, the channel has created an internal lab for transmedia storytelling extensions, like 2020's Emmy Award–winning web series *Ethics Training with Kim Wexler*, an extension of the series *Better Call Saul* (itself a spin-off of *Breaking Bad*).

Major Key Performance Indicators—Television

1. Weekly ratings
2. +7- and +10-day on-demand ratings
3. Distribution license sales or presale

4. Cable, premium, or streaming network licensing or syndication presale

5. Performance of syndicated content on streaming services

6. Brand and advertiser interest

7. Home entertainment sales (digital)

8. Consumer product sales

9. Game, publishing, and other licenses

10. Earned media (word of mouth, buzz)

11. Fan base activity

12. Social media activity

Streaming Media: Reaching an Audience Anywhere, Any Time

Industry	Outreach	Creative Execution	Sustainability	Longevity
Streaming	Low	High	Medium	High

Over the next few years, all of the television partners described in the last section may become streaming partners, as streaming syndication and owned streaming networks subsume the broadcast television landscape completely. That said, the different mindsets of the two groups profoundly affect how they engage with transmedia extensions.

Streaming companies grew from the same multiplatform landscape as the early-2000s transmedia renaissance. They are different from television content partners because they are technology companies first, content companies second. Quantitative analysis is the core of business decisions made by these groups. For independent creators seeking to partner with major streaming groups like Netflix or Amazon, or distribute on streaming content platforms like YouTube or Twitch, lessons can be learned by evaluating how the biggest players in this field would consider a new project or extension.

These networks rely on subscribers. Since the 2010s, the broad interest that they have in creating appealing libraries of content has led to a flourishing of streaming-backed, long-form series and films—but very few of these stand out as having substantial and compelling transmedia extensions. Major players like Netflix, Amazon, Hulu, and YouTube regularly launch shows, but they rarely invest in creating content that lives outside their platforms. The extensions that have been created have been promotional, like *The Man in the High Castle*'s reimagined 1960s album collaboration with Sam Cohen and Danger Mouse; sponsored, like Microsoft's *Camp Know Where* campaign with *Stranger Things*; or focused on selling IP-related consumer products.

Transmedia extensions are few and far between when commissioned by streaming networks themselves, but for IP owners of content distributed through streaming networks, the need to develop audiences and facilitate the discovery of their content through multiplatform outreach can make the difference between success and invisibility. While groups like Netflix have made seemingly reluctant promotional forays into advertising transmedia campaigns and announced an interest in games, the budgets, ambitions, and long-term commitments for these initiatives have been significantly lower compared to game, television, and film companies.

How Streaming Groups Determine Success

Creative Execution

User experience is a term rarely used in movie studios and television networks, but it is critical to understanding the reasons why streaming networks make creative decisions. The behavioral goals of these companies are paramount: attract subscribers, get them watching, and keep them watching. Producers who create for these networks have access to and engage with audience-research groups that give detailed insight into the "who, what, and why" of audience engagement in similar content, and potentially even directions on how to optimize their shows' pacing to enhance "bingeability." Some investment in projects that are explicitly top-rated shows on streaming networks, like Netflix's *13 Reasons Why* (a teen drama focused on the ripple effects of a suicide), have been initiated as marketing investments to develop fan bases or partner with major groups like Microsoft for corporate service responsibility, like *Camp Know Where*, a *Stranger Things*–themed remote summer camp program for STEM education.

Outreach and Engagement

While out-of-home advertisements (things like billboards or ads in public-transit stations) for Netflix and Amazon shows were ubiquitous in the late 2010s, these networks advertise only a small percentage of their total catalogs. This is a small percentage of even their new release content. Their

ability to market and recommend new content to viewers in their streaming applications is so high that their promotional investments focus on
shows with the highest mass-market potential, usually with an eye toward
drawing new subscribers, developing brand prestige, or establishing their
firms as content companies on par with or above the level of existing movie
studios and TV networks.

Sustainability

Budget numbers for streaming companies are closely guarded trade secrets
(Katz, 2019), but figures that have been released publicly indicate that these
networks are investing in content at or above the budgets for movie studios
and television networks (Summers, 2020). This heavy investment is directed
only toward content that can live on the streaming platform, and for creators of work that retain ownership of their projects and wish to expand
their content across platforms, streaming networks rarely add budgets or
retain licensing interests in ancillary licenses. That provides opportunity
to create extensions for projects with existing distribution agreements, but
which are not supported with budgets from their distributors.

Longevity

The agile test-and-learn mindset common to modern technology companies is present at all of the major streaming services that fund content.
One important strategy is to extend and expand content that works into
on-platform spin-offs, like Netflix's drug-trafficking-themed action-dramas
Narcos and *Narcos: Mexico*, which are built to create series story arcs that last
for three seasons before being refreshed or sundowned. For Netflix's competition, platform-exclusive properties like Amazon's *The Man in the High
Castle* or Hulu's *The Handmaid's Tale* aim to replicate the success of the business models for prestige television networks (e.g., HBO, Starz), which focus
on promotional experiences that drive subscribers to their services rather
than seeking to keep their attention with other types of experiences.

Major Key Performance Indicators—Streaming

1. Viewers per show
2. Subscribers
3. Show completion rate

4. Episode completion rate

5. Show abandonment rate

6. Binge-ability

7. User ratings (varies per network)

8. Time per viewing session

9. Press coverage

10. Industry awards

11. Fan base activity

12. Social media activity

13. Partnership interest from major potential sponsors.

Games: Interactive Experiences for Long-Term Fan Development

Industry	Outreach	Creative Execution	Sustainability	Longevity
Games	Low/Medium	High	Medium	Medium

The gaming industry contains both massive corporations wielding budgets in the tens of millions and scrappy independent start-ups that find global success based on a small team's hard work in their spare time. While many AAA game franchises are built with an eye toward sequels and ongoing growth, the overhead and complexity of developing these productions often leave little room for multiplatform or transmedia investment. Transmedia investments for AAA game properties tend to be internally licensed, building creative projects with internal teams that reach marketing goals.

Each of the different levels of the gaming industry, from independent to console to multiplayer, could be the focus of its own section here (or, indeed, its own chapter in this book), but understanding where in the industry a potential partner operates is critical to evaluating whether the goals of a particular project mesh with a creator's. Games and streaming networks are both highly data-centered industries, and decisions are made as much as possible based on information about audiences and their behavior. Games are play-tested, optimized, and adapted constantly throughout their development process. Their performance in the market is no less researched and scrutinized.

How Gaming Groups Determine Success

Creative Execution

Some of the most notable transmedia game franchises are fictional story-worlds like Half-Life, Assassin's Creed, Final Fantasy, and Uncharted. These franchises often operate as full divisions or quasi-independent business units within game companies, like 343 Industries at Microsoft Game Studios, which oversees the Halo IP. These IP-centered groups have expanded their storyworlds through narrative and nonnarrative extensions like books, comic books, laser-tag experiences, and even feature-length films. Entire games have been released as downloadable content (DLC) add-ons for other titles, like *Halo 3: ODST*. When extensions are created, they often mirror the first-person perspective of the user, focusing on location-based gaming experiences, though in recent years, more successful film adaptations have been developed following characters through game universes, like *Halo 4: Forward Unto Dawn* and *Halo: Nightfall*.

In contrast, games are also created as extensions for film or television-driven storyworlds, sometimes commanding budgets as large as feature films or becoming stand-alone storylines in franchises based on their success.

Licensed games are a huge category within the game industry, focused on for-hire or licensed games commissioned by film and television studios to support major releases. For decades, these games were considered lack-luster rehashes of film scripts, but when creatively executed as stand-alone projects that are good game experiences, while simultaneously expanding game storyworlds, they can become major narrative series on their own, like *Star Wars: The Force Unleashed*.

Massively multiplayer online games (MMOs) and massively multiplayer online role-playing games (MMORPGs) are among the most complex games to produce and maintain. The number of MMOs created or played by many users at a given time is fairly small, but some successful titles have been created to serve fans of science fiction series or franchises like Battle-star Galactica, allowing players to explore the wider storyworld, and SyFy's *Defiance*, which interwove weekly TV episode storylines with related in-game challenges. Earlier blockbuster MMORPG titles like *World of Warcraft* attracted players en masse and launched a wide range of licensed extensions, including books, comics, consumer products, and films.

In the 2010s, high-speed internet became more accessible to at-home players and thereby enabled the rise of esports and team-based multiplayer games, which have overtaken complex RPG worlds and drawn in younger generations of players. Games like *Overwatch, League of Legends, Roblox,* and *Fortnite* all saw phenomenal success on their core platforms and, like other streaming platforms and online businesses, their primary goals are to get people to log in and to keep them logged in.

Outreach and Engagement

Because AAA developers often take years to produce a single game, maintaining or pulsing buzz with fans, and potential fans, is a critical part of games outreach. Game companies research and engage with fan communities more directly than other industry cohorts because productions have the capacity to update the content of gameplay based on player feedback. Unlike film or television, the most satisfying versions of these productions are created with audience feedback. Promotions begin for new titles more than a year ahead of a project's release, often teased three or four years before a project is ready for purchase or download. Big releases cluster around major conferences like GDC, PAX, E3, or company-led gatherings like BlizzCon or Microsoft Ignite. The long gaps between game releases have inspired major alternate reality games (ARGs) like Halo's *I Love Bees* and led to spin-off game experiences that, while they are considered marketing expenses, could easily be their own product groups, like Halo's touring paintball fields and immersive experience, *Halo: Outpost Discovery.*

Sustainability

While significant budgets are expended on the creation of new games, additional budgets are reserved for the refinement, expansion, and development of games once they are released to audiences. These budgets, while substantial, have to compete with other priorities, like marketing and promotion. Once a game's world is established with a successful title and a stable fan base, project extensions on additional platforms are licensed with third parties, prioritizing revenue. Consumer products, comic books, and book publishing licenses are extensions with strong track records for games.

Longevity

Long-term success is a critical concern for the leading platform titles of a game property, whether creating or maintaining a persistent game platform or utilizing and developing the game engine and code base used to create the initial titles of a game. Because video game development requires significant up-front costs, ensuring that they can extend for multiyear or even multidecade life cycles is a major consideration, as are any methods that can recoup costs and drive new attention to titles mid–life cycle. Extensions to these worlds come in two varieties: short-term promotional or revenue plays and long-term storyworld development aimed at expanding the fan base of a property. Console games are standout examples of franchise transmedia storytelling, and titles that have established storyworlds have seen their audiences grow and licensing revenues expand—Pokémon, Grand Theft Auto, and The Witcher, for example. Other AAA titles that have attempted a more anthology-focused format, creating new rules for their storyworld in every title—like Prince of Persia—have been unable to maintain audience interest in recent decades.

Major Key Performance Indicators—Games

1. Unit sales
2. Subscription sales
3. Downloads
4. Microtransactions
5. Time spent in games
6. Daily active users
7. Time per session
8. Play testing
9. Focus groups
10. In-game biometric player analysis
11. Other platform and consumer product license sales or presales
12. Earned media (word of mouth)
13. Fan base activity
14. Social media activity
15. Dwell time (experiential)

Conclusion: How to Build a Community of Interest

It's fun to sit and develop storyworld concepts and explore an idealized production in your head, but it is much harder to bring these complex projects to life. In my own experience, 80 percent of the failed projects that I've encountered have failed because they didn't consider the needs of the partners that would bring their project to life.

There are a wide range of industries and genres that this chapter does not address, but that also have distinct and clear goals and workflows worth exploring: independent film, podcasting, advertising, children's media, educational games, consumer products, livestreaming, and sports media, to name a few. They all have their own goals, KPIs, and industry standards. They all can be framed according to the needs that this chapter explored for film, television, streaming media, and games: creative execution, outreach and engagement, sustainability, and longevity. And of course, the fundamental question and challenge remains: *will an audience actually want to engage with the project?*

Determining which companies, if any, are the right partners and allies in a transmedia practitioner's community of interest is a per-project decision. The level of financing, the ambition of the distribution, and the creative execution necessary to engage audiences are distinct to each production, and these parameters guide the project's artistic parameters.

Partners will view every project through the lens of their commercial motivations. In most cases, partners in the community of interest don't or can't invest in the totality of a transmedia project, but they *can* make decisions about a part of the project's whole: a film, a television series, a marketing campaign.

It takes a lot of footwork on the part of a transmedia producer or creator to find that community of interest, but it's part of every commercial production, transmedia or otherwise. While the adage "It's all who you know" is true at its core, it is also possible to get to know people in the industry by reaching out and asking them for advice. Like every other creator, even with a wide breadth of credits to recommend me, I strike out more often than I succeed when I'm trying to connect with people. Outreach takes time and persistence.

For creators that love experimentation and have a mindset open to developing their work closely with audiences, transmedia techniques provide a unique way to build productions. As media systems continue to transform, the opportunity for experimentation that transmedia techniques provide is invaluable for testing and learning what audiences will actually enjoy, as well as how to connect with them through experiences that are genuinely appealing.

References

Katz, Brendon. 2019. "How Much Does It Cost to Fight in the Streaming Wars?" *Observer*, October 23, 2019. https://observer.com/2019/10/netflix-disney-apple -amazon-hbo-max-peacock-content-budgets.

Keegan, Rebecca. 2017. "James Cameron on *Titanic*'s Legacy and the Impact of a Fox Studio Sale." *Variety*, November 26, 2017. https://www.vanityfair.com/hollywood /2017/11/james-cameron-titanic-20th-anniversary-avatar-terminator-fox-studios -sale.

Ryan, Maureen, and Cynthia Littleton. 2017. "TV Series Budgets Hit the Breaking Point as Costs Skyrocket in Peak TV Era." September 26, 2017. https://variety.com /2017/tv/news/tv-series-budgets-costs-rising-peak-tv-1202570158.

Summers, Megan. 2020. "The 10 Most Expensive Netflix Original Movies, Ranked by Budget." *Screen Rant*, September 29, 2020. https://screenrant.com/netflix-most -expensive-original-movies-budgets.

US Department of Justice and Federal Trade Commission. 2017. "Antitrust Guidelines for the Licensing of Intellectual Property." https://www.justice.gov/atr/IPguidelines /download.

Transmedia Crosstalk: Maureen McHugh Yeager and Caitlin Burns

Bob Beard: You've both been in the industry for years and have worked on some major media properties—and I know you both contributed to the Halo universe, Maureen through *I Love Bees* for *Halo 2* and Caitlin through other transmedia work for the franchise. Have your paths crossed before?

Caitlin Burns: I actually came in later on Halo; *I Love Bees* was totally legendary, my work started around *Halo 3*, so the expectations set by the *I Love Bees* project had already set really high bars creatively. Even now, it influences the path of conversations about creative choices and structure.

Maureen McHugh Yeager: I am so tickled to hear that it was influential. When we did the project, we were told many times that it wouldn't be considered canonical [to the Halo universe], and then later they told us they liked it so much that it was.

BB: Maureen, your chapter deals with the experimentation that birthed a new medium, and Caitlin, your chapter explains how these experiments have been institutionalized and codified over the years. When something like *I Love Bees* becomes canonized, I imagine there's tension between narrative experimentation and the mandate to monetize.

MMY: When we were working on *I Love Bees*, we were very lucky that Bungee [the game studio that developed *Halo*] was open and engaged with what we were doing. They didn't really know what an ARG was because no one did. It was expensive, of course. And experimental.

CB: I have to say that it's a little weird to suggest that these works weren't institutionalized at the time; while they were definitely experimental, they were still commissioned by major film and game companies.

Still, most of the experimental projects I've developed came out of marketing budgets. If they did well, they often got production budgets, but reaching people in new ways tends to be seen as supportive of bigger-budget experiences.

But yes, much of the current media landscape is extremely structured: mature systems that people see through the lenses of their silos again. For example, social media used to be an incredibly weird and experimental place. Now there's a "way to do social media right" and while a lot of "how to play" in those systems is clear, it's also very fertile ground for disruption.

So much of these interactive projects have been in cycles and waves, where experimentation with the audience happens for a while, then an audience is built and more static experience systems are maintained. Then someone comes in and shakes everything up again.

For me, it all comes down to how people are playing with other people. When I'm setting up experiences, I'm trying to set parameters that people can dive into, and probably break until they fit a human experience.

MMY: Obviously for me, the big issue is the affordances of the different platforms. For example, a first-person shooter game doesn't exactly allow you inside a character's head and doesn't create that internal narrative. A novel, comic, or traditional movie can deliver that, but doesn't allow you to *do* things. I love the idea that someday we'll have sophisticated enough AI [artificial intelligence] systems that game worlds are more narrative.

CB: For me, I'm less interested in AI on a personal creative level and more interested in shared human spaces. Your chapter, Maureen, shows that a lot of the magic comes from what people do with the experience that you don't expect. An AI can support that, but when you get three humans in a room, that's where the wildest stories happen for me.

BB: What do you see as the next exciting space for transmedia, as both producers and participants?

MMY: I would be watching augmented reality and transmedia. Augmented reality is clunky now, with big headsets, and using a headset makes a chunk of the audience nauseous, but the ability to "paint" a different reality in my own space feels as if it's going to further reduce the distance between the audience and the storyworld. If they can get [augmented reality] more accessible and more fun, it's an exciting technology.

CB: To avoid writing another chapter on the future of transmedia, I'll comment on some trends I'm seeing in my own practice now.

Inclusion is at the forefront of conversations, and ten or fifteen years ago, it would have been an afterthought. It's expected that characters will have diverse backgrounds and perspectives, and finding meaningful story space for those characters and perspectives is more important than ever.

The economics and contractual structures that are the base of experiences are about to be disrupted—NFTs [nonfungible tokens] and smart contracts are likely to be shifting a lot of assumptions about how audiences are allowed to participate with intellectual properties. This is not the first time people have said this, but economics of NFTs are already influencing decisions inside big studios and publishers. It will be interesting, to say the least.

Also, to Maureen's point, you can play most experiences on the same device now—AAA games, TV shows, first-run movies, TikTok, all while talking to your friends simultaneously. That layering is going to influence work and its structures, *and* require that each experience stand out against the rest to really grab attention.

MMY: It will also be interesting to see if transmedia migrates away from fantastical worlds. I mean, I don't know that I want transmedia stories set in the same world as [the 2021 HBO series] *Mare of Easttown*, but I'm sure I could take a stab at it.

3   There Is No Such Thing as a Transmedia Text: Transmedia as Practice

Paweł Frelik

In this chapter, Paweł Frelik takes up a fundamental notion of our editors' introduction and chapter 1, by Maureen McHugh Yeager, and a theme in many other chapters in this book: that transmedia is culturally pervasive, which makes it difficult to bound or define in an analytically productive way. Frelik responds to this "conceptual morass" by arguing that nearly all texts that span multiple media can be described in terms of adaptation, remediation, paratextuality, and transmediality—but that these labels are not boxes that contain texts but rather "ways of thinking about texts, and strategies of approaching them," which sensitize critics and audiences to particular features and relegate other features to the background. For Frelik, transmedia logics and other types of relationships among cultural texts are processes of creation and interpretation and tacit agreements among media producers and their audiences, rather than essences. This sense of "transmedia" as a verb, a doing, provides theoretical grounding for many chapters in this book that frame transmedia as a participatory process of co-creation and collaborative meaning-making, from Lee Emrich's course on Shakespeare as a transmedia phenomenon (chapter 9), to Katherine Buse and Ranjodh Singh Dhaliwal's narrative experiments within the Foldit citizen-science project (chapter 11), to Jennifer Palilonis's piece about creating new stories and communities of interest around men's volleyball (chapter 10). In the closing section of this chapter, Frelik focuses on The Prophecy, a short film created for the EVE Online video game universe, to demonstrate how approaching a single text through each of these four different frames opens up unique possibilities for interpretation and enjoyment. This emphasis on a niche cultural experience that is extremely meaningful, but only to members of a small discourse community, picks up a thread that runs throughout this collection: examining the dynamics of transmedia experiences that activate the cultural literacies of hyperspecific communities. We see this in the chapter by Dilman Dila, on local audiences and interpretive traditions in Uganda (chapter 4), in Kayla Asbell et al.'s chapter on UTOPIAN HOTLINE and using hybrid digital-physical experiences to create uniquely intimate experiences (chapter 6), and in Buse and Dhaliwal's chapter on Foldit, a community as intense and internally complex as EVE's. These examples exemplify how transmedia, a form so often associated with big-budget media franchises like the

Marvel Cinematic Universe (MCU), also has unique affordances for drawing on deep, situated knowledge from more constrained communities of fan-creators, lay critics, and other highly engaged participants.

As of April 2021, among the top fifty highest-grossing films globally, there are four based on original scripts: *Avatar* (2009) at no. 1, *Titanic* (1997) at no. 3, *Zootopia* (2016) at no. 44, and *The Lion King* (1994) at no. 50. The remaining forty-six titles are adaptations, sequels, and spin-offs from preexisting sources. The earliest title on the list is *Jurassic Park* (1993), accompanied by only three more from the same decade and another six from the 2000s, but no fewer than nine titles—almost 20 percent of all of the ones recorded—were released in 2019. Over the years, such statistics have led many to bemoan the state of originality in American filmmaking, including the director Martin Scorsese, who, in 2019, penned a harsh opinion piece in the *New York Times* about the Marvel movies. On the other hand, the four-hour-long *Zack Snyder's Justice League* (2020), which sits at the center of the DC cinematic universe, has been discussed in terms of auteurism (Hellerman, 2021).

Aesthetic judgments notwithstanding, the list clearly demonstrates that the last three decades have marked a massive shift in the patterns of cinematic production and audiencing. And film is not unique in that respect; similar trends can be observed in other media, too, although arriving at semiobjective lists based on finance may prove a bit more difficult for television, comics, or video games. Still, among the ten most streamed television series of 2020, the newest was in its third season (*Ozark*), and most of the titles are well past season five. As I am writing this in August 2021, the most positively reviewed big-budget video game of the first three quarters of the year is *Mass Effect Legendary Edition*, a remaster of the acclaimed role-playing trilogy (2007, 2010, 2012).

It is clear that, in the early twenty-first century, a dominant mode of experiencing cultural texts is that of seriality. Instead of one-off experiences, however unique and memorable, cultural texts—and I use the term "text" in the sense current in cultural studies, where it may denote a novel, a film, or a comic book, but also a music video, a rock album, or a video game—are presented to audiences in groups and strings. Seriality is not, naturally, a late-twentieth-century invention. Many Victorian novels were first made available in newspaper or magazine installments. Cinema was not even a decade old when it hit the mother lode with screen adaptations of novels and stage performances. In the early twenty-first century, any medium can spawn serial progeny: films, television series, comic books, video games, or even toys and amusement park franchises. When The Matrix, one of the first truly complex networked narratives, debuted in 1999, much of the initial success was undercut by the fact that the audiences were not used to jumping across media divides (from feature films to comics to video games and animated shorts) to make sense of the story. A mere two decades later, large demographics of viewers, readers, and players effortlessly move between multimedia texts, tracing narratives and constructing coherent universes.

Fandoms are particularly adept at it, even if their enthusiasm and obsessive love of trivia have also been consciously fostered in a culture of tested intellectual property (IP) and, at times, exploited by producers. In academia, researchers and media scholars have been simultaneously invested in establishing relationships between such texts and proposing hierarchies, whereby each text contributes something to an overarching story, but they are not all created equal. The frameworks for such classifications have not been commensurate with one another, since some focus more on narrative continuity and others on production networks. In addition, academic distinctions are rooted in various critical schools, some attendant to the socioeconomic aspects of such texts and others more committed to aesthetic distinctions divorced (relatively, anyway) from the market.

Some of these distinctions have been more inclusive than others, too. While sequels and transnational remakes refer to very specific relationships between texts, a collective survey of definitions of the four most encompassing of these categories—transmedia, adaptations, remediations, and paratexts—can conceivably lead nonspecialist readers to a conclusion that they are nearly synonymous and that a significant majority of texts that are elements of transmedia networks are also—at the same time—instances of the other three. At the same time, academic discussions regarding the distinctions between these categories have been nothing short of intense.

Needless to say, the theorizations of transmedia have been very diverse, but also too numerous to even mention here, and their relationship to the other three has been contentious. Christy Dena's work is of particular interest in that respect. In her doctoral dissertation (2009), she sought to frame the importance of larger networks within which transmedia could be understood beyond theorizations, shifting the focus to cultural producers and to transmedia as a practice rather than a set of "end-point characteristics," such as expanding a story across media (2009, i). In the context of this chapter, her erudite 2018 piece "Transmedia Adaptation: Revisiting the No-Adaptation Rule" seems particularly relevant since the widespread exclusion of adaptations from the realm of transmedia, which she masterfully maps, remains grounded in often unexamined assumptions and comes at a cost to critics and scholars who adhere to it. Elsewhere, Matt Hills (2018) discussed the negotiations of transmedia and paratexts, while Marc Ruppel (2012) approached the role of remediation in some transmedia texts.

This chapter is a provisional attempt at a reconciliation within this conceptual morass. Building on Dena's as well as other scholars' arguments, I propose that almost any cultural narrative (potentially including those customarily labeled as "nonfiction") that spans more than one medium can be described as an instance of one of the four categories describing networked texts: adaptation, remediation, paratextuality, and transmediality. In other words, none of these terms addresses some inherent features of the text in question or reflects any of its objective aspects. Instead, these categorizations can be more productively regarded as ways of thinking about texts and strategies of approaching them. Practically, each of the four terms translates into a set of questions, which elicit answers that can reveal or illuminate certain aspects of a given text and its relationships with other texts around it. None of these perspectives function inherently better than the others, but the explosive proliferation of textual production in the last hundred years in general, and the last three decades in particular, demand some stable points of reference. For producers and audiences alike, these four lenses offer ways to make some sense of the noise of contemporary cultural production, but the choice of one of them determines the terms for examining a given text and allows specific insights, including its formal and cultural operations.

Discussions of aesthetics, lines of influence, complex interactions among cultural texts, and the pleasures that we draw from them are important, but approaching them as somehow essentialist leads to conceptual confusion and pointless debates. In their place, this chapter offers a path through discussions of transmediality, adaptations, remediations, and paratextuality that emphasizes their formal elements. The way of thinking proposed here can help order some of the contradictions inherent in theoretical frameworks, but it can also help media creators and audiences think through how texts connect to other texts, and how different audiences can find diverse pleasures in them.

I will first provide a brief overview of the common understandings of these four concepts. Drawing on the new genre theory that in the last few decades has treated genres as audience practices rather than inherent objects (e.g., Mittell, 2001), I will identify the aspects of texts that allow for formulating questions, which then underpin each of the perspectives. I will then test this framework, applying this new understanding of each of the four perspectives to the case study of *The Prophecy* (2014), a digital short film. I will conclude by outlining some of the investments—among audiences, critics, producers, and other people and groups—that underpin the use of these perspectives.

Among the four perspectives, adaptation is probably the broadest and oldest, but I will begin with transmedia, as it is the focus of this book. Compared to the others, transmedia is relatively new, but it has already accumulated a critical mass of theorization and conversation, both within cultural industries and academia. Its most recognized definition comes from Henry Jenkins, who began to theorize it as early as 2003 but most recognizably articulated it in his *Convergence Culture: Where Old and New Media Collide* (2006). Using the example of The Matrix, Jenkins describes a transmedia story as one that "unfolds across multiple media platforms, with each new text making a distinctive and valuable contribution to the whole. In the ideal form of transmedia storytelling, each medium does what it does best—so that a story might be introduced in a film, expanded through television, novels, and comics; its world might be explored through game play or experienced as an amusement park attraction" (95–96). Crucial to his understanding of transmedia is the phenomenon of media convergence, a turn-of-the century development rooted in a number of economic and technological practices. Later, Jenkins expanded this definition and reconceptualized the term into an umbrella for a number of logics: transmedia storytelling exemplified by The Matrix is thus accompanied by "transmedia branding, transmedia performance, transmedia ritual, transmedia play, transmedia activism and transmedia spectacle" (Jenkins, 2011).

Jenkins's work also provides a launchpad to a dazzling spectrum of transmedia scholarship, exemplified by Matthew Freeman and Renira Rampazzo Gambarato's magisterially systematic *Routledge Companion to Transmedia*

Studies (2018), among other sources. Parallel to Jenkins's sustained work on transmedia, the term has become a buzzword in a number of contexts, from marketing (Cartwright, 2013) to heavy-duty narratological theory (Thon, 2018). Perspectives offered by different understandings of transmedia have also been used to account for practices outside its immediate geographical origin and temporal frame and applied to non-Anglophone (Wall, 2019) and pre-late-twentieth-century cultural phenomena (Freeman, 2016; Léger-St-Jean, 2012).

From the moment of its rise into visibility, it has been clear that transmediality overlaps and collides with other perspectives used in the study of media texts, the most widespread of these being adaptation, which has the longest history of cultural and industrial practice, but also with academic theorization. Within the latter, because of its tenure, it has accumulated the widest range of conceptualizations, ranging from the very specific to the very broad. Early theoretical approaches to adaptations, which focused on adaptations of predominantly literary originals, emphasized the degree of fidelity of the transfer and judged them in that context (Newman and Graff, 1985; Peary and Shatzkin, 1977). The term was understood rather narrowly, often relying on the overt identification of the umbilical connecting the original and its derivative. In more recent academic work, adaptive relationships have been conceived much more liberally. In her authoritative *A Theory of Adaptation* (2013), Linda Hutcheon suggests that not only plots, but also themes and storyworlds, can be adapted; Deborah Cartmell and Imelda Whelehan (2007) include various types of intertextuality; and Kathleen Loock and Constantine Verevis (2012) extend the category of adaptations to remakes and sequels.

Remediation, the third of the four frameworks, was first used in this sense by Jay Bolter in *Writing Space: Computers, Hypertext, and the Remediation of Print* (1991), but its most common understanding was developed to encompass audiovisual media by Bolter and Richard Grusin (1999) to account for the flow of stories between media forms. Instead of focusing on the narrative, it turns our attention toward the medium itself and its material, institutional, and social limitations and affordances, as well as the influence that these material circumstances exert on the shape of the story. Consequently, remediation perspectives are less interested in the cultural or political signification of the narrative in itself, and more in how the shift of the narrative from one medium to another affects it because of institutional and technological limitations and affordances.

Last but not least, the concept of paratexts was originally proposed by Gérard Genette (1997) to account for elements of books that, while not integral parts of the text, affect the reception of that text. These include the cover, title page, foreword, blurbs, and footnotes, but also more external objects, such as interviews with the author. Genette developed this interpretative framework for works of literature (his principal examples were seventeenth- and eighteenth-century books), but in the last two decades, it has been adopted in media studies by such scholars as Jonathan Gray in *Show Sold Separately: Promos, Spoilers, and Other Media Paratexts* (2010) and Sara Pesce and Paolo Noto in *The Politics of Ephemeral Digital Media: Permanence and Obsolescence in Paratexts* (2016). These scholars emphasize the importance of paratexts in shaping audience reactions. This constitutes a dramatic shift in thinking since, for all its role in influencing textual reception, Genette's paratextuality was still rooted in the hierarchical distinction between the central text and its secondary accoutrement.

Like almost all attempts at cultural groupings, transmedia, adaptations, remediations, and paratextuality have been repeatedly conceptualized and reconceptualized. In that, these categories bear certain similarity to genres, whose changing history of theorization offers very instructive analogies. For a long time, genres were considered "ontologically objective" formations. This approach may work for such genres as sonnets or haikus, which are defined by their structure. However, where the genre definition relied on narrative properties, as it does in most contemporary genres across media, this structuralist vantage also necessitated the invention of new labels, such as science fiction Westerns or cybergothic, thus threatening a potentially unchecked proliferation of genres, to the point of analytical uselessness.

The way out of this has been what is now collectively known as the new genre theory (although it is hardly "new" in 2021), developed by scholars interested in the questions of genre across a spectrum of disciplines and fields from semiotics and rhetoric (Freadman, 1988) to film studies (Altman, 1984) to so-called popular genres (Bould and Vint, 2009; Rieder, 2010). In these approaches, genres are not fixed cultural entities, but rather loose and dynamically shifting constellations of texts that respond to varying agendas and circumstances. They are also in constant motion, solidifying into existence and dissolving into a corpus of texts in synchrony with the needs of each definer. Consequently, the American shore ode and the Korean revenge film are as clear in their descriptiveness as they are tentative and contingent. They may hypothetically be joined by financial thriller, Russian noir, and Argentinian gothic, genres which may be nonexistent as of now, but their logic of formulation is clear. If organizing texts in genres is like organizing computer files, then the old genre theory demanded that they be placed in separately named folders (and, in some cases, that the files be replicated so that they could be placed in more than one folder at the same time). The new genre theory, instead, proposes keeping all these files in one or very few top-level folders, but tagging them with a number of labels. Accordingly, Ridley Scott's film *Blade Runner* (1982) could be tagged as cyberpunk, science fiction, detective, neo-noir, romance, and probably several others. Each of these genre tags signals attendance to certain elements of the text, but this attention does not preclude other vantage points and does not make exclusive demands to claim the text for one of them only.

The categories of transmedia, adaptation, remediation, and paratextuality can be, I propose, treated productively in a similar manner. Each text possesses a number of properties, which can be divided into two principal classes. These properties are also independent of the specific type of narrative—so it does not matter if the text is a Western, a horror story, or a romance.

The first class of these properties can be described as individual and internal. They characterize the text as a stand-alone object or as "a document," a specific instantiation of the text, which is different from what N. Katherine Hayles calls "work" and "text" (2003, 265). These properties include the text's materiality, including all technological limitations and affordances (e.g., podcasts or video games); length, which can be measured temporally or numerically (e.g., feature films versus short films; novelettes versus novels); medial properties, such as the sound system, color palette, or font (e.g., virtual reality (VR) games versus "screen" video games); and, finally, the text's narrative and its constituent elements, such as the setting, protagonist, temporal frame, and dramatic scenario. These properties decide, to a large extent, which medium a given text is perceived as belonging to, as well as which genre it is seen to be part of.

The second class of each text's properties is relational and external—they situate the text within a larger ecology of other texts. In other words, these characteristics can be assessed only when the text is juxtaposed with other texts that are related through either formal and internal properties or narrative and aesthetic commonalities. Of course, it is not unusual for two texts to possess common features and yet not be perceived as relatable, beyond the most general ways. George Lucas's *American Graffiti* (1973) and George Romero's *Crazies* (1973) are both independent movies produced outside the Hollywood studio system and released in the same year, but there are few reasons to consider them as being related in any way. Similarly, Isaac Asimov's *Foundation* (1951) and China Miéville's *Embassytown* (2011) are both science fiction novels but have little in common.

As noted earlier, though, the contemporary cultural landscape is populated by texts that are interlinked in various ways, and the properties in this second class describe the nature of this interlinking. They include the temporal position in any grouping of texts, based on the straightforward sequence of release or publication; a medial identity or difference from other related texts (e.g., a film based on a novel); narrative continuity with or discontinuity from other texts (e.g., a sequel; a remake; a text set in the same shared world); a hierarchical relationship with other related texts within cultural contexts and institutional structures (e.g., a trailer promoting a TV series; a short film preceding a feature title); the character of authorship and its position within cultural contexts and institutional structures (e.g. professional versus amateur/fan-created); and industry and institutional anchoring of the text (e.g., a transnational remake).

The two classes of properties presented here are provisional and, depending on the text, more categories could be added. While the first class is less interesting in the present discussion, since it describes any text in isolation from other texts, the second is crucial for thinking about transmediality, remediation, adaptation, and paratextuality. It is the properties from this second class that are mobilized in various configurations when we consider a given text to be an instance of one of these four frameworks. The distinction between the four frameworks can be conceived of as defined by the questions about the relational properties. The act of referring to a text as a transmedia node, a remediation, an adaptation, or a paratext thus reflects greater attention to some relational properties and less focus on others. Of course, each property in the second class can be used to characterize more than one of these four perspectives, making them practices in which the selective interest of the interlocutor, rather than the inherent qualities of the text, determine the label pinned on it. Thinking about a given text in one of these four ways entails paying attention to some aspects and disregarding others, or asking certain questions that are pertinent to the discussion at hand but leaving others for other discussions.

Consequently, approaching a text as part of a transmedial network typically compels us to focus on its narrative continuity with and medial difference from other texts, but also on the nature of authorship, where fan-made texts can be considered on a par with those produced within corporate structures. As mentioned earlier, the classic example of a strong transmedia text used by Henry Jenkins in *Convergence Culture* (2006) is The Matrix, in which familiarity with all the nodes is a prerequisite for a full understanding of the second and third feature films. For instance, *The Second Renaissance* (2003), a short animated film that is part of the collection *The Animatrix*, sheds a completely new light on the origin of the story and possibly complicates viewers' sympathies in the conflict between humanity and machines. An equally compelling argument can be made in favor of treating the extended Star Wars universe as a sprawling transmedia story. Its coherence and continuity are, in fact, rigorously maintained, but unlike in The Matrix, the degree of integration among the various nodes is far more relaxed: the nine feature-length movies do not in any way require knowledge of the hundreds of Star Wars novels and comics.

At the same time, transmedia approaches, both strong and loose, pay less attention to the temporality of production since the publication or release date is not important in a rhizomatic network of interrelated nodes. This does not preclude some sense of hierarchy—the three Matrix and nine mainline Star Wars movies remain firmly at the center of their respective transmedial worlds, after all. At the same time, the pleasure of the text informed by the transmedial perspective is derived from tracing the connections among the various nodes in the narrative network, even if some of these nodes contribute less than others.

The perspective of remediation privileges insights into medial differences of subsequent texts through which a story circulates. It may also investigate industrial and institutional anchoring of the text, as well as consequences of technological contexts as they influence both the shape and reception of the text. At the same time, questions of narrative consistency or accretion of the story across texts, which are crucial for transmediality, are of less importance.

The paratextual framework centrally focuses on the hierarchical relationship of the text under consideration to other texts, and its narrative relationship to them. Fan-made texts have often been discussed using this framework, too. At the same time, paratextuality takes for granted the media diversity of various categories of paratexts in relation to the main text, which is so important in remediation.

As stated previously, adaptation is the most inclusive of the four categories, and consequently, depending on the situation, can draw on any combination of all relational properties in the second group. As Linda Hutcheon (2013) suggests, the main impulse informing any act of adaptation is the interplay between familiarity and novelty. These can be balanced and rebalanced across time, media, and producers' positioning in cultural circulation.

As always, a case study demonstrating theoretical propositions helps, so the next section will look at how the various relational properties of a text can be used to approach it from any of these four perspectives. *The Prophecy* is a short film attached to the fictional universe of *EVE Online* (2003), a massively multiplayer online game (MMO) set 21,000 years in the future. *EVE Online* is, in many ways, an exceptional title. It is one of the few specifically science fiction–themed MMOs. While not the largest by any standards, its player base has fluctuated around half a million over the past few years. Unlike most other games of its class, in which gamers are scattered across many servers, all players interact on the same server (although there is a separate one for China only), resulting in a more complex network of allies and enemies. *EVE Online* is also arguably one of the most difficult video games ever produced, with an infamously steep learning curve and a 50 percent new-user attrition rate. The biggest challenge for many players is the complexity of gameplay, which involves constant calculations and strategic planning. For Darren Jorgensen (2010), this makes *EVE Online* a quintessential science fiction game—not because of the thematic skinning but because of the "numerical verisimilitude" that undergirds the game and which he sees at work in much "hard" science fiction.

Produced by CCP Games, the makers of *EVE Online*, for the 2014 annual fan convention held in Iceland, *The Prophecy* masquerades as a faux-trailer. Despite its categorization as "a fan fest trailer," it does not really announce any specific product; instead, it aims to reinforce awareness of the company's constellation of titles, which, apart from the flagship game, at that point included *Dust 514*, a first-person shooter game for the PlayStation 3 console, and *EVE Valkyrie*, a spaceship dogfighting game for the Oculus Rift VR headset, then in development. Since May 2014, the trailer has garnered over 1.7 million views on YouTube alone.

The Prophecy can be approached from all four critical perspectives discussed here, none of which seems to be more relevant or more revealing about its circulation than the others. Inarguably, *The Prophecy* is a remediation of the game world developed in *EVE Online*. Due to its brevity, it offers a narratively nonconsequential glimpse of the main game's universe, but its filmic spectacularity is probably its most attractive aspect. In less than four minutes, it showcases a wide array of techniques used in contemporary digital image-making: hyperrealistic digital animation, extra-diegetic onscreen updates accompanied by skeumorphic sound, diegetic three-dimensional (3D) software interfaces, kinetic action sequences, multiple audio-planes, and, first and foremost, spectacular images suggesting the awing scale of spacecraft, constructions, and events.

EVE Online's primary mode of engagement is flying spacecraft, and the user interface assigns the player a free-floating point of view capable of movement in all directions and zooming in and out. In combination with multiple overlays, windows, and menus, the gameplay requires constant attention to multitasking and switching between varying levels of data concerning one's ship, targets, other players, and the space itself. The constant real-time negotiation of all these parameters imposes significant demands on the player. As a remediation, *The Prophecy*'s filmic mode, with a unified perspective managed through a basic array of shots of varying length and fairly standard crosscutting, offers a much more relaxed experience. Viewing movies is, of course, far from passive, but compared to the intense engagement of the MMO and its demanding point of view, the short's audiencing draws on the cultural experience of media older than online video games. In that, it operates like many other promotional and advertising texts, making the game engagement seem easier by orders of magnitude than it really is. In the world of digital gaming, remediations of the storyworld that deemphasize the difficulty of the gameplay are fairly common. Trailers promoting games often comprise extensive cut scenes—cinematic interludes during which players yield control of the in-game world and can literally sit back. Game packaging features detailed visualizations of fictional characters, often with facial close-ups, even when there are none in the games themselves. Both *The Prophecy* and *EVE Online* are enacted on the users' screens, but they trigger radically different cultural competencies: where *EVE Online* demands a type of coordination and cognition that could even be described as appropriately posthuman, *The Prophecy* falls back on spectating practices that are over a century old.

The short can equally productively be read as a node in the transmedia world of EVE. As far as video games are concerned, its medial constellation is not particularly expansive; it features a comic book, three tie-in novels, and three other video games (with another no longer active) set in the same universe. This core universe is enhanced in a series of short films, similar in character to *The Prophecy*, which CCP Games has released over the years. *EVE Online* fandom is also known for posting hundreds of gameplay footage films, including those documenting memorable in-game events such as what is known as the Bloodbath of B-R5RB, an online battle involving thousands of players in a single star system. The battle unfolded over twenty-one hours and is recognized as one of the largest in gaming history. Since *The Prophecy* is a faux-trailer, its connection to the rest of the universe is distinct but largely nonconsequential. One of the player organizations featured in it, the Drekar Alliance, has never existed in the actual game but has been often used in promotional materials to stand in for any powerful bloc of players. At the same time, the commanders of the rebel forces represent factions and corporations extant in the game. The same goes for types of spacecraft shown, including large Titan-class ships and the titular Prophecy fighters. The space gate shown in the short does not exist either, but its speculative technology is consistent with other similar gates routinely used in the gameworld. As a transmedia node, *The Prophecy* is thus fairly insignificant. The micronarrative extends, or rather promises an extension of the core megatext, barely sketching several events with no consequences for the main narrative of the game. Instead, its cinematic third-person-perspective visualization provides a more personal glimpse of *EVE Online*'s game world, which is usually presented through a distant, godlike perspective.

The Prophecy is also a paratext of *EVE Online*—and a model one at that. While it is not an integral part of the game, it extends and details its world, even if its interventions are fractional. Even the fact that it is merely one of a number of similar shorts that CCP Games has released over the years, usually to coincide with the annual fan convention, makes it hierarchically marginal. In his original conceptualization, Genette (1997) emphasizes that paratexts often act as entryways into the text proper. This is certainly true of *The Prophecy*, whose dual task was to provide some "comfort content" for existing players and to provide one of many possible entryways into *EVE Online*'s microculture. Writing about media paratexts, Jonathan Gray (2010) notes that contemporary audiences consume many more paratexts than texts, and this too seems to apply to *The Prophecy*, whose number of views on one platform alone is triple the number of all players of the game. Finally, paratexts usually come with a short expiry date of circulation. *The Prophecy* still continues to accrue views on YouTube, but the pace of this accretion slows every year.

Treating *The Prophecy* as an adaptation, the broadest of the four categories discussed here, may entail several lines of inquiry. It can be viewed as an adaptation of *EVE Online*'s storyworld, and such analysis would partly overlap with the questions raised in the transmedial treatment. At the same time, the traditional transmedial perspective focused on narrative does not address the motivations of its production. In *A Theory of Adaptation* (2013), Linda Hutcheon also raises questions about the different modes of reception over time: as the main game evolves along with its annual shorts, *The Prophecy* may become more of a historical record of its evolution, while its active role in the game's universe weakens.

My selection of *The Prophecy* as a case study is, of course, intentional: not because of its larger cultural significance, of which it has very little, but because it readily lends itself to approach from all four perspectives. This does not mean that every media text that is part of a wider ecology can be productively dissected in a similar manner. Each of these perspectives is really a set of questions about specific aspects of the text; all of them can be asked, hypothetically, but in some cases, the responses will not be very illuminating or, in others, they will be trivial and obvious. Consequently, for some media texts, only one or two of these perspectives can be truly productive.

For example, although marketed as tie-in novels, Jennifer Lynch's *The Secret Diary of Laura Palmer* (1990) and Scott Frost's *The Autobiography of F.B.I. Special Agent Dale Cooper: My Life, My Tapes* (1991) can easily be read as crucial elements of David Lynch's Twin Peaks transmedia narrative, which predates the use of that term but is a quintessential example of the practice. They can just as easily be treated as the television series' paratexts, although arguing that they are merely entryways into the world of Twin Peaks can be problematic since both provide important elements of the story's puzzle. On the other hand, thinking about both as remediations would not be very useful since their medial form—a codex book—is precisely what they purport to be narratively. Neither would approaching them as adaptations yield any interesting insights, since the former only shares the general milieu of the late-twentieth-century US with the series, and the latter's original contribution can be better appreciated when juxtaposed with the film *Twin Peaks: Fire Walk with Me* (1992).

The AMC/Netflix crime television series *The Killing* (2011–2014) can be most immediately analyzed as a transnational adaptation of the Danish original *Forbrydelsen* (2007–2012), and the comparison of the changes between them can provide interesting insights into the differences between Scandinavian and American politics, as well as audience expectations (the original is, arguably, much darker and more pessimistic than the remake). At the same time, approaching the American remake as a paratext of the original does not seem to be particularly productive. Finally, the two do not fit most known definitions of transmedia, and neither can they be treated as remediations so long as one understands the term as contingent on a change of medium.

The selection of one of the four approaches also depends on a definition of the medium. *Blade Runner 2049* (2017), along with the three shorts that preceded its release—*2036: Nexus Dawn, 2048: Nowhere to Run,* and *Blade Runner Black Out 2022*—comprise a transmedia narrative, which also, retroactively, includes the original *Blade Runner* (1982), but not the three tie-in novels written by K. W. Jeter, which continue the narrative of Ridley Scott's film in a way that became inconsistent with the director Denis Villeneuve's later sequel. Whether they can be approached as remediations depends on whether one considers short film a medium distinct from feature film (I do).

If we assume that the denomination used to describe texts and their mutual relationships is largely a matter of practice contingent on the circumstances of analysis rather than on the discovery of inherent qualities, it becomes less important to establish definitively whether a given text is, for instance, a transmedia node or a paratext. At the same time, it seems far more productive, for our thinking about these texts and their circulation, to consider why a given perspective is used to talk about it. In other words, if transmedia, remediation, paratextuality, and adaptation are ways of using texts, their use says little about the nature of discussed texts, but it says much about the cultural and cognitive investments of people and groups seeking to make meaning from, around, with, and about them.

All four perspectives require departures from medium-specific thinking about texts and promote thinking in more ecological or systemic terms. More than ever before, contemporary media texts exist in relationships with one another that are dynamic and contingent on the diverse but also conflicting stakes of artists, publishers, producers, marketing specialists, and audiences, which themselves are hardly uniform. The assignation of one of the four categories to a text is thus intensely interesting as a way of thinking through the agendas of those using the categories. Given the vast landscape of contemporary culture, these stakes can be complex and sometimes contradictory, so perhaps limiting the inquiry to transmedia, a central theme of this book, is in order.

What are, then, the investments signaled by classifying something as a transmedia text? Their disentangling must begin with noting that "transmedia" as a label has been used as both a commercial lens for producing and disseminating products and an academic concept for analyzing contemporary culture. As the former, in the early 2010s, it became a buzzword in marketing speak (Cartwright, 2013), much the same as the prefix "cyber-" connoted cutting-edge cultural production two decades earlier and still continues to reverberate (albeit not quite so ubiquitously) at the outset of the 2020s. As the latter, transmedia has become a contentious concept whose investments begin with demarcating it from other cultural categories. Early on, Henry Jenkins (2009) differentiated transmedia from adaptation, "which reproduces the original narrative with minimum changes into a new medium and is essentially redundant to the original work," a statement to which probably every scholar of adaptations would take exception. This exclusionary border policing stands in stark contrast with the otherwise broad use of "transmedia" by Jenkins himself, but also by many other theorists and practitioners.

One possibility is to read this new insistence on the ubiquity of transmedia as motivated by its in-the-now-ness. Adaptations trigger associations with bringing novels to screen, a practice that still remains common. But, in the contemporary cultural environment, media proliferate, and each medium comes with its own communities of practitioners, its own audiences, and its own toolboxes of production and distribution. Thinking about contemporary cultural texts in terms of transmedia retains the autonomy of these media worlds. Even without the perspective of fidelity, adaptive pairings are forever locked into a relationship in which the original constitutes the point of reference. Paratextuality can never shed its prefix suggestive of not-quite-ness and subordination to the central text. Remediation always suggests a point of departure against which change is measured. It is only transmedia that, in its essential sense, signals the retainment of each node's equality with others—even if, in practice, there is always a text in the transmedia network that is more central than others.

Historically, adaptation frameworks were entangled in hierarchical disputes while, in the third decade of the twenty-first century, the very concept of the original is suspect. A transmedia approach resists hierarchies and resonates with horizontal networks that can expand indefinitely. Thinking about relationships between texts transmedially entails subverting hierarchical dependencies. Even the move away from thinking about The Matrix as a quintessential transmedia text—it was, after all, deeply embroiled in big budgets and big-media players—demonstrates commitment to the "trans-" prefix in all its resonances and political consequences. There are certainly contradictions inherent in this commitment, as it clashes with actual industry practices, box-office expectations, and corporate creative control, all of which create a potential for a truly transmedial, sprawling, ontologically flat narrative and undercut it at the same time. But the utopian potentiality of such a narrative persists, despite the many limitations. The flexibility of models, contexts, and technologies evident in the global transmedia ecosystem may well speak to the persistence of the concept.

References

Altman, Rick. 1984. "A Semantic/Syntactic Approach to Film Genre." *Cinema Journal* 23, no. 3 (Spring): 6–18.

Bolter, Jay David, and Richard A. Grusin. 1999. *Remediation: Understanding New Media*. Cambridge, MA: MIT Press.

Bolter, Jay David. 1991. *Writing Space: Computers, Hypertext, and the Remediation of Print*. New York: Routledge.

Bould, Mark, and Sherryl Vint. 2009. "There Is No Such Thing as Science Fiction." In *Reading Science Fiction*, edited by James Gunn, Maureen S. Barr, and Matthew Candelaria, 43–51. London: Palgrave Macmillan.

Cartmell, Deborah, and Imelda Whelehan, eds. 2007. *The Cambridge Companion to Literature on Screen*. Cambridge: Cambridge University Press.

Cartwright, Jamie. 2013. "Transmedia Storytelling: A New Way to Fuel B2C Inbound Marketing." *Business 2 Community*, November 2, 2013. https://www .business2community.com/marketing/transmedia-storytelling-new-way-fuel-b2c -inbound-marketing-0662954.

Dena, Christy. 2009. "Transmedia Practice: Theorising the Practice of Expressing a Fictional World across Distinct Media and Environments." PhD dissertation, University of Sydney.

Dena, Christy. 2018. "Transmedia Adaptation: Revisiting the No-Adaptation Rule." In *The Routledge Companion to Transmedia Studies*, edited by Matthew Freeman and Renira Rampazzo Gambarato, 195–206. New York: Routledge.

Freadman, Anne. 1988. "Untitled: (On Genre)." *Cultural Studies* 2, no. 1: 67–99.

Freeman, Matthew. 2016. *Historicising Transmedia Storytelling: Early Twentieth-Century Transmedia Story Worlds*. New York: Routledge.

Freeman, Matthew, and Renira Rampazzo Gambarato. 2018. *The Routledge Companion to Transmedia Studies*. New York: Routledge.

Genette, Gérard. 1997. *Paratexts: Thresholds of Interpretation*. Translated by Jane E. Lewin. Cambridge: Cambridge University Press.

Gray, Jonathan. 2010. *Show Sold Separately: Promos, Spoilers, and Other Media Paratexts*. New York: New York University Press.

Hayles, N. Katherine. 2003. "Translating Media: Why We Should Rethink Textuality." *Yale Journal of Criticism* 16, no. 2: 263–290.

Hellerman, Jason. 2021. "Does 'The Snyder Cut' Prove Auteur Theory?" *No Film School*, March 24, 2021. https://nofilmschool.com/zack-snyder-auteur-theory.

Hills, Matt. 2018. "Transmedia Paratexts: Informational, Commercial, Diegetic, and Auratic Circulation." In *The Routledge Companion to Transmedia Studies*, edited by Matthew Freeman and Renira Rampazzo Gambarato, 289–296. New York: Routledge.

Hutcheon, Linda. 2013. *A Theory of Adaptation*, 2nd ed. New York: Routledge.

Jenkins, Henry. 2006. *Convergence Culture: Where Old and New Media Collide*. New York: New York University Press.

Jenkins, Henry. 2009. "The Revenge of the Origami Unicorn: Seven Principles of Transmedia Storytelling (Well, Two Actually. Five More on Friday)." *Confessions of an Aca-Fan*, December 12, 2009. http://henryjenkins.org/blog/2009/12/the_revenge_of _the_origami_uni.html.

Jenkins, Henry. 2011. "Transmedia 202: Further Reflections." *Confessions of an Aca-Fan*, July 31, 2011. http://henryjenkins.org/2011/08/defining_transmedia_further _re.html.

Jorgensen, Darren. 2010. "The Numerical Verisimilitude of Science Fiction and EVE-Online." *Extrapolation* 50, no. 1 (Spring): 134–147.

Léger-St-Jean, Marie. 2012. "Mid-19th-Century Cheap Novels: Speeding towards Global Mass Transmedia Culture." Academia.edu, 2012. https://www.academia.edu /1702239/Mid_19th_Century_Cheap_Novels_Speeding_Towards_Global_Mass _Transmedia_Culture.

Loock, Kathleen, and Constantine Verevis, eds. 2012. *Film Remakes, Adaptations and Fan Productions: Remake/Remodel*. London: Palgrave Macmillan.

Mittell, Jason. 2001. "A Cultural Approach to Television Genre Theory." *Cinema Journal* 40, no. 3 (Spring): 3–24.

Newman, Charles, and Gerald Graff. 1985. *The Post-Modern Aura: The Act of Fiction in an Age of Inflation*. Evanston, IL: Northwestern University Press.

Peary, Roger, and Gerald Shatzkin. 1977. *The Classic American Novel and the Movies*. New York: Frederick Ungar Publishing.

Pesce, Sara, and Paolo Noto, eds. 2016. *The Politics of Ephemeral Digital Media: Permanence and Obsolescence in Paratexts*. New York: Routledge.

Rieder, John. 2010. "On Defining SF, or Not: Genre Theory, SF and History." *Science Fiction Studies* 37, no. 111 (July): 191–209.

Ruppel, Marc Nathaniel. 2012. "Visualizing Transmedia Networks: Links, Paths and Peripheries." PhD dissertation, University of Maryland, College Park.

Scorsese, Martin. 2019. "I Said Marvel Movies Aren't Cinema. Let Me Explain." *New York Times*, November 5, 2019. https://www.nytimes.com/2019/11/04/opinion/martin -scorsese-marvel.html.

Thon, Jan-Noël. 2018. *Transmedial Narratology and Contemporary Media Culture*. Lincoln: University of Nebraska Press.

Wall, Barbara. 2019. "Dynamic Texts as Hotbed for Transmedia Storytelling: A Case Study on the Story Universe of The Journey to the West." *International Journal of Communication* 13 (May): 2116–2142.

4 Aunty Santa's Story and the Making of a Transmedia Artist

Dilman Dila

While many of the essays in this volume seek to define and explain the logics that undergird our increasingly transmediated existence, this chapter by the Ugandan artist and filmmaker Dilman Dila raises a philosophical question about the effects of transmedia on cultural knowledge and notions of personal identity and authenticity. In keeping with chapter 1, by Maureen McHugh Yeager, Dila first defines transmedia in relation to earlier media forms, mapping connections between contemporary, oft-commercialized transmedia experiences and historical examples of networked stories, including folklore, song, poetry, dance, and riddles. He argues that receiving a story and participating in its co-creation are fundamental components of human sociality, in that acts of retelling, iteration, and reenactment affirm one's individual identity while also engendering a sense of belonging to a larger whole. Communal storytelling for both identity performance and social cohesion is a common theme throughout this volume, directly referenced in the case study given in chapter 5, by Yomi Ayeni, in his participatory steampunk transmedia experience, and visited again in later chapters detailing the use of transmedia storytelling in educational interventions, most notably in chapter 11, by Katherine Buse and Ranjodh Singh Dhaliwal, in their discussion of the citizen-science community around the educational and research-based game Foldit. In each of these examples, the sometimes anarchic energies of the audience must be balanced with the often-more-focused intent of creators, leading to surprising trajectories and unexpected results. This tension between constrained transmedia experiences amenable to measurements and quantitative assessments of impact and decentralized, wild forms of networked stories reflecting the diversity of human expression lies at the heart of Dila's essay and is a provocation for readers to consider throughout the rest of the volume.

Searching for Aunty Santa's Story

A physical disability gave me a traumatic childhood. It's a past that I dare return to only in stories, because stories kept me alive back then. They still do. I must've been eight years old when I heard the first story that, in retrospect, helped me survive. My mother's best friend, Aunty Santa, visited and told me of a book whose plot was something like this: Two boys look alike but live in different worlds; one is poor and suffering while the other is comfortable and happy. One day, Suffering Boy switches places with Happy Boy, and for a moment, Suffering Boy thinks that his nightmare is over. But he soon discovers that Happy Boy's life is worse than his, so he escapes back to his own world.

I believe that Aunty Santa told me this story to help me make sense of the world. Of life. She had to, because the need to pass good stories around is hardwired in every human. When you hear a great story, you can't hold it in. You want to retell it to your neighbors, to give that good book to your friends, to share that beautiful movie with your loved one, to sing that song to your spouse, hoping that the story will affect their lives, whether in a grand way that causes behavioral change or in a simple way that puts a smile on their faces. This need gives transmedia storytelling its foundation. Aunty Santa, upon reading about a suffering boy who wished he had another life, must have thought that I needed to hear about it, and she was right. I loved the tale! I wanted to know more about Suffering Boy—his name, his town, his parents, all the little things that either Aunty Santa had left out or that I hadn't grasped—because I saw myself in Suffering Boy. Aunt Santa promised to bring me the book next time she visited, but when she returned, she said, "Oh, I couldn't bring it for you. The library wanted it back."

That was the first time that I heard the word "library," and I immediately thought of it as a place where stories are kept. I lived in Tororo, a sleepy town in Uganda about three hours from our capital city, Kampala. It had a small public library, an understocked colonial relic. The schools that I attended had libraries too, full of old books. I spent a lot of time in them, searching for Aunty Santa's story and failing to find it, until my early twenties, when I came upon Mark Twain's *The Prince and the Pauper*. Then, I thought, I'd finally found it.

When I think about transmedia, I think about this rich kid–poor kid story in its myriad versions. It affirms the universality of human experiences. When a story is good, when it has some kind of impact, it will forever be retold, remixed, and readapted to suit the realities of different peoples and cultures; it becomes an essential tool to help us make sense of life. Such a story, then, ends up not belonging to any particular person or community, and this is exemplified in the many folk stories around the world that share similar characters and plots. For a while, I thought Aunty Santa's story started with Mark Twain. But then I saw how he introduced the book: "I will set down a tale as it was told to me by one who had it of his father, which latter had it of HIS father, this last having in like manner had it of HIS father—and so on, back and still back, three hundred years and more, the fathers transmitting it to the sons and so preserving it." So it was a kind of folktale that Mark Twain wrote down, though we now think of it as Twain's story.

I have mixed feelings about this, for while writing, and now technology, has given us the means to concretize stories—to have one version that lives unchanged for centuries, even millennia, as seen in the Bible, the Koran, the Hindu Vedas, and other ancient writings—it also inhibits oral storytelling, which was the first kind of transmedia. It does not allow for the story to evolve each time that it is told, to reflect diverse realities in different communities, and in a way this leads to a negative form of conservatism and the oppression of those who oppose such texts. But that's an argument I'll make in another essay. For this chapter, I want to focus on story ownership since transmedia, as we know it today, is a form of storytelling dominated by corporations.

Kibanda and the VJs

Tororo in the 1980s had the right settings to host a transmedia storytelling experience, but one that didn't rely on the digital tools and technologies that have become synonymous with present-day transmedia. The most important characteristic that we can use to describe transmedia is that the story is a chameleon, existing in multiple platforms and changing each time to reflect the reality of each storyteller, who is also part of the audience or who has a very close relationship with the audience. As such, the story and its larger storyverse are communally owned. Digital technology and the internet today have made it easy to develop formal structures, like fan fiction and alternate-reality games, around this characteristic, but in Tororo in the 1980s, we experienced transmedia without giving it a name.

The country had only one TV station, which came on the air in the early evening and shut down by midnight. Reception was often poor, and we saw more fuzzy black lines than actual pictures. State-owned radio was on all day, but it was dominated by news, which we never trusted. We instead relied on "Radio Katwe," named after a suburb of Kampala, whose residents were famous for copying and making locally relevant versions of technology like electric stoves and water heaters. Perhaps that's why gossip and unofficial news came to be named after it. For entertainment during power blackouts, we huddled in the tiny kitchen as supper cooked, reciting old stories and urban legends that I presume, in the distant future, will be thought of as folktales. We told of people who eat zombies and of people like John Akii-bua, who could outrun a car (Akii-bua had set a world record while winning Uganda's then-only Olympic gold medal in 1972). Our town had a cinema at another colonial relic, The Social Center, but shows were intermittent and expensive, so video halls, called *bibanda* (the plural form of *kibanda*), cropped up. These tiny rooms, often former retail shops, were always so packed that you'd leave drenched in your neighbor's sweat. An old TV set sat at one end of the room atop a video deck, providing the only light, and the audience sat on wooden benches, choking on cigarette smoke.

Bibanda gave rise to a new genre of film, unique to this region of Africa, the "translated film," which is the ultimate transmedia experience in that it marries oral storytelling with modern-day, technology-based storytelling. All films that came into the country were in English or dubbed into English, which a majority of people barely understood. For a while, the most popular genre in *bibanda* was action films; they were easy to follow even without understanding the dialogue. Over time, audiences wanted to know exactly what was happening, so someone came up with an idea for live translation. These translators were nicknamed VJs (video jockeys), and they would sit beside the TV set with a microphone and PA system to explain the plot. Some VJs barely understood English, let alone the Western accents, so what they told the audience would often diverge from what was happening on the screen. Yet, their translation had to make narrative sense, and in the end, they would have concocted a new storyline. Sometimes the VJs made up lengthy backstories for the characters, and the goal often was to make the audience laugh, even if it was a horror film, which served to further skew the plot. They would also localize the characters, businesses, and places with Ugandan names and equivalents, and the audience enjoyed the experiences so much that today these translations are dubbed into the films. This, of course, interferes with the original soundtrack. You have, for example, six seconds of the VJ speaking, and then the soundtrack crashes in for like a second, then maybe another three seconds of the VJ, creating a staccato that adds to the otherworldly feel of this new kind of cinema.

In the 1980s and early 1990s, with our access to films being limited, those who watched these films retold the stories to those who could not. Often the stories took on a life of their own, as the narrator would make out like the events happened to them or to someone they knew; such retellings created many new stories set in the same storyverse.

One that easily comes to mind are stories that sought to explain why China never participated in the World Cup. One of these, Google tells me, was not unique to my town and was deplorably racist: that Chinese people look alike, so they could replace all their players during halftime, causing the team to be banned from the tournament. Most of these China/World Cup yarns were pure fantasy. I first heard one from a truck driver whose job took him all over East Africa, and he told us how he watched a Chinese football club in Nairobi. When one of the players kicked the ball, the Kenyan goalkeeper instead saw a lion charging and fled, leaving the net exposed. Other versions that I heard later had the ball turning into fire. Another person told us of meeting a Chinese man who was so gifted in kung fu that when he kicked the ball, it disappeared into the clouds, and he drank a cup of tea while he waited for it to fall back to Earth.

Several years after first encountering these stories, I watched a film called *Shaolin Soccer*, and then I understood that it either gave birth to or utilized these soccer myths. While writing this chapter, I tried to verify these memories, but internet searches only bring up Stephen Chow's 2001 parodic film of the same name. I can't find one that must have been made in the 1980s, or the 1970s, or perhaps earlier, that I watched as a child. Is my memory wrong? Did I watch a kung-fu-soccer fantasy film before 2001? Or were these simply urban legends about the world's most popular game that went on to find a home in an early-2000s comedy film?

Ultimately, a transmedia story does not revolve around a single character, or even a specific set of characters or a handful of plot lines. Instead, plots are nonlinear, with vague beginnings and endings, such that endless permutations of characters and plots can be derived from the thread that holds them all together in a single storyverse. When I first read Amos Tutuola's novel *The Palm-Wine Drinkard* (1952), I did not know about his process in creating it, but I recognized many stories in the book at once because I'd heard them before. Later, I learned that he had traveled around Nigeria collecting folk stories, which he compiled into the book. Yet it stands as an original work of fiction because Tutuola introduced a new character, the "palm-wine drinkard," whose quest to find a dead palm-wine tapster sets him on a collection of adventures. The central character and his quest serve to emphasize that these stories belong in one narrative universe. The same can be said of the Arabian Nights, and of many folktales from around the world, which tether together stories from oral cultures using a fairly lightweight central narrative, like the hare in many Luo stories playing a cunning character. So when I see Chinese soccer fantasies, or urban-legend tales from the era of Idi Amin's rule in Uganda (1971–1979), I see a series of loosely related anecdotes that can, and have been, anthologized into a single narrative. This is possible because they come together to form one narrative universe.

David and the *Rise and Fall of Idi Amin*

The first film that I remember seeing was *Rise and Fall of Idi Amin* (1981), at The Social Center before the *kibanda* phenomenon, before there was anyone standing beside the screen to "translate" Idi Amin's story. The Social Center was packed. People stood in the aisles and in any available space. I spent most of the film squeezed between legs, and every now and then, my older brother David lifted me onto his shoulder so I could glimpse the screen, and he put me down when I got too heavy. David was killed sometime in 2001. He was living in Kitgum, in northern Uganda, far from us in the East, when Lord's Resistance Army (LRA) rebels kidnapped him and frog-marched him to Sudan. On the way, he said that he was tired and the rebels killed him on the spot. Learning about his death made me wonder if my first experience of cinema had any meaning.

But Uganda's traumatic past holds a lot of meaning when we attempt to define transmedia, which I see as a phenomenon where a common experience triggers a deluge of stories. This could be something as simple as a film that captivates the imagination of viewers globally and ignites a fandom, or as dark as a genocide; stories spring up to document the event for those who did not experience it, and, above all, to help us make sense of it all so the business of life can continue.

That day, with The Social Center so densely packed, I wasn't the only one who couldn't see the screen. Many of us had to rely on a relayed narration from those who could. At one point, the audience gave a collective gasp of horror and people whispered to each other, "He [Idi Amin] is eating his son's heart." When I rewatched *Rise and Fall* many years later, I couldn't find a scene like this, though there is one that shows Amin eating the raw flesh of Chief Justice Ben Kiwanuka. By then I'd already heard so many stories about Amin; I'm not sure if these informed the film or if the film contributed to the stereotypes and misinformation.

I've encountered some of these tales in works of literature. In George Seremba's play *Come Good Rain* (1993), which documents how the playwright survived death during Amin's reign, there's a story of a woman dating a soldier. When she asks the soldier to take her to shop for luxuries, he brings her to a mass grave and tells her, "Here is a shopping center. Take what you want." In Seremba's play, this is a sad story, but it was a comedy when I first heard it—told to make us laugh at the woman. Many stories from Idi Amin's times, as with most of the traditional horror stories from Ugandan communities, are told as humor, maybe as a way for the society to process the collective trauma that it suffered at the hands of the dictator's trigger-happy soldiers.

Julius Ocwinyo's novel *Fate of the Banished* (1997) also tackles Uganda's traumatic past and includes anecdotes that I had heard from oral sources long before. In Ocwinyo's novel, I found one version of the story in which an athlete kicks a ball into the clouds. This time, it is a Ugandan soldier fighting for the British in Singapore during World War II; while playing football for leisure, he executes such a powerful kick that he sends the ball beyond the clouds, leaving time for him to roll up and light a cigarette before the ball falls back onto the pitch. I didn't like this novel. Unlike Seremba's play, which made the story I'd heard seem fresh by presenting it in a different genre, shifting from gallows humor to dismal, quotidian horror, Ocwinyo's novel was a word-for-word replay of what I'd heard before, so I felt cheated.

The Drive to Become a Transmedia Storyteller

Transmedia, at its core, is multiplatform storytelling, where a story, or a story experience, starts in one format and evolves when retold in another. Arguably, transmedia has always been there, as long as humans were telling stories, from cave dwellers whose tales mixed oral techniques with song and paintings; to more complex civilizations, where people gathered under the full moon to sing and dance and celebrate; to the modern era, where we consume stories in theaters or in the secluded comfort of our homes. We tend to ascribe a new term to this experience because today, digital technology has made it possible to create formal structures around it, and because corporations are deploying it as a way to keep audiences in their grasp.

In this traditional sense, then, transmedia does not rely on a single narrator; instead, it is what I call "communal storytelling." Today's mainstream transmedia shares this characteristic, with corporations employing hundreds, even thousands, of artists to create a transmedia piece like the Marvel Cinematic Universe (MCU). The difference is that mainstream transmedia might have a single individual, or a small group of individuals, at the helm dictating the outcome, and the plot lines usually have little room to organically evolve in response to audience experiences and to reflect the diverse lived realities of different audiences.

However, given that advances in technology enable a single artist to comfortably work in many kinds of media and formats, it is possible to have a sole creator of a transmedia story. I think of myself as a multidisciplinary artist who has written books of fiction, created digital arts, done photography, and made films, among other formats, and it was only logical that I would eventually end up creating a story that spans all these different kinds of media.

At first, I only wanted to be a writer, and by the time I set my mind on this, at the age of fifteen, I was aware of two kinds of stories: those with recognizable authors and those that had taken on a life of their own and had been stripped of all kinds of authorship, such that they'd become communal and, if they were old enough, "folk stories."

In retrospect, I wanted to be a writer to prove that I was not useless, which is how my parents, my family, and the society saw children with disabilities. I realized early in life that I had to excel in something for people to think differently about me. I must have been six, or seven, certainly, long before I heard Aunty Santa's story, when I drew a picture of a car, and one woman, a visitor from my father's side of the family, was amazed. She showed the drawing to others, and they swooned over the details. Someone said, "He even put in the number plate!" and I did not wonder why this detail was supposed to be important because I was reeling from the realization that they weren't looking at me with pity or disgust, but with awe.

This became even more apparent in secondary school, where I was a laughingstock until I joined the writing club and became a "news reader." At first, of course, no one would let me. But since I was one of the few really good literature students, I gained a key position in the writing club and then appointed myself news anchor. I forced myself to step onto the stage during a school assembly, and I ignored the booing. I didn't deliver news about mundane happenings at the school, but about offbeat stuff that they had never heard during an assembly, like a story about boys who had been caught stealing boiled cassava at the Eastern Market. The students loved it! When I finished, they clapped and cheered for a long time, and I became a top celebrity in my last two years. I wanted that kind of thing for the rest of my life.

For a long time, I thought the only thing I'd do was write, but I discovered that I could not make a living at writing—not in a country without a well-developed publishing industry. For a moment, I faced the possibility that I wouldn't become a writer, and hence I would never prove my worth. Seeing that I might be stuck in day jobs, where I wasn't treated with respect because of my disability, I became desperate to find a way to earn a living making art.

In the early 2000s, Nollywood, Nigeria's unique and vibrant homegrown film industry, blossomed in Africa, and seeing people watching and buying video tapes, CDs, and DVDs of these movies told me that I could make a living working in film. So I broadened my ambitions beyond writing and learned the craft of filmmaking. I was working in a developing film industry where most of the crew lacked formal training, so I ended up learning much more than just writing and directing. I learned photography, music composition using digital workstations, and video editing, and this increased my skills and fostered my ability to work in many kinds of media. Along the way, because I create science fiction films, I needed photorealistic visual effects, and so I learned computer-generated imagery (CGI), using an opensource software suite called Blender—in turn, this opened my eyes to digital arts. Now, I started to create not only animated films, but also graphic novels, and I discovered even more ways of making money. I thought of publishing poetry only after the internet made it possible to make money writing it. I turned some of my poems into transmedia pieces, combining verse, video art, and graphic art, albeit without much monetary success. But it was a learning process, and it showed me that it is possible to create transmedia and multiplatform art as a solo artist.

Jopolo and *Robots of the Pearl*: Transmedia Art Pieces

While I work in many platforms, right at the initial idea stage, I know where a story will end up: whether it will be a short story, a film, a novel, or something else. But as I developed my skills in these different platforms, I started to think of stories that could be told in multiple ways. One of these started life as a short film, which I then adapted into a radio play, *Toilets Are for Something Fishy*, and it was longlisted for the BBC Radio International Scriptwriting Competition in 2014. I later rewrote it as a stage play, and then as a feature film, though it is yet to be produced in either of those more cost-intensive formats.

Other than that, I never gave much thought to multiplatform stories or mixed-media stories until I noticed how advances in digital technology were influencing consumer behavior. Given trends in smartphones, mobile devices, augmented reality, and VR, it's easy to imagine a near future where the lines between formats are blurred—that it will be possible to, for example, produce interactive books that blend text, graphics, comics, video, and audio. Social media has already made the microfilm a trend, with amateurs producing films that are only a few dozen seconds long, and some news agencies, like Al Jazeera, featuring documentaries that mix video and text, rather than relying on traditional voiceover, to optimize for consumption on social media. Since I primarily depend on my art for a living, I fear that a time will come when the films I make or the books I write will not have a market. As a result, I'm determined to change with the times and learn new skills in emerging media.

In 2018, I saw a call for projects from KLAART, an arts festival in Kampala, and I came up with an idea for an interactive and immersive piece. At first, I wanted it to be an augmented-reality experience, but I could not access the right technology to experiment, and so I settled for a transmedia piece, *Robots of the Pearl* (2019), a social commentary on maternal health issues in Uganda. I used digital art to re-create scenes from precolonial Uganda, like cesarean section operations performed by native doctors, as well as scenes from the present day, like one about government plans to import doctors from Cuba as a reaction to a strike by local doctors over poor working conditions and payments. In these images, I rendered digital characters onto photographs and added text narrations that told stories and gave background information, along with video documentaries of families who had lost someone during childbirth. Each piece was a stand-alone, and yet when consumed together, they told a wide-ranging, nonfictional story about health care in Uganda.

I didn't think I was creating a transmedia piece. I was only trying to solve a problem: how to portray the history of health care in Uganda in an interactive and engaging manner. In 2020, when I pitched another art project to South Africa's National Arts Festival, I still was not thinking of work in this vein as transmedia. This was at the height of the COVID-19 pandemic, and the festival had moved online, so they were seeking art pieces for online consumption. I thought of a graphic novel, *Jopolo*, about space travel as told in ancient African stories. But unlike most graphic novels, *Jopolo* (2020) is designed as a website, and it uses the technique of interactive maps to place links on images, making the experience nonlinear, with multiple storylines, allowing readers to jump from one story point to another. It also includes animations, videos, and texts, some of which are like infodumps to provide background information while others are excerpts from old anthropological books. Despite all of this cross-media complexity, *Jopolo* is still very much a work in progress. My dream is to create this labyrinth of a story, a kind of game where a reader tries to guess the plot.

Working on *Jopolo* made me painfully aware of how limiting it is to create transmedia as a single artist, without any budget or resources. Big corporations can pay hundreds of artists to bring their transmedia projects to life. They also have the budget to market their stories and create fandoms. Then the fans contribute to the stories without the big corporation paying them a penny, and yet the fans can't earn money from their creations because they are using copyrighted material to make them. In a way, these corporate transmedia replicate the structure of communal stories, but, crucially, without the element of communal ownership.

The Transfusion-Confusion Boy and the Future of Storytelling

Someone once forwarded a story to my email about a five-year-old boy who gives his blood to save his sister from leukemia, believing that the transfusion would kill him in the process. Like Aunty Santa's story, it pulled at my heartstrings. Though by then I was in my early twenties and the impact was not as profound, I found it intriguing because it spoke of a form of sibling love that I had never experienced. I wanted to know more—all the details that the chain email didn't provide—but I found nothing until many years later, when I remembered it and googled the key words: "five-year-old boy," "transfusion," "sister," and "leukemia." A link to the fact-checking website Snopes came up, and I saw that not only was the story made up, but it had been circulating for nearly 100 years.

This, since it appears to be a single story told across many platforms with little variation, might not strictly fit my definition, or many others, of trans-media. However, while Snopes was able to dig up its earliest documented appearance—a film in 1925—I suspect that it had been going around for a long time before that. Retelling the story in film and literature, along with its virality on the internet, gave it a sort of permanence where there is little variation, even after 100 years, especially because it is retold in platforms that offer persistent documentation. In contrast, stories passed down orally undergo significant variations across time and place because oral storytellers have greater room to readapt the tale.

Whenever I hear an ancient story, I ask myself, "Where did this come from?" I've been asked that same question a few times, from audience members who watch my films and can't imagine anyone like me thinking up such a yarn. When my first collection of short stories, *A Killing in the Sun*, came out in 2014, someone asked, "Did you write this?" When I said yes, she said, "But you didn't grow up in Uganda. You must have grown up in Europe." She couldn't believe that I grew up in a small town three hours' drive from the city, because modern history makes it hard for people to imagine a boy from Tororo writing science fiction or making films like *What Happened in Room 13* (2007), a dark comedy about crime and adultery. But I ask this question because I'm aware that whatever ancient story I've encountered has traveled a long, long way, over a long, long time; its origin is blurred, and I really want to know: Who dreamed it up first? Was it based on any shred of truth?

Transmedia has come to be associated with the technological platforms of the digital era, but only the label is new. Storytelling has always been a transmedia experience, for stories power human civilizations. Once a story came to a community, they owned it, even if the origins were foreign, and they retold it over generations to reflect their realities and histories. In this way, stories have played a vital role in enhancing a sense of belonging, passing on essential knowledge and skills, and giving meaning to life. A defining property of transmedia storytelling is diverse stories existing in multiple platforms but nevertheless forming one narrative universe, as we saw in *The Palm-Wine Drinkard* and in the Arabian Nights.

The second key property of transmedia is that the crafting and shaping of stories is not limited to content producers. Transmedia stories include the interpretations and experiences of users and audiences, as we can see in fandom culture around popular works. Fans create their own versions of a story by using Photoshop, painting, creating memes, writing fan fiction or making fan films, and more. In the days of our ancestors, the creation and telling of stories was rarely a single-author phenomenon. It was a collective effort, and participation from the community, the listeners, was an important part of the storytelling experience.

Around 2012, I accompanied a friend to Gulu, a city in northern Uganda; she was trying to collect Acholi folktales and put them on her website. "We have to preserve our culture," she told me. "These stories are dying out." I brought a camera and helped her to film some of the stories. She was appalled when she heard children retelling folktales, but including modern-day items like soda and vehicles in them, and she was even more horrified when she heard them talk about "fire-breathing lizards," which never appear in Acholi mythology. The Acholi were coming out of nearly two decades of horrible war, and I tried to explain that perhaps the children were not thinking of dragons, which they probably had never heard of, but something else that came about because of the trauma of living in terrible conditions in refugee camps. Sometimes a fire would burn down half the camp, leaving them homeless. My friend was not open to such interpretations. She wanted the old stories to remain "pure."

She is not alone. Every now and then, someone puts out a book with a collection of folktales from a particular culture, purportedly to preserve them. This is a valid response to centuries of colonialism and racist ideology undermining African cultures—and yet, oral stories were, and still are, never static. They change from community to community, over time and across generations, which explains why, even among the Acholi, Awili's story varies from village to village. It's about a proud girl who ends up marrying an ogre, and her sister, a person with a disability, who saves her. Some villages sing the songs differently, and some give the sister a different disability. In the one I grew up listening to, she was blind. In others, she has mobility issues because of a malformed leg.

I don't know exactly where I stand in all this, but I think I'm somewhere in between, supporting efforts to preserve the original folktales but also encouraging a retelling of new versions based on current realities.

Perhaps this desire to preserve folktales comes from interactions with media and technology that offer permanent and unchangeable documentation, like books, or perhaps from the current trend to copyright stories. Given how flagrantly Western corporations appropriate other cultures' stories for profit, perhaps it is important to have them in written form so their origins can easily be traced.

Though it seems like technology, especially the internet, has made it possible to enjoy ancient human traditions of readily adapting, retelling, and sharing stories we love, capitalism and the global consolidation of media conglomerates have constrained and complicated the process with strict rules of ownership. Some stories, like *The Lord of the Rings* and *Game of Thrones*, have become global phenomena, creating new universes that inspire people to dream, but the freedom to readapt these stories to fit any culture and any reality is severely limited.

It is not far-fetched to imagine a future where all stories belong to capitalistic entities. We can glimpse this possible future scenario today in #inktober, an annual challenge where artists from all over the world participate by creating one ink drawing each day during the month of October and then sharing it online. But then, corporate sponsorship led to the emergence of official #inktober suppliers selling brushes and ink sets, which many artists could not afford. And the artist who started the hashtag copyrighted it, ostensibly to protect it from abuse. He relied on the artificial intelligence (AI) of online stores like Amazon to enforce the copyright, and suddenly artists found that they could not sell their own artworks. While Snopes tracked down the origin of the leukemia-transfusion story, AI systems could potentially do a far more efficient job, and it is possible that even if a story contains only a section that is vaguely similar to another story, the author could be punished.

In 2011, I made a thirty-minute documentary film, *The Sound of One Leg Dancing*, about a Nepali dancer, an amputee who participates in a national competition. The documentary contained a few moments where the subject is dancing to songs by other artists. When I uploaded it onto YouTube, Google's AI flagged the film for copyright violation. I got a notice stating that the music company that owns these songs could run ads on my video without my consent, even though the songs in question were in the documentary for less than two minutes. Furthermore, I would not be allowed to monetize the film. I could not argue fair use, and I could not use the email discussions I had with this music company at the time that I was making the documentary saying that I did not need contractual permission, given the nature of the film. I decided to pull down the documentary.

For me, copyright laws are essential because they protect my works and enable me to earn a living from my creations—and yet I have mixed feelings about them, for I fantasize about the past, where stories were free and communally owned. I know that times have changed, that we operate in a system that requires copyright law to protect an artist, but perhaps we need a new paradigm within which to enshrine these laws. For one, I think it would be a good thing if corporations and other nonhuman entities were prohibited from owning art. And anyone should be free to adapt, copy, and share a work of art, maybe under a system like what we have with Creative Commons, giving the original creator attribution and, if the derivative work is a commercial success, royalties. This might help to preserve storytelling as a shared endeavor, as it has been in human societies since the beginning of time.

Transmedia has become an important concept in modern art, but it leaves me worried about the future of storytelling. While art has always been a commodity of some sort, capitalism has turned it into a factory product. It scares me to imagine what it might be like if all the tools and platforms for consuming and telling stories are owned by corporations—if all stories are owned by profit-minded people rather than the people and groups who love those stories and derive meaning from them.

Transmedia Crosstalk: Paweł Frelik and Dilman Dila

Bob Beard: Welcome both of you to this chat. I'd love to hear how these chapters struck you.

Paweł Frelik: Well, the VJing practice totally blew my mind! Like, totally, transmedia before transmedia!

Dilman Dila: Hehehe, it's still a phenomenon that feels fresh, even to us who have lived with it for all this time. We see people talking in real life as if they are VJing, complete with the sound effects of an interrupted soundtrack.

PW: Fantastic! How widespread is it, or has it been, in other countries?

DD: It's now in nearly all East African countries. I know for certain that in Rwanda it is as big as in Uganda. Not sure how much it is in Kenya and Tanzania, but I hear it is there. In Rwanda, it is more organized, like in Uganda.

BB: It's certainly interesting as concretized media form now, but it also works as a type of literacy, or perhaps a cultural currency. Paweł, how does that square with your essay?

PF: I think it does—it's a perfect example of taking a cultural text (here, a film) and using it in the way that is localized, or that simply resonates with a given community.

DD: Yes, it fits well with your view on adaptations. And I think ultimately adaptation is what makes transmedia.

PF: The closest is an adaptation, but it's also a remediation. After all, a specific tech infrastructure does play a role in this practice.

DD: Yeah . . . though I believe tech is the one thing that keeps changing. We are always adapting stories to suit our own experiences, and in the VJing case, they are using a tech that is new to that society to perform that adaptation.

PF: I also kind of thought of the room arrangement as a kind of tech—like, that TV set, a microphone, and so on.

DD: Oh, the room arrangement was not prethought, I think. In most cases, it was people putting good use to unused spaces in their town, like shops that Indians had left after Idi Amin expelled them, and which stayed empty for decades. Very much like the birth of Nollywood, where a businessperson had a lot of blank videotapes, and was looking for means of disposing of them. Again, there's adaptation for you. With Nollywood, they must have taken stories that were circulating around orally and put them on videotapes.

PF: Now that I think about it, this wouldn't be another perspective like the four I discuss in my chapter, but something that lives on the same level as transnational remakes, or video game adaptations.

DD: Oh yeah . . . sometimes I think of it as video game adaptation, but in real life.

PF: And also like a stand-up commentary on the film, especially where the VJ changes the mood—you mention, I think, people making funny comments about scenes in horror movies.

BB: It seems what you're both talking about here is the focus on people as the sites of transmediality. In commercial, predominantly Western and Disney-fied transmedia, there's a hierarchy of participation: play only in this section of the sandbox, with only this set of tools. But VJing has a different set of "rules" and practices, pivoting the meaning-making from the text to the audience.

PF: Hm, interesting. Yeah, That sounds accurate. Also, I sense there is a changed hierarchy.

DD: I think fandoms try to do that in a way, shifting the pivot from text to the audience, but have so far been unsuccessful about it.

PF: Well, in some ways, they have, I think. But to me, the main difference is the immediacy. Most transmedia reworkings are objects that can only be experienced or inspected after their creation. VJing is in the moment. It is a reworking that is happening and being audienced at the same time.

BB: As media scholars and creators, how do you feel about VJing as a mode of transmedia? What are the strengths and possibilities beyond these localized sessions—or are they meant to be fleeting and immeasurable?

PF: I find them massively invigorating! Sure, the practice of recording them is a move in the direction of commodifying them, but the immediacy and fleetingness of the original practice seems to me almost subversive. Especially in a world which is obsessed with collecting and archiving data.

DD: I think of them as products of their times, sort of, and there will always be versions of them in the future. So they came about as a necessity, to fill a gap, and then they became part of urban cultures. I think they sort of stand for what transmedia is: humans adapting stories to reflect their own experiences.

PF: Yes, that makes sense. In some ways, especially recently, they may be copying some commercial practices, but the original VJing seems to be very community-based, or community-oriented—even if this community comes into existence only for a limited period of time during the screening.

BB: In its original formulation, it seems liberatory too—as it's not dictated or predetermined by media producers, distributors, and conglomerates. Of course, once it becomes "institutionalized," there'll be another disruption or innovation.

PF: Yes, totally! As William Gibson wrote, the street finds its own uses for things.

DD: Yeah. There will always be an underground version of something.

PF: I can only restate: this really blew my mind, so thank you, Dilman, for writing about this!

DD: Thank you too, for your piece! It did make me put a lot of my thoughts in their place.

5 Transmedia Experientialism and Social Cohesion (A Work in Progress)

Yomi Ayeni

The role of a transmedia creator, whether managing a multimillion-dollar intellectual property (IP) or applying storytelling in the classroom, is to set the conditions for an actionable story. A narrative without a network to shape and share it will wither from inattention. Likewise, the boundless, collaborative energy of an audience must be met with a story that invites not just consumption but participation. In this chapter, the writer and producer Yomi Ayeni shares his experience dual-wielding the creative and organizational tools that animate Clockwork Watch, an alternate-history transmedia experience spanning print media, in-person events, and third-party partnerships, unfolding over the past decade. As introduced earlier in this book by Caitlin Burns (chapter 2), the longevity of Ayeni's project can be attributed to his active and careful stewardship, which provides old and new audience members multiple entry points to reflect on and enhance the story's thematic goal of confronting historical erasures and injustices through collaborative engagement. The storyworld explores themes of inequality and oppression, lightly glossed by elements of the fantastic via robots and neo-Victorian technologies, but it is designed such that audience participation becomes an additional narrative element—generating surprising, unscripted vignettes and opportunities for shared empathy by bringing real-world concerns into the fiction, from local economies to feminist activism. The liberatory potential of enacted stories is similarly taken up in chapters 14 and 15 by Zoyander Street and Terra Gasque, respectively. Ayeni also discovers that social activity within a transmedia storyworld, whether through puzzle-solving, role-play, or co-creation, has educational potential as well, inspiring both self-directed and peer-to-peer learning opportunities; in chapter 9, Lee Emrich embraces a similar logic of horizontal pedagogy in their chapter on remixing Shakespeare in the classroom. Although Clockwork Watch is an ambitious undertaking, Ayeni highlights how a transmedia experience can be delivered without the use of sophisticated social media tools or complex and expensive online content management systems, which are often a barrier for entry for many organizations and creators, especially those working with young people. In chapters 8 and 12, respectively, Francis Quek et al. and Ruth Wylie et al. discuss similar efforts at creating socially intensive but technologically modest learning experiences with a foundation in transmedia storytelling and collaborative play.

It's almost impossible to give a definitive answer when asked what the term "transmedia" means, but in this chapter, I will try by exploring lessons learned and experiences gained from projects that I have created. To start, it is an experience, a little like life, with all the various actions, random interactions, experiences, occurrences, and connections made in the context of one storyworld.

Whenever participants interact with aspects of a transmedia narrative, it should co-create a randomness that is unique, organic, and realistic. To fully experience this effect, one has to be an active participant in the story, be open to connecting with others, and immerse in whatever the scenario dictates.

My practice involves creating holes within a transmedia production where I relinquish direction of the story to participants, inviting them to become co-creators with an opportunity to explore. This is where the real storytelling begins, as people realize that they have a choice—reaching for a smartphone to capture the moment or going with the flow and diving deeper into the experience. This creates an opportunity for the story to become a personal and visceral journey, and one that can lead to positive change.

It took a while for me to finally accept that I'm a storyteller. The vocation started while working as a journalist in the BBC TV newsroom, handling stories from all over the world and structuring them into bite-sized chunks that the general public could assimilate. The emergence of the internet changed my world; I went back to college to study for a master's degree in interactive multimedia, finished the course, and wrote the BBC newsroom's first consultation document on incorporating internet content into news bulletins.

I left college with the firm belief that the viewing audience was tired of a never-ending diet of passive entertainment, and yearned for content that would engage their minds, bodies, and souls. So I set out to create things that weren't platform dependent, didn't require an appointment to view, and had built-in feedback, so participants could see the story change as a result of their interactions within the storyworld. I had high hopes that technology would free us from being tethered to the TV—that we could carry our media around with us, and even choose when, how, and where we consumed content.

How I Have Come to Understand Transmedia

There's a certain irony in the fact that I spent years in the newsroom turning complex pieces of information into easy-to-understand chunks for broadcast, only to realize that news was just another form of storytelling. This eureka moment reminded me of the bedtime stories that my Gran used to read to me every night, and how I role-played so many of them with friends. Some remain cherished memories, while others are most definitely unacceptable and offensive in retrospect—but either way, lessons were learned. As my interest shifted from news toward how nonlinear storytelling can be mapped to real-life experiences, I became motivated to harness the power of interactive stories to shift people's attitudes and expand their perspectives.

I vividly remember playing "Cowboys and Indians" and piecing together every exciting nuance gleaned from the latest TV adventure of *The Lone Ranger*, but it's hard to believe that I was oblivious to the negative portrayal of Native Americans and other marginalized ethnic minorities in similar TV formats. At some point in my youth, I began to feel a sense of unease and knew there was something wrong with the way Black people were portrayed in shows like *Tarzan* and books like Hergé's *Tintin in the Congo*. I often wonder why I didn't develop some degree of political awareness earlier in life, having been introduced to the brutal colonial past of several Western countries through my role-play. But I was just a kid; I grew up, went to college, started the thing called "life," and left behind role-play—or so I thought.

When I was finishing my master's program, a friend gave me a copy of the technology theorist, entrepreneur, and *Wired* magazine cofounder Kevin Kelly's book *Out of Control: The New Biology of Machines, Social Systems, and the Economic World* (1994) for my birthday. In this book, Kelly describes how a beekeeping neighbor experienced being part of a honeybee colony by slotting his head into the middle of a moving swarm. Becoming part of a mobile hive, while being of independent mind, coupled with the certainty of being out of control, presented many questions (some of which I still haven't been able to address), and it got me thinking about co-creating narratives with active and independently minded participants. Could a member of the public become part of a story by simply attending a theater production? Was this any different from my childhood role-play, apart from the risk of being stung? And how could I turn a simple story into something that attracted participation, inspired people to do good things, and hopefully rewarded everyone involved?

I came to the conclusion that the bee story was in fact akin to a form of role-play: the participant beekeeper had a unique experience that influenced his knowledge and understanding of bee behavior. I wanted to create stories that offered similar experiences.

Transmedia offers a feedback loop of participant reactions with the various elements of the storyworld. These dispersed, even random elements can then be incorporated back into the central narrative. This chapter addresses my work in practice, exploring how I have instigated projects with social impact through co-created and shared experiences. Looking back, I would say that the door to this line of thought opened while I was a DJ playing funk and soul in London clubs. The dance floor was the sandpit where everyone's dreams and aspirations melded into one narrative that flowed throughout the night. It was a shared experience shaped by a multitude of interactive elements, not just the DJ or the music. It puzzled me as to how so much anxiety, sadness, worry, and trouble could be left at the door, and the alchemy by which people came together in a harmonious environment where they enjoyed one another's company. I soon switched to playing house music, and the dance floor narratives in that scene attracted even more people across differences of race, gender, sexual orientation, and class.

Does Practice Make Perfect?

I channeled the inspiration from reading Kelly's *Out of Control* into my first reality TV project, *E-Trippers* (2000), where we sent teams of participants on globe-trotting adventures, while viewers at home controlled almost every aspect of their lives. During development, I knew audience involvement was important, and capturing their attention from the start was pivotal. So we launched a web portal and invited interested candidates to submit a short travelogue introducing their local neighborhood. The public voted on who they thought was best suited as TV presenters, and contestants with the highest number of votes were invited to an audition, which was filmed as part of the show.

On the surface, *E-Trippers* seemed simple enough: Teams filmed themselves completing a series of tasks submitted by the audience. But there was a catch; after all, this was a game show, and there's always a "sting." If a team failed to complete three tasks in a row, it was replaced by contestants dropped from our first round of auditions. My objective was to let the audience live vicariously through every step of the participants' adventures and then become immersed through their attempts to control the course of the TV show. The co-created content was assembled into a cohesive story and broadcast on network TV. In 2001, I pushed the envelope further with *Global E-Missions*, which handed more control to the audience by allowing them to interact with contestants out in the field through social media, and rewarding them with daily video updates from the contestants, filmed and shared from locations around the world. *Global E-Missions* won the 2002 Broadcast Magazine Award for Best Use of New Media.

These series also became, happily, an unexpected platform to launch careers in media. In *E-Trippers*, we selected contestant candidates who were outliers—people who would hopefully endear themselves to the viewing (and interacting) public not through obvious star power, but through their inadequacies, flaws, and insecurities. You might call them "rough diamonds," but by the end of the series run, we had several seasoned broadcasters. As of 2021, one former contestant is the world's leading motocross commentator, another is a global name in the online gaming community, and another is a leader in the world of technology.

There's a million different ways of telling a story, including letting the audience become part of the narrative, which is why I liken transmedia storytelling to a living organism. A transmedia story reacts in different ways depending on a multitude of factors: location, time of day, story context, and even how it responds to a specific trigger, such as opening a door, deciding whether to walk through the doorway, leaving the door open, or even slamming it behind you. Transmedia flows, twists, and bends unlike any other form of narrative; I consider it to be a unique beast and approach it with cautious expectation every time.

This form of storytelling is best explained as an experience based on how a participant's background, personal beliefs, and perceptions influence how they respond to series of prompts within an interactive narrative. This means any two people in an experience may have the same initial interaction, but their responses will mostly be different.

After years of tinkering, I've come to understand that each narrative element in a transmedia story should be unique and independent, should solicit engagement, and should incentivize further participation.

Transmedia storytelling is easily confused with cross-platform, cross-media, or "360 programming," all of which repeat the same story across multiple platforms (e.g., a story told by TV show, collected on DVD, delivered as an audiobook, and perhaps an online presence). In contrast, transmedia has proven to be a gateway to a world of possibilities, where there could be alternate experiences and story threads, co-created narrative elements, immersive live events, and much more.

Over the years, I've even experimented with positioning participants as narrative elements, built into the architecture of the experience; I love how their unpredictable contributions lead to unimaginable developments in the story. They are living artifacts and also shapers of the story, co-creating with every interaction.

The Story

Regardless of how amazing the interactive and participatory mechanics seem, the story, being the backbone of the transmedia project, needs to be strong. It has to entice the audience to explore and unlock the various narrative elements. Most transmedia stories are fictional, but I believe that these experiences can also be based on an element of fact and introduce participants to subjects or topics that could easily be a turnoff in other modes.

One example is *Violette's Dream* (2008), an alternate reality game that I created for Gamecock Media to support the launch of *Velvet Assassin*, a next-generation computer game inspired by the real-life story of Violette Szabo, a British-French Special Operations Executive agent during World War II. My task was to generate interest around the game while it was still in development, but I was also mindful that people are sensitive about stories that could potentially glamorize the horrors of war. I focused on extending Violette's life story and legacy in a way that seemed realistic, and decided to mobilize participants on a real-life adventure in search of hidden (fictional) Nazi treasure and (real) gold bars. As the game was still in development, I knew our early adopters wouldn't be gamers, so I focused my attention on communities that liked solving puzzles, World War II enthusiasts, and most important, anyone who liked the idea of searching for hidden treasure. At first, interest was modest, but participation went stratospheric when the first real gold bar was found in a storage unit in Texas. Then a second piece of treasure was discovered in the left-luggage storage at London's Victoria Station. I was disheartened when plans to hide elements of the treasure hunt in the actual computer game were dropped because the game's publisher had been bought by a rival company.

I tend to choose subjects that are close to my heart, and I'm particularly inspired by projects that address a need within our society. *Violette's Dream* focused on quandaries around the past and history, questioning how we should remember and honor the legacy of people who have sacrificed their lives to create a better future, and what happens when time passes and that legacy is challenged by consumerism, social media, and the simple process of getting on with life.

My technique is a little like an escape room experience, where a problem is concealed in the middle of a story in the hope that participants will co-create a solution via role-play. It's what I'd call "story engineering," and it does work.

Engaging an audience in a participatory project presents unimaginable dynamism—it's impossible to know what to expect. The collective mind reacts like a mad box of frogs, probing every aspect of the storyworld, unearthing hidden gems, and often mistaking one thing for something totally different. There will always be red herrings here and there in order to mislead, and this flexibility inspires me to craft twists and turns in my work. Then I wait patiently to see where and when the secrets are discovered. There was a one puzzle in *Violette's Dream* that went unsolved, and that had me slightly worried. The participant leading our treasure hunt went off on a wild-goose chase, wasting a significant amount of time chasing a dead end. To my surprise, he eventually surfaced with a detailed response from a US Navy cryptographer working on a nuclear submarine.

My work is classed as "grassroots," and this gives me the freedom to expand and adapt on the fly, the flexibility to script holes in my narratives, and at junctures invite the audience to physically step into the storyworld that I've created. It remains a collaborative process, like the beekeeper participating with the swarm.

While I wouldn't necessarily encourage people to waste time chasing leads that go nowhere, anyone new to my creations should be prepared to probe the darkest recesses, or at least question the natural order of things as they seem.

Breathe (2009)

In *Breathe*, I put a few of my theories into practice and focused on pushing the boundary of immersive participation further by involving the audience in an immersive world that ran parallel to their day-to-day lives. *Breathe* was set up to see whether a film could encourage participants to create, develop, and bring to life their own characters within my story, and thereby help to co-create the narrative. The end objective was that the audience would eventually take ownership of the story as it neared its climax. Assisted by a small production team, we set about finding out whether a transmedia film could mimic real life and solicit audience participation over a long period.

When the project launched at Power to the Pixel, the digital arm of the 2009 London International Film Festival, delegates and participants stepped in and out of the story by simply attending the screening's after-party, a separate nightclub event, or a drinks party where interactions were recorded and edited into the weekly episodic releases.

The audience was invited to explore the seedy underbelly of London's nightlife in the hope of solving a series of mysterious deaths, infiltrating a hedonist group and exposing their deadly antics. The interactive story was crafted to forge a community of caring individuals who would feed information to the police to help prevent another death. This was a daring challenge, owing to how the community regard the police in such matters. During the project, we leaked a recording of a dangerous initiation ceremony to participants, and what followed was a heated online debate over whether the video should be sent to the police character. The community decided not to share the video, but over time, as participants warmed to the police character, they started to funnel information to him via phone calls.

To unearth the shady background of our hedonist group, we hosted a daylong treasure hunt along the River Thames, where a global audience used the image-sharing platform Flickr and other forms of social media to guide one participant through a series of hurdles, puzzles, and locations as they collectively deciphered Latin inscriptions on old Roman sundials. They were tasked with finding the sundials and then choosing the first character from each Latin inscription, which would reveal a location in London. Seems simple enough—apart from the fact that one of the sundials was destroyed in the Great Fire of London in 1666. We introduced the Latin-translation element halfway through the narrative, as a way of slowing things down and hopefully attracting more people to the story. I was surprised to find out that many of the people playing had studied the language at college!

One aspect that we hadn't considered was the impact that continuous online communication would have on the lone on-ground participant's phone—that is, until we got a message that said, "My phone is about to die." Unfortunately it did, leaving both the online followers and the story in limbo.

Breathe was structured with multiple facets so participants could immerse themselves to the point of steering the story. Our principal actors were contactable via telephone, which was attached to a Skype account so we could record calls. Halfway through the project, a participant called Paul Giffney solved one of our puzzles and was rewarded with details of a secret expedition. He joined the hedonists on a mission to assassinate a mole who had been leaking their activities to the police. The person was hiding on the roof of a twelve-story apartment block in London. After the event, Paul compiled a comprehensive dossier of the group's activities and presented his findings to the actor playing a police officer. Details of the midnight raid, as well as how he infiltrated the group, were eventually made public in a recorded phone conversation between Paul and the police officer, which was edited into the final segment of the film.

Throughout the project, there were rarely instances where participants felt compelled to reach for their phones to document what they were experiencing—even Paul's dossier was a mix of content gleaned from hidden websites, personal interactions, and puzzle-solving rather than a collection of videos and images from his phone. Participants understood that interactions were part of the story, and the payoff was seeing if their presence or actions affected the narrative and made it into the next episode of the drama.

Breathe was self-funded. The collaboration with Power to the Pixel/London International Film Festival helped to extend its reach. Our web presence saw a huge spike in traffic as word of mouth spread about how participants could interact with the narrative and help solve a murder mystery. At the same time, the team managed to keep the story localized within our target community: Power to the Pixel delegates, alternate-reality game fans, murder-mystery enthusiasts, and nightclubbers. We aimed to keep news of the project contained, just as it would have been if the fictional scenario were real. The reason for this decision wasn't solely creative; it also helped to keep costs under control. Our core objective was to see if we could successfully spread a film experience across multiple live events, locations, telephone numbers, and fictional characters, while sustaining the interest of immersed participants for three weeks, and I'm pleased to say that we achieved this.

The project also gave me a chance to question the definition of what constitutes a "cinematic experience" and why it solely applies to one-time screenings with run times of seventy-five minutes or more. Other forms of narrative immersion emerged around *Breathe* and directly challenged the primacy of that model. For example, in April 2009, almost six months before the project launched, an online radio station called UKDance started streaming music and cryptic messages related to *Breathe*. Our team used word of mouth and social media to draw attention to the station, which picked up a small and dedicated following of dance-music listeners from the UK, the US, Australia, and Greece. There was no way of telling whether these listeners really knew what the project was about, but many tuned in for long periods.

The cinematic part of *Breathe* launched in November 2009 with several screenings at the Greater London Council Chambers and a simultaneous launch on YouTube. Upon arrival at the screening, people were confronted by Nica Cooper, a character from *Breathe*, who was convinced that someone at the event could help her and the police solve the mystery of her brother's death. The drama that ensued was filmed and edited into one of the three thirty-minute episodes, which were released alongside thirteen live, immersive events over a three-week period. Did that make *Breathe* a feature or a series of shorts? I eventually came to understand that classifying *Breathe* as a feature film was wrong. I considered calling it a "co-created nonlinear experience," and then I settled on "co-created feature-length experience." We were able to give participants multiple "wow" moments, and by incorporating footage from our live events in each screened installment, we created an "appointment-to-view" ethic that extended the cinematic experience.

While fragments of *Breathe* exist online, the main story resides in the minds of those who experienced it. The success of the project suggests that people were tired of being spoon-fed content: they wanted to be tested, surprised, and rewarded, so this became one of my goals.

A World Run by Clocks

The *Clockwork Watch* story started at a New Year's Eve party in 2007, when I was asked to help a group of friends host a local Burning Man event, which we called "Seductive Alchemy." Playing on the steampunk theme, we went all-out on the creative. The party was huge: more than 1,000 people turned up in neo-Victorian attire, but surprisingly I was one of just a handful of Black people in attendance, which felt wrong.

As a DJ, I'd hosted many parties in and around London, each with a diverse crowd, but something about this particular event jarred with people of color. I realized that they weren't comfortable with the idea of role-playing colonialism, even though that was far from what we were doing at the party.

So I decided that steampunk was the appropriate vessel to critically explore aspects of the UK's colonial past. While the genre looked amazing, it was a "no-go" area for many non-White people. Despite its sartorial verve, it was evident that celebrating a period synonymous with the slave trade would never appeal, especially as the role-players in the early days of steampunk were predominantly White.

Clockwork Watch was designed to nudge a participatory audience into exploring our history in a nonconfrontational way. The story was set at a time when clockwork mechanics were the latest technological advancement. The world that I created was a warped reflection of our past: humans were living in harmony and everyone was equal, but sentient humanoid mechanical slaves, "Clockwork Servants" or "Clockworks," were the oppressed laboring class. The project used color to invite critical engagement: all the Clockworks dressed in black attire, prompting people to consider whether there was a racial aspect to the color-coding. The story introduced a world on the cusp of industrial change: role-players immediately identified the manufacture of these Clockwork Servants as a threat to society, both because the Clockworks might rise up and touch off violence and because the oppression of Clockworks in an otherwise egalitarian society might create a template for expanding exploitation to other groups.

In 2009, we hosted a second "Seductive Alchemy" on New Year's Eve. The theme was the same, but the narrative started online with the publication of a series of letters between two fictional young ladies. One described how excited she was to live in London, while the other lamented her boring country life; they were both eager to meet up for the Queen's New Year's Eve Ball, where there would be lots of eligible young men in attendance. The dialogue was inspired by Jane Austen's *Pride and Prejudice*.

Attendees were informed of the online correspondence ahead of ticket sales, which helped set the scene for the event. The letters also contained references to the injustice and suffering that Clockwork Servants endured, especially in London. To keep the conversation flowing during the event, we incorporated a device called Talkaoke—a pop-up talk show where anyone could air their views around the table of chat. Attendees shared their opinions of the world that we'd created and commented on the diversity of our crowd—there were more people of color in attendance. I felt this was just the beginning of an adventure.

By 2011, I had mapped my vision for *Clockwork Watch* across graphic novels, immersive events, role-play, and a printed newspaper. It was to have no online characters, no mobile phones, and zero Twitter, Instagram, or Facebook presence. I was intent on making sure that the project relied heavily on human connection, instigated by reading printed comic books and role-play at live events. *Breathe* had depended heavily on social media, and I felt that certain nuances of the story had been lost in translation. *Clockwork Watch* presented an opportunity to craft something different. To the best of my knowledge, no one else had explored the history of colonialism through the medium of a co-created story; it could be a platform through which participants could explore their own idiosyncrasies, hangups, or questions about our history. I was determined not to let technology get in the way of the experience. The story had to be told on a level playing field, where anyone could be a participant. Everything that participants needed to take part in the story was available in written form or could be accessed by attending one of our immersive live events.

Clockwork Watch was my first attempt at writing a graphic novel; I had no literary track record, I wasn't particularly well known in the steampunk scene, and I hadn't published a book or a bevy of essays beforehand. After getting several rejection letters from agents and publishers, I'd already realized that self-publishing was the only way that the story could be told, so I focused my attention on crowdfunding to generate a buzz. The steampunk community loved the idea, and many people shared the crowdfunding call-to-action on social media. I raised enough to pay an editor and illustrator and to print the first 500 copies.

My first obstacle was to build on my past success and offer the audience the freedom to explore the narrative, as I had done in *Breathe*. I needed to find a way to incorporate this aspect into *Clockwork Watch*, and I felt that the best way to achieve this was to place my audience within the story ahead of publication. One of the crowdfunding perks was a chance to be included as a character in the book, which quite a few people liked, and that was how I started to build my audience.

In an attempt to give the project a more dynamic appeal, I created three narrative paths with different arcs: Herakles, the Clockwork; Janav Ranbir, the Protagonist; and Saccadius Cartwright, the Alchemist. Each path told the same story from a different perspective. Later that year, *Clockwork Watch* won the 2012 IndieGoGo Best Crowdfunded Graphic Novel Award.

Several minutes into the launch of our first immersive event, a participant stormed out of the venue, found a print shop, designed and created some leaflets, and returned to proclaim himself the leader of "The Spanner," a new trade union movement set up to protect the jobs of real people from the Clockworks. This unplanned moment of participant creativity was a major turning point. We collaborated with The Spanner to stage an immersive experience at the Latitude Festival, where a demonstration by striking trade unionists prevented the viewing public from entering a showcase of Clockwork automata.

Very early on, the Clockwork Servant arc proved popular. The storyworld's online newspaper, the *London Gazette*, was inundated with articles from role-players, each talking about the negative impact that Clockwork technology was having on their daily lives. Many of these pieces were reactions to strategically placed signposts created to nudge the story along, and this meant that I often found myself reacting to participants' contributions. At first, I assumed that managing the co-created content would be an easy task, but the quality of content being submitted was amazing, and some of it simply demanded to be incorporated into the central story.

London Gazette Special Report: And If You Wrong Us, Shall We Not Revenge?

Dear Sir,

To be truthful, I sympathise with the Clockwork Twins, I do. Had I been subject to Zachary's perpetual torment then I would have most likely found a much messier and nastier way to end him than dragging him to The Thames.

After all, what creature with a mind of its own would not retaliate when sufficiently provoked? The lad knew exactly what he was doing and deserved what he got. Locking Clocks in boxes! What was he thinking? Even if they weren't jailbroken it's a publicity minefield. If there was ever a more fitting illustration of the word cretin then I do not know of it. Unfortunately upon opening The Den one of the conditions of limiting Hargreaves' operations within the East End was appointing his odious nephew as manager.

Good Riddance.

We now have two frightened, lost and deadly children roaming the city. God help them.

Ella Mayhem

Holding Space for Others to Create Stories

At the start of *Clockwork Watch*, I envisaged creating space for role-players to develop characters and scenarios. The newspaper stories were a great addition to the narrative. Some were folded into our world, while others ran parallel to the project, but Haley Moore's *Laser Lace Letters* actually nudged the story in a different direction.

Haley's contribution introduced the Angel Corps, a rabble-rousing, all-female airship squadron appointed by Queen Victoria herself. Within a matter of weeks, Haley had developed a whole series of stories based around their rowdy exploits.

Laser Lace Letters was told through handwritten letters, puzzles, and newspaper cuttings, all anchored in *Clockwork Watch*. To complete the project, Haley needed access to a laser cutter to make a series of cameo ornaments, so she launched a crowdfunding campaign that we supported, and she raised enough to buy the laser cutter, quit her day job, and set herself up in business. *Laser Lace Letters* is just one of the co-created offshoots from the *Clockwork Watch* story.

The transmedia, co-created aspects of this project have developed through all kinds of interesting partnerships and collaborations: connections and resonances with Black Lives Matter, integration with a real-world beverage, museum exhibits that blur fictional and actual histories, and a local partnership in the town of Kendal, in the north of England.

Black Lives Matter

Clockwork Watch remains a space where participants are given a chance to collaborate and interact with the story in their own self-directed ways. These co-creations are restricted to written contributions and role-play, which I believe help participants connect real-world themes and experiences with the plight of the Clockworks, such as the fight for equal rights, with hints of the suffragette movement. By sheer coincidence, the colonial arc in *Clockwork Watch* started to gain traction just before George Floyd's murder in Minneapolis and the massive global expansion of the Black Lives Matter movement.

A collaboration with the artist and scientist Dr. Geof Banyard led to a fundraising campaign selling a badge calling for more diversity in steampunk. Funds raised were donated to Il'laramatak Community Concerns, a nonprofit organization in Kenya set up to protect young girls from retrogressive practices that violate their human rights, such as underage marriage and female genital mutilation. Each badge was packaged in a colorful card and accompanied with the following statement:

> We love the creativity of steampunk, playing with fiction and elements of Victoriana and history to create vibrant fantastical worlds. But one of those elements is colonialism, and colonialism has caused harm.
>
> We also love the inclusivity of steampunk, the celebration of creativity and creating above all else. But sometimes it can appear that steampunk celebrates colonialism, and that can make people who have been harmed by colonialism feel excluded.
>
> We think we can have steampunk without celebrating colonialism, that we can use the frothing creativity of steampunk to make it clear to others that we reject colonialism and that they might like playing with us. So we're going to do stuff. And you're going to do stuff too. Because together we reckon that we can make our steampunk even more beautiful and inclusive.

Hodgson's India Pale Ale

Beyond the published *Clockwork Watch* graphic novels, there have been quite a few physical manifestations of the story; all have been collaborations, with each helping to move the story along. We even stepped back in time to highlight the real heritage of an alcoholic beverage that hasn't been tasted since Queen Victoria's reign. Hodgson's Brewery, in Bow, is rumored to have created the world's first India Pale Ale when a consignment from the brewery was sent by ship to India. The duration of travel, temperature change, and unsettled movement turned the drink pale. It was one of the first beer exports of its kind in the Victorian age.

I was offered creative custodianship of the Hodgson's brand, which presented the opportunity to introduce, and interrogate, an element of colonial-era nostalgia that participants loved. A special batch of the beer was brewed for our immersive theatrical shows; this sparked interest in the reenactment community, members of which wanted to taste a beer that hadn't been brewed since Queen Victoria was alive. There are no plans to make the beverage commercially available.

Museum Partnerships

The *Clockwork Watch* story was adopted by the Royal Observatory and National Maritime Museum in London, which were keen to explore the arrival of our main characters, the Ranbir family, from India, as part of *Longitude Punk'd* (2014), an exhibition to mark the 300th anniversary of the Longitude Rewards, offered by the British government to devise a method of determining a ship's longitude at sea. *Clockwork Watch* featured in a yearlong exhibition of fantastical inventions created by steampunk artists, placed alongside real historical objects in a showcase blurring the boundaries between art and science, fact and fiction. We presented drawings, dresses, jewelry, dioramas, and a host of bizarre gadgets, all purporting to solve the problem of determining longitude at sea.

A further collaboration between *Clockwork Watch* and Wyn Griffiths of Middlesex University led to the creation of "Globe of Dislocation," which manifested as an abandoned airship navigation unit positioned beside the prime meridian. According to our story, the piece was allegedly used by the Astronomer Royal, Nevil Maskelyne, as part of an abortive longitude experiment. Visitors were invited to investigate how the Victorian vessel came to crash in Greenwich. We also hosted several live events from the *Clockwork Watch* storyworld, where participants interacted with the character Tinku Ranbir, who explained the trials and tribulations of colonial England and what life was like for an Indian family living there.

Town of Kendal

In 2018, *Clockwork Watch* collaborated with the Lakes International Comic Art Festival and the Dramatic Arts Department at Kendal College to engage the students in an exercise that would give them "pride of place and purpose" in their community. I was asked to create a narrative that would help to stem the "brain drain" from this small town in the north of England and encourage students to stay in the town instead of moving to a big city after graduation.

We collaborated to localize the story in a way that would involve the whole town and tap into Kendal's history. One of my long-term ambitions was to explore Victorian heritage within the framework of the education system, and this partnership presented the ideal opportunity.

Over the course of several workshops, we developed a new arc to celebrate the centenary of women's right to vote, as enshrined in the Representation of the People Act of 1918. To make it relevant, we focused on the National Union of Suffrage Societies, which was formed in Kendal circa 1908. Another participant-initiated project, Haley Moore's Angel Corps, offered a perfect connection for this local activation.

The process involved five months of online newspaper articles written by the students, referencing the townsfolk's displeasure with Her Majesty's decision to offer Angel Corps a new squadron headquarters on the outskirts of Kendal.

We knew that the online content would have little penetration with the locals, so we printed a six-page edition that was handed out on street corners in Kendal. The paper documented Angel Corps' daring adventures in far-flung places, as well as their determination to fight misogyny and sexism whenever the opportunity presented itself.

Here's an extract from one of the contributions by students of Kendal College:

London Gazette Special Report:

Dear Sir,

Recently, I had the privilege of interviewing select members of the Angel Corps. We spoke about many things; however, I found a certain recruit's views about equality and reasoning for becoming part of the Angel Corps particularly interesting.

> "I originally had heard about Angel Corps through rumours in school. It was a very controversial topic at the time so teachers did not like us to talk about it. There was one girl in my class whose Aunt was in the Corps. A lot of the boys and girls would tease her for it, calling her names and saying horrible things like 'I bet you'll turn out aggressive just like your Aunt and the other Angels.'
>
> I think that there was and still is a lack of understanding about the Corps in many ways and quite frankly I think that it boils down to the lack of communication and/or miscommunication about them. I believe that a lot of children's opinions are very much influenced by their parents' views of the group.

I hope that when we arrive in Kendal, despite the split views that are coming from locals, we will influence the young women (and everyone else) into creating a safer and fairer environment to live in as that is our main goal partially because Kendal will become our home base, meaning we will soon be joined as part of the community ourselves."

We employed our connection with the local community to place posters about the Angel Corps Homecoming Parade in every shop window on Kendal's high street. The students created a local group called the Machine Liberation Front (MLF), in support of the Clockwork Servants' rights, and held street-corner protests.

My speech at the launch event for the Kendal collaboration was hijacked by disgruntled members of the MLF demanding equality, which set the scene for multiple flash points across the town throughout the day. Angel Corps set up a recruitment pop-up and welcomed people off the street who were eager to learn more about their story.

At sunset, Angel Corps assembled in front of Kendal's war memorial before leading a huge procession to the nearest pub, where they arrested the sexist bar manager and declared a free bar—which, as it happened, was another opportunity to serve Hodgson's India Pale Ale.

When the Plan Comes Together

Well, that is how a New Year's Eve rave became the creative inspiration for a transmedia comic book series featuring West African slave trade, Egyptian pyramids, Caribbean sugarcane plantations, and the Buddhas of Bamiyan, all to immerse readers and role-players in the legacy of colonialism.

At the start of *Clockwork Watch*, my objective was to use transmedia storytelling as a vessel through which people could explore the wrongs of colonialism in an environment that sidestepped unproductive responses fed by guilt. I had grand plans to create video games, books, comics, and a feature film—in fact, my very first treatment of the story was for a film. But despite all of these plans, the majority of the successes can be attributed to the open-ended nature of my work and the communities that have supported the project. Every aspect of the co-created content is open to the public via a Creative Commons license, which offers contributors the freedom to expand their creative input beyond the realms of my work.

Clockwork Watch is a story perpetually in progress, as is my exploration of transmedia storytelling. There will be another four books in the series, with at least two more immersive theatricals planned. I believe that we can use the story to build a caring, supportive, and understanding form of steampunk that addresses and grapples with the legacy of colonialism rather than merely aestheticizing it.

As for *Breathe*, the second part of the story is almost good to go. It is set in another country, and it delves deeper into the fragile ego of our technology-dependent society. Only time will tell whether the co-created, free-flowing narrative will work as well in 2021 as it did in 2009. Getting buy-in from the audience requires being simultaneously proactive, reactive, and agile, which is not always possible when developing a project for a client, and that is why I believe that *Breathe 2* will also be self-funded.

I strive to make my projects as realistic as possible, meaning that if a story is based on a four-year love affair, I pace the narrative accordingly and keep it alive for a lifelike duration. *Violette's Dream* ran for three weeks, just long enough for participants to collaborate on a global treasure hunt, whereas *Clockwork Watch* is the story of a society coming to terms with the legacy of colonialism, a process that promises to take much longer. One advantage of transmedia storytelling is not having to make all of the elements accessible at the same time: in the case of *Clockwork Watch*, I believe that the story will be finished in four more years, making it a fifteen-year project.

There are a million different ways of telling you a story, including letting you be part of one.

Wish me luck.

References

Kelly, Kevin. 1994. *Out of Control: The New Biology of Machines, Social Systems, and the Economic World*. New York: Basic Books.

Longitude Punk'd. 2014. Royal Observatory Greenwich, UK. https://www.artfund.org /whats-on/exhibitions/2014/04/10/longitude-punkd-exhibition.

6 *UTOPIAN HOTLINE*: Transmedia and the Future of Arts Practice

Kayla Asbell, Denis Butkus, Alex Hawthorn, Rubén Polendo, and Ada Westfall

In this chapter, five members of the Theater Mitu collective describe the collaborative process of creating and performing UTOPIAN HOTLINE, a multiplatform transmedia work bridging the physical and digital, with media extensions including a telephone hotline, recorded music, live performance, and a web archive. Theater Mitu's work exemplifies a style of transmedia creativity explored in many chapters throughout this book—especially Ioana Mischie's Tangible Utopias project and Yomi Ayeni's locally rooted steampunk storyworld (described in chapters 16 and 5, respectively)—wherein the architect of the experience creates an arena that invites and builds on audience input and contributions. This model of storytelling, which is also described in the context of co-creative classroom environments by Francis Quek et al. in chapter 8, is more improvisational than many highly orchestrated transmedia experiences, which key on intricately designed puzzles and carefully rehearsed relays among interconnected texts. Like Ayeni, Theater Mitu embraces a mode of transmedia production that connects open, globally accessible digital gateways with more intimate in-person experiences—a particular take on transmedia that stresses interchanges between the abstract and the concrete, not just among a variety of somewhat-fungible digital media forms. For both Mitu and Ayeni, the value of this physical element—trading broad global accessibility for an intensity of synchronous experience—is that it can powerfully forge communities, establishing more durable relationships among audience members. The UTOPIAN HOTLINE experience also joins Terra Gasque's discussion of tabletop role-playing games (TTRPGs) in chapter 15 in describing transmedia experiences as providing solace during challenging times, in the face of individual, community, or societal trauma. Developed and initially staged during the COVID-19 pandemic, UTOPIAN HOTLINE was a restorative collective experience for its authors, as well as its audience members who contributed to and connected with the project via telephone, and later through its live performances. Building on the analytical and definitional work done by Paweł Frelik in chapter 3, Theater Mitu's work suggests that some transmedia projects are distinctive not because of their particular repertoire of media texts and relays, but rather because of the collective experience that they generate, which travels among different instantiations and temporalities, enabling new forms of social interaction and community formation.

Rubén Polendo: Intro

How do you perform time—not only our experience of it, but our relationship to it? This has been a key point of exploration for the work of Theater Mitu. As a permanent group of multidisciplinary, interdisciplinary, and transdisciplinary artists, the exploration of time pervades our work. In helming this conversation as director and company founder, I've found it essential to create a framework of givens as we navigate these ambitious explorations. The most salient of these givens is the conscious move away from a trifurcated narrative of time.

Societal norms have invited us to view time as threefold: present, past, and future. But that linearity is a construct, while the latter two frames are inextricably attached to imagination. We experience time as a simultaneity. Even if we begin with the trifurcation of time, we experience all three spheres simultaneously and continuously. In this moment, for example, I can hold a space of memory (past) and a space of vision (future)—both of which inform this momentary embodiment (the present). This type of simultaneity is mythologized by a whole range of spiritual practices, employed in the visions of our best futurists and science fiction makers, and reaffirmed by physicists and astrophysicists.

There is a further commonplace assumption that time is a horizontal, linear experience, inescapably linking one moment to the next. But what if we disrupt that assumption of horizontality to reflect a vision of time as simultaneous? What if we shift the view of horizontal time experience to a vertical one? This theoretical leap is not that unfamiliar—it better reflects a more experiential idea of time. We can see this even at a mundane level: I can sit in a house built in 1940, holding a computer assembled in 2020, sitting in a chair from 1960, articulating my plans for 2023. In one moment, all these times are existing. Yes, there are gaps, variables, and possibilities that are filled by imagination and emotions—but in that moment, my experience of time is vertical, simultaneous. In addition, in that scenario, there is not one past, but many; there is not one future, but a range of them. This plurality adds still another dimension to our understanding of time. So, if we argue that simultaneity, verticality, imagination, emotion, and plurality are key in our experience of time, how do we perform this?

We have engaged these ideas most rigorously and directly in our latest collaborative project, *UTOPIAN HOTLINE*. Conceived as a multiplatform, transmedia work, *UTOPIAN HOTLINE* is ultimately a meditation on the future (with the acknowledgment that said meditation inevitably holds the present and the past). The project exists simultaneously across an active telephone hotline (inviting callers to leave messages for the future), an album of original music (available online and on vinyl), a live performance installation (in which performers and audience are tethered together by headphones), and a virtual archive of voicemails (which exists in an interactive environment hosted on the project's website; see Theater Mitu, 2021a).

The work engages technology in the most capacious sense. It invites technology as medium and object; as archivist and witness; as performer and collaborator. As the goal of this project is to generate a work with a diverse range of access points, it seems appropriate that this chapter includes an array of voices: those of several makers of, and collaborators on, *UTOPIAN HOTLINE*. What follows are testimonies from Theater Mitu company members that reveal our transmedia arts practice on this project. We will travel through our multiplatform approach by having each company member discuss a distinct access point of *UTOPIAN HOTLINE*. Our hope is to provide a case study about the future of transmedia arts practice, as well as glimpses into how Theater Mitu's process responds to and interacts with the simultaneity of time.

Denis Butkus: The Telephone Hotline

The idea for the telephone hotline access point of *UTOPIAN HOTLINE* came from research into early projects involving telephones, like the artist John Giorno's *Dial-A-Poem* (1968–2012) and Allan Bridge's *Apology Line* (1980–1995). Giorno's *Dial-A-Poem* revolutionized how poetry was disseminated and consumed by recording the luminaries of the day reading their work into the phone (featured poets included Allen Ginsberg, Patti Smith, Amiri Baraka, and many more). Callers would dial the hotline and listen to more than 200 recordings on reel-to-reel tape recorders at random; you can listen today thanks to the San Francisco Museum of Modern Art (Giorno, 1968/2012). For Bridge's *Apology Line*, the interaction involved anonymous callers leaving messages on a new piece of technology: an answering machine. Bridge posted flyers around New York City advertising "an anonymous telephone line where strangers could come clean about their wrongdoings, ranging from infidelity to murder" (quoted in Given, 2021).

Inspired by the work of Giorno and Bridge, Theater Mitu could achieve two goals: collect a variety of anonymous messages answering a simple question about the future, and use these collected messages as source material for a new transmedia project. The collection of anonymous messages alone was interesting as a research action; the secondary goal of using these messages somehow in a work of transmedia was territory that the company had never explored.

> *Hi. I'm calling y'all back. A more perfect future is continuously in flux. A more perfect future is change. Change is God. A more perfect future is God—but not in that way, you know? Love y'all.*

This is the first voicemail that Theater Mitu received on the beta version of the Utopian Telephone Hotline set up in Portland, Oregon (Butkus, 2020). We received it on July 26, 2020, after much waiting and wondering about whether the idea was going to work. A few weeks prior, during a developmental laboratory for the project, I had clumsily set up a telephone number with an outgoing message in a recorded robotic voice:

> *Hello*
> *Thank you for calling the Utopian Hotline*
> *We are collecting anonymous responses to help us build a better tomorrow*
> *At the tone, please leave a message answering the question: can you imagine a more perfect future on Earth?*

I had then spent the better part of a week hanging rudimentary posters on telephone poles around my neighborhood in southeast Portland. I treated it as a game, and it was a welcome distraction from the unfolding pandemic engulfing the world. I would dress in all black and mask myself up before heading out on my single-speed Raleigh bike, a playlist of 1990s grunge in one ear. I didn't want anyone to know who was hanging these posters, and every time I would hang one, I'd look around to make sure that no one was watching. There was something about this anonymity that was freeing and important in the moment. It created space for me to think about the future of our species and our place in the universe. These posters were made up of an old 1950s sci-fi image of outer space with Saturn in the lower-right corner, blinking stars in the background, and a comet shooting across the top. I added the telephone number and a cheeky "Leave a message!"

Figure 6.1
The original *UTOPIAN HOTLINE* poster, first hung around southeast Portland in the summer of 2020.

exclamation in the upper left of the poster. I centered text in the middle of the poster that repeated the question from the outgoing message on the hotline: "Can you imagine a more perfect future on earth?" I had doubts as to whether this would work. Would anyone call and leave an actual voice message answering the question? After receiving this first message, I was thrilled. The person initially called and left a questioning "Hmmmmm-mmm?" and then called back! I knew the moment that I heard the first full voice message that this was an exciting and innovative mode of collecting responses, and one that Theater Mitu could use as we developed the *UTO-PIAN HOTLINE* project.

Receiving this first voicemail was a revelation to me about Theater Mitu's transmedia process and how we use media and technology to connect with the simultaneity of time. There was an intimacy, an immediacy to every-one who called and left messages. People spoke of God, of faith, of dreams, of worries, of the future. It was a chorus of voices that anchored me and my process during the development of the project in a very real present, while reaching into both the past and the future. We succeeded in col-lecting approximately seventy-five unique voicemails in Portland, which encouraged us to deploy the telephone hotline in Brooklyn, where the com-pany makes its home. We create and premiere all our work at MITU580, a renovated warehouse that we have turned into an interdisciplinary arts venue. The same poster pictured here was placed around Carroll Gardens, Gowanus, and Park Slope in the lead-up to the performance of *UTOPIAN HOTLINE* at MITU580 in September 2021. The telephone hotline remains active today, receiving on average three to five new messages each week. To date, we have collected hundreds of messages, and they range in form and content from the silly to the profound. The hotline has become a conduit to access the other elements of the project: an album of original music, a virtual archive of voicemails, and the live performance of *UTOPIAN HOT-LINE*. You can call the hotline today and leave your own message for the future at (646) 694-8050.

I have been fascinated by the Voyager Project by the National Aeronau-tics and Space Administration (NASA) since I was a little kid, especially the Golden Record. The idea that a group of people working in collaboration could collect an archive of 115 images encoded in analog form, spoken greetings, recorded music, and human brainwaves, etch them onto a gold disk, and fling it out into the universe, without any expectation of ever seeing it again or receiving anything in return, is at once so hopeful and so devastating to me. It is an incomplete and problematic archive of life on Earth and offers us a chance to look at the past, present, and future—and see everything that they missed! The Voyager Project had two goals: the scientific study of our solar system, and carrying a message on the Golden Record that captures a moment of time back on Earth, a brief and incomplete narrative of us. The fact that these probes are still going, speeding away in interstellar space while sending signals back to Earth, gives me hope that these messages have meaning. These two probes are now the farthest objects that humans have sent into the universe. Some futurists believe that we will eventually be the ones to retrieve them—that our technology will advance to such a degree that we will catch up with *Voyager* 1 and 2. For me, they are a fixed point in the past, moving at 17 kilometers per second, while sending messages to us in the present. Unique unto themselves, they offer both a warning and a hope for a better future. These probes, and the copies of the Golden Record that they contain, continue to show us how far we have come, how much we have changed, and how much more work still needs to be done as they speed away from us into the unknown.

Voyager's Golden Record of 1977 and Mitu's telephone hotline of 2020 both represent a link between the power of sending a message and the responsibility of receiving it. Whether it is the thought experiment of imagining who might receive the messages on the Golden Record when *Voyager* is recovered, or simply taking out the phone in my pocket, calling a number on a poster, and leaving a voicemail to the future—these actions help me cope with an uncertain moment, full of anxiety, and give me a chance to pause and wonder if anyone is out there and if they are listening. Voyager's Golden Record served as a point of inspiration, helping us to innovate our process beyond live performance. It helped us conceptualize *UTOPIAN HOTLINE* as being at once a telephone hotline, a vinyl album, a live performance, and a virtual archive of voicemails. Through each of these access points, unique details emerge, and the audience is asked to reckon with their future and piece together a story born out of their personal experiences in relationship to our work. As makers, this is what the pandemic wrought out of us: it forced us to use our tools in a new way, to explore the power of the device as a creative activator and use transmedia arts practice to interact with the simultaneity of the past, present, and future. *UTOPIAN HOTLINE* is the message that Theater Mitu launched into the universe.

Hopefully, this message will be found one day and heard by a future inheritor of this precarious present.

Kayla Asbell: The Performance

Theater Mitu uses multiple modalities of technology and forms of media, woven into all our work. The company members who create each piece also function in myriad ways, using all the skill sets and interests that they bring with them through the entire process—from the first day of incubating a piece until the very last performance. The piece that ultimately became *UTOPIAN HOTLINE* had lots of time to incubate and remain in the liminal space of dream and ideation. We talked for a long time about wanting to do a piece surrounding the idea of utopias: What do they mean? What type of person tries to craft a utopia? By creating a utopia, does that inherently mean there are people who cannot be a part of it, or who need to be silenced? We all salivated at the idea of creating a piece surrounding these topics, and we all had entry points that we wanted to probe and investigate through this effort.

From the start, there were those who wanted to delve into the world of religion and spirituality, members dedicated to throwing themselves into the world of space exploration, and those who wanted to talk to inventors, futurists, and technological visionaries. I wanted to dig into the world of cults and the utopias that they attempt to create (or at least advertise as such). We all began researching furiously, going down internet rabbit holes, talking to experts—any way that we could get our hands on information.

As we develop a piece, we use the term "laboratory" for our coworking sessions together. These are times for exploration and experimentation with content and the technology that we will use, misuse, and hack in our development of the piece. In the lab, we create what we call "autonomous installations," where we make individual pieces (containing our own content, technology, and other research materials), share them with the group, and then open these pieces' ingredients up for others to use in their experiments. At the first lab session for *UTOPIAN HOTLINE*, the room was abuzz as every company member presented their own experiments. We'd only gotten a few days into it when COVID-19 really hit in the US. After much uncertainty, we decided to shift to digital for the remainder of this laboratory, as company members spread across the globe to hunker down for the storm.

We had never conducted a laboratory over a digital platform (hell, I'd never even heard of Zoom before that moment), but we all were determined to share ideas despite the distance—we would start each day discussing and dissecting the research that each of us had done, and then go off to our newfound laboratories: our own apartments. Without our usual technology and home to work in—Mitu's lighting, audio, and video equipment are all housed at our MITU580 space—we used what was at our disposal. Some members began to develop apps that others could use remotely; some began to create websites where people could record and archive text, audio, video, and image messages; some made short films or created movement pieces that we could watch from our screens.

One of the main components of my artistic practice is making music. I do it almost exclusively in a collaborative setting, though—I've played in punk and rock and roll bands for many years, and my bandmates and I all riff off each other and create songs together. The pandemic took that option off the table. So I started to create a makeshift analog studio in my bedroom. My bands had only ever recorded analog; we either recorded live straight to magnetic tape for vinyl or used a tape machine. Using my scrappy home studio, I embarked on creating my first solo compositions in the name of *UTOPIAN HOTLINE*. Theater Mitu is the only artistic home I've had where I can mix my style of music and theater in an unadulterated way, and now I had an opportunity to explore how to weave those things together in a way undiscovered even to myself. I composed two songs for the piece that started out when I was still exploring the idea of cult-created utopias. At first, they retained the punk essence that I usually create from musically. I shared them with the group, and they joined the archive of work that each of us was creating in the laboratory.

As time went on, and quarantine restrictions lifted, we began meeting in person—each of us having our own little island-laboratories spaced around MITU580. *UTOPIAN HOTLINE* began to morph and develop and take shape as our ideas and experiments all intertwined and entangled and informed one another. As we emerged from the isolation and loneliness of quarantine, the piece started shifting to the idea of space—the vast unknown—and questioning if we are indeed alone in the universe or if there is, in fact, someone or something out there to commune with. If there is something out there, what message would we send them? What message would we send to the future in a time when the future here on Earth seemed just as unknown as the vastness of space?

The topic of space travel lends itself to using cutting-edge technology, and those Mitu members with technical prowess and acumen set off to experiment in that way. However, we also kept coming back to the Golden Record, that etched disc blasted into space decades earlier with blinding optimism to an audience entirely undiscovered and unknown. This became the touchstone of the piece—and with the idea of vinyl entering the room, my musical ideas began to form. We were asking lofty questions, but they also felt so incredibly intimate. When asking about space and if we are alone in the universe, we were also asking, are we alone *here and now*? As the performance aspect of *UTOPIAN HOTLINE* developed, we decided that it would involve only four performers and audiences of twelve, with performers and audience members alike sitting on a pink carpet tethered together by headphones. This would evoke the feeling of a small, intimate listening party—a moment where we could share not only the research and things we had created, but also the feeling that we could find communion in the shared loneliness that the past year had subjected us to, and the feeling that there is indeed, either in a distant landscape or closer by, someone out there who can listen and speak back to us. The songs that I had written before altered and shifted in my mind. When I first wrote them, they were utopian manifestos from the perspective of a cult member, but now I could see that the pervasive themes in all the cult research, much like our exploration of space, were isolation and loneliness, and the desire to find a community that could and would listen. The songs began to take on the feeling of lullabies, like a song that you would record from your bedroom straight onto a tape player, to be shared only with the closest of friends or lovers (Asbell, 2021). It got me thinking about the times someone had directly conveyed a message of loneliness, of longing for connection, of looking for something more, through audio—and from that, I added a piece about my grandmother and me playing records for one another over the phone while we were separated by distance. Over time, *UTOPIAN HOTLINE* became not only an esoteric, philosophical, scientific piece; every company member involved also brought something deeply personal and vulnerable.

After we had shaped and created the piece, it was time to perform within it. I was one of four tasked with this role. We covered the floor in the MITU580 space with soft pink carpet; audience members were given pillows to sit on and headphones to listen through; a projection screen cloaked the ceiling; and at the center of the room, the four performers manipulated objects upon an illuminated table in what felt like part ritual, part laboratory experiment, part meditation, and part nostalgic record-listening party. We spoke into the microphones in soft, soothing tones straight into the ears of the audience seated encircled around us. It was all about creating a balance between vulnerable connection with the audience by speaking to them directly with eye contact, while also using the various pieces of technology—audio and video from countless different sources, both digital and analog—to create a distance, a disembodiment, to allow the audience to go on their own meditative journeys about space, loneliness, and the future. The mixture of analog and found recordings allowed the audience

Figure 6.2
A live performance of *UTOPIAN HOTLINE* in Theater Mitu's MITU580 space in Brooklyn, New York.

to be lost, at times, in a reverie of nostalgia, and then be swept into contemplations of the future. As a performer, I felt more like a guide than a character or a storyteller. My role, and the role of the other three performers, was to interact with the technology, essentially as a collaborator, and allow the communication between the technology and us to lead the audience to ponder and ask themselves what messages they would like to send, whether it be to a distant future, unknown entities in space, loved ones, or their past or future selves.

Ada Westfall: The Album

At any given intersection within Theater Mitu's creation process, my artistic practice hinges on a plurality of disciplines, techniques, hardware, software, and media. At its most effective, inspiration leaps from one context to the next, shedding and accruing details as it translates cut-up source material into, for example, an extrapolated lyrical scheme, into MIDI data sequenced in a digital audio workstation, into an aural set of instructions created to cue performers in a series of dancelike actions. A particularly apt example of this is the creation of *UTOPIAN HOTLINE*'s song "Together Alone" (Westfall, 2021) and its accompanying movement sequence—a dance of sorts in which four company members perform the song by playing and pausing a collection of handheld tape decks, reel-to-reel recorders, and an answering machine, where the song's melody is sung into phone receivers atop a lo-fi hip-hop beat created by different combinations of the tapes' audio loops. (The phones' number pads are even "dialed" to create a discordant harmonic counterpoint and physical gesture.) Tracing back this segment to its genesis allows us to take inventory of the transmedia movements required to bring the idea to life.

As always, the seed for this performance installation took root in the soil of our accrued research matériel; by noticing recurring motifs in the texts, interviews, and images that we collected, I began to mull over how the devices that humans have invented to connect with one another become icons for the existential loneliness from which we yearn to escape. The somewhat outdated image of a phone receiver tethered by a looping cord to its cradle and keypad resounded in my mind as an almost plaintive musical instrument: the morose whine of its dial tone (so quiet, it's audible only when the pinholes of the phone's receiver are pressed to the ear); the clicks and polyphonic yelps of its keys when dialed; the nervous clatter of the handset when removed or replaced in its plastic cradle; and the shrinking, distorted quality imparted to one's voice by the receiver's microphone, not to mention its continual descent into obsolescence and audio decay.

I imagined a song that could be performed using outdated, landline-style phones. By extrapolating the phone-as-instrument, I began to picture auxiliary instruments filling out a larger "band": an answering machine, which produces sound (the recorded voices of people who were never present) only in response to direct manipulation of the machine's buttons. And from there, other versions of tape recorders and playback devices. What if we could have the image of a whole "band" onstage, with no sign of a traditional band? Furthermore, I noticed a recurring theme in our research about the way that togetherness and aloneness seem to emerge out of one another. We exist on this planet together, but it's possible that we may be the only life out here: we're alone together. Conversely, it's when we're apart from one another that we use phones as a way of bridging the distance between us. On the phone, we share communion in our isolation; we are together alone.

From here, I switched hats from conceptual artist to lyricist. Using our research as my guide, I synthesized these themes into a few stanzas, following an impulse to keep my sentiment as simple as possible, since it would have to remain legible over the visual and logistical complexity of the technical and choreographic feat that lay ahead: "alone together / together alone / connect me, operator / to where a home is still a home," and so on. These lyrics then needed to be set to a melody and layered over the audio loops that would emanate from each tape recorder when its start and stop buttons were pressed. So, in addition to exercising my discipline as a composer, I needed to function as sound designer: I delved into Ableton Live (my digital audio workstation of choice) and my library of audio samples and began arranging the sounds that I found into a few measures that could loop indefinitely (something popular music producers often call a "groove" or "beat"). I pulled audio samples of dial tones, busy signals, modems prattling away, pleasant and coldly prerecorded operator voices, and answering machine beeps, plus a collection of drum/percussion loops and synth patches. Recalling techniques employed by Brian Eno, David Byrne, and Talking Heads in the creation of their record *Remain In Light*, I layered these sounds, weaving them together so that if they are muted and unmuted in different combinations, different "sections" of the song may be created subtractively and additively—even though each individual instrument is effectively playing the same thing over and over, ad infinitum.

Leaping back into the analog world, I then had to acquire the physical phones and tape recorders and arrange them in a mise-en-scène for the performers to manipulate and sing into. This required "hacking" the microphone in the phones' handsets and wiring and installing a ¼-inch output jack so that the resulting audio signal could be routed to the ears of the audience (a process that involved disassembling, gutting nonessential components, soldering and rewiring, dremeling out the enclosures, and drilling holes for the output jacks). The project also required rhythmic "guide" tracks to be piped into the performers' in-ear headphones so that they would know when to press which buttons on each specific device, keeping everyone in time like a metronome or click track. Back in Ableton Live, I slowly but surely solved the organizational puzzle of how to prompt the performers to recreate my composition by starting and stopping each machine, recording myself speaking cues: "Device A . . . 3, 2, 1, GO!" "Device B . . . 3, 2, 1, STOP!" and so on.

Finally, with the phones, tape decks, and answering machine arranged and modified as needed, and with the instrumental tape loops and in-ear guide tracks completed, we were ready to attempt a prototype run-through of my creation. At this point, everyone involved needed to act as audio engineers and choreographers. Using our in-ear tracks as guides, we plotted out the paths and button presses that each performer would undertake—including singing the lead vocal and "playing" the keypads on each phone. We documented this prototype performance on video as part of our laboratory process and, later, once we had decided it would become part of the final version of UTOPIAN HOTLINE, this allowed us to reconstitute the performance and modify it to fit the parameters and needs of the larger piece—including accommodations for our new set, light-emitting diode (LED) lighting cues, and a large rear-projected surface that hangs above the action. There is no direct path to the completed installation that could be traveled in only one discipline or medium. Research begets concept begets composition begets technical needs begets staging, and so on.

This process continued as Theater Mitu developed the idea of creating a vinyl record as an additional access point to the UTOPIAN HOTLINE project. Part homage to Voyager's Golden Record and part dream of the company to create an artifact of our collaborative process, the album includes

Figure 6.3
Cover art for the *UTOPIAN HOTLINE* album.

selections of messages received on the telephone hotline along with original music created by myself and other company members. I'm most proud
of the way that the *UTOPIAN HOTLINE* album coheres audio segments from
several creators, despite their tracks' eclecticism. Comprising a variety of
generative strategies, compositional points of view, orchestrative tones, and
tensions with genre and idiom, it still feels like a collection of material that
belongs together. The album feels as much like an exercise in curatorial
selection (Theater Mitu acting collectively as archivist) as an expression of
pure creative impulse (Mitu acting as midwife to the births of its company
members' musical brainchildren). "Found" audio collected from the hotline
voice messages and tape recordings of interviews conducted by company
members commingle with slickly produced pop ("Radiate"), lo-fi hip-hop
("Together Alone"), electronic ambience ("Arrow of Time"), ethereal indie
("Nothing There to See"), and even a cover tune that reworks and recontex-
tualizes a mostly forgotten single from a 1970s also-ran (Gilbert O'Sullivan's
"Alone Again (Naturally)"). And because of its situation in relation to the

UTOPIAN HOTLINE theatrical experience, our vinyl record can be viewed as a kind of soundtrack, as a companion piece, as a concept album, a prompt, a response, a riff on NASA's Golden Record, a research archive, documentation of a creative process, a concept album, or even a parlor-room curio— an objet d'art (Theater Mitu, 2021b). But no matter how it is viewed—or listened to—its individual tracks link and form a sensitive inquiry into the dark, twinkling maw of space and time; it begs a status update on humankind's present condition, as well as our trajectory aboard Spaceship Earth as it hurtles into both the future and empty regions unknown.

The material that doesn't make it into a Mitu show is nearly as important as the stuff that does. What an audience experiences when they come to see one of our works is really an expression of a much larger conversation that the company is having and has been having for a long time. It is the sum of processing hours upon hours of interviews conducted and transcribed, texts researched and read, images organized, group discussions engaged in, and creative impulses made manifest and documented. The act of creation is how we synthesize our material and how we synchronize our intentions around it. Sometimes, even though we need to excise an entire category of inquiry from the conversation (as happened with the subject of religious cults within *UTOPIAN HOTLINE*, for instance), the echoes of that conversation continue to reverberate through the elements that "make it."

What's most inspiring to me about working with Theater Mitu is the ability to develop works of art over longer periods of time—often years—in community with a family of artists whom I've come to know and trust across quite a bit of time and project after project. We struggle and problemsolve together, we teach and learn together, we work and relax together, we build and tour and research and discuss together, and the list goes on and on. Because of our laboratory process, the work that's done on a Mitu piece is as structured as it is freeing. Rigor and research are allowed to collide freely with impulse and intuition and emphasis is placed on iteration. The challenge is, in one sense, to become an idea-generating machine, never resting with the last success or failure, but always attempting to wring the next experiment out of one's brain. This process is as exhausting as it is addictive, and that's ultimately what keeps me coming back for more.

UTOPIAN HOTLINE has been a particularly successful endeavor for Mitu because we are a company who yearns for a dialogue with the various communities in which we find ourselves—an impulse that is often walled in by the limited nature of a subject or by a particular time or locality. But examining the subject of loneliness in this piece by looking at the totality of human experience—asking universal questions about the nature of our existence in space and time and about the hopes we collectively harbor about what the future might bring—has allowed us to transcend the usual limitations and speak to any and every community with confidence that the conversation is relevant to anybody we set our sights on. The format of the telephone hotline itself allowed us to break down another barrier: that of anonymity. For the first time, we were able to collect research and interview material from people who will never be known to us. It is exciting to let the immense diversity of offerings made to our hotline act both as guides in our creative work and as sentiments that we can catalog, archive, and reflect to our audiences—which may well include people we'll never know called in!

Alex Hawthorn: Virtual Archive

Theater Mitu could not be sure, in the fall of 2020, if an in-person performance would be possible the following year. And, even if it was, would anyone want to come? How could we remain connected to our community in a time of isolation? Even remaining connected as a company was more difficult than ever before. The development process that emerged during *UTOPIAN HOTLINE* became less linear than usual, and a transmedia practice in itself: our collaborative labs took place both remotely and in person (as fluctuating case rates allowed), work on the accompanying album was remote and asynchronous among the artists contributing tracks, and we kept a running discourse of research and references on a group message thread. This fractured, rhizomatic nature was inherent to the creation process, with work on one part of the project naturally influencing other parts.

This development process is perhaps most legible through a *systems aesthetic* lens, to use a term coined by Jack Burnham in an article for *Artforum* in 1968: "The scope of a systems esthetic presumes that problems cannot be solved by a single technical solution, but must be attacked on a multi-leveled, interdisciplinary basis" (Burnham, 1968, 34). In the case of *UTOPIAN HOTLINE*, approaching the project as a work of transmedia enabled us to decenter the live performance and recenter the research. The process became both an exploration of different modalities through the lens of our research, and a reframing of the research through the lens of different modalities: a telephone hotline, a vinyl record, a performance.

As an interdisciplinary artist, I found this recentering very exciting. While I have never felt limited or constrained on a Mitu project, there has always been the understanding that we were all co-creating toward a live performance. With *UTOPIAN HOTLINE*, however, that guideline was dissolved and replaced with the question of how best to connect with our audience. Mitu has always engaged with communities worldwide as part of our research, training, and touring work, and so it was important to us that *UTOPIAN HOTLINE* provide an opportunity to connect with our global community through digital and asynchronous media. The virtual archive is a perfect example.

While developing work for the live performance, we had lengthy discussions about the creation of an installation piece: a phone booth that someone could enter and record a message on our telephone hotline. As with any group design process, there were a wide range of ideas and intuitions. One day, I was feeling stalled on a particular piece of creation and wanted to switch my focus to something else. I opened Unity, a video game development program, and began to create a virtual space, aesthetically mirroring our physical space at MITU580: a pink carpet, a low overhead rectangular projection surface. I placed Bell public telephones in concentric circles, emanating out from the middle of this world. Each telephone contained a single voicemail that we received on the hotline—making manifest, virtually and visually, our archive of voicemails, the trove of primary research that we were collecting. This virtual archive resonated with the group when I presented an initial draft, and the idea of a physical installation project was tabled in favor of this virtual option.

I was not sure it would be so well received. I first presented a nonnarrative "open world" Unity project to Mitu during a laboratory for an earlier project, *REMNANT*, as an exploration of how sound can be presented in a virtual environment. My proposal did not make it into the project: it was missing the aesthetic linkage to our work. When Mitu engages with technology, we do so on our own aesthetic terms. We rarely use a piece of technology for its intended purpose, choosing instead to imbue it with a new operational capacity: a telephone becomes a microphone, a projection surface becomes a light source. We weren't interested in "video game–ness"; we were interested in what kinds of emotional and aesthetic conjuring could take place within a virtual world. As an environment without physical constraints, we could create a landscape that was simultaneously familiar and foreign, defined and abstract. An expanse of pink carpet. A sea of telephones, each one with a message from a stranger.

This balance of the familiar and the foreign is present in all our work. The weirding of space and time, to pull the cultural theorist Mark Fisher into this conversation, "cannot only repel, it must also compel our attention" (Fisher, 2016, 17). Mitu lives in this weirdness, placing disparate objects and sensorial experiences next to each other to disrupt people's settled concepts of time and place:

> The sense of wrongness associated with the weird—the conviction that this does not belong—is often a sign that we are in the presence of the new. The weird here is a signal that the concepts and frameworks which we have previously employed are now obsolete. (Fisher, 2016, 6)

Mitu's aesthetic and dramaturgy present a world so grounded that one has to assume that it has always been that way. This is in part due to the nature of Mitu as a permanent company of artists: we iterate on our form from project to project, defining and refining what it means for something to "be a Mitu piece." This intangible quality, this instinct, is our constant guide and is in a state of constant co-creation. Some aesthetic linkages are more obvious: reel-to-reel tape machines have been in our work since at least *HAMLET/UR-HAMLET* (2015), if not earlier. Other elements of our works may seem disparate, but are, by nature of being codesigned by this group of artists, all formed from the Mitu aesthetic.

This group aesthetic sense sets us apart from many in the theater world and places us more in line with the art world. In theater, great value is placed on the dramaturgical justification of choices, and while our work is thoroughly researched and considered, we respect and trust our intuition, as it draws on each artist's years of work with the company. That intuition is the manifestation of the Mitu aesthetic within each artist.

A telephone hotline, a vinyl record, a performance, a virtual archive: each modality of *UTOPIAN HOTLINE* acts as a spoke connected to a central hub of research, crafted from a central aesthetic sense, all to explore the question, "How do we imagine a more perfect future?" For Mitu, I see our future continuing in a transmedia practice, exploring new modalities and revisiting old ones, with an aim to continue building and connecting with a diverse community around the world. I, for one, cannot wait to see what we make.

Rubén Polendo: Outro

How you do you perform time? Or rather, how do *we* perform time? As a company, we cannot engage in any generative strategy without deeply considering process. For Theater Mitu, this is our first step of interrogation. We shift away from the monochromatic and asphyxiating inheritance of theater and performance practices and look at a vast range of forward-thinking arts and research practices. We investigate how these practices create processes with which to explore time. We invite visual artists and game designers, composers and architects, filmmakers and astrophysicists, technologists, and theologians to aid us in disrupting our practice.

Using transmedia to create collaborative work provides the freedom to not be bound by discipline, thereby disrupting the hegemonic norms applied to work that challenges the status quo. Our role is to be the access point that reveals to our audiences a new way of participating in our culture. We use transmedia as a method for interrogating the world, which extends beyond the field of theater, and can be applied to any process that calls for the creation of collaborative projects that defy categorization and pursue innovation across fields of practice. Ultimately, we invent a process that holds hybridity and innovation as pillars for the work—this is what connects us with practitioners in other fields, beyond theater, whose work is also examining this moment in time and our relationship to it. In so doing, we invite artists to create, reflect, and respond to the past, present, and future by sharing our work with those who know us and especially those who do not.

> I would dress in all black
> and mask myself up before heading out
> on my single-speed Raleigh bike,
> a playlist of 1990s grunge in one ear.

We create a room where the weird, the strange, the deconstructive, and the constructive all have equal voice. With a foundation on the firm ground of our extensive research, we trust artistic instinct and follow it down nuanced routes, acknowledging that our process is an embodied one and it does not exist in a vacuum. Within the details of our embodied practice is a desire to reimagine what it is to be human and so discover new ground.

> This required "hacking" the microphone in the phones' handsets and wiring
> and installing a ¼-inch output jack so that the resulting audio signal could be
>   routed

to the ears of the audience (a process that involved disassembling, gutting nonessential components, soldering and rewiring, dremeling out the enclosures,
and drilling holes for the output jacks).

We engage broadly with media and invite a constant interrogation of it is a tool, a pathway, a trace, a disconnector, and a unifier. We offer it up as open-source material for interpretation and reinterpretation.

I opened up Unity, a video game development program,
and began to create a virtual space,
aesthetically mirrored to our physical space:
a pink carpet, a low overhead rectangular projection surface.

We engage audiences in a relational modality rather than the transactional and sedentary modes in which audiences are traditionally engaged. The work invites audiences to witness, interact, embody, and travel through the many access points. We abandon the expected role of storytellers, and instead invite our audiences to become active storymakers.

As a performer, I felt more like a guide
than a character or a storyteller.
My role, and the role of the other three performers, was to interact with the
technology, essentially as a collaborator . . .

And above all, we acknowledge the impossibility in our work, an impossibility that reaffirms that the performance of time for us as a company is not a goal, but rather a journey—one filled with simultaneity, verticality, plurality, emotion, and limitless imagination.

Hi. I'm calling y'all back. A more perfect future is continuously in flux.
A more perfect future is change. Change is God.
A more perfect future is God—but not in that way, you know?
Love y'all.

References

Asbell, Kayla. 2021. "Nothing There to See." MP3/FLAC audio. Theater Mitu, Brooklyn, NY. https://theatermitu.bandcamp.com/track/nothing-there-to-see.

Burnham, Jack. 1968. "Systems Esthetics." *Artforum* 7, no. 1: 30–35. https://www.artforum.com/print/196807/systems-esthetics-32466.

Butkus, Denis. 2020. *PDX Hotline: 503-662-7263*. Theater Mitu, Brooklyn, NY.

Fisher, Mark. 2016. *The Weird and the Eerie*. London: Repeater Books.

Giorno, John. 1968/2012. *Dial-A-Poem: 641-793-8122.* San Francisco Museum of Modern Art, Media Arts Collection. https://www.sfmoma.org/artwork/2017.386.

Given, Molly. 2021. "New York City-Based Project 'The Apology Line' Hears Compelling and Chilling Confessions." *amNY,* January 25, 2021. https://www.amny.com /news/new-york-city-based-project-the-apology-line-hears-compelling-and-chilling -confessions.

Theater Mitu. 2015. "*HAMLET/UR-HAMLET.*" https://theatermitu.org/works/hamlet -ur-hamlet.

Theater Mitu. 2021a. *UTOPIAN HOTLINE.* https://utopianhotline.com.

Theater Mitu. 2021b. *UTOPIAN HOTLINE.* MP3/FLAC audio and vinyl album. https://theatermitu.bandcamp.com/releases.

Westfall, Ada. 2021. "Together Alone." MP3/FLAC audio. Theater Mitu, Brooklyn, NY. https://theatermitu.bandcamp.com/track/together-alone.

Transmedia Crosstalk: Yomi Ayeni and Denis Butkus

Bob Beard: What strikes me about these two chapters is the choice to enlist audiences as co-creators. Certainly, this is a hallmark of transmedia, but I think it's more explicit in your projects, which use live theater as the mode of interaction. What is it about role-playing and the theater that facilitates this? What are the affordances of this medium, versus something mediated via text or online interactions?

Yomi Ayeni: Theater offers a different dimension. It signifies *play*. When accompanied by participation, it cuts against inhibitions.

I guess people have a choice: they can be spectators, or take a leap of faith and become part of the story. It's a bit like visiting a museum, which has a fourth wall, whereas public art often offers a different experience.

Denis Butkus: For me, the theater is a portal—it's a doorway where you enter an alternate plane of consciousness. For us at Mitu, I think we are actively trying to disrupt the fourth wall.

YA: Yes! You successfully did that all the way, starting with the poster, phone number, answerphone, then leaping to the performance.

DB: Yomi, could you talk about how you create holes in your productions? I feel like we share that as a tool, or as an essential part of our respective practices.

YA: I look at life through the metaphor of a newspaper. Each different publication presents a unique spin on the headline of the day. This always plays to the political leaning of the reader, who reacts to it in a particular way. Our narratives play to the participants' tribal affiliations. This leads to some playing the hero, while others will most likely take the role of the villain. I create space for all of them to imagine what they'd do in a particular situation.

DB: Do you attempt to anticipate your participants' reactions?

YA: Not as such. I usually exhaust that aspect within the first few minutes, when the unusual and unplanned start happening. I couldn't imagine how a *New York Times* reader would react to a story, whereas I may just get an inclination about how a musician would.

I'd drive myself crazy trying to anticipate every possible reaction. That's the beauty: I eventually become a participant.

DB: We also rely on instinct. There's always a chance to go off course, to jump to a new thing, depending on our instincts. I think that's something that is trained out of a lot of artists: the power of the immediate impulse.

Following those impulses can turn into gesture, text, a phone number, a newspaper very quickly.

YA: How easy was it to move from platform to platform with the project? Was there a fear that people wouldn't understand the process, apart from the initial leap of faith with the answerphone?

DB: The process unfolded very organically and asynchronously over about two years, with multiple parts of the various projects being made at the same time. We are always in a state of creation and articulation. The one informs the other.

The phone number is so easily accessible. Everyone knows how a phone works. That's when things really changed.

YA: I think that was where the fourth wall disappeared. Was *UTOPIAN HOTLINE* a cathartic process? Do you think it would have been different if the world hadn't pulled a handbrake with COVID?

DB: I don't think *UTOPIAN HOTLINE* would have existed without the pandemic. It would have been an entirely different process. There were moments of catharsis, but mostly it was a process of revelation. The piece, the material, the people revealed to us so many things about our current predicament.

BB: What have the two of you learned since embarking on these projects? Have these projects changed your practices?

DB: I think it has expanded all of us at Theater Mitu. *UTOPIAN HOTLINE* gave us a big dose of hope during a very trying time. We got to see that reflected in our audience, and that was really impactful, as it helped us think beyond discipline. I think a lot of us have been put into boxes and that makes us afraid to try new things, but after *UTOPIAN HOTLINE*, we realized that we can do this, that we have a deep transmedia practice, and that feeds us to explore unknown territory and discover new skill sets and new inspirations.

YA: *Clockwork Watch* was a story that I felt needed to be told, explored, and participated. It was a chance for me to tell a story that would otherwise not have been told if I hadn't self-published. Of course, the parts that would have broken my brain were handed over to the participants, and they created a real world, which led to supporting young women in Kenya.

That transmedia world is now helping young women dream, a little like how *Clockwork* has helped me dream.

DB: That's what I mean about this medium's power as a portal: you actually transform in the doing of your work! Maybe that's the new form of catharsis—transformation?

YA: Yup—gain insight, transform, grow, and learn. All of it.

II Methods, Techniques, and Teaching Approaches

7   Cultivating Youth's Hope in STEM through Speculative Design

Camillia Matuk

Taking up speculative design as a teaching methodology, Camillia Matuk describes how imagining possible futures can serve students in terms of introducing core science, technology, engineering, and math (STEM) concepts, but also inspiring a sense of optimism for a future that includes them. This approach articulates what often goes unsaid: teaching is a utopian enterprise, a practice of hope that in the K–12 context reaches young people during major milestones in their personal development. Speculative design foregrounds the generative power of alternate futures to interrogate the present and open up new possibilities: new stories can create new worlds and serve as canvases for imagination. Matuk's description of pedagogy designed to unite STEM and futures thinking has parallels in Ruth Wylie et al.'s work on Frankenstein as a teaching tool (chapter 12). Both that chapter and this one consider the role of scientific creativity and responsibility as key aspects not only of learning as a process of acquiring knowledge but also self-learning and identity formation. Shared imagination can also be a powerful vehicle for shared learning, and the communities of learning that Matuk describes also evoke the informal learning that takes place around the Foldit citizen science platform in Katherine Buse and Ranjodh Singh Dhaliwal's discussion in chapter 11. What Matuk argues for most passionately is the value of speculative design and futures thinking in advancing desired learning goals. This framing of value and how to evaluate success offers a compelling comparison to Caitlin Burns and other writers in part I of this book, who all address how to measure the impact and success of their transmedia narratives. In the STEM classroom, that impact is superficially obvious in domain-specific measures such as knowledge retention, but the longer-term impact on identity and efficacy can unfold over years or decades, fueled by the power of imagination. Taken as a genre, speculative fiction also provides a hook and a lens for teaching, sensitizing learners to particular ideas and perspectives in texts and granting them particular forms of transmedia narrative agency. That approach and the collaborative ethos of design fiction intersect with Lee Emrich's discussion of teaching Shakespeare as a highly contemporary, hands-on transmedia activity (chapter 9), as well as Terra Gasque's exploration of how transmedia works hold space for and invite collaborative imagination from their audiences (chapter 15).

The Need for Hope in STEM

> Kids have a concern for the world around them. Seeing that it's being harmed feels bad. Seeing brick walls doesn't help. There's tension and anxiety. Kids are feeling paralyzed and overwhelmed by the hopelessness. It used to be that we could talk about species successes and promising conservation efforts. But people have been working on these problems for a long time, and things are still broken. There's a lack of confidence in the fact that science is valuable. Then they hear other messages that it's great to be a scientist. There's something about students' hopefulness about science, and their decision to enter science as a career.

The words here were spoken by a high school science teacher, paraphrased from a unit-planning conversation with me and my colleagues. Over her twenty years of experience as an educator, she noticed her students' growing awareness of how the problems of decades past remain problems today. More than ever, they need to be convinced of the value of pursuing science, technology, engineering, and math (STEM). Her comments reflect a shortcoming of STEM education, wherein hope is not often nurtured but is clearly critical to STEM participation.

STEM participation—that is, interest and engagement in STEM content (e.g., processes of infection or of climate change) and practices (e.g., prediction, experimentation, explanation, and revision)—can spur youth to pursue STEM careers later (Dabney et al., 2012; Tai et al., 2006). By middle school, however, there is a startling decline in youth's interest in STEM, which can be difficult to reawaken (Potvin and Hasni, 2014a; 2014b), and an increase in pessimism with regard to the future of STEM (Hicks and Holden, 2007). Unsurprisingly, this decline in STEM interests coincides with the shift from a focus on participation during elementary school to a focus on performance in middle school (Cavas, 2011). It also coincides with fewer informal learning opportunities aligned with youth's existing STEM interests (Alexander, Johnson, and Kelley, 2012). What is particularly distressing about these trends is that interest and its related states—engagement, motivation, and positive attitudes—influence learners' attention, goals, and degree of learning (Hidi and Renninger, 2006), and predict learners' academic achievement better than traditional aptitude measures (Cavas, 2011; Pan and Gauvain, 2012; Reid and Skryabina, 2002; Singh, Granville, and Dika, 2002). Unfortunately, the spread of misinformation through misguided fear and misleading political messaging about such critical aspects of health and policy as vaccines, masking, and climate change (Lawton, 2020) contributes to the public's shaken confidence in STEM. At the same time, research has found that even as mistrust and cynicism peaked in youth (fifteen to twenty-nine years old), their hopefulness about the future was related to greater life satisfaction—an outlook that may translate into productive educational and life choices (Myllyniemi and Kiilakoski, 2017). Together, this research suggests that youth's hope in STEM, and in its possibilities for ensuring a better future, must be intentionally nurtured.

What This Chapter Aims to Do

This chapter describes *speculative design* as an approach to promoting youth's hopefulness in STEM. Through this approach, learners speculate about socioscientific issues through transmedia storytelling, and in so doing engage with the possibilities and implications of STEM. In the sections that follow, I describe the theoretical rationale for this approach, share my and my colleagues' efforts in this area, and discuss the practical implications of speculative design in STEM learning contexts. Ultimately, this chapter argues that approaches to STEM learning that emphasize imagination, and that help learners to realize a degree of agency, can be effective in fostering youth's hope in STEM.

Grounding STEM Learning in Youth's Concerns

STEM education tends to be guided by *how* and *why* questions. It focuses students on studying solved problems and applying ideas that have already been shown to be true, such as: "How do plants get energy?" (Espinoza, Orvis, and Brophy, 2020) and "Why do we have seasons?" (Sung and Oh, 2018). While such approaches are necessary and important, they can fail to capture the creative and imaginative dimensions of STEM. They can also be far from youth's real concerns, which can prevent them from recognizing the relevance of STEM to their lives.

When my team and I asked a group of seventh-grade students their thoughts on the future of STEM, they shared numerous worries (figure 7.1). For example, they feared that people's ambitions in STEM would backfire and cause inadvertent harm. Students shared their concerns that genetically "modif[ying] people to be perfect could go wrong in many ways," that robots might "get too smart and take jobs and overpower humans,"

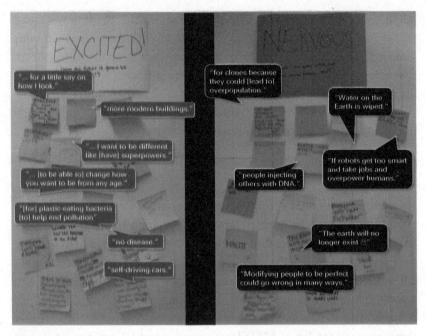

Figure 7.1
Sticky notes on a whiteboard created by a group of seventh-grade students during a
workshop activity in which they were prompted to name what makes them excited
and what makes them nervous about the future of STEM.

and that humans might deplete natural resources to the point that the
Earth would "no longer exist." However, students also shared hopes in
STEM as a route to healthier and more desirable lives, including agency
over their bodies (e.g., that genetic engineering would allow them "a little
say on how I look" and "to [have] superpowers") and over their environment (e.g., to end overpopulation and disease). These ideas reflect youth's
concerns that advances in STEM will outstrip our ethical responsibilities.
They also resonate with existing research on students' worries for the future
(Hicks and Holden, 2007; Lee et al., 2020; Matuk et al., 2021b), and with
the concerns of the public more generally (e.g., Anderson, Rainie, and
Vogels, 2021; Rainie, Anderson, and Vogels, 2021). At the same time, they
demonstrate youth's hope for the role of STEM in a better future. Their
ideas are reminders that scientific advances happen within social systems
that implicate cultures, ethics, and values. They raise questions about how

well STEM education prepares youth to engage with the social aspects of STEM, now and in the future.

A Future-Oriented Approach to STEM

One approach to preparing students to handle future socioscientific issues is to explicitly prepare them to engage with the future (Wilenius and Pouru, 2020). Indeed, "Humans can only work to build a future if they can first imagine it" (Ellyard, 1992; see also Jones et al., 2012). Some education researchers have drawn on futures studies to ensure this preparation. As an interdisciplinary field of innovation, futures studies involves critically examining the trends of today and developing alternative future scenarios that strike a balance between plausibility and imagination. This process values and develops several skills, including skills in empathy and perspective taking, systems and holistic thinking (ARIES and Australian Government Department of the Environment, Water, Heritage and the Arts, 2009; Cohen, 2007; Dale and Newman, 2005; Morris and Martin, 2009; Sterling, 2009; Sterling and Thomas, 2006; Strachan, 2009; Warburton, 2003); critical thinking (ARIES and Australian Government Department of the Environment, Water, Heritage and the Arts, 2009; Hurlimann, 2009; Jones, Selby, and Sterling, 2010; Parker, Wade, and Atkinson, 2004); anticipatory or foresight thinking (ARIES and Australian Government Department of the Environment, Water, Heritage and the Arts, 2009; Barth et al., 2007); interdisciplinarity (Barth et al., 2007; Cherry, 2005; Rieckmann, 2012; Strachan, 2009); and dealing with complexity, uncertainty, and ambiguity (Bateson and Ackoff, quoted in Ramage and Shipp, 2020; Tomkinson, 2009).

Ahvenharju, Minkkinen, and Lalot (2018) synthesized these competencies in a review of futures studies research to define *futures consciousness*, a construct that describes one's awareness of the bidirectional relationships between present and future. Futures consciousness, in other words, is an understanding of how the future should guide the actions that we take today (Pouru-Mikkola and Wilenius, 2021). For example, one might use predictions of the future of climate change, as well as goals for that future, to inform mitigation actions that can be taken today. More specifically, futures consciousness can be defined in terms of several dimensions (Ahvenharju et al., 2018), including *agency beliefs*, beliefs that one's actions can influence the future; *systems perceptions*, awareness of how everything is interconnected and the ability to make predictions based on an understanding of interacting components of a system; *openness to alternatives*, the ability to imagine probable, possible, and preferable futures; and *empathy*, the attention to ethical and moral responsibility.

Speculative transmedia design can be an approach to futures education. It can be particularly valuable for fostering hope, as it pivots learners away from solving problems with STEM, to instead pursuing future possibilities of STEM. In the next section, I describe examples of how speculative design can be used to promote STEM learning.

How Does STEM Learning through Speculative Design Look?

Speculative design is an approach to building futures literacy that aims to provoke critical discussion of the connection between present and future. Speculative design is distinguished from traditional design in that it is critical, not affirmative; aims to find, not solve problems; aims to ask, not answer questions; aims to address the world as it could be, not as it is; and aims to make us think, not buy (Dunne and Raby, 2013). Through playful experimentation and improvisation, speculative designers critically consider the present and build plausible images of future possibilities to inspire action.

There is a long tradition of thinkers engaging with the future, most prominently through science fiction, and notably, including contemporary authors of color who use their craft to engage critically with issues of justice and identity (e.g., Alyssa Wong, Craig Strete, and Nnedi Okorafor). Speculative design also includes the design of tangible objects. In one example, the designer Medan Levy's four-dimensional-printed *Neo Fruit* (2019) envisions a future of artificial food that fulfills the human need for aesthetic, sensory food experiences, while cautioning against agricultural practices that lead to food devoid of nutrients. In another example, Lucy McRae's *Solitary Survival Raft* (2020) is a reaction to the rejection of human touch brought on by forces including COVID-19 and digitalization. This inflatable structure offers visitors a reactive buffer against the world that simultaneously encompasses and comforts the body (figure 7.2).

There are diverse possible approaches to, and products of, youth learning from speculative design. To begin their ideation, youth might start with a general theme, a story prompt, or an existing story (a comic, novel,

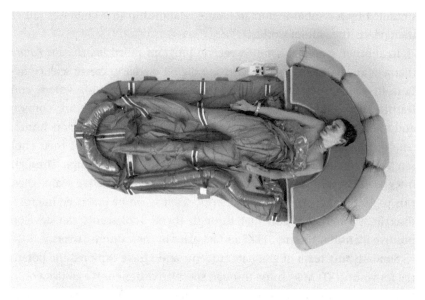

Figure 7.2
Solitary Survival Raft, from the exhibit *Real Feelings* at Haus der elektronischen Kün-
ste, Basel and MU Hybrid Art House, Eindhoven, Netherlands. Credit: Lucy McCrae.
Source: https://flic.kr/p/2jvBLtU; CC BY-NC-ND 2.0.

movie, or game), and through a transmedia creation process, spin off a new
story of their own (Matuk, Hurwich, and Amato, 2019; Matuk et al., 2020).
Their speculative design artifacts might take the form of creative writing,
dramatic play, art, and digital or tangible inventions. The few examples of
existing research on learning from speculative design offer promising evidence of promoting youth's critical stances on environmental, social, and
economic systems (Holbert, Dando, and Correa, 2020; Jones et al., 2012),
and for developing their identities in relation to STEM (Jiang et al., 2020).

For example, in one out-of-school program, Black female youth explored
the genre of Afrofuturism using the fictional world of Wakanda from the
film *Black Panther* as a starting point (Holbert et al., 2020). They discussed
and reflected upon their own personal stories related to social inequity and
the environment, and in consultations with guest artists, created artifacts
from imagined futures. One young woman, inspired by her love of both
nature and city skyscrapers, used cardboard, light-emitting diodes (LEDs),
wire, and fabric to build a model of her vision of a future neighborhood

sustained by a symbiotic human-nature relationship that embraces rather than rejects the natural world.

In another example, a multiweekend program called *Imagine the Future* (Jiang et al., 2020) had adolescents use digital media to create science fiction. In teams, they engaged with guest scientists and sci-fi writers, and learned to use digital media platforms to create interactive art, comics, and infographics. In teams, they authored original science fiction stories, conducting research to strengthen the scientific credibility of their chosen themes (e.g., time travel, space exploration, and cloning). Through integrated literacy activities, and through their collaborative team roles, this project demonstrates that authentic science can be practiced in cross-disciplinary activities, and that through them, adolescents can develop positive identities toward STEM and its place in their future careers.

Similarly, my team of graduate students and I have explored the potential for youth's STEM learning through speculative design. We guided youth through methods in speculative design (Matuk et al., 2020) over a five-day workshop format that involved introducing them to socioscientific issues through stories from the *World of Viruses* comic books (figure 7.3), story prompts (table 7.1), and news stories such as that of the scientist He Jiankui, who defied ethics in research to create the first gene-edited AIDS-resistant babies (Dyer, 2020); developing evidence-based, future scenarios based on these issues; and designing, testing, and refining artifacts before exhibiting them to an external audience.

Our workshop themes included "Viruses and human health," "Robots and AI," "Climate change and natural disasters," and "Genetic engineering." Meanwhile, youth took on interdependent roles (e.g., world builder, concept artist, or science researcher), and we guided them in designing artifacts that included board games, tableaux vivants, and tabletop role-playing games (TTRPGs; figure 7.4). With each workshop implementation, we iterated on our facilitation, refining the activity framing, facilitation strategies, and learner scaffolds. We also examined youth's learning through field observations, pretest/posttest surveys, and focus-group interviews.

Next, I illustrate youth's experiences with speculative design through a vignette based in part on my and my team's observations of participants in one of our workshop implementations, and also on ideas from existing speculative fiction experiences geared toward youth. The vignette highlights how speculative design can provide multiple routes to engaging diverse

Figure 7.3

A page from *Phantom Planet* (Powell et al., 2011), a comic book that imagines the future of HIV. The comic was used as a prompt during a speculative design workshop with young people.

Table 7.1.
Two examples of story prompts given to prompt youth's designs of science-themed, speculative, role-playing games.

(iii)   Sneak into the Surveillance Site
The government and corporations surveil everything people do. So much is known of each person that [artificial intelligence (AI)] algorithms can predict their future actions. Police have begun to use a controversial new technology to identify people likely to commit crimes, and to arrest them before they have even committed the crime. As a result, criminals have had to resort to advanced technologies to hide their traces and avoid detection.

You are a group of criminals committing a heist against one of the most well-guarded hi-tech facilities in the world. Your team of experts will need to work together to overcome the most powerful security and surveillance technology available in the future if they want to not only succeed, but escape without being detected.

Keywords: mass surveillance, smart cities, hacking, predictive algorithms, fatalism, electronic police state, cybersecurity, cybercrime

Questions to discuss:
1. Is it acceptable to use technology to surveil people? How much surveillance is OK, and under what circumstances?
2. What surveillance and security technologies currently exist? How might these evolve in the future?
3. What future advanced technologies might exist in the future to commit these crimes?
4. How do these technologies work?
5. How do you steal data? How do you protect it?
6. What is a firewall? How do they work?
7. What is cybercrime? How is it similar to regular crime? How is it different?

(iv)   Beat the Biohackers
Conflicts have been growing between "classic" humans, and a new group of "neo-humans," who have augmented themselves with cybernetics, genetic enhance-ments, and other methods. As the conflict grows more unstable and dangerous, you are members of one of these two groups that has decided to take matters into your own hands. After locating an enemy base, you are a team of experts who is going to go into the headquarters and shut down the enemy resistance, once and for all.

Keywords: Bioengineering, cyborgs, transhumanism, gene splicing, stem cells, xenobiology

Questions to discuss:
1. Who is right: Pro- or anti-technology?
2. What risks come with augmenting ourselves? What benefits?
3. Where is the line—at what point are we or are we not human?
4. What is the purpose of technology? Who determines its purpose?
5. Should the use of technology for human enhancement be regulated? To what extent? Who should decide how / what is regulated?
6. Does technology inherently change us? What parts of us are "real" or imagined?

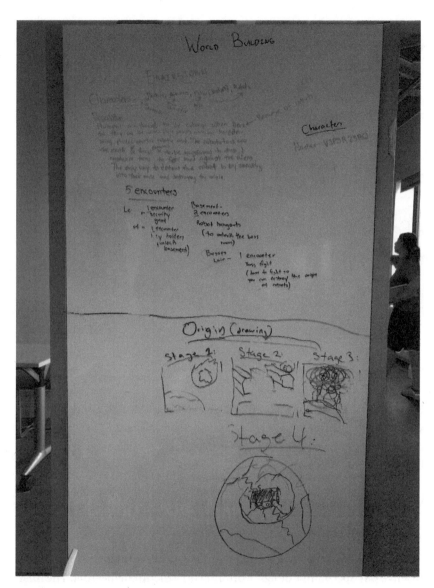

Figure 7.4
Youth's designs-in-progress at one of the author's speculative design workshops.

Figure 7.4
(continued)

learners with STEM: through art and storytelling; through connections to youth culture; through personally and socially relevant STEM ideas; and through higher-level, generally applicable practices such as systems thinking, prediction, and explanation.

Vignette: Organ Cloning in the Future

Asking "What If?"
Sam, Ali, and Mo are participating with twelve other middle school youth in a five-day speculative design workshop on genetic engineering. The final product, they are told, will be a tableau vivant: a staged photograph of a key scene from their visions of the future. They spend the first few sessions studying professional examples of speculative design and engaging in interactive speculative design exercises. During these exercises, they share their hopes and concerns about the future of genetic engineering. Ali wonders, "What if you could clone Einstein and raise him as your child?" This leads

the group to a conversation about the malleability of genes. Meanwhile, Sam is fascinated by the idea of body enhancement, based on her infatuation with the TV series *The Flash*, in which the main character achieves superhuman speed following a lab explosion. Her interest spurs a discussion of ethics in genetic engineering and its impacts on equity in the workforce and in sports.

In this conversation, some youth raise concerns over the fairness of people having different advantages, as well different access to those advantages. Others question whether the potential advantages gained through genetic modification are different from other kinds of advantages that already exist, such as variations in socioeconomic status or one's personal connections to people in power. Scientific misconceptions also emerge from this group discussion. For example, one participant asks: "Would your clone have the same memories as you? Would they be the same age as you?" Through these and other questions, facilitators are able to see youth's reasoning and correct their understanding as needed.

Using Science to Build a Credible Storyworld

Following these introductory activities, facilitators guide youth through a design process in which Sam, Ali, and Mo brainstorm and converge on an idea for their story and begin worldbuilding. They envision a hypothetical society 200 years from now, wherein organ cloning is a common procedure: Those who can afford it clone their organs in their youth and transplant these later in life, achieving a kind of immortality. Meanwhile, the life spans of those who cannot afford the procedure shorten due to other conditions of this future, including the impacts of climate change and the evolution of viral diseases. As the team develops their idea, Ali, who enjoys creative writing, takes charge of putting the team's ideas on paper.

Sam, whose interest in *The Flash* has already encouraged her casual research on the topic of body enhancement, leads the team's research. She reads science news articles, watches video explanations of genetic engineering, and collects her teammates' questions to pose to the expert facilitators. She documents this information and incorporates it into her team's developing story to make their ideas more believable. As they construct this future vision, the team discusses the ethical responsibilities of government and medical professionals, as well as the impacts of this future on people occupying different roles in this society.

Crafting a Future Vision

To prepare their tableau vivant, Sam, Ali, and Mo decide to create a model of the organ cloning machine. While other teams have decided to explore digital film and three-dimensional (3D) printing to create their artifacts, Mo, who has been an avid cardboard sculptor since preschool, convinces the team to use cardboard, paint, and other craft supplies. Their machine has a slot into which a medical professional can insert a card containing genetic information and a window through which one can view the organ as it is being fabricated.

The team discusses which key scene from their story they wish to stage, what that scene should contain, and how to compose it to best convey the necessary detail and desired tone to an audience. Once in agreement, they assemble props, create costumes, and position themselves in their roles while a facilitator captures photographs from different angles, from which they will select their final piece. In their tableau vivant, Sam is a surgeon transplanting the cloned kidneys of Ali, the patient, with Mo, the technician, operating the organ-cloning machine (figure 7.5).

To complete their final piece for a public exhibit and website, Sam, Ali, and Mo write a design statement that explains the socioscientific issues that they sought to comment on, the rationale behind their design decisions, and the reaction they hope to provoke in their audience. They include a reflection on the consequences of this potential future, and they conclude that their vision is simultaneously dystopic and utopic. Sam, Ali, and Mo refine each of their design artifacts through group critique sessions, during which they present and exchange feedback on their pieces among peers and facilitators.

The youth leave the workshop with their interest piqued in genetic engineering and its possibilities. For weeks afterward, when they encounter news of recent STEM advances, they find their minds wandering into *what if* scenarios and playing out potential storylines for the impacts of those advances on society in the future.

Why Speculative Design Might Activate STEM Learning

As shown in the vignette in this chapter, speculative design learning environments can attend to the cognitive, motivational, and active dimensions of learning (Durik, Vida, and Eccles, 2006), which lend them the potential to engage learners not just in disciplinary practices and knowledge,

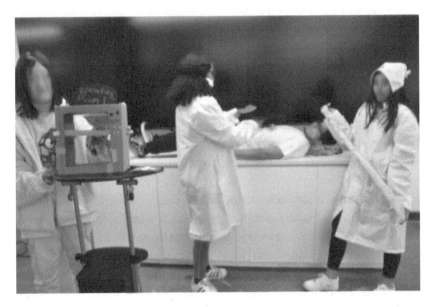

Figure 7.5
Youth constructing a cardboard organ-cloning machine and staging a tableau vivant of their vision of the future.

but also in developing an emotional investment in STEM, a hopefulness about its potential, and an awareness of its implications for social justice. Several features of speculative design position it well to offer learners these experiences.

Constructionist and Design-Based Learning

One valuable feature of speculative design is that it involves learners in sorting out and representing their ideas through construction with tangible materials. In line with constructionist theories of learning (Kafai and Burke, 2015; Papert and Harel, 1991), learners can engage with big ideas (e.g., scientific phenomena, ethics, or social dilemmas) through their design of public artifacts—that is, through the construction, presentation, critique, and refinement of ideas represented by tangible materials. Learner-designed artifacts are opportunities for both learning and assessment. They are objects *through* which to learn, in that designers externalize their understanding through their designs; objects *with which* to learn, in that audiences can reflect on and learn from the designer's model; and objects *from which* to know learning, in that designers' understanding is made visible for assessment (Clark et al., 2009). In addition, the process of storymaking, as with the general process of design, engages learners in authentic professional practices grounded in disciplinary content (Fortus et al., 2004; Games, 2010; Kafai and Burke, 2015; Kolodner et al., 1998, 2003; New London Group, 1996). Design can also foster self-efficacy in a domain—that is, the belief in one's ability to succeed—which makes learners more successful at task choice, engagement, effort, and persistence (Schunk, Meece, and Pintrich, 2013).

Narrative Contexts for Socioscientific Reasoning

Another feature of speculative design is that it engages learners in using narrative as a tool for reasoning. Stories and narrative are implicated in memory, understanding, and identity (Lombardo and Cornish, 2010; Zeidler, Herman, and Sadler, 2019) and used in various fields of inquiry (Botha and Pretorius, 2017; Heinonen and Balcom Raleigh, 2015; Miller, 2007; Slaughter, 1996). Building narratives engages such scientific and reasoning practices as posing questions about natural phenomena (Cohn, 2000) and relating abstract ideas to real-life situations (Leavy, 2020). Moreover, integrating stories and literacy practices into science instruction has been shown to improve students' performance in science (Ke et al., 2020;

Liu, Lin, and Tsai, 2011; Markauskaite and Goodyear, 2017; Yang, 2005) and to elicit youth's domain curiosity (Dickey, 2011).

The storytelling aspect of speculative design makes it an ideal context for reasoning about socioscientific issues. In line with frameworks for teaching science through socioscientific issues (Zeidler et al., 2019), speculative design can promote critical discussion of complex societal problems that implicate both the scientific and moral reasoning that will be essential in navigating STEM advances of the future. In the vignette in this chapter, for example, youth described the advances that they wished to see in the future of genetic engineering, but at the same time balanced those wishes with discussions of the impacts of those advances on all who might be implicated.

Interdisciplinarity and Connections to Youth's Non-STEM Interests

As with futures studies more broadly (Eccles, 1994), socioscientific reasoning is multidisciplinary and interdisciplinary. By drawing on multiple disciplines, speculative design can potentially connect STEM to youth's interests in the arts, social sciences, and language arts (Hidi and Renninger, 2006; Potvin and Hasni, 2014a), notably at a time in life when their interest in these domains increases (Hidi and Renninger, 2006; Potvin and Hasni, 2014a). As illustrated in the vignette, speculative design offers youth various ways to contribute to the development of an idea, such as through creative writing, science research, and design; it also offers multiple entry points into STEM, such as through popular culture, ethics, and social issues. As such, it responds to calls for STEM learning environments that integrate youth's interests and connect their formal and informal learning experiences (Ito et al., 2013; National Research Council, 1996). These efforts are based on research that finds that exposure to a discipline's ideas across contexts of youth's lives can activate STEM learning, foster dispositions that empower learners to identify as contributors to STEM, and prepare them for lifelong STEM learning (Ito et al., 2013). Experiences such as these can cultivate youth's adoption of disciplinary ideas, values, and ways of doing STEM, which may be key to broadening STEM participation (Ahn et al., 2014; Clegg and Kolodner, 2013).

How Speculative Design Promotes Futures Consciousness

Next, I elaborate on how the features of speculative design described in this chapter—design-based learning, narrative reasoning, and interdisciplinarity—

support youth in developing along the dimensions of futures consciousness (Ahvenharju et al., 2018) that are essential for engaging with future socioscientific issues.

Agency beliefs are beliefs in one's ability to act, and they are tied to identity. Agency requires an optimism about the future and a sense of purpose and responsibility over it (Lombardo and Cornish, 2010). The interdisciplinary and collaborative nature of speculative design expands youth's views of what STEM entails (e.g., imagination as well as discovery), the domains to which it is relevant (e.g., economics, psychology, design, and social science), and the roles that they can take up in STEM (e.g., writers, artists, and future thinkers). Other research has found that youth's collaborative creation of narratives can promote identity development by evoking discussions of identity (Beghetto, 2009; Bonsignore et al., 2016), and blending different epistemological frames can expand the resources and knowledge available to youth (Matuk et al., 2021a), promote content connections across contexts that aid in knowledge transfer (Levy-Cohen and Matuk, 2017), and enable youth to develop interests and identities relevant to STEM. By providing youth with more ways to identify with and participate in STEM, it is possible to foster a sense of agency to act on issues that matter to them.

Systems perceptions is an awareness of the interconnectedness of the world. With respect to socioscientific issues, systems perceptions involves recognizing causal links and patterns across the economic, cultural, and policy dimensions of an issue in relation to scientific evidence, as well as being able to explain and predict outcomes for different stakeholders in a system (Sadler, Barab, and Scott, 2007). Without systems perceptions, learners can overlook the true complexity of issues (Liu et al., 2011; Yang, 2005). Stories can help by grounding causal reasoning in concrete situations, allowing learners to recognize the personal and societal relevance of the issues and draw on intuition to predict and understand outcomes. Epistemic tools can support learners' systems perceptions by promoting knowledge construction and justification (Markauskaite and Goodyear, 2017), but such tools must be framed in ways that encourage students to fully appropriate them, such as by embedding them within authentic and relevant tasks (Ke et al., 2020).

Openness to alternatives is the ability to imagine probable, possible, and preferable futures (Miller, 2007). It requires curiosity and imagination (Lombardo and Cornish, 2010), critical questioning, and an ability to identify ways that issues of the present might extend into the future (Heinonen and Balcom Raleigh, 2015). Stories can serve as simulations with which learners may test and make predictions by imagining how scenarios may play out. For example, youth might create stories to speculate on the impact of climate change on geopolitics, or on how data privacy policies will affect law enforcement (Botha and Pretorius, 2017). An openness to alternatives may also be related to agency and confidence in STEM, as it requires identifying possible sequences of events, which highlights how choices in the present have consequences in the future (Slaughter, 1996).

Empathy is a concern for others. It puts intention behind the other dimensions of futures consciousness and accounts for an individual's sense of ethical and moral responsibility (Heinonen and Balcom Raleigh, 2015). Stories can evoke empathy by allowing a virtual embodiment of characters' experiences (Cohn, 2000) and immersion in fictional worlds, in which an audience can explore issues from alternative perspectives that are otherwise out of reach (Leavy, 2020). Collaboratively creating stories can also engage youth in perspective taking (Bonsignore et al., 2016). It is within this empathy dimension of futures consciousness that speculative designers strive to imagine better futures (Bell, 2011).

Whether one engages with a dystopian or utopian future, speculative design is ingrained with a sense of hope: It aims to spur critical reflection and to highlight the agency that designers and their audiences have to shape probable futures into preferable ones (Johannessen et al., 2019). Using stories to engage youth in making tangible representations of their worlds allows them to manipulate and form those representations in desired ways, and to thus embody the agency that youth have to shape, reify, and redefine their realities. We also found that through our workshops, youth come to view design abilities as personally achievable rather than limited to those with innate skills (Levy-Cohen, Matuk, and Pawar, 2017; Levy-Cohen and Matuk, 2017). This finding shows that adequate support for design activities can create pathways toward STEM for youth who may not have chosen to participate otherwise.

Observations of Youth's Learning from Speculative Design

Our research on youth learning in speculative design contexts has generated several insights to inform both theory and practice. For example, we observed how the performative aspect of speculative fiction, embedded in cycles of design and critique, could support youth in scientific practices such as argumentation and explanation. The process of worldbuilding—which involves specifying aspects of the geography, history, and culture of the context in which a story takes place—prompted youth to compose and present ideas for feedback from an audience of peers and facilitators. This encouraged them to find and incorporate evidence to revise and strengthen explanations for their story decisions (Matuk et al., 2019). For example, one youth participant, whom I shall refer to by the pseudonym Chi, had conceived of and presented his idea for a "guardian angel" character in a game about HIV. Prompted by facilitators' feedback, Chi researched the science of bird wing evolution and T-cell transfer—a treatment for cancer that he imagined might be extended to also treat HIV—and developed a backstory for how this character came to have wings. Eventually, he developed the following explanation:

> The HIV monster was diagnosed with HIV and his brother wanted to help out and in order for him to help out he thought it would be best if he gave him T-cells. So he gave him T-cells but sadly, he didn't have enough and his reproduction of T-cells, weren't, wasn't massive enough so this is like later on in the future but not far ahead when there's like a cure. But they just found the cure. So they used birds to add for genetic, uh gene editing to extract T-cells and add it into human, which caused to mutate the human body cells.

This example shows the value of publicly refining ideas. By presenting versions of his ideas in progress to peers and facilitators, Chi made his ideas available for critique and open to guided refinement. This example also demonstrates the value of building a scientific explanation within a narrative context. The idea for his character motivated Chi to go deeper into understanding and explaining the science, in order to build more narrative and scientific credibility.

We also found that youth's iterations on their designs reflected refinements to their understanding of the underlying STEM concepts (Hovey, Matuk, and Hurwich, 2018). For instance, in one virus-themed workshop, youth created story-based games with the intention of aligning player actions (e.g., collecting objects, making choices) with science concepts. One team's initial design reflected a misconceived view of vaccines as curative viral infection. In their initial game, players would "vaccinate the sick" to "remove symptoms" and "cure" them. Following facilitators' encouragement to research the mechanism of vaccines more deeply, the team iterated on its design. Eventually, they came to one that reflected the preventive nature of vaccines, in which players had "chances to get different vaccines to prevent different diseases," and some of these vaccines "prevent one, some prevent three or four" diseases. They also ensured that each player would shepherd a group of characters, some of whom may or may not become infected, in order to avoid the game ending too soon. This observation shows the value of the process of designing an artifact for engaging with science ideas. In particular, it highlights the importance of the medium and genre of their storytelling—in this case, a TTRPG—for driving the development of the team's conceptual understanding of the science.

Issues and Guidance for Supporting STEM Learning through Speculative Design

Speculative design requires balancing imagination and plausibility, which presents the potential for rich learning, as well as conceptual and practical challenges. On the one hand, plausible stories and plausible scientific explanations share much in common, including logical coherence and a basis in evidence (Clarke, 1962/1973). Each requires learners to draw upon practices such as prediction, evidence-based argument, and systems reasoning. Moreover, the construction of each emphasizes iterative refinement, with scientific explanations being refined to incorporate new data interpretations, and stories being refined to achieve the desired audience reaction.

Yet, while there are many learning opportunities at the intersection of storytelling and science explanation, there are also tensions that facilitators must anticipate. For example, while stories can provide intuitive contexts within which to reason about science phenomena, including the complex systems that are inherent in socioscientific issues, they can also oversimplify complexity to the point of misrepresentation. This tension is apparent in the fact that we ask audiences of scientific explanations to bring a healthy skepticism, while we ask audiences of stories to suspend disbelief.

As an illustration of this tension, I observed that youth, with exceptions, are prone to incorporate science only superficially into their speculation and to create underdeveloped narratives, flawed designs (e.g., games that are too easy or difficult), and artifacts that overlay science (e.g., through the addition of "fun science facts" that have no consequence to the story), rather than integrating science into the narrative. Youth also struggle to make design decisions that balance their aesthetic preferences with scientific backing. For example, one team, which was creating a TTRPG, conceived a game character who travels between people's shadows. In spite of facilitators' encouragement to incorporate a science-based explanation of how an object might be teleported, the team chose to maintain this more poetic, albeit vague, notion of "shadowstepping." Examples such as these point to the potential conflict in speculative design between crafting good stories and building strong scientific explanations. However, these examples also illustrate the need to guide learners through a design process that invites the revision of ideas.

In the next section, I describe some practical guidance for addressing these challenges in facilitating STEM learning through speculative design.

Prioritize Desired Learning Goals

Speculative design requires the coordination of multiple kinds of domain and practical knowledge, including a deep enough understanding of unfamiliar scientific phenomena, of the craft of storytelling, of different expressive media and story genres, of design processes, and of working on open-ended projects in cross-domain collaborative teams (Khaled and Vasalou, 2014). Without sufficient ability in these areas, learners are limited in terms of the forecasts that they can imagine and articulate. At the same time, it can be tempting, due to a desire to do justice to the richness of the relevant domains, and given the limitations of time and resources that are characteristic of most structured learning contexts, for facilitators to overload learners with expository instruction. Unfortunately, this approach can cause confusion about the goal of the activity and prevent anything more than superficial engagement with ideas.

To ensure that learners' experiences are rich and authentic, designers should keep activities tightly aligned with desired outcomes. In preparing a speculative design learning experience, facilitators might consider these questions: What are the essential learning goals? What are the essential design practices that will help learners to achieve those goals? Is it important for learning outcomes to be the same for all learners, or is it acceptable—or even desirable—for individual learners to have different learning experiences as a result of their participation? Once specified, these goals can be used to decide how to frame the purpose of the workshop; how to structure the roles that youth will play in their teams; which activities and ideas to exclude; and how to place emphasis on the activities and ideas that are included.

Cultivate Design Thinking and Prioritize the Process of Design

As illustrated earlier, the artifacts that youth create reflect their thinking, and youth refine their thinking through iteration on those artifacts. Design fixation, by which designers become overly attached to ideas such that they avoid iteration and improvement (Leahy et al., 2018), can also lead to learners being fixated in their conceptual beliefs. In my experiences, some youth are willing to abandon initial design ideas upon learning new science information. They integrate that new understanding into their design iterations, and ultimately they create more effective designs (Hovey et al., 2018; Matuk et al., 2016). Meanwhile, other youth can become so fixated in their initial design ideas that they resist changing them, even upon being introduced to new or contradictory science information. To keep youth open to revising their ideas, it is important to cultivate a culture of design thinking. This can be done by modeling and prioritizing the process of design, such as by providing opportunities for learners to present and critique work-in-progress with an audience and to reflect and iterate upon their designs, and by praising and showcasing process-related over product-related outcomes.

Prioritizing the design process has an additional benefit of making learners' thinking visible. The meaning of speculative design is often clarified and given added dimension in light of the process and rationale for its creation. Learners' speculative design artifacts will vary widely in form, and will not necessarily show the origins and trajectory of their inquiry, the decisions that helped them to craft their message, or the reactions that they intended for these messages. Documents of learners' processes through written artifacts can offer context, explanation, justification of the designers' choices, and reflection on their process, and they can be displayed alongside the finished pieces.

Understand the Learning Affordances of Different Genres and Media

Speculative design learning experiences are most effective when they connect to and build on learners' prior knowledge, interests, and culture, and when the themes, media, and genres used are within learners' realm of experience. A proper understanding of the learning affordances of different genres and media in speculative storymaking can moreover allow facilitators to take the best advantage of those affordances.

For example, certain genres (e.g., sci-fi, fantasy), media (digital, analog), and forms (tableaux vivants, comic books) present different opportunities to align with the nature of the focal topic or domain. Creating a TTRPG, for instance, immerses the designer in reasoning about the personal and social contexts of a phenomenon, predicting the multiple probable outcomes given different interacting variables, and appreciating the implications of events from the perspectives of multiple players. Meanwhile, creating a tableau vivant, while it also involves a degree of worldbuilding, and thus systems reasoning, emphasizes the audience's emotional reactions to an idea.

Different genres and media also have implications for broadening participation. In particular, certain aspects of speculative design and of the traditional artifacts with which it is associated (e.g., science fiction and games) have traditionally been associated with male creators and consumers (Richard, 2017). It has been my team's experience that our opt-in role-playing game and sci-fi workshops have tended to attract young men, whereas our more general STEM and storytelling workshops have attracted youth of all genders. Knowing this, it is important for the sake of broadening participation to highlight the aspects of speculative design that have the potential for broad appeal, such as creative writing, communication, and collaboration.

Final Words

This chapter has described speculative design as an approach to developing youth's futures consciousness and confidence in STEM. By moving youth from asking *how* and *why* to instead asking *what if*, speculative design can connect STEM to youth's personal experiences and concerns; draw on their interests in creative and imaginative domains (e.g., through creative writing, design, and futures thinking); broaden views of what counts as STEM by offering diverse pathways for participation; and address the urgent need to foster youth's hope in STEM. There are many practical considerations in designing and facilitating youth's STEM learning through speculative design that merit further research. However, our experiences thus far suggest that speculative design can develop important abilities in youth to draw upon multiple disciplines and perspectives to reason about complex socioscientific issues, which can prepare them to engage with both the present and future of STEM with foresight, imagination, and empathy.

References

Ahn, June, Tamara Clegg, Jason Yip, et al. 2014. "Seeing the Unseen Learner: Designing and Using Social Media to Recognize Children's Science Dispositions in Action." *Learning, Media and Technology* 41, no. 2: 252–282.

Ahvenharju, Sanna, Matti Minkkinen, and Fanny Lalot. 2018. "The Five Dimensions of Futures Consciousness." *Futures* 104, 1–13.

Alexander, Joyce M., Kathy E. Johnson, and Ken Kelley. 2012. "Longitudinal Analysis of the Relations between Opportunities to Learn about Science and the Development of Interests Related to Science." *Science Education* 96, no. 5: 763–786.

Anderson, Janna, Lee Rainie, and Emily A. Vogels. 2021. "Experts Say the 'New Normal' in 2025 Will Be Far More Tech-Driven, Presenting More Big Challenges." *Pew Research Center*, February 18, 2021. https://www.pewresearch.org/internet/2021/02/18/worries-about-life-in-2025.

ARIES and Australian Government Department of the Environment, Water, Heritage and the Arts. 2009. *Education for Sustainability: The Role of Education in Engaging and Equipping People for Change.* Sydney: Macquarie University Sydney. http://www.aries.mq.edu.au/publications/aries/efs_brochure/pdf/efs_brochure.pdf.

Barth, Matthias, Jasmin Godemann, Marco Rieckmann, and Ute Stoltenberg. 2007. "Developing Key Competencies for Sustainable Development in Higher Education." *International Journal of Sustainability in Higher Education* 8, no. 4: 416–430. https://doi.org/10.1108/14676370710823582.

Beghetto, Ronald A. 2009. "Correlates of Intellectual Risk Taking in Elementary School Science." *Journal of Research in Science Teaching* 46, no. 2: 210–223.

Bell, Wendell. 2011. *Foundations of Futures Studies: Human Science for a New Era: Values, Objectivity, and the Good Society.* Piscataway, NJ: Transaction Publishers.

Bonsignore, Elizabeth, Derek Hansen, Anthony Pellicone, et al. 2016. "Traversing Transmedia Together: Co-designing an Educational Alternate Reality Game for Teens, with Teens." *IDC '16: Proceedings of the 15th International Conference on Interaction Design and Children*: 11–24.

Botha, Anthon P., and Marthinus W. Pretorius. 2017. "Future Thinking: The Scarce Management Skill." *2017 Portland International Conference on Management of Engineering and Technology (PICMET)*. https://doi.org/10.23919/picmet.2017.8125327.

Cavas, Pinar. 2011. "Factors Affecting the Motivation of Turkish Primary Students for Science Learning." *Science Education International* 22, no. 1: 31–42.

Cherry, Nita Lilian. 2005. Preparing for Practice in the Age of Complexity. *Higher Education Research & Development* 24, no. 4: 309–320.

Clark, Douglas, Brian Nelson, Pratim Sengupta, and Cynthia D'Angelo. 2009. "Rethinking Science Learning through Digital Games and Simulations: Genres, Examples, and Evidence." *National Academy of Sciences Workshop on Learning Science, Computer Games, Simulations and Education,* Washington, DC. https://sites.nationalacademies.org/cs/groups/dbassesite/documents/webpage/dbasse_080068.pdf.

Clarke, Arthur C. [1962] 1973. "Hazards of Prophecy: The Failure of Imagination." In *Profiles of the Future: An Enquiry into the Limits of the Possible,* rev. ed. New York: Random House.

Clegg, Tamara, and Janet Kolodner. 2013. "Scientizing and Cooking: Helping Middle-School Learners Develop Scientific Dispositions." *Science Education* 98, no. 1: 36–63.

Cohen, Bert. 2007. "Developing Educational Indicators that Will Guide Students and Institutions toward a Sustainable Future." *New Directions for Institutional Research* 134: 83–94. https://doi.org/10.1002/ir.215.

Cohn, Dorritt. 2000. *The Distinction of Fiction.* Baltimore: Johns Hopkins University Press.

Dabney, Katherine P., Robert H. Tai, John T. Almarode, et al. 2012. "Out-of-School Time Science Activities and Their Association with Career Interest in STEM." *International Journal of Science Education, Part B* 2, no. 1: 63–79. https://doi.org/10.1080/21548455.2011.629455.

Dale, Ann, and Lenore Newman. 2005. "Sustainable Development, Education and Literacy." *International Journal of Sustainability in Higher Education* 6, no. 4: 351–362.

Dickey, Michele. 2011. "Murder on Grimm Isle: The Impact of Game Narrative Design in an Educational Game-Based Learning Environment." *British Journal of Educational Technology* 42, no. 3: 456–469.

Dunne, Anthony, and Fiona Raby. 2013. *Speculative Everything: Design, Fiction, and Social Dreaming.* Cambridge, MA: MIT Press.

Durik, Amanda M., Mina Vida, and Jacquelynne S. Eccles. 2006. "Task Values and Ability Beliefs as Predictors of High School Literacy Choices: A Developmental Analysis." *Journal of Educational Psychology* 98, no. 2: 382–393.

Dyer, Owen. 2020. "Chinese Researcher Who Made CRISPR Babies Is Sentenced to Three Years in Prison." *BMJ* 368: m11. https://doi.org/10.1136/bmj.m11.

Eccles, Jacquelynne S. 1994. "Understanding Women's Educational and Occupational Choices: Applying the Eccles et al. Model of Achievement-Related Choices." *Psychology of Women Quarterly* 18, no. 4: 585–609.

Ellyard, Peter. 1992. "Education for the 21st Century." Christchurch: New Zealand Principals Federation Conference.

Espinoza, Cecilia, Kathryn S. Orvis, and Sean P. Brophy. 2020. "Learning the Electron Transport Chain Process in Photosynthesis Using Video and Serious Game." *Journal of Biological Education*, 1–21. https://doi.org/10.1080/00219266.2020.1808511.

Fortus, David, Charles Dershimer, Joseph Krajcik, Ronald W. Marx, and Rachel Mamlok-Naaman. 2004. "Design-Based Science and Student Learning." *Journal of Research in Science Teaching* 41, no. 10: 1081–1110.

Games, Ivan Alex. 2010. "*Gamestar Mechanic*: Learning a Designer Mindset through Communicational Competence with the Language of Games." *Learning, Media and Technology* 35, no. 1: 31–52.

Heinonen, Sirkka, and Nicolas A. Balcom Raleigh. 2015. *Continuous Transformation and Neo-Carbon Energy Scenarios*. Turku: Finland Futures Research Centre, University of Turku.

Hicks, David, and Cathie Holden. 2007. "Remembering the Future: What Do Children Think?" *Environmental Education Research* 13, no. 4: 501–512.

Hidi, Suzanne, and K. Ann Renninger. 2006. "The Four-Phase Model of Interest Development." *Educational Psychologist* 41, no. 2: 111–127.

Holbert, Nathan, Michael Dando, and Isabel Correa. 2020. "Afrofuturism as Critical Constructionist Design: Building Futures from the Past and Present." *Learning, Media and Technology* 45, no. 4: 328–344.

Hovey, Christopher M., Camillia Matuk, and Talia Hurwich. 2018. "'If You Add Too Much Science, It Gets Boring.' Exploring Students' Conceptual Change through Their Game Design Iterations." In *13th International Conference for the Learning Sciences, ICLS 2018: Rethinking Learning in the Digital Age: Making the Learning Sciences Count*, edited by Judy Kay and Rosemary Luckin, 1575–1576. London: International Society of the Learning Sciences.

Hurlimann, Anna C. 2009. "Responding to Environmental Challenges: An Initial Assessment of Higher Education Curricula Needs by Australian Planning Professionals." *Environmental Education Research* 15, no. 6: 643–659.

Ito, Mizuko, Kris Gutierrez, Sonia Livingstone, et al. 2013. *Connected Learning: An Agenda for Research and Design*. Irvine, CA: Digital Media and Learning Research Hub.

Jiang, Shiyan, Ji Shen, Blaine E. Smith, and Kristin Watson Kibler. 2020. "Science Identity Development: How Multimodal Composition Mediates Student Role-Taking as Scientist in a Media-Rich Learning Environment." *Educational Technology Research and Development* 68: 3187–3212.

Johannessen, Leon Karlsen, Martina Maria Keitsch, and Ida Nilstad Pettersen. 2019. "Speculative and Critical Design—Features, Methods, and Practices." *Proceedings of the Design Society International Conference on Engineeering Design* 1: 1623–1632. https://doi.org/10.1017/dsi.2019.168.

Jones, Alister, Cathy Buntting, Rose Hipkins, Anne McKim, Lindsey Conner, and Kathy Saunders. 2012. "Developing Students' Futures Thinking in Science Education." *Research in Science Education* 42, no. 4: 687–708. https://doi.org/10.1007/s11165-011-9214-9.

Jones, Paula, David Selby, and Stephen Sterling. 2010. "Introduction." In *Sustainability Education: Perspectives and Practice across Higher Education*, edited by Paula Jones, David Selby, and Stephen Sterling, 1–16. New York: Routledge.

Kafai, Yasmin B., and Quinn Burke. 2015. "Constructionist Gaming: Understanding the Benefits of Making Games for Learning." *Educational Psychologist* 50, no. 4: 313–334.

Ke, Li, Troy D. Sadler, Laura Zangori, and Patricia J. Friedrichsen. 2020. "Students' Perceptions of Socio-scientific Issue-Based Learning and Their Appropriation of Epistemic Tools for Systems Thinking." *International Journal of Science Education* 42, no. 8: 1339–1361.

Khaled, Rilla, and Asimina Vasalou. 2014. "Bridging Serious Games and Participatory Design." *International Journal of Child-Computer Interaction* 2, no. 2: 93–100.

Kolodner, Janet L., Paul J. Camp, David Crismond, et al. 2003. "Problem-Based Learning Meets Case-Based Reasoning in the Middle-School Science Classroom: Putting Learning by Design(tm) into Practice." *Journal of the Learning Sciences* 12, no. 4: 495–547.

Kolodner, Janet L., David Crismond, Jackie Gray, Jennifer Holbrook, and Sadhana Puntambekar. 1998. "Learning by Design from Theory to Practice." *Proceedings of the International Conference of the Learning Sciences* 98: 16–22.

Lawton, Graham. 2020. "Science in Crisis." *New Scientist* 246, no. 3281: 12–14.

Leahy, Keelin, Colleen Seifert, Shanna Daly, and Seda McKilligan. 2018. "Overcoming Design Fixation in Idea Generation." In *Design as a Catalyst for Change—DRS International Conference 2018*, edited by Cristiano Storni, Keelin Leahy, Muireann McMahon, Peter Lloyd, and Erik Bohemia. London: Design Research Society. https://doi.org/10.21606/drs.2018.v1.

Leavy, Patricia. 2020. *Method Meets Art: Arts-Based Research Practice*. 2nd ed. New York: Guilford Press.

Lee, Katharine, Nathalia Gjersoe, Saffron O'Neill, and Julie Barnett. 2020. "Youth Perceptions of Climate Change: A Narrative Synthesis." *Wiley Interdisciplinary Reviews: Climate Change* 11, no. 3. https://doi.org/10.1002/wcc.641.

Levy, Medan. 2019. *Neo Fruit.* https://meydanish.wixsite.com/portpoliome/concept.

Levy-Cohen, Rinat, and Camillia Matuk. 2017. "What Children Learn from the Game Design Process." Paper presented at the 13th Conference of the International Society for Design and Development in Education, Berkeley, CA, November 2017. https://www.researchgate.net/publication/320839960_What_children_learn_from _the_game_design_process.

Levy-Cohen, Rinat, Camillia Matuk, and Shashank Pawar. 2017. "'Game Making Is Harder Than I Thought': Game Design Driven by Children's Own Interests." Poster presented at the 10th Annual Subway Summit on Cognition and Education Research, New York, January 2017. https://www.academia.edu/30997111/_Game_Making_Is _Harder_Than_I_Thought_Game_Design_Driven_By_Childrens_Own_Interests.

Liu, Shiang-Yao, Chuan-Shun Lin, and Chin-Chung Tsai. 2011. "College Students' Scientific Epistemological Views and Thinking Patterns in Socioscientific Decision Making." *Science Education* 95, no. 3: 497–517.

Lombardo, Tom, and Edward Cornish. 2010. "Wisdom Facing Forward: What It Means to Have Heightened Future Consciousness." *The Futurist* 44, no. 5: 34–42.

Markauskaite, Lina, and Peter Goodyear. 2017. *Epistemic Fluency and Professional Education: Innovation, Knowledgeable Action and Actionable Knowledge.* Dordrecht, Netherlands: Springer.

Matuk, Camillia, Talia Hurwich, and Anna Amato. 2019. "How Science Fiction Worldbuilding Supports Students' Scientific Explanation." *FL: Proceedings of FabLearn 2019*: 193–196. https://doi.org/10.1145/3311890.3311925.

Matuk, Camillia, Talia Hurwich, Jonathan Prosperi, and Yael Ezer. 2020. "Iterations on a Transmedia Game Design Experience for Youth's Autonomous, Collaborative Learning." *International Journal of Designs for Learning* 11, no. 1: 108–139.

Matuk, Camillia, Talia Hurwich, Amy Spiegel, and Judy Diamond. 2021a. "How Do Teachers Use Comics to Promote Engagement, Equity, and Diversity in Science Classrooms? *Research in Science Education* 51, no. 3: 685–732.

Matuk, Camillia, Rinat Levy-Cohen, and Shashank Pawar. 2016. "Questions as Prototypes: Facilitating Children's Discovery and Elaboration During Game Design." *FabLearn '16: Proceedings of the 6th Annual Conference on Creativity and Fabrication in Education*: 111–114. https://doi.org/10.1145/3003397.3003417.

Matuk, Camillia, Rebecca Martin, Veena Vasudevan, et al. 2021b. Students Learning about Science by Investigating an Unfolding Pandemic." *AERA Open.* https://doi.org /10.3886/E151305V1.

McRae, Lucy. 2020. *Solitary Survival Raft.* https://www.lucymcrae.net/solitary-survival -raft.

Miller, Riel. 2007. "Futures Literacy: A Hybrid Strategic Scenario Method." *Futures* 39, no. 4: 341–362.

Myllyniemi, Sami, and Tomi Kiilakoski. 2017. "Tilasto-osio [Quantitative Results]." In *Opin Polut ja Pientareet: Nuorisobarometri 2017* [Roads to learning: Youth barometer 2017], edited by Elina Pekkarinen and Sami Myllyniemi, 9–117. Helsinki: Ministry of Education and Culture, Finland, Youth Research Society and State Youth Council. https://tietoanuorista.fi/wp-content/uploads/2018/03/Nuorisobarometri_2017_WEB .pdf.

Morris, Dick, and Stephen Martin. 2009. "Complexity, Systems Thinking and Practice: Skills and Techniques for Managing Complex Systems." In *Handbook of Sustainability Literacy: Skills for a Changing World*, edited by Arran Stibbe, 156–164. Cambridge, UK: Green Books.

National Research Council. 1996. *National Science Education Standards*. Washington, DC: National Academies Press. https://doi.org/10.17226/4962.

New London Group. 1996. "A Pedagogy of Multiliteracies: Designing Social Futures." *Harvard Educational Review* 66, no. 1: 60–93.

Pan, Yingqiu, and Mary Gauvain. 2012. "The Continuity of College Students' Autonomous Learning Motivation and Its Predictors: A Three-Year Longitudinal Study." *Learning and Individual Differences* 22, no. 1: 92–99.

Papert, Seymour, and Idit Harel. 1991. "Situating Constructionism." *Constructionism* 36, no. 2: 1–11.

Parker, Jenneth, Ros Wade, and Hugh Atkinson. 2004. "Citizenship and Community from Local to Global: Implications for Higher Education of a Global Citizenship Approach." In *The Sustainability Curriculum: The Challenge for Higher Education*, edited by Cedric Cullingford and John Blewitt, 63–77. New York: Routledge.

Potvin, Patrice, and Abdelkrim Hasni. 2014a. "Analysis of the Decline in Interest towards School Science and Technology from Grades 5 through 11." *Journal of Science Education and Technology* 23, no. 6: 784–802.

Potvin, Patrice, and Abdelkrim Hasni. 2014b. "Interest, Motivation and Attitude towards Science and Technology at K-12 Levels: A Systematic Review of 12 Years of Educational Research." *Studies in Science Education* 50, no. 1: 85–129.

Pouru-Mikkola, Laura, and Markku Wilenius. 2021. "Building Individual Futures Capacity through Transformative Futures Learning." *Futures* 132. https://doi.org/10 .1016/j.futures.2021.102804.

Powell, Martin, Peter Angeletti, Anisa Angeletti, and Thomas Floyd. 2011. *Phantom Planet*. Lincoln: University of Nebraska Press. https://worldofviruses.unl.edu/comics -apps.

Rainie, Lee, Janna Anderson, and Emily A. Vogels. 2021. "Hopes about Developments in Ethical AI." Pew Research Center, Washington, DC, June 16, 2021. https://www.pewresearch.org/internet/2021/06/16/2-hopes-about-developments-in-ethical-ai.

Ramage, Magnus, and Karen Shipp. 2020. *Systems Thinkers*. Basingstoke, UK: Springer Nature.

Reid, Norman, and Elena A. Skryabina. 2002. "Attitudes towards Physics." *Research in Science and Technological Education* 20, no. 1: 67–81.

Richard, Gabriela T. 2017. "Video Games, Gender, Diversity, and Learning as Cultural Practice: Implications for Equitable Learning and Computing Participation through Games." *Educational Technology Research and Development* 57, no. 2: 36–43.

Rieckmann, Marco. 2012. "Future-Oriented Higher Education: Which Key Competencies Should Be Fostered through University Teaching and Learning?" *Futures* 44, no. 2: 127–135.

Sadler, Troy D., Sasha A. Barab, and Brianna Scott. 2007. "What Do Students Gain by Engaging in Socioscientific Inquiry?" *Research in Science Education* 37, no. 4: 371–391.

Schunk, Dale H., Judith R. Meece, and Paul R. Pintrich. 2013. *Motivation in Education: Theory, Research, and Applications*. New York: Pearson College Division.

Singh, Kusum, Monique Granville, and Sandra Dika. 2002. "Mathematics and Science Achievement: Effects of Motivation, Interest, and Academic Engagement." *Journal of Educational Research* 95, no. 6: 323–332.

Slaughter, Richard A. 1996. *The Knowledge Base of Futures Studies*, vol. 1. Melbourne: Futures Study Centre/DDM Media.

Sterling, Stephen. 2009. "Ecological Intelligence: Viewing the World Relationally." In *Handbook of Sustainability Literacy: Skills for a Changing World*, edited by Arran Stibbe, 77–83. Cambridge, UK: Green Books.

Sterling, Stephen, and Ian Thomas. 2006. "Education for Sustainability: The Role of Capabilities in Guiding University Curricula." *International Journal of Innovation and Sustainable Development* 1, no. 4: 349–370.

Strachan, Glenn. 2009. "Systems Thinking: The Ability to Recognise and Analyse Interconnections within and between Systems." In *Handbook of Sustainability Literacy: Skills for a Changing World*, edited by Arran Stibbe, 84–88. Cambridge, UK: Green Books.

Sung, Ji Young, and Phil Seok Oh. 2018. "Sixth Grade Students' Content-Specific Competencies and Challenges in Learning the Seasons through Modeling." *Research in Science Education* 48, no. 4: 839–864.

Tai, Robert H., Christine Qi Liu, Adam V. Maltese, and Xitao Fan. 2006. "Planning Early for Careers in Science." *Science* 312, no. 5777: 1143–1144. https://science.sciencemag.org/content/312/5777/1143.short.

Tomkinson, Bland. 2009. "Coping with Complexity: The Ability to Manage Complex Sustainability Problems." In *Handbook of Sustainability Literacy: Skills for a Changing World,* edited by Arran Stibbe, 165–170. Cambridge, UK: Green Books.

Warburton, Kevin. 2003. "Deep Learning and Education for Sustainability." *International Journal of Sustainability in Higher Education* 4, no. 1: 44–56.

Wilenius, Markku, and Laura Pouru. 2020. "Developing Futures Literacy as a Tool to Navigate an Uncertain World." In *Humanistic Futures of Learning: Perspectives from UNESCO Chairs and UNITWIN Networks,* 207–210. Paris: UNESCO.

Yang, Fang-Ying. 2005. "Student Views Concerning Evidence and the Expert in Reasoning a Socio-scientific Issue and Personal Epistemology." *Educational Studies* 31, no. 1: 65–84.

Zeidler, Dana L., Benjamin C. Herman, and Troy D. Sadler. 2019. "New Directions in Socioscientific Issues Research." *Disciplinary and Interdisciplinary Science Education Research* 1: 1–9.

8 Supporting Children's Creative Storytelling across Media Formats

Francis Quek, Niloofar Zarei, and Sharon Lynn Chu

In this chapter, Francis Quek, Niloofar Zarei, and Sharon Lynn Chu start from a different epistemological perspective, arguing that the cognitive process of story-telling is itself a form of transmedia because it engages perception, language, and expression. Working from these fundamentals in the frame of learning science, the authors share the results of a series of experiments in imaginative storytelling with elementary-school students. Children have rich imaginative capacities to envision stories and characters, and in these activities, they oscillated among different forms of enactment, discussion, and revision together. The research explored several conditions, including the media of writing, screen animation, and puppetry to create or inscribe imagined narratives in the world. While participants in the writing process seemed to step through clearly defined stages of ideation, composition, and revision, those in the others moved more fluidly between the different stages. Echoing other contributions to this volume, such as those by Jennifer Pali-lonis and Yomi Ayeni, the authors found that the unique affordances and contextual details of the media involved play a crucial role in how children tell stories. Their efforts to empirically measure this kind of transmedia imagination also resonate with Caitlin Burns's and Camillia Matuk's efforts in chapters 2 and 7, respectively, to observe and "count" transmedia storytelling according to metrics that are accessible and comparable beyond the contexts of their original sites and media. At the heart of this chapter is the question of how transmedia functions as a form of collaborative imagination. Scientific measurement can offer some insights into the detailed mechanics and taxonomies of action, using approaches like discourse analysis and gestural observation. But the chapter also touches on a kind of alchemy, the "magic" in imagination that Dilman Dila and Ioana Mis-chie talk about in different storytelling contexts (chapters 4 and 16, respectively), and that builds STEM connections and insights in Ruth Wylie et al.'s discussion (chapter 12). This line of argument underscores the power of storytelling as a fundamental cognitive capacity, a sort of universal metalanguage akin to the way that Dila talks about storytelling from cultures of orality to the hypernetworked communities of the digital age. That capacity also unites diverse audiences in many contexts, and Quek, Zarei, and Chu's work here illuminates one of the core themes of this volume as a whole: they offer a glimpse of the building blocks

of transmedia practice, and collaborative imagination, that now infuse so many
aspects of contemporary culture.

> When I was sick and lay a-bed,
> I had two pillows at my head,
> And all my toys beside me lay,
> To keep me happy all the day.
>
> And sometimes for an hour or so
> I watched my leaden soldiers go,
> With different uniforms and drills,
> Among the bedclothes, through the hills;
>
> And sometimes sent my ships in fleets
> All up and down among the sheets;
> Or brought my trees and houses out,
> And planted cities all about.
>
> I was the giant great and still
> That sits upon the pillow-hill,
> And sees before him, dale and plain,
> The pleasant land of counterpane.
>
> —Robert Louis Stevenson, "The Land of Counterpane"

Language and expressive writing are foundational skills that underlie the entirety of human learning and education. The development of these skills is critical in elementary education in the crucial developmental period from grades 3 to 5, when children undergo tremendous cognitive, social, and emotional changes. The education system recognizes these changes, for example, by having instruction typically done with physical manipulatives (e.g., base-10 blocks, tangrams, color tiles) in mathematics up to grade 3, after which children are expected to transition to symbolic abstractions in grade 4 gradually (Gajdamaschko, 2005). In language arts, children are required to transition from "learning to write" to "writing to learn" in the third grade. This poses a challenge for many children, as the ship of their nascent imagination is often dashed against the shoals of their inability to form or express their ideas adequately. Left unaddressed, this situation worsens as children progress to higher grades, to the point that according to the report of the National Assessment of Educational Progress, only 24 percent of students achieve a "proficient" writing level in grade 8 (National Center for Education Statistics, 2012; Valkenburg and Beentjes, 1997). Since early intervention is more effective than later remediation, there is an urgent need to support children's writing and language development in the grade 3–5 period.

Writing is not a disembodied process of symbol assembly. Good writing and storytelling evoke the embodied imagination of the reader or listener by invoking lived experiences and understanding. Hence, to write well, authors call upon their own embodied lived experiences in their imagination and communicate these in ways that their readers will connect with and understand. The process may be construed as that of transcribing the analogic imagination into language-based form in the written medium. For children in the eight-year to eleven-year age range, this transformation is particularly challenging. We describe a body of work examining how children may be supported to transform embodied imagination into various expressive media forms including animations, video, vocal storytelling, and writing.

Writing involves the use of language to express ideas. It may be divided into three parts: (1) having something to write about, (2) having knowledge of formal language mechanics (e.g., grammar, sentence formation, vocabulary), and (3) having the skill to translate this content into formal language. In a sense, all writing is "transmedia"—encoding into symbolic writing that begins with analogic imagination. This chapter explores how children may be supported to navigate this transmediation through an explicitly embodied approach, moving from imagination to embodied enactment, to externalized visual presentation, and finally to written expression. The various research studies described in this chapter focus on all the steps of this progression. First, we look at how children externalize their imagination into visual media. Next, we investigate the physical means that may support more creative visual externalizations. And finally, we look at the process of transmedia writing, where children watch the visual media that they created and write their stories.

The Conundrum of Imagination: Bridging Imagination through Visual Media

An elementary school teacher in one of our studies describes the challenge and frustration of teaching children to write: "When [students] edit sentences they do fine. But ask them to do something, create something on their own, and they're like uh . . . uh . . . I don't know where to start." This seems strange in the light of children's imaginative play. Children evidence no paucity of imagination in pretend play (Russ and Wallace, 2013), as illustrated by the Robert Louis Stevenson poem with which we opened this chapter.

In this chapter, we present a strategy for bridging the gap between the rich imagination of children and the expression of that imagination through media transformation. Writing is an involved process that incorporates at least four basic stages: planning or prewriting, drafting (writing), revising (redrafting), and editing (Seow, 2002). Prewriting is one of the most important stages of writing, wherein thoughts are stimulated for getting started (Seow, 2002), and during which the author makes ideas "writing-ready" (Nicolopoulou, 2008) by, for example, evaluating story topics, constructing chains of events or logic, adding details that support the topic, addressing narrative order, thematic centering, causal links (Meyer, 1995), and other actions. A writing-ready form commonly used by experienced writers is the inveterate outline. Advancing children's language abilities to be writing-ready requires specific pedagogical processes. Yore, Bisanz, and Hand (2003) note that "Writing is . . . a learning tool that involves students in far more than a mere demonstration of knowledge. Rather, the act of writing . . . is seen as a process of constructing understanding and building knowledge: the minds-on complement to hands-on inquiries." In science, "hands-on inquiries" are often used to help children transform knowledge from theory into a usable form (Blumenfeld et al., 1991, 712).

A typical strategy is to separate the question of "what to write" from "how to write," as illustrated in figure 8.1. The jumble of things that the writer wants to say (A) is first organized into an intermediate "writing-ready form" (C) that the writer encodes into prose (B). For adult writers, (C) often takes the form of the outline. This exemplifies theories of distributed cognition (Hollan, Hutchins, and Kirsh, 2000), whereby human cognition relies tremendously upon external representations to anchor and catalyze thoughts and ideas (Kirsh, 2013). Developmentally, children aged eight to eleven are just transitioning from more concrete modes of thinking to the abstract (Adey and Shayer, 1990; Piaget, 1973). Although there is some variation in the age of this development, the progression toward a greater capacity for abstraction is broadly recognized in education (Adey and Shayer, 1990). Hence, it is illogical to expect children to employ abstract outlines to organize their stories, to then present in a more concrete

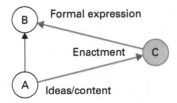

Figure 8.1
Writing-ready forms.

expressive form. To address this, teachers use tools like graphic organizers (Meyer, 1995) and story maps (Reutzel, 1985) to help children with narrative structure and organizing abstract ideas. However, to our knowledge, tools that help children to transform imagination into a writing-ready form are lacking.

In our transmediation approach, children engage their powerful capacity for imaginative pretend play with their bodies (Goldman, 1998) to act out or enact their ideas. This enacted imagination is captured through technology and transformed into cartoon videos, which then serve as external representations or writing-ready forms to help the children in their writing. This approach is illustrated in figure 8.2. Given children's interest in media (Ofcom, 2012), they are motivated to not only actualize their ideas but also to iteratively review their animated cartoon snippets. Essentially, the children take the initiative to review, edit, and refine their ideas in the prewriting phase. Such iterative refinement is rather uncommon without teacher intervention in the typical writing process at school.

We seek to bridge the chasm that separates ideas and the writing activity through enactment and feedback. The source of ideas may be the product of fantasy, or it could be grounded in some form of knowledge that may be acquired through instruction and learning. In a writing assignment for social studies, for example, this may be information about a period of history. Such "factual" writing requires the student to deconstruct the information from the source material and reconstruct it to tell the story in a cogent and meaningful way. In a word, the approach engages children to *reimagine* what they are writing, not to simply regurgitate facts.

In this chapter, we begin by summarizing a body of research on narrative creation and expression of third-to-fifth-grade children. Then, we present a series of innovations and studies by which we enable children to

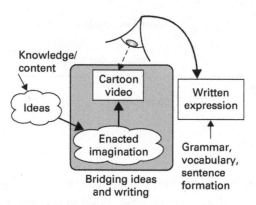

Figure 8.2
Bridging imagination through media transformations.

materialize imagination into intermediate media forms and engage in this transmediation process.

Enacting in Media Storytelling: Screen Animations and Puppets

Beyond the obvious form of the story produced (e.g., movie or book), the medium in which one creates exerts powerful influences on the process of storytelling. For example, Cochran-Smith's (1991) studies performed during the popularization of personal computers show that children exhibit evidence of "speculative thought," the tendency toward "impermanent writing," and the positive effect of "discouraging premature closure of divergent ideas" during the writing process when typing into a word processor as opposed to writing with pen and paper (111). Mayer (2001) argues that using both visual and verbal channels through multimedia in learning improves our creative problem-solving abilities.

The Medium for the Message: Enacting in Animations
Externalizing and expressing imaginative stories is a transmedia activity for children. Here, we consider imagination as the first medium and ask the question: How do differences in the second medium—the output medium of authoring—affect a child's process of storytelling? To answer this, we conducted a study looking at how children construct stories using a piece of simple animation software that allows them to enact their stories on a

computer screen (Chu, Quek, and Lin, 2011). We used the commercially available software Frames, from Tech4Learning, which allows children to select graphical story elements (e.g., a dog), insert them into a story screen, and move them on the screen with a mouse. Objects can either be obtained from a library or created using drawing tools. They can be manipulated through dragging, rotating, flipping, or resizing. Stories can be organized as a series of still frames (like a storyboard with sound). Authors can specify the duration that each frame stays active when the animation is played, so they can create the illusion of motion by varying the placement of objects in consecutive frames. The child can provide voice-overs or voice enactments that are co-temporally recorded with the story animation. Recorded media segments comprising screen animations with the voice-over can be played back immediately after they are created. We compared children recruited in an after-school program in two conditions: one group constructed their stories in an animated fashion, while a second group constructed their stories by typing into "storybook pages" (Microsoft PowerPoint slides configured to look like pages in a storybook; see figure 8.3). Our goal was to investigate the effect of an externalization medium on children's processes of story creation and planning.

The Study

Eight children in third or fourth grade took part in the main study. The bulk of the study consisted of asking the children to create stories using

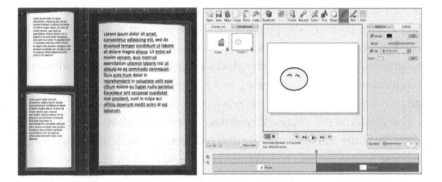

Figure 8.3
Screenshots of PowerPoint slides created with a storybook template (left) and Frames animation software (right).

the two media: animated stories created using Frames and textual stories created using PowerPoint, presented as a set of storybook slide templates (figure 8.3).

After each session, the participants took part in a postactivity interview where they were asked to retell the story they created in that session. The study was carried out within-subject in two counterbalanced sessions over two days to prevent the children from becoming fatigued by creating two stories in one session. To enable us to study the creative process, they worked in random groups of two or three, as social interaction motivates the externalization of thoughts into speech. In the first session, two pairs of participants created animated stories and two pairs produced PowerPoint storybooks. In the second session, two of the participants were not able to take part in the study, resulting in two groups with three children in each. One group used Frames and the other used PowerPoint. Each group worked on a separate computer and had a voice recorder positioned to capture the conversation during the story creation process. This procedure resulted in a total of six stories: three animations and three storybooks.

The children were given story starters and were asked to complete the stories. We wrote two story starters that satisfied three criteria: they were appropriate for the developmental age of the children in terms of language and content, they were not close to experiences that only some of the children might have gone through before, and they were more action-oriented than emotionally driven. The starters had similar themes and were both around half a page in length, with standard formatting. The first related the story of living soap bars that have been placed in the cupboard by a family. One day, the protagonist, a blue soap bar, decides to leave the cupboard to see the outside world. His cousin, a green soap bar, wants to accompany him. The starter introduces a set of living red, blue, yellow, and green colored pencils that belong to a girl named Amy. They live in a box on Amy's desk. One day, they decide to visit the outside world.

We analyzed the process of creation in both media by doing a careful analysis of the discourse among the collaborative student teams using a purpose coding approach (Nakatani et al., 1995), which groups individual utterances in the discourse into chains of references. The chains can be at the object level (talking about a subject), at the meta level (talking about the talk or managing the discussion flow), and at the para level (referencing objects and persons that are physically present). Meta- and para-level chains are particularly useful to determine turning points in the children's discussions. The coding was conducted by four coders, who were each first allotted a transcript to analyze according to the purpose hierarchy coding scheme. Then they conferred and resolved any serious discrepancies in their understandings of the discourse. We found that an object code in our case could refer either to talk about the "story" or the "tool." The transcripts were then redistributed among the coders and coded again with new understandings of the coding scheme.

Next, using Guilford's classical theory of creativity (Guilford, 1950; 1967), we characterized utterances that contribute to the story construction process as being divergent or convergent. In our coding process, propositions of story ideas that depart from previously presented material, either in the story starter or by other group members, were classified as divergent. Convergent thinking involves the application of critical processes by which one evaluates sets of ideas (possibly, generated by divergent processes) to arrive at a solution, possibly "the correct one" (Runco, 2003, 432). We coded discourse contributions that propose story ideas that draw from, build on, and/or follow what was presented before by the starter or another child as being convergent. We also coded a third element that we labeled "seeding." The emergence of a story idea was categorized as seeding when it consisted of a proposition that did not draw from what has been presented before in any form. All such ideas that were suggested were classified as seed ideas, whether or not they made it into the final story. We did not assess the originality (a form of idea divergence) of the story ideas during the coding process. A convergent idea is one that helps to tie the story together. Convergent ideas could be as original, and sometimes even more original, than a divergent idea—but if the idea drew from material presented previously, it was still coded as convergent. The coding was done mainly in terms of how an idea shaped, directed, or influenced the path of the creation of the final story product.

The Findings

The most significant finding of this study is that children in the two conditions engaged in markedly different processes in their story creation. In the written story sessions, children employed what can be characterized as a more formal, four-stage process: generating ideas, encoding into the tool, working on aesthetics, and correcting language (see figure 8.4). The idea generation

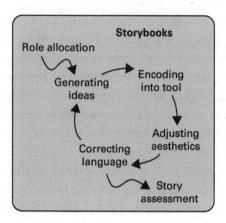

Figure 8.4
Creative process for storybooks.

stage saw greater argumentation that framed the storyline. This was followed by the encoding process, where the story was typed into the PowerPoint story-book. Adjusting aesthetics was basically a formatting exercise. The children then reviewed their writing, sometimes by reading it aloud, as they corrected grammatical and spelling errors at the end of the process.

In creating the animated stories, children employed a far more fluid process. Unlike the generally linear staging in the PowerPoint story creation, the process took the form of smaller iterative cycles of generating ideas, previewing the story, assessing the story, and fixing and adjusting the final product (see figure 8.5). Idea generation and encoding became less distin-guishable as the children used the tool to help formulate their ideas. In this stage, the children were more inclined to openly state what they were thinking of doing. Previewing was more tightly related to idea generation, providing instantaneous feedback for new ideas to be added. Assessment and fixing (using tool functions such as undo, timing, placement) were tightly blended with previewing.

Next, we sum up five main themes that distinguished animated-media authoring from the common writing process:

1. *Microactivities:* The story is told using microactivities of creating differ-ent elements (e.g., sounds and objects). Even as the pieces of the story were created in a seemingly piecemeal fashion, the children were able to keep a coherent storyline. They were able to articulate the overall story plan when

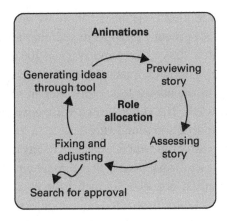

Figure 8.5
Creative process for animations.

asked and even without prompting. For example, one of the children said, "on this one [referring to a frame] he needs to say 'Bye,'" showing that she already had a picture of the story development in mind while creating the previous frame. Such short evaluation-editing loops also created more opportunities to maintain consensus throughout the creation process and constitute microunits of negotiation among team members that shape the narrative that the children are creating collaboratively.

2. *Activity-driven integrated story generation:* Story creation occurred in terms of specification of actions within the interface and without. Children responded to the multiple cues and modes of stimuli enabled by the Frames animation tool to make sense of the story, for instance, through the *placement of elements*, the *choice of objects* to include, and *voice enactments*. By placing and moving objects in the setup of each story frame, the children molded the development of the story. For example, to show that the main character is leaving his family behind to go on his adventure, a child verbalized: "That guy needs to be way up. Those guys need to be right there." Action-based story creation was often accompanied by extensive gesturing and pointing at the screen. Space and time became a kind of "medium" where the children's imagination was materialized. The children were more exploratory about story possibilities provided by the software and often chose objects for their stories by browsing the software's object library. While it may be argued that the provision of ready-made "sources of ideas"

in the library serves to limit users' imagination, we saw how the children used the selections as epistemic prompts to scaffold individual and group creative activity (Eales, 2005; Jacucci and Wagner, 2007). The processes of browsing and object selection became points of creative negotiation. One group found a dog in the library, leading to a dog in the story saving the green crayon after it fell. The children used voice enactments extensively to create character speech and sound effects. This, in itself, is unsurprising since it is difficult to carry the symbolic element of any narrative arc in animation alone. What was remarkable is that throughout the story creation process, the children did not seem to discuss the overall arc of the story verbally. In many instances across the animation sessions, the children communicated story development through the process of creating sounds: determining what to record, practicing the speech or sound effect to be recorded, recording the sound, and deciding where to place the sound. The animation storytellers seem to be thinking collectively through the tool.

3. *Qualitative focus:* The animation storytellers devoted much focus to precise, qualitative details through the shaping of aesthetics (e.g., color, speed, size, and thickness). For instance, children discussed whether a book in the story should be rectangular or square, worked to determine a book's size and color, and conversed about which breed of dog should appear. One group recorded a line of character dialogue four times to get it right in terms of volume, clarity, speed, and other characteristics. While such attention to detail took a significant proportion of the time, we noted that this time was spent adding texture to the story. In the written storybook case, aesthetic considerations like selecting font size and paragraph settings consumed an equivalent amount of time without adding to the narrative.

4. *Broader imagination:* Engaging in the animated story creation appeared to deepen the encoding of the story, leading to better retention and broader imagination beyond the bounds of the story product. In the interviews conducted after the sessions, there was a significant difference in the fidelity with which the children who completed storybooks could retell their story, as compared to those who completed animations. For animated stories, the children could retell their story with an accuracy of 63.3 percent (based on the number of propositions covered in the retelling over the total number of propositions in the "narrative digest" of the story), whereas in the case of the written stories, they did so with an accuracy of only 41.8 percent. In fact, two of the children could not remember any of the propositions at all

when asked to recount their storybook stories, while two others recounted their animation stories with full coverage of all the propositions.

5. *Serendipitous creativity:* The activity-based nature of the animation creation process led to idea generation by accident at various times, a strategy that was not present in the storybook authoring. This finding was also observed by Eales (2005) in a study of the ad hoc creative process of a professional artist using digital software to produce her works of art. In the creative process of the artist, the computer "often introduces unexpected or accidental effects and elements, generally helping to create the compositional problem" (11). While one group was trying to draw a cupboard in the Frames software, they accidentally created a brown shape, which they then imagined to be a shelf instead. The following conversation among two group members demonstrates this serendipitous creativity:

A: Oh . . . how did that happen?

B: Ooh, that's good, actually

A: That's good, yea . . . it's like a shelf

B: Shadow. The shelf on it.

A: Yea we've got a shadow with the shelf. We can move the suitcase up there so he can be reaching down there . . .

Figure 8.6 shows the proportion of the types of utterances that we found in our discourse analysis. We found that more seeding (by 22.13 percent) occurred in the storybook sessions, indicating that somewhat more ideas were put forward during the creation of the storybooks. However, the degree of both divergence and convergence of ideas was greater in the animated story condition (by 14.8 percent and 7.32 percent, respectively). These results may be explained by the five themes described here. For example, low seeding may have been caused by constraints imposed by the software, such as the search for objects in the library. On the other hand, the activity-driven property of the creative process may have encouraged greater divergence and convergence by providing more discussion and decision points.

Hennessey (2007) describes motivation as one of the key factors in creative behavior that needs attention. Amabile's principle of internal motivation for creativity (1982) states that internal motivation (e.g., satisfaction or interest) leads to the creative process, but external stimuli such as expectations and the offering of rewards hinder it. We thus need to look at children's reactions to the use of animation for creative activity.

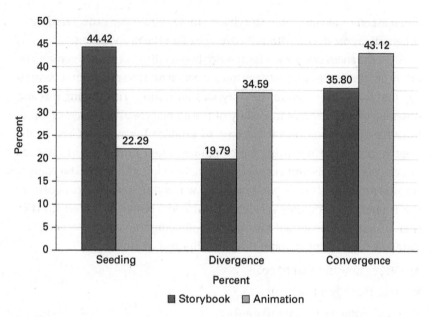

Figure 8.6
Seeding, divergence, and convergence by medium.

A number of observations provide support for us to posit that story authoring using animation was more motivating for the children. The storybook sessions, which lasted on average twenty-eight minutes (153 speaker turns), were much shorter than the animation sessions, which lasted an average of forty-eight minutes (417 speaker turns). The children became bored and restless quickly when making the storybooks, as we observed, and as illustrated by the following extract from one of the group's conversations: "That's all we have to do. We just have to write a middle and an end. Hurry, let's write the story so we can get outside." Conversely, children in the animation sessions showed excitement and enthusiasm: gesturing, acting out, and expressing eagerness to present their story to others. Two children, in fact, explicitly remarked to their group during the sessions:

A: This is fun

B: I know

And later:

A: [B's NAME], isn't this fun?

B: Yea . . .

The groups creating animated stories wanted to keep going even when they were being picked up at the end of their after-school period. Several students requested that the researchers return another day to let them finish their stories. Engagement in the creative process is a key component of the writing process. The progression from enactment to being able to retell the story is a necessary first step to children's successful writing. The results presented here demonstrate that the animated medium has a strong potential to support children in cross-media narrative creation and writing.

Enacting through Instrumented Puppets

In a second study, we investigated creating media through video-edited recordings of instrumented puppet enactments (Chu et al. 2015). The study took the form of storytelling workshops where children, working in pairs, would plan a story, make a set of "lighted characters," and perform the stories in a Maker Theater (see figure 8.7).

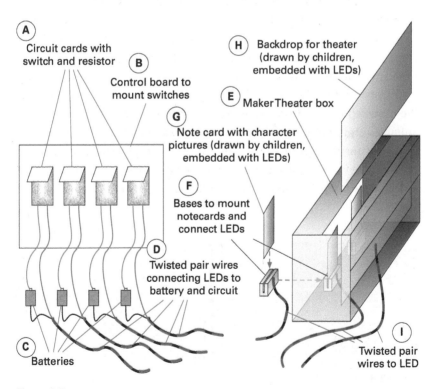

Figure 8.7
Maker Theater setup.

Using basic electronics comprising paper switches (A), batteries (C), wires, and light-emitting diodes (LEDs) (I), the children made paper-card puppets that were inserted into cardholders (F), which could be manipulated in a Maker Theater Box (E) using sticks attached to the cardholders. In essence, the children were making stick puppets. LEDs controlled by four switches on a control board (B) would control the LEDs that can be embedded either in the backdrop (H) of the Maker Theater or in the paper-card characters (G). As with the animated storytelling discussed earlier in this chapter, the children voice-enacted their characters or narrated their stories by recording their voices as the story was being performed. Examples of scenes from two Maker Theater stories are shown in figure 8.8. The children were free to decide what their LEDs signified in their stories.

We conducted a series of three Maker workshop studies with children aged eight to eleven who were free to construct any story they wished and create their own characters. The children were first shown how to construct simple LED circuits with the paper switches and introduced to the Maker Theater. Then they were organized into groups of two or three to discuss how they would use the electronics and the Maker Theater to construct a story that would be recorded and edited into videos. One child would manipulate the stick puppets, another child would operate the control board, and all the children in the group would provide voice enactments. We observed many of the same features that we saw in the screen-based animated storytelling described before. For example, the children engaged in microconstruction of the stories and iterative previewing and refinement. There was significant attention to detail, which added to the texture of the videos. The children exhibited strong motivation in creating their stories.

Figure 8.8
Screenshots of puppet-story videos.

A key question we asked is: were the children able to incorporate the technology into their stories in meaningful ways? After all, participants were encountering electronics for the first time, and there was the added difficulty of creating the electronic apparatuses while constructing the stories. We analyzed the stories constructed, along with video and audio recordings of the process of collaborative story construction. The children employed the LEDs and electronics creatively in four ways:

1. As a symbol standing for something else (e.g., a laser weapon blast for a superhero character; or in conjunction with speech to show which character was talking with the voice-over; or to show that a character is thinking; or to accompany actions like walking, signaling a character's affective state, like being hungry or tired)
2. As an instrument of focus (e.g., to represent a spotlight in a beauty pageant story, or to draw attention to something happening in the theater)
3. As a means of imparting structure (e.g., to flag beginnings of events like a race, to signal a scene change, or to mark the climax of a story)
4. As qualifiers (e.g., to show that the tiara of the beauty pageant contestant is shiny)

The studies show how children are able to appropriate novel physical electronics-embedded media to generate meaningful video story outputs through enactment using their hands. This illustrates how the translation of imagination through enactment can take a broad range of forms and become evident in multiple types of media, from the in-screen animations of our first study to instrumented puppetry. The common thread is that media forms that engage embodied expression support children's construction of stories, possibly as a waypoint on the path from idea to written expression.

Enacting with Bodies

In the previous section, we looked at how children use various mediums and physical means to create stories. Our studies demonstrate that children use different mediums in different ways when creating stories, and that the creation process varies based on the medium in which the story is crafted. We also found that children can use specific affordances of mediums meaningfully, even if the medium is new and previously unfamiliar to them—for example, using LEDs in story creation. Physical media allow children to externalize story ideas. In this section, we focus on body-based play and how children use play to bridge imagination with expression. We are interested in how imagination becomes a medium and how this medium allows for further imagination through the creative process.

Children's imaginative play occurs very naturally: children use their bodies as actors in pretend enactments, in a sense moving from the third person–dominant perspective of digital and puppet enactments into a first person–dominant perspective. In this section, we will describe a series of explorations to understand how such enactive storytelling may support expression in digital media, and ultimately in written form. Children seldom engage in pretend play with their bodies alone, in the abstract. Pretend play is almost always engaged using external accoutrements such as props or toys (Pulaski, 1973). In a series of studies, we explored how various types of props, backgrounds, and character representations influence children's story writing. In addition, we studied the kinds of structural supports that children need to externalize their imagined worlds through various media transformations to written media.

The Toys of Our Imagination

Playthings are seldom real things. Safety and practical considerations are obviously of concern in the construction and selection of toys. However, the use of props and proxies may serve a more fundamental (and possibly developmental) purpose in pretend play. Vygotsky describes the role of "object substitution" in play as serving an important purpose of separating the object (the toy or prop) from its real purpose or function and transferring it to another (the real object that is imagined) (Vygotsky, 1978; see also Gajdamaschko, 2005; Moran and John-Steiner, 2003). Pederson, Rook-Green, and Elder (1981) emphasize that objects can support a child's imagination by helping the child to move "from action in response to objects present in the perceptual field to action generated and controlled by ideas" (759).

How might physical objects support imagination? What form should these objects take? McLoyd (1983) investigated the effects of play objects of different structures on the pretend play of children aged 3.5 and 5 years. High-structure objects consisted of a miniature version of objects, the "identity and functions of which most preschoolers are aware" (e.g., dolls and trucks). Low-structure objects were "less specific and unique" objects, at least for preschoolers (e.g., boxes and pipes) (627). His results showed that high-structure objects generated more pretend play themes. For older children, however, Pulaski (1973) found that unstructured toys like Play-Doh and crayons encourage more imaginative play than structured toys like Barbie dolls.

How might toys be brought into the loop of story creation in media? More significant to the focus of this volume, what kinds of physical objects may support not just play, but also the construction of a stable storyworld that may be expressed in various media forms? In previous studies (Chu and Quek, 2013b; Chu et al., 2013), we explored the effectiveness of various types of external objects or props to support the externalization of imagination. Children were given a story framework and asked to enact and then narrate the story episodes that were left out. Three kinds of props were available to the children to represent an object that they imagined holding. We called these cultural, generic, and arbitrary props (see figure 8.9). Cultural props looked exactly like the objects that they were imagining (e.g., a fully formed pickax toy to represent a pickax object in the imagined story). Physical or generic objects resemble the imagined object in general shape (e.g., a T-shaped object to represent a pickax). Arbitrary objects are nondescript objects that the child holds (e.g., a short Nintendo Wii controller that can represent anything from a pickax to a battle flag). In all cases, the child would engage in the enactment in front of a big-screen TV that displayed a graphical rendering that closely resembled the cultural prop. As the child enacted with each prop, the movement of the prop was tracked, and the graphical object was rendered on the screen as though it was wielded by a phantom hand.

Twelve children (eleven aged nine years, one aged ten years) were recruited for a study in which a story was read aloud to them. The story was divided

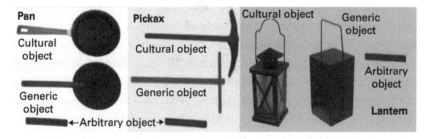

Figure 8.9
Object types used in the enactments.

into episodes; each episode took five to seven minutes to read aloud. The story follows the adventure of three dwarfs in a high-fantasy setting who encounter a series of challenges while traversing a network of caves. During each episode, the story was paused, and the children enacted the story segments that addressed the challenges presented. These enactments were open-ended so the children could engage their imagination for the particular scene. The only constraint was that the children had to solve the problem presented in the scene using a tool (a frying pan, a lantern, or a pickax). The children were given one of three props (cultural, generic, or arbitrary) to represent the tool that they would use in each segment. The challenge segment may begin with the prompt: "[Dwarf's name] is frying/digging up/swinging the [target object]. Can you act out how he/she is using the frying pan/pickax/lantern?" In all, each child would enact nine story episodes with the props (three graphical objects [pan, pickax, lantern], multiplied by three prop conditions). While the children were told to act out the prompt presented, they were free to interpret the prompt in whatever way that they saw fit.

We were particularly interested in studying imagination in the process of its evocation when using the objects in enactment. We measured and analyzed imagination using the Methodology for Assessing Imagination in Action (MAIA), as detailed in Chu and Quek (2013a). MAIA measures "broader imagination," defined as including "any form of extension and association made beyond (visual, auditory, tangible, etc.) materials that had been presented to the child for the task at hand." MAIA specifies that qualitative data from various sources, including story enactments, scene drawings, and oral recall interviews, should be triangulated to identify common elements. So, for example, if an element (e.g., a mushroom in a frying pan) is present across all three data sources (enactments, scene drawings, and oral recall interviews) conveying the same story scene, then it is assumed that that element is a stable component of the child's imagination of that story scene. To analyze the video enactments, we first create a repertoire of the Micro Actions (MAs) in the enactment. These are defined as individual minimal action units (e.g., a single downward swing of the pickax, a flip of the frying pan, or an upward glance). Next, we identify a repertoire of vignettes composed of sequences of MAs. These are defined as the repeated sequences of MAs performed by the child. For example, one child swung the pickax downward several times, then swept it sideways, followed by doing a picking action with her other hand. This sequence, repeated several times, was identified as a vignette: she was imagining breaking rocks loose, clearing the debris, and picking up diamonds from the loosened rock pile. More complex vignettes indicate more elaborate physical imaginations. In addition to the MA and vignette coding, we asked the children to draw pictures depicting the scenes that they enacted, and we elicited oral retellings of the story scenes. These enable us to assess the consistency of the imagination. The detail of the story, quantity and quality of elaboration, and consistency across depictions are consolidated to produce a Broader Imagination score.

When we compared the complexity of the embodied vignettes in the three prop specificity conditions (cultural (C), generic (G), or arbitrary (A)), we found that the generic object provides the best support for imagination expression based on the broader imagination scores. This finding has important implications for designing toys that are intended for transmedia expression. While the majority of toys that are available commercially fall into the category of cultural toys, our results suggest that such toys may contribute to a kind of functional fixedness that limits imagination. For example, a child with a fully expressed *Star Wars* lightsaber, complete with lights and lightsaber sounds, may be hard-pressed to imagine it as a pirate's sword or a walking stick.

Backgrounds and Avatars

We continue our systematic exploration of media formation through the body by looking at how this body is embedded in the imagination/media and how it appears. The story environment can provide the context for the enactive imagination, acting as a support for the child in the imaginative process to feel a presence in the storyworld and prompting them with details that they can include in their story. Another important property of digital enactment is the representation of the characters in the story environment—or the *avatars*. In the sections that follow, we summarize our research on these aspects of the storytelling environment and examine how various designs may contribute to stronger story outcomes, higher engagement for children, and an enhanced overall story creation experience.

Enactment Context

Enactive imagination takes place within a context. As children engage in pretend play, they create an imaginary world where the story occurs. Digital media can be designed to afford a sense of embodied presence in children, making them great tools to support imaginative storytelling. To explore this space, we studied how the presence of a graphical backdrop in the enacted scene may affect the story creation process for children, the quality of the imagination, and the resulting transmediated story (Chu and Quek, 2014). We ran a study in the form of a storytelling workshop session for six children in the age range of eight-to-ten years. Each child created and enacted two stories: one with a digital context-relevant background displayed, and one with a blank background.

We found that digital contextual structures like backgrounds can have an engaging effect on children, resulting in them having an easier time getting started and staying on track during the storytelling task. Despite this positive effect, we also found that the stories in the blank background condition had more structure and more elaborate storylines. Kirsh's concept of "mental projection" (2009, 2312) furnishes a possible explanation for this observation. He theorizes that external representations and physical structures can support and catalyze the thinking process. For example, imagining a game of chess while looking at an empty chessboard is easier than trying to do so without the external anchoring of the empty chessboard. However, there is also a cost associated with keeping these external representations in memory. Therefore, using external projection makes sense only if this extra cognitive resource expenditure can be allocated. In the case of our study, it might be that projecting mental imagery onto the background incurs a cost to the children to deconstruct these elements, which prevents them from creating a more complex story arc. This is not the issue in the blank background condition, where the child is able to freely draw upon memory and knowledge to create the narrative they desire.

Avatars and Self-Representation

Another aspect of enactment-driven media is how the presentation of the children's avatar may affect the imagination encoding/externalization process. Previous work has shown that avatars can have a significant effect on how the users perceive virtual environments, thus affecting their performance in the virtual environment. Yee and Bailenson (2007) introduce the *Proteus effect*, which describes how avatars can induce a self-transformation in the users, through which they may behave more confidently as their virtual selves than in the real world. In the context of creative applications, the body of previous work is more limited. Nonetheless, there are research works showing a similar pattern to the Proteus effect in creative environments, where embodying creative avatars, such as that of famous artists or scientists, results in a higher level of creativity in the user's performance (Guegan et al., 2016). Another thread of work investigates the effect of avatar similarity on users' performance. Bailey, Wise, and Bolls (2009) show that similarity between the appearance of a user and their avatar can result in users being more engaged in the activity presented, fostering a sense of self-identification with the character and an embodied presence in the virtual environment. There has been less work in the context of virtual environments focused on nurturing creative performance, rather than goal-based outcomes such as games. Given the extensive body of work on the significance and impact of avatars in multimedia environments, an important question is raised on whether we can support children's story creation process across various media through appropriate avatar design.

We investigated the role of avatar design in transmedia story authoring for children (Russ and Wallace, 2013). Specifically, we investigated whether an avatar representing a character in the story would support the child's imagination more effectively in the story enactment, as well as improving their performance when writing their enacted story. We developed a story creation tool where children could create stories by creating story scenes and adding details (e.g., title, background, character, and object) to each scene. They could then use the software to record a video for each scene, enacting the story in that scene while using a prop representing a physical object in the narrative. Once all the scenes in the story were recorded, they could play their whole story and watch its playback like a movie. We designed the software to afford two types of avatars: The story-relevant avatar, resembling the story character (in the case of our study, the story character is a cowboy/cowgirl), and the self-avatar, resembling the user—a direct video stream of the user during enactment.

We conducted a two-session study where twenty children (age eight-to-twelve years, mean age 9.5 years) used our story creation system to create, enact, and write stories in both avatar conditions. Each session took approximately ninety minutes. In each session, the interface used one of the avatar conditions, and the order of the conditions was counterbalanced among the participants. The children were given a one-line story starter and asked to complete the story. Once they had recorded a complete story video using the interface, they could watch the recorded video and make revisions if desired. Next, we asked them to write their story on paper. While writing the story, they were allowed to rewatch the video if needed. This resulted in two pairs of videos and written stories per participant. However, four participants were not able to complete parts of the study protocol, so they were not included in the data analysis.

We compared their enactment videos and written stories in terms of narrative complexity, coherence, and richness. We used the MAIA framework (Chu and Quek, 2013a; see the section "The Toys of Our Imagination" in this chapter for details on the MAIA coding methodology) for coding the enactment videos. The videos were coded for action vignettes, as well as the idea digest in the spoken dialogue. The written stories were coded by the research team based on Grosz and Sidner's discourse analysis method (1986). The written stories were also scored by an elementary school teacher for expert assessment based on the Personal Narrative Rubric (Texas Education Agency, 2011).

Our results show a conundrum in avatar design for cross-media narrative authoring applications. On the one hand, the self-avatars seemed to create a higher sense of self-identification with the character, as its appearance resembled the child. This, in turn, resulted in a higher level of embodied presence in the story environment. We observed that the children were able to express themselves more freely through their bodies in the self-avatar condition and created more action vignettes and more complex actions. On the other hand, the story-relevant avatars resulted in richer written stories. Going back to David Kirsh's (2009) concept of mental projection (see the section "Enactment Context" in this chapter for details), we can posit that the projected story character in the story-relevant avatar created an externalized scaffold for the child's imagination of the story character, freeing their cognitive resources to focus on other aspects of story-writing activity, like crafting richer stories using more complex language.

There is, therefore, a clear transmedia aspect to avatar design in story enactment and authoring tools, depending on the type of media that it is designed to support. If the focus of the tool is to support the enactment activity, self-avatars might be a more suitable choice due to the higher self-identification, while for supporting more complex expressive formats such as writing, a story-relevant avatar can provide the necessary scaffold for mental projection, resulting in richer writing.

Conclusion and Next Steps

Our work on children's storytelling using multimedia tools and body-based enactment demonstrates the importance of storytelling in supporting children's self-expression and creativity. We have also investigated how several aspects of the authoring tools and enactment activity can be altered to motivate and engage children in the process of story creation. Our focus in many of these studies has been on oral storytelling and retelling as the medium in which children produce their stories. The rationale is that such oral storytelling is an important waypoint to effective writing. Furthermore, our studies show that transmedia storytelling can be a powerful tool to support children in learning. Our enactment-based approach to transmedia storytelling was shown to be an effective means of supporting children in their progress toward higher levels of abstraction in their thinking and expressive abilities.

Throughout this chapter, we have presented a series of studies investigating various aspects of children's transmedia storytelling activities. First, we demonstrated the crucial role of medium in the storytelling process. Next, we presented the framework for enactment-scaffolded writing. In this model, the transmediation process that occurs by using enactment as a writing-ready form provides a scaffold that allows children to express themselves more effectively in the subsequent written form. Finally, through various studies on modifications in the enactment setup, we demonstrated that different affordances of the enactive medium could affect the scaffolding that it provides for storytelling.

We end this chapter by discussing some possible directions for future work. In our studies, we focused mainly on supporting children in the creation of the writing-ready forms of their imagination. However, given the various characteristics of enactment and written mediums, children might not always succeed in fully transforming imagination into written stories. For instance, how should the written story be structured, as compared to the enacted story? And what other pieces should be added during the transmediation process? While every writer faces these types of questions when engaging in writing, these challenges are more significant for children. In addition to prewriting tasks, there seems to be a need for support during the process of transforming media to achieve a successful narrative creation across mediums. In classroom settings, this dynamic guidance is provided through teachers' feedback in conferencing time. How to realize this technique in the context of authoring tools is an open research question.

References

Adey, Philip, and Michael Shayer. 1990. "Accelerating the Development of Formal Thinking in Middle and High School Students." *Journal of Research in Science Teaching* 27, no. 3: 267–285.

Amabile, Teresa M. 1982. "Children's Artistic Creativity: Detrimental Effects of Competition in a Field Setting." *Personality and Social Psychology Bulletin* 8: 573–578.

Bailey, Rachel, Kevin Wise, and Paul Bolls. 2009. "How Avatar Customizability Affects Children's Arousal and Subjective Presence during Junk Food–Sponsored Online Video Games." *Cyberpsychology, Behavior, and Social Networking* 12, no. 3: 277–283.

Blumenfeld, Phyllis C., Elliot Soloway, Ronald W. Marx, Joseph S. Krajcik, Mark Guzdial, and Annemarie Palincsar. 1991. "Motivating Project-Based Learning: Sustaining the Doing, Supporting the Learning." *Educational Psychologist* 26, no. 3–4: 369–398.

Chu, Sharon Lynn, and Francis Quek. 2013a. "MAIA: A Methodology for Assessing Imagination in Action." Paper presented at the CHI 2013 Workshop on Evaluation Methods for Creativity Support Environments, Association for Computing Machinery, Paris.

Chu, Sharon Lynn, and Francis Quek. 2013b. "Things to Imagine With: Designing for the Child's Creativity." Paper presented at the Interaction Design and Children meeting, Association for Computing Machinery, New York.

Chu, Sharon Lynn, and Francis Quek. 2014. "The Effect of Visual Contextual Structures on the Child's Imagination in Story Authoring Interfaces." In *IDC '14: Interaction Design and Children 2014*, edited by Bo Stjerne Thomsen, Lars Elbæk, Ole Sejer Iversen, Panos Markopoulos, Franca Garzotto, and Christian Dindler, 329–332. New York: Association for Computing Machinery. https://doi.org/10.1145/2593968.2610484.

Chu, Sharon Lynn, Francis Quek, Luke Gusukuma, and Theresa Jean Tanenbaum. 2013. "The Effects of Physicality on the Child's Imagination." In *C&C '13: Proceedings of the 9th ACM Conference on Creativity & Cognition*, edited by Ellen Yi-Luen Do, Steven Dow, Jack Ox, Steve Smith, Kazushi Nishimoto, and Chek Tien Tan, 93–102. New York: Association for Computing Machinery. https://doi.org/10.1145/2466627.2481205.

Chu, Sharon Lynn, Francis Quek, and Lin Xiao. 2011. "Studying Medium Effects on Children's Creative Processes." In *C&C '11: Proceedings of the 8th ACM Conference on Creativity and Cognition*, edited by Ashok K. Goel, Fox Harrell, Brian Magerko, Yukari

Nagai, and Jane Prophet, 3–12. New York: Association for Computing Machinery. https://doi.org/10.1145/2069618.2069622.

Chu, Sharon Lynn, Francis Quek, Michael Saenz, Sourabh Bhangaonkar, and Osazuwa Okundaye. 2015. "Enabling Instrumental Interaction through Electronics Making: Effects on Children's Storytelling." In *8th International Conference on Interactive Digital Storytellling, ICIDS 2015*, edited by Henrik Schoenau-Fog, Luis Emilio Bruni, Sandy Louchart, and Sarune Baceviciute, 329–337. Cham, Switzerland: Springer. https://doi.org/10.1007/978-3-319-27036-4_31.

Cochran-Smith, Marilyn. 1991. "Word Processing and Writing in Elementary Classrooms: A Critical Review of Related Literature." *Review of Educational Research* 61, no. 1: 107–155.

Eales, R. T. Jim. 2005. "Creativity in Action: Some Implications for the Design of Creativity Support Systems." In *CHINZ '05: Proceedings of the 6th ACM SIGCHI New Zealand Chapter's International Conference on Computer-Human Interaction: Making CHI Natural*, edited by Beryl Plimmer, 9–14. New York: Association for Computing Machinery. https://doi.org/10.1145/1073943.1073945.

Gajdamaschko, Natalia. 2005. "Vygotsky on Imagination: Why an Understanding of the Imagination Is an Important Issue for Schoolteachers." *Teaching Education* 16, no. 1: 13–22. https://doi.org/10.1080/1047621052000341581.

Goldman, Laurence R. 1998. *Child's Play: Myth, Mimesis and Make-Believe*. New York: Routledge.

Grosz, Barbara J., and Candace L. Sidner. 1986. "Attentions, Intention, and the Structure of Discourse." *Computational Linguistics* 12, no. 3: 175–204.

Guegan, Jérôme, Stéphanie Buisine, Fabrice Mantalet, Nicolas Maranzana, and Frédéric Segonds. 2016. "Avatar-Mediated Creativity: When Embodying Inventors Makes Engineers More Creative." *Computers in Human Behavior* 61: 165–175. https://doi.org/10.1016/j.chb.2016.03.024.

Guilford, J. P. 1950. "Creativity." *American Psychologist* 5: 444–454. https://doi.org/10.1037/h0063487.

Guilford, J. P. 1967. *The Nature of Human Intelligence*. New York: McGraw-Hill.

Hennessey, Beth A. 2007. "Creativity and Motivation in the Classroom: A Social Psychological and Multi-cultural Perspective." In *Creativity: A Handbook for Teachers*, edited by Ai-Girl Tan, 27–45. Singapore: World Scientific. https://doi.org/10.1142/9789812770868_0002.

Hollan, James, Edwin Hutchins, and David Kirsh. 2000. "Distributed Cognition: Toward a New Foundation for Human-Computer Interaction Research." *ACM Transactions on Computer-Human Interaction* 7, no. 2: 174–196. https://doi.org/10.1145/353485.353487.

Jacucci, Giulio, and Ina Wagner. 2007. "Performative Roles of Materiality for Collective Creativity." In *C&C '07: Proceedings of the 6th ACM SIGCHI Conference on Creativity & Cognition*, edited by Ben Shneiderman, Gerhard Fischer, Elisa Giaccardi, and Mike Eisenberg, 73–82. New York: Association for Computing Machinery. https://doi.org/10.1145/1254960.1254971.

Kirsh, David. 2009. "Projection, Problem Space, and Anchoring." *Proceedings of the Annual Meeting of the Cognitive Science Society* 31: 2310–2315. https://escholarship.org/uc/item/51s3c9bn.

Kirsh, David. 2013. "Thinking with External Representations." In *Cognition Beyond the Brain: Computation, Interactivity, and Human Artifice*, edited by Stephen J. Cowley and Frédéric Valée-Tourangeau, 171–194. London: Springer-Verlag. https://doi.org/10.1007/978-1-4471-5125-8_10.

Mayer, Richard E. 2001. *Multimedia Learning*. Cambridge: Cambridge University Press.

McLoyd, Vonnie C. 1983. "The Effects of the Structure of Play Objects on the Pretend Play of Low-Income Preschool Children." *Child Development* 54, no. 3: 626–635. https://doi.org/10.2307/1130049.

Meyer, Diane Jean. 1995. "The Effects of Graphic Organizers on the Creative Writing of Third Grade Students." Master's dissertation, Education Resources Information Center. https://eric.ed.gov/?id=ED380803.

Moran, Seana, and Vera John-Steiner. 2003. "Creativity in the Making: Vygotsky's Contemporary Contribution to the Dialectic of Development and Creativity." In *Creativity and Development*, edited by R. Keith Sawyer, Vera John-Steiner, Seana Moran, et al., 61–90. Oxford: Oxford University Press. https://doi.org/10.1093/acprof:oso/9780195149005.001.0001.

Nakatani, Christine H., Barbara J. Grosz, David D. Ahn, and Julia Hirschberg. 1995. "Instructions for Annotating Discourse." *Harvard Computer Science Group Technical Report TR-21–95*. http://nrs.harvard.edu/urn-3:HUL.InstRepos:26506433.

National Center for Education Statistics. 2012. *The Nation's Report Card: Writing 2011*. Washington, DC: Institute of Education Sciences, US Department of Education. https://nces.ed.gov/nationsreportcard/pubs/main2011/2012470.aspx.

Nicolopoulou, Ageliki. 2008. "The Elementary Forms of Narrative Coherence in Young Children's Storytelling." *Narrative Inquiry* 18, no. 2: 299–325.

Ofcom. 2012. *Children and Parents: Media Use and Attitudes 2012*. London: Ofcom. https://www.ofcom.org.uk/research-and-data/media-literacy-research/childrens/october-2012.

Pederson, David R., Anne Rook-Green, and Joy L. Elder. 1981. "The Role of Action in the Development of Pretend Play in Young Children." *Developmental Psychology* 17, no. 6: 756–759. https://doi.org/10.1037/0012-1649.17.6.756.

Piaget, Jean. 1973. *The Language and Thought of the Child*. New York: Routledge. Originally published in 1923.

Pulaski, Mary A. 1973. "Toys and Imaginative Play." In *The Child's World of Make-Believe*, edited by Jerome L. Singer, 74–103. New York: Academic Press.

Reutzel, D. Ray. 1985. "Story Maps Improve Comprehension." *The Reading Teacher* 38, no. 4: 400–404.

Runco, Mark A. 2003. *Critical Creative Processes*. New York: Hampton Press.

Russ, Sandra W., and Claire E. Wallace. 2013. "Pretend Play and Creative Processes." *American Journal of Play* 6, no. 1: 136–148.

Seow, Anthony. 2002. "The Writing Process and Process Writing." In *Methodology in Language Teaching: An Anthology of Current Practice*, edited by Jack C. Richards and Willy A. Renandya, 315–320. https://doi.org/10.1017/CBO9780511667190.044.

State of Texas Education Agency. 2011. "Grade 4: Personal Narrative Writing Rubric." State of Texas Assessments of Academic Readiness. Texas Education Agency. https://tea.texas.gov/sites/default/files/Rubric-WritingGr04.pdf.

Valkenburg, Patti M., and Johannes W. J. Beentjes. 1997. "Children's Creative Imagination in Response to Radio and Television Stories." *Journal of Communication* 47, no. 2: 21–38. https://doi.org/10.1111/j.1460-2466.1997.tb02704.x.

Vygotsky, Lev S. 1978. *Mind in Society: The Development of Higher Psychological Processes*. Cambridge, MA: Harvard University Press.

Yee, Nick, and Jeremy Bailenson. 2007. "The Proteus Effect: The Effect of Transformed Self-Representation on Behavior." *Human Communication Research* 33, no. 3: 271–290. https://stanfordvr.com/mm/2007/yee-proteus-effect.pdf.

Yore, Larry, Gay L. Bisanz, and Brian M. Hand. 2003. "Examining the Literacy Component of Science Literacy: 25 Years of Language Arts and Science Research." *International Journal of Science Education* 25, no. 6, 689–725. https://doi.org/10.1080/09500690305018.

Transmedia Crosstalk: Camillia Matuk, Francis Quek, and Sharon Lynn Chu

Bob Beard: This is an interesting pairing, as you're both addressing questions of how youth create stories and the utility of narratives for sensemaking.

Francis Quek: If you take the perspective that all intelligence is narrative, you can put everything under the same umbrella. We take the perspective that narrative is a foundational skill in learning, for all things, and that the ability to create narratives needs to be scaffolded. We need to have something to say, and some way to say it. So, in our article, we talk about this congealing of imagination into expressive form as the start of any chain of media transformations. All these require that you somehow engage imagination as a way to deconstruct understanding, and retell these in your own way in a medium of your choice.

Camillia Matuk: That is really interesting. A question that arose in my research is how different genres of narrative—sci-fi, adventure, humor—seem to interact with certain ways of approaching science. For example, some students who imagined science with a sci-fi framework engaged with it via apocalyptic themes. Might they have done the same if they were imagining a drama, or a comedy? I'd be curious to know your perspectives, Francis and Sharon, on how domain-agnostic one can be when thinking of the range of stories a writer can imagine.

Sharon Lynn Chu: In our findings, the approach is domain-agnostic. But I agree that the imagination of the writer is not.

FQ: Of course, every imagination is concrete. That is the whole perspective of embodiment. So, our approach has to engage concrete imaginations, irrespective of field.

BB: Camillia, you talk about speculative design as a way to iterate on students' thinking, to get them out of their fixed beliefs. How do you see notions of enactment and embodiment from Francis and Sharon's research contributing to this, especially in the domain of STEM [Science, Technology, Engineering, and Mathematics]?

CM: Yes, the enactment and embodiment idea was intriguing, and the findings of their studies made me rethink the approach my team initially chose with our workshops. In particular, I was interested to see how storytelling *through* media and enactment seemed to support a more emergent approach to children's storytelling. It made me wonder how my youth participants may have differently approached their stories had we not encouraged a more standard design process, but instead given them the materials and storytelling forms right away.

Within a STEM domain, and particular with a speculative approach, I can see how using enactment and embodiment could have many affordances for helping students to work out the possible, probable, and preferable futures, since it may simulate context-bound decision-making and actions, which they can then return to and reflect upon. Perhaps this approach would be less burdensome for youth compared to just sitting and thinking of those possibilities. At the same time, I notice that youth of a certain age, especially middle school–aged, can be very self-conscious. Not everyone is eager to be in the spotlight, and would probably cringe at the idea. To put this into practice with this age group, I think there would have to be a lot of work done to make youth feel at ease with one another and with themselves.

SLC: We have seen this kind of self-awareness from older children about enactment. But that's why our approach proposes a digital enactment method where the child sees a cartoon character of themselves as they enact. That diverts the focus of attention, and children tend to be less self-aware.

FQ: As we progress in our learning, the embodied processes of imagination become more and more internalized. We think that it is all "in our head"—but even these internalized processes are grounded in embodiment.

The theory is that we *always enact*. But some of the enactment is internalized. However, external processes can always help—that is why we want to encourage learning using virtual, augmented, and mixed realities.

BB: If we're looking to stories as a tool for sensemaking and new storytelling technologies as a way to bring these enactments forward, what other domains are you excited about? Where else can you imagine these methods being applied for great impact?

SLC: In the past, we have thought about applying our approach to science learning, actually. I think that would be an exciting domain. We focused our previous work on language learning. It could be interesting to look at how these theories can be applied to other more abstract domains like math.

CM: I've seen and heard of these approaches in various domains that look really exciting and promising—for example, civics, education, or climate change. Basically, in any complex domain or context that involves social implications, this approach is promising for giving people some agency in imagining better futures, and possibly deciding on actions they may take in the present to achieve those futures.

9 Transmedia Shakespeare: Critical Approaches and an Annotated Syllabus

Lee Emrich

Lee Emrich's chapter brings a deeper historical perspective to this volume, situating transmedia as an intellectual framework that can be used effectively to read and teach literature that is centuries old. By approaching William Shakespeare as a transmedia phenomenon, a complex storyworld that engages questions of authorship, authenticity, identity, cultural performance, and the power of narrative, Emrich gives their students a valuable toolkit for working with the Bard in a world that he now shares with social media and the Marvel Cinematic Universe (MCU). Emrich is not unique in reminding us of transmedia's long history, and their approach here echoes the contributions of Paweł Frelik and Dilman Dila (chapters 3, and 4, respectively) in linking transmedia to rich, and ancient, traditions of storytelling. By framing this perspective as pedagogy and providing an annotated syllabus, Emrich also offers a set of practical starting points for prospective creators and academics to approach transmedia projects. Perhaps the most powerful move that the chapter models is how it performs its own study of transmedia performance, tagging the classroom itself as a key stage for transmedia storytelling and the orchestration of media. This move echoes the way that Maureen McHugh Yeager and Yomi Ayeni (chapters 1 and 5, respectively) reflect on how transmedia narratives enact and perform their own validity and reality to their audiences. Emrich's approach to Shakespeare also gives readers (and their students) a way to contend with the complex debates around authorial intent and meaning-making, particularly relating to diversity, equity, and justice. Emrich points to recent controversies over inclusive and diverse casting for Shakespeare plays, establishing connections to the projects that Kirsten Ostherr and Zoyander Street describe in chapters 13 and 14 of this volume, centering the needs and values of marginalized populations and considering how transmedia stories can resist othering, silencing, and exclusion. The stakes of these debates are high precisely because these stories still feel real and meaningful to so many people, so many inhabitants of the Bard's storyworld (which encompasses the character, life, and times of Shakespeare himself, of course). Like so many other chapters in this volume, Emrich's teaching approach reminds us that all stories are negotiated across platforms and media, passing through the hands, minds, and hearts of many people. As contemporary media forms multiply, questions of relevance and authenticity that have always dogged Shakespeare and his characters have grown only more urgent to study and debate.

Transmedia Shakespeare is the narrative and construction of Shakespeare's proliferation across media forms, beginning with the inception process for the plays themselves, which were never neatly contained within one medium. This chapter details how transmedia approaches both create and undo, as well as celebrate and resist, the numerous effects of Shakespeare's multimedia presence and proliferation. As I will describe here, my experiences suggest that promoting Transmedia Shakespeare in the classroom is an important avenue for addressing Ayanna Thompson's contention that Shakespeare's works are often treated as "spinach" literature, seemingly unquestionably beneficial to students and society (Thompson, 2019). Following Thompson's lead, an essential component of Shakespearean transmedia literacy practices should be the acknowledgment and inquiry into Shakespeare's deleterious operations in the promotion of White supremacy, imperialism, sexism, and other modes of domination and subordination, as well as the role that mediation plays in perpetuating or disrupting these operations. Ultimately, Transmedia Shakespeare topples the cultural monolith of Shakespeare by centralizing the disrupted and dispersed history, authorship, and reception of his works.

Transmedia Shakespeare

Shakespeare is a powerful but difficult lens through which to consider the debates within transmedia studies, particularly the never-quite-settled definition of transmedia storytelling. Henry Jenkins popularized transmedia studies with his definition of transmedia storytelling in 2003, which he defined as "a process where integral elements of a fiction get dispersed systematically across multiple delivery channels for the purpose of creating a unified and coordinated entertainment experience. Ideally, each medium makes its own unique contribution to the unfolding of the story" (Jenkins, 2010, 944). Warren, Wakefield, and Mills (2013) define transmedia as "a single experience that spans across multiple forms of media" (67). Both of these definitions acknowledge the multiplicity inherent in transmedia storytelling, even as they both maintain an attachment to singularity and control: "single experience," "systematically," "unified." Although both framings suggest that the role of solitary author—a lone figure holding all the story threads—is now dispersed among content creators, producers, corporate executives, and consumers, there remains within these definitions of transmedia storytelling a localization of control of the narrative. This singularizing drive seeks to reduce ownership of the story to a definable unit: a person, group of authors, media conglomerate, and so forth. Suggesting that narratives can be controlled allows Jenkins to argue for systematicity and intentionality in the mediation of the narrative.

But in the world of Shakespeare, systematicity and localization of control present a ghostly veneer that dissipates upon close inspection. Marie-Laure Ryan pushes back against Jenkins's "top-down approach" in defining transmedia storytelling, arguing that most instances of transmedia storytelling begin from "the bottom up" (2015, 2). Ryan argues:

> The term "transmedia storytelling" suggests that narrative content forms a unified story, which means a self-contained type of meaning that follows a temporal arc leading from an initial state to a complication and resolution . . . This is not how transmedia storytelling works. Transmedia storytelling is not a serial; it does not tell a single story, but a variety of autonomous stories, or episodes, contained in various documents. What holds these stories together is that they take place in the same storyworld. (2015, 4)

Adaptation studies and media studies in Shakespeare gesture to a worlding of Shakespeare where characters, historical contexts, the figure of "the Bard," and all their adaptions and mediations infuse each other with additional meaning. Jennifer Hulbert, Kevin J. Wetmore, Jr., and Robert L. York argue that due to the proliferation of Shakespeare in new media forms, "we no longer have 'Shakespeare' but rather 'Shakespeares'" (2006, 1). When looking at the historical record, Shakespeare's singularity as the author of the plays attributed to him, as well as the stability of the plays themselves, have never been a guarantee and are in fact still changing. Margaret Jane Kidnie's powerful work in *Shakespeare and the Problem of Adaptation* argues precisely for the lack of any stable "original" Shakespeare play: "a play, for all that it carries the rhetorical and ideological force of an enduring stability, is not an object at all, but rather a dynamic process that evolves over time in response to the needs and sensibilities of its users" (2009, 2). There is no single a priori source from which a Shakespeare play stems; a play is itself the performance of its own scattered production history and adaptation. Similarly, given the disputes about the authorship of Shakespeare's plays, the idea that there is anyone in control of Shakespeare's narratives or the narrative of Shakespeare's life is a fiction. The myth of Shakespeare is that we know who and what Shakespeare is.

More recently, Jenkins has begun to trouble the impetus of singular control by arguing that transmedia studies, fan studies, and adaptation studies teach us that the line between consumer participation and authorship is becoming more and more blurred (2017, para. 10). Katherine Rowe asks, "What can we learn about Shakespeare's works when we pay close attention to the different media in which we encounter them?" and goes on to say that "the answers to this question are as varied as the media formats through which audiences around the world have encountered those works since the late sixteenth century" (2016, 1907). The proliferation of media landscapes and Shakespeare go hand in hand, as Shakespeare's cultural authority is often relied upon to test or legitimate new forms of technological expression (Rowe, 2016, 1909).

But Shakespeare's works have always been transmedia stories—that is, they have never belonged to a single medium. They have structurally crossed media from their inception, beginning as separate, scrawled play parts, then turned into rehearsals with numerous actors, then into a performance with an audience, turned into a printed, quarto playscript, then perhaps into a pirated performance at another playhouse, then cropping up as a textually different quarto playscript, then turned into a solemn folio tome, canonized as part of an author's oeuvre. And the proliferation and transmediation has only continued. Due to this constant play and presence across media, Shakespeare is one of the ur-transmedia figures of our day. Ryan argues that "if transmedia development is to extend further, it must be dictated by some narrative necessity, rather than being treated as inherently desirable" (2015, 16). The narrative necessity of Shakespearean transmedia storytelling is to reveal that he and his works have always been and continue to be a transmedia story of multiplicitous authorship without a clearly defined single point of origin—except for this figurehead of "Shakespeare," who is, in fact, also not a stable or certain entity.

Transmedia Shakespeare in a Transmedia Classroom

The classroom is a primary site for interrogating the thorny questions surrounding Transmedia Shakespeare; classrooms themselves can be approached as transmedia productions. Paul Teske and Theresa Horstman (2012) argue that the typical lecture-based classroom is like the modern theater, in which audiences sit as receptacles for the performance of the instructor. They describe student-centered learning as a way of altering teacher performance in the classroom to share agency—a breaking of the proverbial fourth wall. They argue that "transmedia storytelling as a dynamic content method . . . entail[ing] adaptations or extensions of stories that add new dimensions to plot, characters, and themes" is another way of ensuring greater student/audience participation (Teske and Horstman, 2012, 5). Their "breaking the fourth wall" pedagogy is similar to Laura Fleming's notion of "transmedia learning," where "storytelling techniques combined with the use of multiple platforms to create an immersive learning landscape . . . [enable] multivarious entry and exit points for learning and teaching" (2013, 371). But Teske and Horstman, like Fleming, like Jenkins, are still invested in retaining control of the narrative. They define transmedia storytelling as "a story that is told in pieces through various mediums so as when brought together through the experience of the participant, *it tells a complete whole*" (Teske and Horstman, 2012, 5; emphasis added). Fleming argues that a course or classroom itself *is* that complete, whole transmedia story: "It is the unifying concept of the learning environment that is important since that can become a landscape for learning that has few, if any, boundaries" (2013, 371).

The completing, unifying impact on the narrative is the shared agency between the students and the instructor, as well as the temporal bounding of the course, which, inevitably, must come to an end. The narrative necessity, to use Ryan's term, of most university-level transmedia courses is the creation of transmedia literacy beyond the classroom. But, in a course on Transmedia Shakespeare, the narrative necessity should also be the transmedia story of the instability inherent to Shakespeare and his plays. To teach Transmedia Shakespeare is to keep adding facets to his transmedia story, so Transmedia Shakespeare in the classroom should (paradoxically) include the recognition that no classroom can ever show or produce "a complete, whole" Shakespeare play.

In preparing the course design for this Shakespeare class, my goal was to think through how particular media and transmediations affect our interpretation and analysis of narratives, as well as to provide as much multimedia access to Shakespeare as possible. Michael Griffith and Matt Bower state, paraphrasing Annette Lamb (2013), "Transmedia environments . . .

ask readers to seek out content, explore information in different contexts, evaluate ideas across formats, and interact with other readers. They are non-linear, deeply immersive, intersubjective, and require student evaluation of content" (326). As such, another goal of the class was to promote community formation and active learning—getting the students interacting with each other and the materials as much as possible. I designed group activities and assignments to allow them to reconstruct historical narratives and build new stories of their own.[1]

Assigned Texts and Course Annotations

Having argued for an overarching and ineluctable transmedia approach to Shakespeare, I will now provide a detailed course description with specific commentary on the conversations and texts included in my own Transmedia Shakespeare course. What follows is a breakdown of the course into its six units, with a narrative of class discussions, activities, questions, and texts for each unit. After the narratives, which provide critical approaches and reflections, I have listed the assigned texts that students were asked to read for each section of the unit. Each unit examines a different facet of the imbrication of Shakespeare and transmedia, in the hope that instructors and students will feel agency to explore and question the process of Shakespearean worlding in many ways. I have broken the course into units and sections, rather than weeks and days, to make it easier for other educators to adapt these materials for their own courses and schedules. This course initially ran as a six-week summer course taught on Zoom due to the ongoing COVID-19 pandemic. Some units are annotated in greater depth than others; when possible, I indicate changes that I would make in future iterations of the course.

Unit 1: Shakespeare and "Shakespeares"
The continuing proliferation of Shakespeare extends the global reach of his work, but the hegemonic presence of "Shakespeare" can also obscure viewing his history and his plays as always-already-transmedia constructions. The first unit focused on challenging students' perceptions of Shakespeare and his plays as cultural, historical, and textual monoliths. We began with the students' experience of transmedia pedagogy and inquiry into how Transmedia Shakespeare is a prescription for uncertainty, an avenue for interrogating the role of the Bard culturally as well as authorially.

The course began with a discussion of Emma Smith's idea of "gappiness" from her 2020 book *This Is Shakespeare*. Students were introduced to the concept by listening to Smith's interview with Barbara Bogaev on the *Shakespeare Unlimited* podcast, hosted by the Folger Shakespeare Library. They also read Henry Jenkins's article "Adaptation, Extension, Transmedia" to learn about transmedia storytelling. We discussed "gappiness," which Smith defines as "this breathing space that there is in Shakespeare: all the things that we don't know, the space there is for our creativity" (2020), alongside Jenkins's explication of the differences and similarities between transmedia studies and adaptation studies.[2] Students also learned about the early modern theatrical profession, discussing the major playing companies, theatrical and printing processes, theaters, and patrons. This got them thinking about the collaborative, networked context of playwriting and performing in early modern theater.

Students then got a "grounding" in London geography and location of the playhouses via two key virtual sources: they wandered modern London to find early modern sites using the ShaLT (Shakespearean London Theatres) Project and then traversed early modern London using *The Map of Early Modern London* site. I also acquainted students with the dominant social concerns and political figures in Shakespeare's England, using the British Library's series of articles on early modern London, which are especially helpful because they include primary documents, images, and material artifacts that encourage students to think about the tangibility of history and its mediation.

Articles from British Library read/relied on in class:

"Cities in Early Modern England" by Liza Picard

"The Social Structure of Elizabethan England" by Liza Picard

"William Shakespeare"

"Shakespeare's Playhouses" by Eric Rasmussen and Ian DeJong

After this introduction to the historical world of Shakespeare, we worked on an in-class assignment through which students experienced Shakespeare's biography and authorship as a transmedia production. Using the *Shakespeare Documented* database, I formed the students into groups, and each group was assigned one primary document from the late sixteenth century that referenced Shakespeare as either citizen or author. Here are the documents I used for this in-class assignment, meaning these were not among the preassigned readings for this unit:

Shakespeare's Biography

> Parish Register of Holy Trinity Church, Stratford-upon-Avon, April 26, 1564
>
> Parish Register of Holy Trinity Church, Stratford-upon-Avon, February 2, 1585

Shakespeare as Pop Figure/Author

> *Greenes, groats-worth of witte*: First printed allusion to Shakespeare as a playwright, 1592
>
> *Palladis tamia*: one of the earliest printed assessments of Shakespeare's works, and the first mention of his sonnets, 1598
>
> *Bel-vedére or The garden of the Muses*: Shakespeare anthologized, 1600
>
> Ben Jonson's "To the Memory of my Beloved the Author, Mr. William Shakespeare"

Shakespeare as Businessman

> *Romeo and Juliet*: second edition with manuscript note "Wil. Sha." beneath the title, 1599
>
> *Love's Labor's Won* listed in a fragment of a Stationer's account book, August 9–17, 1603
>
> Henslowe's diary: including the first recorded performances of *Henry VI* and *Titus Andronicus*, and a possible performance of *The Taming of the Shrew*, 1592–1594

Each group was responsible for providing context for their primary document, and then explaining where the reference to Shakespeare lay, and what information it provided. The series of presentations constituted a performance of Shakespeare's "life" in our own class as the students worked together to analyze the mediation of history through the texts, but it also proved a useful first instance to point out the "gappiness" in historical narratives, as well as in Shakespeare's creative works. Understanding that our access to an author's life is an extended series of connected documents primed them for thinking about Shakespeare, and history itself, as a trans-media production. I left them with the following question: does the lack of certainty regarding the historical William Shakespeare, and the author of the plays attributed to Shakespeare, in part allow and even inspire the transmedia presence of Shakespeare that circulates in our own time?

The last sections of the unit focused on the speculations regarding Shakespeare's sexuality and love life, and delved more deeply into the disputed authorship of Shakespeare's plays. To examine the former, we returned to a particular gap in history from 1585–1592, the "lost years," when Shakespeare essentially drops out of the historical record. Given the sources on either end of that gap, ostensibly Shakespeare leaves Stratford-upon-Avon, and his wife, Anne, and begins his career as a London playwright. The 1998 film *Shakespeare in Love*, set in 1593, relies on this temporal lacuna and even fictionally fills in the London portion of it. To get the students starting to think about the transmedia story of Shakespeare's love life, I presented the concept of "the muse" in early modern poetry, where poets cast themselves as mediums through which creative genius flows: the body of the poet and their words exist to register the affective and sexual pangs of love. To think through a potential historical muse of Shakespeare (again, using *Shakespeare Documented*), we briefly examined "Entry in the Bishop's register concerning the marriage of William Shakespeare and Anne Hathaway" from November 27, 1582, and "The Shakespeare marriage bond" from November 28, 1582. I then introduced the fictional muses of *Shake-speares Sonnets* using LUNA, the Folger Digital Image Collection; the students met Mr. W.H., as well as the fair youth in Sonnet 3 and the mistress in Sonnet 130.

Set to the background of these canonical muses, we discussed *Shakespeare in Love* for its representation of Viola de Lesseps as (another) fictional muse for a fictional "Shakespeare," focusing on the anonymity that she achieves through her disguise as Thomas Kent, a fictional actor, and the hidden, forbidden role she plays in Shakespeare's life. While the film may be an adaptation of the historical life of William Shakespeare, given how little is known of Shakespeare's early time in London, the creation of this new muse figure in a film represents a transmedia extension of history, due to the blurred line between fiction and historical possibility. Using their newfound knowledge of the gappiness of the historical record, students were asked to consider how the character of Viola de Lesseps and the film *Shakespeare in Love* turn Shakespeare's love life into a story traveling across multiple media forms—the film intersecting with, extending, and also resisting the historical documents.

The third section concluded the unit by examining the dispute over the authorship of the plays attributed to Shakespeare. Students read "The Declaration of Reasonable Doubt" and watched interviews with proponents on both sides of the authorship question—those who argue that the historical figure of William Shakespeare did, in fact, write the plays attributed to him, and those who argue that there is space for reasonable doubt about this assertion. They then watched the 2011 film *Anonymous*, which explores the authorship controversy through a fictionalized historical narrative imagining Edward de Vere, the Earl of Oxford, as the author of Shakespeare's plays and poetry. Many students expressed surprise about the dispute, sharing that it was the first they had heard of it. I asked them to think back to the historical documents that they had worked with in the first section of the unit, which could not definitively tie "The Man from Avon" to William Shakespeare. By pointing out the uncertainties of history, the students learned to be thoughtfully uncertain in their own assumptions about Shakespeare and his plays, thus leaving them more open to consider the flow of authorship across media in the rest of the course.

Teaching *Shakespeare in Love* and *Anonymous* and their historical contexts in the first unit of a Shakespeare course powerfully destabilizes what students think they know about Shakespeare, due to both their form and content and the way that they engage the disrupted mediation of history. The playing out of Shakespeare's life across various media forms (digitized documents, historical fiction films, museum articles, YouTube videos, and podcasts) opens up the past as a place that is both real and fictional, and that exists today in scattered remnants that are variously textual, material, and fictional. The familiarity of *Shakespeare in Love*, a winner of multiple Academy Awards, makes it a good opening transmedia experience for the students, in part because its intense visuality brings early modern theater practices to life. *Anonymous* also highlights the coterie of playwrights living and working in early modern London, turning Shakespearean authorship into a contested site of negotiation rather than an easily understood entity. By watching films and engaging with primary historical documents, students experience Shakespearean authorship and history brought to life as unstable entities that flicker into view through various media, but that always require interaction and interrogation.

Materials for Unit 1

Section One: Shakespeare's Biography and Intro to Pop Culture and Transmedia Approaches to Shakespeare

Intro to Popular Culture Approaches to Shakespeare:

Emma Smith on "This Is Shakespeare" from the *Shakespeare Unlimited* podcast hosted by the Folger Shakespeare Library (34:53)

https://www.folger.edu/shakespeare-unlimited/smith-this-is
-shakespeare

Henry Jenkins, "Adaptation, Extension, Transmedia" (2017)

Intro to Shakespeare's Biography:

"Shakespeare's Life and Work"
https://www.youtube.com/watch?v=ZYoGnC66sJY

"William Shakespeare—Playwright | Mini Bio | BIO" (4:43)
https://www.youtube.com/watch?v=geev441vbMI

"Straight Outta Stratford-Upon-Avon—Shakespeare's Early Days:
Crash Course Theater #14"

(An introduction to Shakespeare's Life and Work—Watch until
about the 6:30 mark) https://www.youtube.com/watch?v
=FS2ndY5WJXA

Ben Jonson, "To the Memory of my Beloved the Author, Mr. William
Shakespeare, and what he hath left us" (First Folio 1623)

Supplementary Materials:

Shakespearean London Theatres (ShaLT)
http://shalt.dmu.ac.uk

The Map of Early Modern London
https://mapoflondon.uvic.ca/index.htm

Section Two: Shakespeare's Meet Cutes

Meet Cutes—Shakespeare's Muses:

Katherine West Scheil, "Imagining Shakespeare's Wife" from the
Shakespeare Unlimited podcast hosted by the Folger Shakespeare
Library (35:30)

https://www.folger.edu/shakespeare-unlimited/imagining
-shakespeares-wife

Aviva Dautch, "Shakespeare, Sexuality, and the Sonnets" from the
British Library

https://www.bl.uk/shakespeare/articles/shakespeare-sexuality
-and-the-sonnets

Shakespeare in Love (1998)—film

Section Three: Authorial Disputes—Who Wrote Shakespeare's Plays?

The Case for Shakespeare:

Heminge and Condell, "To the Great Variety of Readers" (First Folio
1623)

"The Shakespeare Authorship Question" Interview with Professor
Jonathan Bate from the Shakespeare Birthplace Trust (15:20)
https://www.youtube.com/watch?v=JXUg0cbEzaE&t=257s
"Did Shakespeare Write His Plays?—Natalya St. Clair and Aaron
Williams"—video on Stylometry (4:06)
https://www.youtube.com/watch?v=K-aAUwAFZlQ

The Case Against:

"An Introduction to the Shakespeare Authorship Question" from
Don't Quill The Messenger: Shakespeare Authorship Explored podcast
https://www.podbean.com/media/share/dir-itgzj-5576ade?utm
_campaign=w_share_ep&utm_medium=dlink&utm_source=w
_share%20(13:08)
The Shakespeare Authorship Roundtable website
https://shakespeareauthorship.org/authors/candidates.html
Read entries on William Shakespeare, Francis Bacon, Christopher
Marlowe, and Edward de Vere, Earl of Oxford
Anonymous (2011)—film
"The Declaration of Reasonable Doubt about the Identity of William
Shakespeare" from the Shakespeare Authorship Coalition
https://doubtaboutwill.org/declaration

Supplemental Readings for "The Case Against":

"Shakespeare Authorship Question: Why Was I Never Told This?"
(5:32) from *DoubtAboutWill* YouTube channel
https://www.youtube.com/watch?v=JyVjR9FNo9w
"Sir Derek Jacobi and Mark Rylance discuss The Declaration of Reasonable Doubt" (29:31) from *DoubtAboutWill* YouTube channel
https://www.youtube.com/watch?v=7ZNYifQfYiE

Unit 2: Political Shakespeare: Shakespeare and Race

The second unit focused on political theater and the theme of "tyranny."
The students read *Julius Caesar* and then learned how the play's transmediation through various performances, news outlets, and reviews highlight questions about race and power within Shakespearean narratives, performance,
and reception.

The first section of this unit covered the play text of *Julius Caesar*,
introducing classical definitions of tyranny alongside discussions of it in

Tudor England. We looked at a censoring statute enacted by Henry VIII that forbade calling the monarch a tyrant, before I further contextualized political theater in Shakespeare's own day by explaining the commissioning of a performance of *Richard II* by the Earl of Southampton on the eve of the Essex Rebellion, near the end of Elizabeth I's reign in 1601. It was especially important to review this moment of early modern political theater directly involving a Shakespeare play because the film that the students watched the week before, *Anonymous*, inaccurately depicts *Richard III* being performed and also suggests that the performance was used specifically to denigrate Robert Cecil, an advisor to Queen Elizabeth I. After sharing that it was, in fact, *Richard II* that was commissioned, I shared the anecdote of Elizabeth I saying, "I am Richard II, know ye not that." Both *Julius Caesar* and *Richard II* are narratives of the downfalls of rulers who are rhetorized as selfish or self-indulgent, so this approach of demonstrating the politicization of theater in Shakespeare's day also contextualized the politicization of *Julius Caesar* in our own time, which we then went on to discuss. It prepared students to think about how audiences mediate plays and plays mediate politics, while serving as a reminder of how films mediate history, which we had covered in the previous unit.

The second half of the unit was inspired by Lauren Eriks Cline's work on *Julius Caesar*. In 2018, I attended the Next Gen Plen at the 46th Annual Meeting of the Shakespeare Association of America, where Cline presented "Audiences Writing Race in Shakespeare Performance," which was later published in *Shakespeare Studies*. When the opportunity arose to teach Shakespeare, the first text that I knew I wanted to teach was *Julius Caesar*, specifically to present her approach to the play. I combined Cline's argument with Ayanna Thompson's arguments on race, reception, and performance, and their approaches framed our media analysis for this unit.

Thompson, in looking at a marketing archive—audience exit surveys for the 1988 Oregon Shakespeare Festival production of *Romeo and Juliet*—as a reception archive, argues that the overwhelmingly White, affluent audience who complained about the "modernization" of the production were in fact reacting negatively to the production's "non-traditional casting," which Thompson defines as "the practice of casting actors of colour in roles originally imagined as white characters performed by white actors" (2017,

158). The students read her essay, and we spent a good deal of time working through the following passage:

> I can imagine that one might argue that I am misreading the surveys and letters of complaint by reading through a specific lens—that of the performance race scholar—which necessarily colours my interpretation of the text(s). I can also imagine that one might argue that I am asking others to look for something that is not there—that I am asking future performance scholars to put race into the centre of their frames of analysis even when audiences resist explicit discussions of it. This, of course, were I a social scientist, would be viewed as a poor methodology. *I am not asking if race impacts an audience's reception; instead I assume that race impacts reception, and I am asking how the impact manifests itself.* I am making this claim because I agree with W. J. T. Mitchell's recent assertion that *race should be treated as a medium through which we experience, read, and interpret our society,* and I think this is especially true for non-traditionally cast productions of Shakespeare. Mitchell argues that "race is not merely a content to be mediated, an object to be represented visually or verbally, or a thing to be depicted in a likeness or image, but that race is itself a medium and an iconic form—not simply something to be seen, but itself a framework for seeing through or (as Wittgenstein would put it) seeing as" (13). Thus OSF's 1988 audience survey and letters of complaint do not explicitly address race as the object being viewed; instead they reveal that race is the medium through which the audience assessed the production.
>
> *If theatre scholars accept Mitchell's claim that race is a medium through which we all experience the world, then our methodologies for reception would necessarily change. Race would inescapably be a part, perhaps even a central part, of our analyses of reception because we would assume that audiences do not, perhaps cannot, make sense of theatrical productions without the medium.* (Thompson, 2017, 168–169; emphasis added)

Thompson argues here that race is an ideological and embodied medium that inflects our intake of narrative, and, within a Shakespeare context, affects and is affected by both the writing of Shakespearean narratives and their reception. Our class used Thompson's argument to contextualize Cline's analysis.

Cline looks at two productions of *Julius Caesar*, the 2012 Guthrie Theatre production and the 2017 Public Theater production, to argue that the politicization of those plays depended upon how different audiences read the race of the actors, and thus which historical figures—Barack Obama or Donald Trump—the two Caesars possibly corresponded to. Cline argues for a shift in thinking from "audience reception to spectator production," and that by "analyzing not only the semiotic codes through which audiences read theatrical signs but also the discursive strategies with which they write narratives of theatergoing, scholars can approach audiences not as failing to see race, but as using techniques of incoherence, opacity, and indirection to construct racial meanings" (2019, 114).

Using Cline's bibliography, I provided the reviews and sources that she mentioned so that students could see the evidence she uses to make her argument, and I also included other videos that furnished background context for the productions and their politicization, which often occurred through comparison of the productions. Cline uses the term "refraction" to describe how audiences experience and produce ideologies of race (2019, 114). My students were fascinated by the idea of thinking about how a play's (and all narratives') refraction through personal experience and cultural contexts is a form of producing and extending the play's narrative. In essence, Cline argues that audience members mediate the characters on stage and the performance's import through their own political affiliations and racial assumptions and biases. In this unit, the students experienced *Julius Caesar*'s politicization through media sources across the political spectrum as a transmedia story of its own; part of that story of politicization was also a transmedia narrative of racial construction created through and between media, historical eras, political landscapes, and audiences.

Materials for Unit 2

Section One: Tyrant-osaurus Rex

Play Text:

Julius Caesar by William Shakespeare

Section Two: Audiences Writing Race; Audiences Writing Shakespeare

Race and Politics in Shakespearean Performance

"Ayanna Thompson—Race and Shakespearean Performance" (Lecture begins at 5:00 mark, ends at 55:50)

https://www.youtube.com/watch?v=G355el-YS1Y

Ayanna Thompson, "(How) Should We Listen to Audiences—Race, Reception and the Audience Survey," from *The Oxford Handbook of Shakespeare and Performance* (2017)

This is the published version of Thompson's lecture on "Race and Shakespearean Performance"—I chose to give the students access to both so that they could choose the medium through which they preferred to encounter Thompson's argument.

Lauren Eriks Cline, "Audiences Writing Race in Shakespeare Performance" from *Shakespeare Studies* (2019)

Videos/Commentary on *Julius Caesar* Performances Mentioned in Cline's Article (TW: Assassination of Caesar is shown)

Guthrie Theater 2012 Julius Caesar (Obama-like Caesar)

"The Acting Company's modern uptake on "Julius Caesar" at CLC—Brainerd Dispatch MN" (3:26)

https://www.youtube.com/watch?v=ej2sP0_0mDE

Oskar Eustis (Director) Makes a Speech before the 2017 Public Theater *Julius Caesar*

"Oskar Eustis before Opening Night Performance of Julius Caesar / Shakespeare in the Park"

https://www.youtube.com/watch?v=1YO_t9ANv7M

Right-Leaning Media: Fox News Reports on the Protests against the Public Theater's 2017 *Julius Caesar*

"Protesters Disrupt Shakespeare in the Park's 'Julius Caesar'" (2:44)

https://www.youtube.com/watch?v=2w6RYCoEeUY

Left-Leaning Media: CBS Reports on the Public Theater's *Julius Caesar*

"Sponsors Pull Support of Play Featuring Trump-like Caesar" (3:11)

https://www.youtube.com/watch?v=XPDP0tD2O14

Right-Leaning Media: Fox News Five Discuss the Public Theater's 2017 *Julius Caesar*

"Fareed Zakaria Raves about Trump-Inspired 'Julius Caesar'" (9:57)

https://www.youtube.com/watch?v=d_BkHvygDQ0&t

Left-Leaning Media: MSNBC Morning Joe Discussion of the Public Theater's 2017 Julius Caesar

"Following 'Ceasar' [sic] Protests, a Talk about Free Speech | Morning Joe | MSNBC" (8:47)

https://www.youtube.com/watch?v=q-ZvGkedDPI

Reviews of Guthrie Theater's 2012 Julius Caesar

"Manage Acting Company and Guthrie Theater Bring 'Julius Caesar' Awkwardly into the 21st Century"—by Jay Gabler—*Twin Cities Daily Planet*

https://www.tcdailyplanet.net/julius-caesar-guthrie-theater
-acting-company-review

"The Acting Company's Version of 'Julius Caesar'" by Eric Grode—
The New York Times

https://www.nytimes.com/2012/04/18/theater/reviews/the
-acting-companys-version-of-julius-caesar.html

"Obama's Ides of March—The Acting Company Production of Julius
Caesar" by Noah Millman—*The American Conservative*

https://www.theamericanconservative.com/shakesblog/obamas
-ides-of-march

"Review—Julius Caesar @ the Guthrie Theater"—*Mpls.St.Paul Magazine*

https://mspmag.com/arts-and-culture/the-morning-after/review
_julius_caesar_the_guthr

Politics and The Public Theater's 2017 Julius Caesar

Right-Leaning Responses

" 'Trump' Stabbed to Death in Central Park Performance of 'Julius
Caesar'" by Daniel Nussbaum—*Breitbart News*

https://www.breitbart.com/entertainment/2017/06/06/trump
-stabbed-death-central-park-performance-julius-caesar

"NYC Play Appears to Depict Assassination of Trump—As seen on
Fox and Friends Weekend—Fox News Insider"

https://insider.foxnews.com/2017/06/11/donald-trump-julius
-caesar-stabbed-death-women-minorities-shakespeare
-central-park

"Blue State Blues: Julius Caesar This Time as a Farce" by Joe B.
Pollak—*Breitbart News*

https://www.breitbart.com/politics/2020/01/17/blue-state
-blues-julius-caesar-this-time-as-farce

Left-Leaning Responses

"Why Outrage over Shakespeare in the Park's Trump-like Julius
Caesar Is So Misplaced" by Alissa Wilkinson—*Vox*

https://www.vox.com/culture/2017/6/12/15780692/julius
-caesar-shakespeare-in-park-trump-public-theater-outrage

Opinion—"A Trumpian Caesar? Shakespeare Would Approve" by
James Shapiro—*The New York Times*

https://www.nytimes.com/2017/06/13/opinion/a-trumpian
-caesar-shakespeare-would-approve.html

"Why 'Julius Caesar' Speaks to Politics Today. With or Without
Trump" by Michael Cooper—*The New York Times*
https://www.nytimes.com/2017/06/12/theater/julius-caesar
-shakespeare-donald-trump.html

Comparisons of Guthrie Theater's 2012 Julius Caesar and The Public Theater's 2017 Julius Caesar

"The Misplaced Outrage over the Public Theater's Trumpian 'Julius
Caesar'" by Sophie Gilbert—*The Atlantic*
https://www.theatlantic.com/entertainment/archive/2017
/06/the-misplaced-outrage-over-a-trumpian-julius-caesar
/530037/

"Character Assassination: Julius Caesar at the Public Theatre"—
Chester Theatre Company
https://chestertheatre.org/character-assassination/

"Trump-like 'Caesar' Causes Freak-out, While Guthrie's '12 Show
Had an Obama-esque Caesar and No One Cared" by Jay Gabler—
City Pages
https://www.citypages.com/arts/trump-like-caesar-causes-freak-
out-while-guthries-12-show-had-an-obama-esque-caesar-and-
no-one-cared/427979593

"Uproar over Trump-Themed 'Julius Caesar,' but None for Obama
Version at Guthrie 5 Years Ago" by Rohan Preston—*The StarTribune*
https://www.startribune.com/trump-themed-julius-caesar-is-talk
-of-theater-world-unlike-2012-obama-version-in-twin-cities
/427990033/

Supplemental Articles

"The Vital Role of Political Theater: Diane Paulus, Branden Jacobs-
Jenkins, and Robert Schenkkan Discuss How the Public Theater's
Recent Production of Julius Caesar Fits into a Grand Artistic Tradition" by Sophie Gilbert—*The Atlantic*
https://www.theatlantic.com/entertainment/archive/2017/06
/the-vital-role-of-political-theater/532371

"Oskar Eustis on Trump, 'Julius Caesar' and the Politics of Theater"
by Michael Paulson—*The New York Times*

https://www.nytimes.com/2017/06/13/theater/donald-trump-
julius-caesar-oskar-eustis.html

Unit 3: Youth Shakespeare

This unit focused on the mediation of Shakespeare's plays for "youthful" audiences, and how what is thought to be age-appropriate or age-accessible mediates conversations and pedagogy around Shakespeare and his plays in particular spaces. I altered our class's transmedia experience of Shakespeare's *Taming of the Shrew* by having the students listen to a podcast before they read the play: an interview with Ayanna Thompson on NPR's *Code Switch*. This interview yielded one of the most potent metaphors for the students' changing conception of Shakespeare's plays and our unsettling of the figure of Shakespeare as a static and unimpeachable pop figure. Thompson argues that theater producers' attempts to redeem for audiences those plays they might see as problematic, by either altering endings, using staging to suggest alternative contexts, or just excusing the plays as being-of-a-different-time-but-still-ok-because-hey-it's-Shakespeare-and-also-we've-moved-on-from-thinking-like-that, are wrong. She argues, instead, that we should begin with the notion that Shakespeare's plays are, and always have been, racist, anti-Semitic, and misogynistic. She states:

> We have a narrative in the West that Shakespeare's like spinach, right? He's good for you. He's universally good for you. When, in fact, he's, you know, writing from the vantage point of the 16th and 17th century. And I hope that we have moved on in the 21st century from some of those ideas . . . I think there are a couple of things that we'd have to fight against, right? One is this idea that Shakespeare is spinach and universally good for you. We have to make that a more complex narrative. Two, we have to allow ourselves to inhabit the full complexity of these plays and to not try and make everything have a happy Disney uplift narrative.
>
> And I think if we get to a place where, you know, Shakespeare's not universally good for you and maybe these plays aren't always necessarily good for us, then we will be in a position where we can maybe rewrite the endings, change the plays, have other plays enter into the major canon and some of them fall out. (Thompson, 2019)

The class's previous consideration of authorial disputes in the first unit had already laid the groundwork for the students to digest Thompson's "spinach" argument. Students latched onto the metaphor, many of them sharing that they had never before been asked to revisit, examine, and rewrite their views of Shakespeare's plays as works of art with inherent value or cultural benefit or supremacy (much as they had never really known the debates around Shakespearean authorship).

Thompson's ideas led to a robust discussion of how students experienced Shakespeare at younger ages and what shape Shakespeare pedagogy had taken in their high schools. Beginning the unit with a podcast recalled how, for many of them, a medium *other* than a play text or live performance was their first experience of Shakespeare; this deliberation would continue in the next unit with *Romeo and Juliet* as, for many of them, Baz Luhrmann's 1996 film *Romeo +Juliet* was a first introduction to the play.[3]

Through this podcast, the students came to realize how their own ages had mediated their understandings of Shakespeare and his plays in the past, but, also, other people's perceptions of their cognitive ability to process or receive particular approaches to Shakespeare's works. Taking up Thompson's "spinach" metaphor, many of them reflected on how they thought high school students were not asked to engage with Shakespeare with enough complexity or nuance to attend to the supremacist logics in and surrounding Shakespeare's works.

Diving into the play text of *Taming of the Shrew*, we took a moment to interrogate the mediating effects of the frame narrative on misogyny in the play. By comparing the folio version of *Taming of the Shrew* with the entire frame narrative provided in the 1594 quarto *Taming of a Shrew*, and reflecting on how many productions remove the frame narrative altogether, students were able to share how the particular version they experienced affected their thoughts on the numerous instances of physical abuse in the play. We ended with a conversation of whether we thought *Taming of the Shrew* is appropriate for "youth" audiences; I greatly appreciated how, in our class, we also had some students who were parents share perspectives on what they would or would not want their kids to discuss about the play in high school. In future versions of the course, I would consider having the students analyze the Folger Shakespeare Library's teaching modules as another media extension of youth Shakespeare.

The second section of the unit continued our transmedia story of *Taming of the Shrew* through an analysis of the 1999 film *10 Things I Hate About You*. Drawing on Hulbert et al.'s claim that "Youth-culture Shakespeare, like all youth culture, is about identity and cliques" (2006, 8), we focused on themes of belonging in the play as what translates so well into the teen film adaptation, given that individuation, domestic transition, and shifting experiences of inclusion and family are often major experiences during teenage and young adult years.

In conclusion, we brought the question back to Shakespeare's belonging in high school classrooms; Hulbert et al. assert how, in youth-culture Shakespeare, the "young viewer/reader/listener is not other or object or the passive member of a one-way transaction, but has agency to engage, reimagine or re-create the plays on his or her own terms" (2006, 4), but we queried just how much this holds true within the power structures of academic classrooms in which syllabi and texts and activities are often determined by the instructor, or at administrative levels even far above them. Like Katherine in *Taming of the Shrew* or Kat in *10 Things I Hate About You*, we reflected on how students' choices were often more about rejecting something familiar or normative than accepting something different. Transmedia Shakespeare can center these discussions of cultural belonging and teenagers' agency, and we can ask: why might we reject Shakespeare, and what does it look like to do so?

Materials for Unit 3

Section One: *Taming of the Shrew* and "Should We Even Teach This Play Anymore?"

Assigned Texts:

"All That Glisters Is Not Gold" by the *Code Switch* podcast by NPR
Interview with Ayanna Thompson on *The Merchant of Venice*, *Othello*, and *Taming of the Shrew*. Students may listen to the podcast in its entirety or skip to Thompson's interview, which starts at 14:45. Transcript is included.
https://www.npr.org/transcripts/752850055

Play Text:

Taming of the Shrew by William Shakespeare
I recommend the Folger Edition, as it includes the Induction.
Taming of a Shrew (1594 quarto from *Early English Books Online*)

Section Two: Youth Shakespeare

Assigned Texts:

10 Things I Hate About You (1999)
"'Smells Like Teen Shakespirit' Or, the Shakespearean Films of Julia Stiles" by Robert L. York (read section on *10 Things I Hate About You* and *Taming of the Shrew*, pp. 67–87)

Unit 4: Remixed, Remediated Shakespeare

In this unit, students learned about hip-hop approaches to Shakespeare, tracing street scenes and city culture in *Romeo and Juliet* and in Ronald Wimberly's 2012 graphic novel *Prince of Cats*. I suggested to the students that although *Romeo and Juliet* is heralded as a story of unparalleled love, the play is equally, if not more so, interesting for its scenes of warfare in Verona between the Capulets and the Montagues and the way that it traces the pitfalls of familial, social, and political hierarchies. We thus approached *Romeo and Juliet* by focusing on Shakespeare in the streets, not the sheets. We tracked what type of action and what type of bodies typically appear in exterior versus interior scenes.[4] Since the students were still excited to talk about the love poetry and the plot of the play, we took time to linger on the abundant use of oxymorons to suggest the emotional struggle that both Romeo and Juliet face, given how their own desires intersect with those of their families. I introduced the concept of "remix" by presenting the students with Aristotle's definition of tragedy and asking them to test its application to the play text. I suggested that Shakespeare was remixing the tragedy genre by elevating romantic affection as a site of tragedy, in addition to action.

The next section of the unit turned to a graphic novel, *Prince of Cats*, which is the story of Tybalt and provides additional focus on characters outside the main romance plot of the play. Romeo is rarely present, as the comic focuses on Tybalt's place within the Capulet family, his care for Juliet, and his skills as a street duelist. The author, Ronald Wimberly, addresses and rejects the tokenization that often occurs regarding Black-created content, so my students and I began our discussion of the comic by watching a You-Tube video of an interview with Wimberly, where he shares his thoughts on how his work is mediated by racial bias:

> Not to mince words but like you know there's a racial paradigm here and every-thing is viewed through that paradigm. Where you might make a work, like, so if I make *Prince of Cats* I'm like yo, look it's this dope thing about this, that and the third and then when someone maybe does like an article on it it's like oh it's like Black characters doing this that and third, it's a hip-hop retelling of Shakespeare and, it's like, not really b! Like that is your racial-ass lens on the work, right? I can't escape it, you know what I mean, that's the world, that's the paradigm that the work exists in. Not only is that the case, but the racial paradigm has created a commodity out of like the racial aspect of it, you know what I mean, like what is the value of it? (Team A-Go-Go, 2018)

I gave space for students to chat about their experiences of inclusion and pedagogy within university classrooms, and we explicitly discussed their thoughts on whether Shakespeare was a figure of and for White culture. We talked about Wimberly's rejection of an art piece's value coming solely from the race of its author, and students were able to share openly and honestly about their own experiences with tokenization, even within higher education classrooms, if they wanted to. We all agreed that *Prince of Cats* could be a key transmedia node for reading *Romeo and Juliet* and in thinking about Transmedia Shakespeare for the way that it refutes White supremacist logics that exist around who Shakespeare belongs to, but also for the way that the graphic novel refuses media tokenization as well. Although the work seems to be one medium, a graphic novel, it is a layered story infused by the multifarious media of hip-hop, which then resist Shakespeare's history of mediation as a figure of Whiteness and White supremacy. John Jennings, in the foreword to *Prince of Cats*, writes, "The genius of Hip Hop culture is the method of production called the remix. The deliberate juxtaposition of seemingly unlike artifacts, assets, beats, what have you, into a cohesive re-mediated cultural expression" (Jennings, 2016). As we explored and experienced Wimberly's text, we found that it indeed, as he says, is not just a "hip-hop retelling of Shakespeare," but a transmedia remix extension and adaptation of *Romeo and Juliet* that also furthers and complicates the transmedia story of Shakespeare's racial views, operations, and belonging.

The comic is set in the mid-to-late-1980s in New York—"an alternate universe New York where dueling is part of the culture, that street culture, that led to the hip-hop and downtown culture of the late seventies, early eighties" (Team A-Go-Go, 2018). To start addressing the remediation and remixing in *Prince of Cats*, we further looked at Jennings' foreword, where he argues that *Prince of Cats*

> isn't just a mish-mash of things he [Wimberly] digs. Yes, it's *Romeo and Juliet* meets Kurosawa meets *The Warriors* meets *Planet Rock*. However, what makes Prince of Cats so innovative is the fact that it acts as a reified index of what Hip Hop culture would manifest itself as visually . . . What makes Wimberly a master of this medium is his visual and intellectual acumen to project equivalence onto myriad types of productions from various cultural sources. (Jennings, 2016)

Wimberly's influences, as Jennings notes them, are *The Warriors*, a 1979 cult film about gang culture in New York City; Akira Kurosawa's *Ran*, a 1985 samurai epic retelling of Shakespeare's *King Lear*; and Shakespeare's *Romeo and*

Juliet—and the primacy of one influence over the other is not, in fact, clear. Jennings argues that the comic doesn't merely reflect hip-hop values—it *is* hip-hop. One aspect of the play that Wimberly specifically wanted to remix was the lack of grief, particularly on Juliet's part but also of the Capulet and Montague families and Verona itself, for the deaths that occur due to street fighting. Wimberly argues that "the lens doesn't really appreciate, sort of, like wow, ok that guy's gone now, they're gone" (Team A-Go-Go, 2018). I read this moment as Wimberly critiquing the media of performance, film, and even the text of Shakespeare's play for failing to fully explore the emotional complexities of the play's street killings: Wimberly states, "I wanted to get more into the price of violence for all involved" (Team A-Go-Go, 2018). *Prince of Cats* extends the emotional world of the play to more fully encompass Tybalt's life and death.

In our class discussion of *Prince of Cats*, we lingered over pages 138 and 139 of the book, where Wimberly presents two alternative endings, each appearing on a page facing the other: one where Tybalt wins his sword duel with Romeo and the other where Romeo triumphs. Chronologically, the Tybalt-triumphant ending is presented first, on the verso, in a series of blue-toned cells which suggests that perhaps this is the ending that Tybalt speculates will occur; and the right hand, or recto page, presents the "original," Romeo-triumphant ending. The two finales are offered without comment, creating an equivalence between them, and the duel between the characters becomes a duel in the medium itself as the pages face off against each other. The narrative reworks Tybalt's death or undeath as the ending of the story, and by concluding this way, Wimberly prevents readers from being distracted from the tragedy of Tybalt's death by the continuation of the romance between Romeo and Juliet. Graphic novels and comics are an intensely fan-driven medium, and hip-hop, in spite of its huge commercial power, is at heart a grassroots, Black, Latinx, and Caribbean community-oriented artistic and economic movement. Through visual hip-hop, Wimberly uses a transmediation of Shakespeare's *Romeo and Juliet* to center questions and conversations about racial, cultural, and familial belonging in Shakespearean worlding.[5]

Materials for Unit 4

Section One: Shakespeare in the Streets

   Play Text:

   Romeo and Juliet by William Shakespeare

Section Two: Remixed, Remediated Shakespeare

Prince of Cats by Ronald Wimberly

"History of Hip Hop in the Bronx—Arts in the City"
    https://www.youtube.com/watch?v=D5ZpQ73R_z4

"The Wisdom of Hip-Hop Gets Respect in a New Museum Exhibit"—by
    Jeffrey Brown; includes a video (7:45) from *PBS News Hour*
    https://www.pbs.org/newshour/show/the-wisdom-of-hip-hop-gets
    -respect-in-a-new-museum-exhibit

"RESPECT: Hip Hop Style and Wisdom" tour of exhibit by trompoly
    studio
    https://www.youtube.com/watch?v=crpmjOTfjzI

"Ron Wimberly Artist Spotlight—Beyond the Longbox"
    https://www.youtube.com/watch?v=ebmUHcus0tI&t

Supplemental Materials:

"Ron Wimberly Interview" on *More to Come* podcast by *Publishers
    Weekly* (49:49)
    https://www.publishersweekly.com/pw/podcasts/index.html
        ?podcast=668&channel=2

Unit 5: What's Old Is New Shakespeare

In the last play-oriented unit, we circled back to history, this time looking
at "original practices" Shakespeare (productions that use theater traditions
from the early modern period, such as costuming, makeup styles, and all-
male casting) as a transmedia research process that remediates historical theater and gender. Students read feminist theory about early modern England
that interrogates the historical construction of gender, and then read early
modern discourse on gender, cross-dressing, and homosexuality. After a
brief lecture on Galen's humoral theory and one-sex model, we worked with
primary documents from the late sixteenth century and early seventeenth
century that specifically reference cross-dressing (including texts by Stephen
Gosson, John Rainolds, and Phillip Stubbes, plus the pamphlets *Hic Mulier*
and *Haec-Vier*). I further elaborated these discussions of gender with C. L.
Barber's argument about festive comedies, and we traced themes of excess,
misrule, and reversal through the play *Twelfth Night*. We spent time thinking
about the *Twelfth Night* characters Toby, Maria, Malvolio, and Feste through
this lens before turning to examining gender role reversal in *Twelfth Night*,

with Olivia as mistress of her household, Viola as a cross-dressed page, and the homoeroticism between Antonio and Sebastian offering numerous avenues for exploring and comparing male and female affective possibility. Linking gender misrule to the concept of carnival revelry and class negotiation, students were struck by how the play abounds with mutability and topsy-turviness that are by no means stabilized at its conclusion.

We drew on our discussion of bodies as mediums, rather than registers, of gender—both in the primary documents and play text—to analyze the Shakespeare's Globe Original Practices production of *Twelfth Night* from 2012, featuring Sir Mark Rylance. After watching the filmed live-stage version, we added new media analyses by examining the role of clothing, make-up, voice, gesture, and props for establishing gender on stage. The students were surprised at how much humor resided in the performance's gender play, and how even though the theatrical experience was so different from what they were used to, they enjoyed watching this staging of the play. We ended with questions about the transmedia creation of theater history in original practices performance research. We looked at how different theaters describe and frame original practices, thinking about how the medium of theater has changed since Shakespeare's time, and considered the following question: are original practices productions adaptations of Shakespeare's works, or are they transmedia productions of theater history, highlighting changes in the theatrical medium? Our analyses of gender, sexuality, and original practices reinforced the idea that the past, like the historical Shakespeare and the authorship of his plays, is constantly being remediated in the present.

We did have a brief discussion about transgender Shakespeare, but it wasn't as robust as it should have been. Driven by our conversations about the diatribes about cross-dressing in the primary documents, students brought up what had been a contemporaneous announcement of a policy shift by Dr. Ben Carson, then US Secretary of Housing and Urban Development, which could allow shelter providers to discriminate against transgender people, allegedly based upon physical characteristics noted by staff. I brought up drag culture and the historical journey of trans drag artists. In future iterations, I would have the students read more specifics on transgender Shakespeare performance, leading with Sawyer Kemp's article "'In That Dimension Grossly Clad': Transgender Rhetoric, Representation, and Shakespeare" (2019) and Alexa Alice Joubin's "Transgender Theory and

Global Shakespeare" (2022). (Joubin's article was not yet available when I taught the course.) Kemp reminds scholars and teachers to approach discussing gender and trans identity in Shakespeare thoughtfully, noting: "If we are going to visit the past to serve the present, it should actually and meaningfully serve those populations whose language, identities, and communities we are borrowing" (2019, 125).

Materials for Unit 5

Section One: The World Turned Upside Down

Background on Sex-Gender Debates in Early Modern England:

"Sexuality and Queerness on the Early Modern Stage" (2017) by Valerie Billing in *A New Companion to Renaissance Drama*, edited by Arthur F. Kinney and Thomas Warren Hopper

"Crossdressing the Theatre, and Gender Struggle in Early Modern England" (1988) by Jean E. Howard in *Shakespeare Quarterly*. (Read pp. 418–425)

"Gender Trouble and Cross-Dressing on the Early Modern Stage" (1996) by David Cressy in *Journal of British Studies* (Read to the end of part 1, pp. 438–445)

Primary Materials Discussing Anti-Theatricalism and Cross-Dressing in Early Modern London:

Selections from:

Stephen Gosson, *Plays Refuted in Five Actions* (1582)

John Rainolds, *The Overthrow of Stage-Plays* (1599)

Phillip Stubbes, *The Anatomie of Abuses* (1583)

Title pages, including woodcut images, of *Hic Mulier: Or, the Man-Woman* (1620) and *Haec-Vir: Or The Womanish-Man* (1620)

Play Text:

Twelfth Night by William Shakespeare

Section Two: Original Practices Shakespeare

Shakespeare's Globe Original Practices *Twelfth Night*, featuring Sir Mark Rylance and Stephen Fry (2012)

"Original Practices" (2016) by Don Weingust in *The Cambridge Guide to the World of Shakespeare* (Read up until the section titled "Developing Original Practices, early on p. 1477)

"What Is Original Practices?" from the Colorado Shakespeare Festival
(2:57)
https://www.youtube.com/watch?v=lyHBjLpFD-I
"Original Practices at Shakespeare's Globe" from *Shakespeare's Globe*
website
https://www.shakespearesglobe.com/discover/blogs-and-features
/2020/04/30/original-practices-at-shakespeares-globe

Unit 6: Class-Created Transmedia Shakespeare

This final unit was designed to both broaden students' knowledge of
Transmedia Shakespeare and scaffold preparation for their final projects,
a create-your-own-Shakespeare project. For the first section, students were
tasked with researching Shakespearean adaptations. I included myself as
a researcher, and since the course had not yet included any discussion of
Shakespearean transmediation into games, my contribution was a description and analysis of the massively multiplayer online role-playing game
(MMORPG) *Arden: The World of Shakespeare*. I tasked the students with
attending to the medium of the adaptation, analyzing how the choice of
medium interplayed with changes in plot, character, and audience interaction. The class findings were gathered into one shared spreadsheet, creating
a kaleidoscope of adaptations that transformed into a snapshot of Shakespearean transmedia worlding. The last section involved the students' final
projects, in which they had to envision and describe, or even create, their
own transmedia adaptation of a Shakespearean play of their choice. The
students not only adapted Shakespeare's plays' narratives, but remediated
the works into newspaper stories, films, novels, graphic novels, and video
games.

Final Thoughts

As this course explored, traditional definitions of transmedia storytelling
that localize the control of a narrative or insist upon systematicity do not
easily map onto Shakespeare. He is a hugely successful and popular author,
but his works have no copyright, there are no royalties going to family
heirs, and there is no single media conglomerate owning and controlling
the narratives of Shakespeare's plays or his life, which make millions each
year around the globe. Transmedia scholars could argue that this might, in

fact, preclude Shakespeare from being a transmedia author himself. But as this course reveals for students, ownership and control over Shakespeare's plays was always tenuous—indeed, as tenuous as some argue is the authorial connection between the historical William Shakespeare and these plays. The fact that Shakespeare's transmedia storytelling has never been fully under control most likely contributes to his hugely prevalent and polyvalent transmedia presence today.

The result is that authorship, ownership, extension, adaptation, transmedia storytelling—they belong to anyone who reads, witnesses, and thinks about the plays attributed to William Shakespeare. Transmedia Shakespeare *is* Shakespeare; Transmedia Shakespeare in the classroom helps students to see the ongoing construction of Shakespeare's narratives and legacy as a project that they themselves get to participate in, speak back to, and alter. The ingenuity and media-play that the students demonstrated in their final assignments indicated that they had grasped the liberatory, analytic potential of Transmedia Shakespeare, while also demonstrating their strong media literacy. Our class became—and yours can become—another node in the network of Shakespeare's transmedia world.

Acknowledgments

I would like to thank the wonderful leadership at the Center for Science and the Imagination at Arizona State University, particularly Ed Finn, Ruth Wylie, Bob Beard, and Joey Eschrich, for their guidance throughout the workshop process, and especially to Joey Eschrich for his brilliant copyedits for this chapter. Additionally, my deepest thanks to Yasmine Hachimi, Katherine Buse, Ranjodh Singh Dhaliwal, and Rebecca H. Hogue for their transformational encouragement and feedback.

Notes

1. Just as we recognize the importance of peer collaboration and coauthorship within the classroom, it is equally important to remember that conversations with our own peers regarding our classrooms and courses are an invaluable source of support and engagement. My conversations about this course with Yasmine Hachimi, my colleague at the University of California, Davis, were invaluable, especially in helping me engage more deeply and meaningfully with the work of RaceB4Race scholarship. RaceB4Race is a community of scholars of color who work on issues

of race in premodern litearature, history, and culture, drawing on and expanding insights from critical race theory. Learn more at https://acmrs.asu.edu/RaceB4Race.

2. In future versions of this course, I would have the students also read the introduction from Margaret Jane Kidnie's *Shakespeare and the Problem of Adaptation* (2009).

3. In his essay "Smells like Teen Shakespirit," Robert York (2006) discusses the disparagement that youth/teen Shakespeare adaptations often receive, with the film *Romeo +Juliet* as one example, for the myriad content and medium distortions that they bring to the play. But he rightfully reminds us that Shakespeare's plays did the same thing to their sources (57–62).

4. We were able to work in our previous unit's discussion of how age mediates our relationship to the plays, and for those students who were reading *Romeo and Juliet* for a second time, they found themselves more impressed by Juliet's strength this time around, and less impressed by Romeo. Funnily, they commented on how they didn't find Romeo as appealing now, specifically because they were a little older than the first time they read the play.

5. I also had the students interact with *Such Tweet Sorrow*, the Twitter production of *Romeo and Juliet*, but I chose to focus on *Prince of Cats* for my analysis here. The archive of *Such Tweet Sorrow* is available online, and the Twitter handles and feed remain available; it's another great piece to consider including in a Transmedia Shakespeare class.

References

Cline, Lauren Eriks. 2019. "Audiences Writing Race in Shakespeare Performance." *Shakespeare Studies* 47: 112–119.

Fleming, Laura. 2013. "Expanding Learning Opportunities with Transmedia Practices: *Inanimate Alice* as an Exemplar." *Journal of Media Literacy Education* 4, no. 2 (2013): 370–377.

Griffith, Michael and Matt Bower. 2013. "Transmedia in English Literature Classes: A Literature Review and Project Proposal." In *Electric Dreams: Proceedings Ascilite 2013*, edited by Helen Carter, Maree Gosper, and John Hedberg, 325–329. North Ryde, Australia: Macquarie University.

Hulbert, Jennifer, Kevin J. Wetmore, Jr., and Robert L. York. 2006. "'Dude, Where's My Bard?': Reducing, Translating, and Referencing Shakespeare for Youth: An Introduction." In *Shakespeare and Youth Culture*, 1–41. New York: Palgrave Macmillan, 2006.

Jenkins, Henry. 2010. "Transmedia Storytelling and Entertainment: An Annotated Syllabus." *Continuum: Journal of Media and Cultural Studies*, 24, no. 6: 943–958. https://doi.org/10.1080/10304312.2010.510599.

Jenkins, Henry. 2017. "Adaptation, Extension, Transmedia." *Literature/Film Quarterly* 45, no. 2. https://lfq.salisbury.edu/_issues/first/adaptation_extension_transmedia.html.

Jennings, John. 2016. Foreword to *Prince of Cats*, by Ronald Wimberly. Berkeley, CA: Image Comics.

Joubin, Alice Alexa. 2022. "Transgender Theory and Global Shakespeare." In *Performing Shakespearean Appropriations: Essays in Honor of Christy Desmet*, edited by Darlena Ciraulo, Matthew Kozusko, and Robert Sawyer. Lanham, MD: Fairleigh Dickinson University Press, 161–176.

Kemp, Sawyer. 2019. "'In That Dimension Grossly Clad': Transgender Rhetoric and Shakespeare." *Shakespeare Studies* 47: 120–126.

Kidnie, Margaret Jane. 2009. *Shakespeare and the Problem of Adaptation*, New York: Routledge.

Lamb, Annette. 2011. "Reading Redefined for a Transmedia Universe." *Learning & Leading with Technology* (November): 12–17.

Rowe, Katherine. 2016. "Shakespeare and Media History." In *Cambridge Guide to the Worlds of Shakespeare, Volume II*, edited by Bruce R. Smith, 1907–1918. Cambridge: Cambridge University Press.

Ryan, Marie-Laure. 2015. "Transmedia Storytelling: Industry Buzzword or New Narrative Experience?" *Storyworlds: A Journal of Narrative Studies* 7, no. 2: 1–19. https://doi.org/10.5250/storyworlds.7.2.0001.

Smith, Emma. 2020. "Emma Smith on 'This Is Shakespeare.'" *Shakespeare Unlimited*, produced by the Folger Shakespeare Library, March 31, 2020. Podcast, 34:53. https://www.folger.edu/shakespeare-unlimited/smith-this-is-shakespeare.

Team A-Go-Go. 2018. "Ron Wimberly Artist Spotlight." *Beyond the Longbox*, January 26, 2018. Video, 9:29. https://youtu.be/ebmUHcus0tI. Transcribed by Lee Emrich.

Teske, Paul R. J., and Theresa Horstman. 2012. "Transmedia in the Classroom: Breaking the Fourth Wall." *MindTrek '12: Proceeding of the 16th International Academic MindTrek Conference*: 5–9. https://doi.org/10.1145/2393132.2393134.

Thompson, Ayanna. 2017. "(How) Should We Listen to Audiences?: Race, Reception, and the Audience Survey." In *Oxford Handbook of Shakespeare and Performance*, edited by James C. Bulman, 158–169. Oxford: Oxford University Press. https://doi.org/10.1093/oxfordhb/9780199687169.013.33.

Thompson, Ayanna. 2019. "All That Glisters Is Not Gold." Interview by Gene Demby and Shereen Marisol Meraji. *Code Switch*, NPR, August 21, 2019. https://www.npr.org/transcripts/752850055.

Warren, Scott J., Jenny S. Wakefield and Leila A. Mills. 2013. "Learning and Teaching as Communicative Actions: Transmedia Storytelling" In *Increasing Student Engagement and Retention Using Multimedia Technologies: Video Annotations, Multimedia Applications, Videoconferencing and Transmedia Storytelling*, edited by Laura A. Wankel and Paul Blessinger, 67–94, Bingley, UK: Emerald Group Publishing.

York, Robert L. 2006. "'Smells Like Teen Shakespirit' Or, the Shakespearean Films of Julia Stiles." In *Shakespeare and Youth Culture*, edited by Jennifer Hulbert, Kevin J. Wetmore, Jr., and Robert L. York, 57–116. New York: Palgrave Macmillan.

10   Teaching Transmedia: An Experiential Approach to the Journalism and Strategic Communication Classroom

Jennifer Palilonis

In this chapter, Jennifer Palilonis describes the process of teaching methods for transmedia storytelling in the context of a strategic communications course. Hearkening back to earlier chapters, Palilonis provides a detailed, process-based description of a transmedia creative effort—in this case, working with students to develop a linked bouquet of texts and activities to encourage public engagement and enthusiasm with boys' and mens' volleyball, on behalf of stakeholders from USA Volleyball and the First Point Volleyball Foundation. Like Caitlin Burns's discussion of transmedia in Hollywood and the entertainment industry in chapter 2, Palilonis presents a case where the impact of media experiences can be assessed statistically, in this case through metrics like social-media follower counts, app downloads, and listener/ viewer counts on podcasts and videos. In strategic communications (and journalism, which Palilonis draws on heavily for her methods and values) as in big-budget entertainment media, clients, stakeholders, and funders often view the success or failure of transmedia projects according to these numerical measures, which means that education and training for aspiring transmedia producers should involve building greater literacy with how to use and understand this kind of data. Moving from industry to learning, the chapter pairs well with Lee Emrich's piece on transmedia Shakespeare (chapter 9) and Camillia Matuk's reflections on transmedia in STEM classrooms (chapter 7), in that it reflects on ways to use transmedia experimentation and design as a vehicle for teaching and learning—and in this case, for public education about themes of sports and gender. The approach that Palilonis and her students took to their volleyball transmedia campaign also connects to Maureen McHugh Yeager's argument in chapter 1 that transmedia texts build communities that co-create and make meaning by marshaling information and aesthetics from a set of multiply mediated narratives. As in Ioana Mischie's later discussion of virtually immersive urban design in chapter 16, Palilonis interprets transmedia projects as interventions in the broader public discourse, seeking to shape attention and interest to specific social ends. Finally, like Kayla Asbell et al.'s UTOPIAN HOTLINE (chapter 6), Palilonis uses transmedia tools to invite people to participate in a multidirectional conversation and create a new social arena, rather than merely presenting a prebaked text for the audience to digest and decode.

Over the past two decades, the media industry has experienced intense and prolonged change. Evolving consumer expectations and behaviors, widespread adoption of digital technology, and the rise of consumer content creators represent transformational changes in the way that stories are told and consumed, as well as how branding messages are developed and distributed. Contemporary media and strategic communication practitioners have access to a wide range of storytelling and branding tactics for building robust messaging to attract, grow, and engage audiences.

Likewise, as transmedia storytelling has evolved, we have seen its regular application expand beyond its origins in collective narrative and transmedia entertainment to educational settings, strategic communication and marketing, journalism, and social activism, to name just a few areas. The notion of building a narrative world that employs the strengths of various platforms to effectively engage diverse audiences in a single story, product, or message has become increasingly valued as consumer attention is distributed across a constantly changing media landscape. Contemporary transmedia also provides educators with a framework for modeling the effective use of different media platforms in the classroom (Jenkins, 2010), as well as building learning environments that engage students in narrative storyworlds. It allows nonprofits, public agencies, and others who wish to mobilize audiences to explore social issues in innovative ways. And transmedia storytelling allows strategic communication professionals and journalists to better engage their publics and attract readers to deep and compelling stories with more context and complexity (Moloney, 2015).

As a result, the number of companies engaged in transmedia—and consequently, the number of jobs for transmedia practitioners—has increased dramatically over the past decade. From news organizations to tech companies and retail businesses, brands are increasingly turning to transmedia to more effectively connect with consumers through distributed storytelling using blogs, videos, games, ebooks, social networks, and more. To work in transmedia, individuals need to understand the ever-shifting communications ecosystem, how to leverage the strengths of various media platforms, and how to apply audience-centered storytelling and design strategies. It's no surprise, then, that teaching transmedia is no small task.

There is no doubt that there is a growing demand for journalists and strategic communication professionals who possess transmedia skills. In a 2020 *International Journal of Communication* article, the professor of transmedia storytelling Kevin Moloney chronicles how the *New York Times* has embraced transmedia in daily news. He notes, "Transmedia storytelling is not a common term among working journalists, even if its logic is becoming as native to the industry as it is in others. Whether or not a news organization is aware of or understands the term and works to engage its advantages, it might deploy transmedia logics intuitively as a response to the current mediascape" (2020). Like commercial transmedia projects—such as entertainment properties like the Marvel Cinematic Universe (MCU), Nine Inch Nails' *Year Zero*, or the Assassin's Creed video game franchise—transmedia journalism and strategic communication are designed to unfold expansively as opposed to repetitively across different media platforms. This is a bit of a twist for traditional news, advertising, and public relations media, as it's more common to see the same story told repetitively across platforms. For example, it's not uncommon to see the same story that appeared in print also appear on a news or magazine website. It's less common, however, to see journalistic or strategic communication stories appear as a series of interconnected narratives, each using the affordances of a specific media platform to tell a different piece of the story. However, in doing so, journalists, strategic communication professionals, and others can create rich, engaging storyworlds, reach a wider audience of consumers, and use the strengths of different platforms to tell complex stories. "By telling interconnected stories, we can embrace the nuance and complexity that exists in any storyworld. Through multiple forms, we can engage the different parts of our story-loving brains. By distributing them across varying channels, we can target the audiences that really matter" (Moloney, 2012).

Moloney's analysis explores three transmedia storyworlds at the *New York Times*. The first is the native (designed as transmedia from the start) transmedia storyworld of *The 1619 Project*, which "aims to reframe the country's history by placing the consequences of slavery and the contributions of black Americans at the very center of [the United States'] national narrative" (Silverstein, 2019). *The 1619 Project* includes an issue of the *New York Times Magazine*, a special section in the Sunday newspaper, a multi-episode podcast series, an essay in the sports section, and a planned school curriculum developed in collaboration with the Pulitzer Center. The second is the emergent (wherein the transmedia properties emerged from traditional beat reporting) transmedia storyworld that began with investigative reporting into the roughly 6,000 New York City yellow taxi medallions, the metal plates that give someone the license to drive a cab. From May 2019 to February 2020, more than twenty stories about the medallion investigation appeared on the *New York Times* website, the newspaper, *The Weekly* television show, *The Daily* podcast, and the paper's *Daily Briefing* newsletter. Moloney (2020) characterizes the third example as a "complex feral transmedia storyworld" represented by coverage of the COVID-19 pandemic, "the transmedia nature of which forms through the life-or-death interest among the public rather than exclusively from the design of the producers" (4687). Again, the *New York Times* distributed coverage of the pandemic across print, website, podcast, newsletter, and television products over many months. Through these pieces, the *New York Times* has masterfully leveraged the power of transmedia to create rich, robust storyworlds that describe complex subjects through the experience of compelling characters, making underlying issues relatable and digestible—a hallmark of good journalism.

Equally interesting are the ways in which transmedia marketing has begun to reinvent public relations strategy. In the digital age, a wide variety of brands have begun to use the rich storytelling potential that transmedia provides to connect with consumers in innovative ways. For example, in 2012, Toshiba and Intel collaborated to create a six-episode web series called *The Beauty Inside* in support of the then-newly released Ultrabook. The series featured fictional characters developed to resonate with a specific demographic of consumers. The campaign quickly went viral, with more than 60 million views worldwide. In 2013, *The Beauty Inside* won the Cannes Lions International Festival of Creativity award. Similarly, in 2014, IKEA released "The Other Letter," a video campaign comprising television advertisements, a YouTube series, and a website to engage families with the IKEA brand. The campaign, which asked kids to write letters to their parents, was viewed more than two million times.

These examples point to a clear trend in media: the ways in which stories are told and consumed are constantly evolving. As a result, journalism and strategic communication educators struggle to keep up with the accelerating pace of the media industry. Today's media professionals must be innovative, nimble, and unthreatened by change, experimentation, and failure. Thus, preparing the next generation of media professionals requires that we equip them not only with foundational skills like writing, editing, photography, and videography, but also with the ability to adapt and innovate. Today's young journalists and strategic communication professionals must be ready to engage audiences on all available platforms, from traditional websites and print products to social media, live events, games, and more. Likewise, to effectively provide students with much-needed practical skills for innovation, educators must move further away from the traditional lecture/assignment/ grade model of teaching and find ways to infuse core learning objectives into applied, experiential courses driven by projects and infused with transferable skills that prepare students for the rapidly evolving industry.

Of course, covering all these bases is no simple task. Compelling trans-media stories or campaigns are complex ecosystems that engage audiences in robust storylines distributed across a variety of media platforms. Under-standing how to harness all these elements requires knowledge and skills that cross a number of core transmedia competencies. To effectively prepare students for careers in transmedia storytelling, their training must cover a range of structural, theoretical, and practical topics. At a basic level, stu-dents must learn to do the following:

- Differentiate storytelling in diverse media forms and channels
- Classify and compare storytelling structures and plot arcs
- Critique transmedia storytelling projects
- Apply transmedia communication strategies across industries
- Identify and explore ethical considerations within a transmedia story
- Plan a complex transmedia communication design
- Execute target-audience research for various media platforms
- Implement organizational skills and project management strategies

On a more advanced level, students should have practical experience that enhances their ability to systematically design, develop, and deploy com-prehensive and engaging transmedia storyworlds. In short, learning to tell transmedia stories requires both theoretical knowledge about how it works and hands-on skills that are best learned through experimentation, prac-tice, and applied experience. However, cram too much practical or theo-retical content into one course, and you risk leaving students with thinly developed skills across a wide range of concepts and an inability to do any one thing well. As a result, educators must find ways to efficiently cover the necessary material while keeping students engaged and motivated.

Experiential learning, which provides students with opportunities to actively engage in real-world projects, establishes a structure for truly meaningful learning to occur. Often referred to as "project-based learning" and/or "immersive learning," experiential learning requires students to apply both theoretical and practical skills to tackling a real problem or opportunity space. Furthermore, experiential learning requires learners both to engage in a hands-on experience and to reflect on what they are learning and how skills learned in a classroom setting can be applied in the real world (Beard, 2010). The ultimate goal is to advance learning outcomes that are specifically focused on employable skills.

When applied to teaching transmedia, strategic communication, and journalism, experiential learning lays the foundation for students to tell real stories that use the strengths of a wide variety of media platforms for real audiences. It provides opportunities to empathize with actual readers and content consumers to better understand how to effectively engage them. And it results in powerful portfolio pieces that allow young professionals to demonstrate that they can effectively apply transmedia strategies. Thus, an effective experiential transmedia storytelling project teaches learners to do the following:

- Plan and execute empathy research that promotes audience understanding
- Plan and execute strategies for creative product development
- Apply audience-centered storytelling and design strategies
- Create a transmedia storytelling strategy
- Build and evaluate creative prototypes
- Analyze audience experience and/or user data
- Present creative work to real-world partners and/or clients.

It's worth noting the practicality of this list. There is, perhaps, no better service that we can provide budding journalists or strategic communication professionals than the ability to apply the skills they are learning in the classroom to a real-world project. To do so effectively, we must align the curriculum with what's happening in industry. According to Jessica Gilbert, the senior director of product and experience for the McClatchy Company, "fostering this kind of learning is truly special and something that will become critical as media experimentation continues" (personal correspondence, April 12, 2019). Gilbert's team at McClatchy, an American publishing company that operates twenty-nine daily newspapers in fourteen US states, designs all digital products and experiences for McClatchy's news organizations, including the *Miami Herald, Kansas City Star,* and *Sacramento Bee.* Gilbert says, "Teaching students to use different storytelling approaches to entice audiences and broaden how they think of consuming information is true innovation. And project-based courses that engage students in real storytelling for real audiences could ultimately help lead to a new way of thinking in and around media organizations, which is and will continue to be critical."

Perspectives like this have become more common among media professionals who recognize that to be successful in the twenty-first century, they can never stop reaching for the next innovation in storytelling. This realization reached traditional university programs in the early 2000s, when the concept of media convergence first took hold. At that time, many journalism and mass communication programs across the US moved away from curricula that aimed to train individuals to specialize in one form of communication—writing, editing, design, photography, videography, among other areas—and instead began to encourage students to diversify their skill sets and learn to develop content for a wider variety of platforms and formats.

Since then, a number of colleges and universities have started offering transmedia storytelling courses and/or programs. The University of Houston's College of Technology offers a Transmedia Marketing certificate program, in which students learn storytelling and worldbuilding techniques to cultivate audience engagement across multichannel content distribution. Likewise, Coursera, the massive open online course (MOOC) provider founded in 2012 by computer science professors at Stanford University, offers two free transmedia courses: "Transmedia Writing" and "Transmedia Storytelling: Narrative Worlds, Emerging Technologies, and Global Audiences."

Transmedia courses can also be found across a number of academic disciplines. Oregon State University's "Transmedia Storytelling" course lives within the College of Business. At Full Sail University, students in the Media Communications program can take a "Gaming and Transmedia Storytelling" course. And several universities offer courses within departments of film and media, creative writing, integrative communications, and other fields. Although all these programs provide theoretical and skills-based instruction, few boast the kinds of intense, immersive learning opportunities that a project-based curriculum provides.

One likely reason for this is that most university courses—whether face-to-face or online—are structured in a traditional format that allows students to earn three or four credit hours over a ten- to sixteen-week quarter or semester. This structure often limits how much a professor can cover. However, an experiential learning model may free educators from the more traditional lecture/assignment/test model of teaching and learning by embedding course content—foundations of transmedia storytelling, narrative structures, worldbuilding, audience engagement, and multiplatform integration—into the context of projects. This approach can be particularly meaningful in journalism and strategic communication classrooms, which are applied fields of study that require practice not only of the craft of storytelling, but also of critical inquiry, critical thinking, problem solving, creativity, and contemplation.

Of course, there are innumerable ways to structure an experiential learning course focused on transmedia storytelling and journalism and/or strategic communication. However, the most effective courses begin with a clear storytelling objective; engage students with a real-world problem, opportunity space, and/or narrative; require students to constantly reflect upon what they are learning and how to apply it, both to the project at hand *and* more broadly in the future; and are led by an instructor who can adeptly walk the line between advising students on the fundamental principles and best practices of transmedia strategy and providing them with the freedom to shape the direction of the project. This freedom is critical to a learning process that embraces experimentation and accepts incremental failure along the way.

This approach has significant teaching and learning advantages. Building students' ownership of the project's trajectory into the course plan engenders motivation. It has been proven time and again that the most meaningful learning occurs when students are fully engaged in process and outcomes (Caine and Caine, 2006; Marton and Säljö, 1976; Nel, 2017). Likewise, requiring students to reflect on the significance and practical applications of what they are learning inspires enhanced critical thinking and problem solving. Reflection cultivates students' self-awareness and "supports learning objectives by expecting students to make astute observations, to demonstrate inductive or deductive reasoning skills and to consider multiple viewpoints, theories, and types of information" (Experiential Learning Office, 2009, 1). Given the practical nature of journalistic storytelling and strategic communication, honing these transferable skills is as important as developing "hard" skills like writing, editing, and design.

Susan Mango Curtis, a professor at Northwestern University's Medill School of Journalism, frequently engages her students in project-based learning. She is a visual-journalism leader and creative thinker with expertise in strategic planning and product management in digital and print. "Graduate and undergraduate students gain a tremendous amount of knowledge when classroom assignments are client-based," she reports (personal correspondence, January 5, 2021). "Real-world experience like this can't be duplicated with regular course assignments. These types of learning experiences challenge students to push the boundaries beyond a typical narrative, seeking new ways to express their creativity, knowledge, negotiation, collaboration, observation, and research on a professional journalistic level. They graduate better prepared for internships and full-time jobs."

Match Point: A Transmedia Case Study

The Center for Emerging Media Design and Development (EMDD) at Ball State University (BSU) in Muncie, Indiana, is home to an interdisciplinary master's degree program and undergraduate minor focused on design thinking, transmedia storytelling, and human-computer interaction. Designed to prepare an advanced, graduate-level workforce, EMDD presents a two-year program that pairs a traditional graduate curriculum with hands-on lab experiences in which students work with public and private partners to envision, design, develop, and deploy large-scale projects at the intersections of storytelling, technology, and experience design. EMDD students and faculty believe in the power of human-centered design and storytelling to solve big problems. To achieve this, the program brings together students with a wide range of undergraduate backgrounds and career experience, including journalists, computer scientists, artists, writers, designers, historians, social scientists, programmers, and more to tackle real-world problems using technology and digital media.

In the first year of study, students take six courses focused on the following:

- Usability and user experience research methods
- Theories and frameworks in human-computer interaction
- Design thinking
- Augmented and virtual reality
- Transmedia storytelling
- Interactive media design and development.

Through these courses, students learn how to plan, develop, deploy, and test communication designs and storytelling across digital platforms. In the second year of study, students take an additional four courses tied to the EMDD Creative Projects and Applied Research Labs, where they research and develop real-world solutions in strategic communication design and digital storytelling for corporations, nonprofits, state agencies, and other partners. Lab teams may include students with a variety of skill sets, including writers, editors, graphic designers, photographers, and others, as appropriate for each project. These labs challenge students to explore user-centered research methods, advanced project management strategies, audience engagement tactics, client relations, and transmedia storytelling strategies. In this way, the EMDD program explores ways to learn, both inside and outside the classroom. The skills taught in EMDD are intended to prepare highly trained professionals for careers in journalism, public relations, advertising, health care, business, education, and more. Ultimately, the center's mission is to advance students' critical thinking and creative problem-solving skills through hands-on, experiential learning.

To illustrate how experiential learning can help students effectively develop strategic communication campaigns that employ transmedia strategies, the following sections explore the course design for a 2020 EMDD project that engaged an interdisciplinary team of undergraduate and graduate students in the development of a robust transmedia storytelling and promotional campaign. Titled *Match Point: The Rise of Boys and Men's Volleyball*, the project centers on a documentary that chronicles growth and opportunities for minority and underserved communities within volleyball, the fastest growing boys' and men's sport in the US.

This project grew from a partnership with USA Volleyball and the First Point Volleyball Foundation, an organization focused on "creating opportunities for young men to develop as players and people by advancing and supporting boys' and men's volleyball across the nation" (First Point Volleyball, 2021). Founded in 2016 by John Speraw, the head coach of the USA Men's National Volleyball Team, First Point Volleyball Foundation represents a grassroots effort to grow boys' and men's volleyball, particularly among underserved and minority populations. Whether it's a new Division I or Division II college program, a budding high school team, or a community initiative in an underserved area, the foundation strives to help establish new programs by connecting donors to boys' and men's volleyball programs across the country.

BSU students engaged in the project were enrolled in one of two courses. Eleven undergraduate journalism and telecommunications students were enrolled in the "Team USA Volleyball Collaborative," taught by Dr. Adam Kuban, an associate professor of journalism, and five graduate students were enrolled in my EMDD Creative Projects Lab course. Both courses allowed students to earn three credit-hours over a sixteen-week semester. The undergraduate course is an ongoing special topics course in BSU's Department of Journalism that allows professors to engage students in real-world projects. In this iteration, Dr. Kuban developed a hands-on course that combined weekly instruction on the foundations of documentary with the collaborative development of an original film. Core learning objectives included the following:

- Understanding key terminology and game strategy associated with a specific sport, which are important skills for budding journalists and sports reporters
- Applying and improving students' multimedia skills associated with documentary storytelling
- Understanding how storytelling campaigns can help nonprofit organizations build their brands and contribute to fan motivation and recruitment campaign efforts

The course also explored:

- How to conduct interviews with sensitivity toward the challenges associated with playing a sport as a member of an underserved community
- How to determine which story arcs comprise the eventual feature documentary
- How to present the arcs in a way that informs but avoids overwhelming viewers
- How to compromise and negotiate with one another regarding subjective production elements such as choice of visuals, music selections, and presence/absence of narration

The graduate course is a required Creative Projects Lab in the EMDD program that engages students in the design and development of novel story forms, interactive systems, news platforms, multimedia apps, and other digital assets in the field of emerging media and communications design. At the end of the class, EMDD students are typically able to demonstrate the ability to design and develop a systematic, comprehensive, and accurate interactive communications product with an external partner. It is important to note that in this case, graduate students had already completed a foundational transmedia storytelling course in which they explored the basic principles of cross-platform storytelling, tools required to publish across various media platforms, and theoretical frameworks for creating transmedia stories.

The undergraduate and graduate courses comprised an interdisciplinary team of students with expertise in the following areas: videography and video editing, writing and reporting, photojournalism, graphic design, interaction design, public relations, advertising, and computer programming.

Together, students in both classes embarked on a four-phase process that included:

1. Defining project parameters, identifying the emerging storyline, and understanding the roles of the First Point Volleyball Foundation and USA Volleyball
2. Engaging in empathy research to identify target audiences and better understand how and where to effectively engage them
3. Engaging in audience-centered prototyping to envision how to best serve each audience segment on distinct media platforms and to identify segment-specific content
4. Developing and implementing the transmedia campaign. This audience-centered approach applied empathy research, transmedia storytelling, and user-centered design to better understand and define the key requirements necessary for building a grassroots transmedia campaign and a robust storyworld.

Phase 1: Define Project Parameters
Regardless of the nature of the experiential learning project, establishing project parameters at the outset is critical to students' ability to hit the ground running and stay focused along the way. One way to structure early phases of a journalism or strategic communication transmedia project is to start with a transmedia design brief. In EMDD, design briefs typically include the following information to set the stage for a project:

• Description of the proposed project and project partner (when applicable)
• Definition of the problem or opportunity space
• Challenge statement
• Key requirements

In the case of the *Match Point* project, the opportunity space was defined over the first week of the semester in the following way:

> Volleyball has emerged as the fastest-growing boys' sport in the U.S. As a result, First Point Volleyball Foundation has emerged as a leader in supporting this growth. Founded in 2016, the organization wants to explore innovative ways to build awareness and raise funding to increase opportunities for boys—particularly those in underserved and minority populations—to play the sport at youth and collegiate levels.
>
> The marketplace is constantly evolving, and the "build it and they will come" model is no longer an effective strategy for engaging a target audience. The 21st-century consumer is well informed, technology-savvy, and fully aware of what's out there. This evolving marketplace needs evolving strategies for building and promoting brands.

Then, to provide a clear and actionable focus from which to launch the project, the graduate student team was presented with a single challenge statement at the start of the semester:

> How might we leverage the rich potential of transmedia storytelling to chronicle the rise of boys' and men's volleyball in the U.S., promote an original documentary, and engage audiences in compelling ways?

Finally, key requirements were established to provide some parameters that would help the teams focus. First, given the nature of the undergraduate course, a thirty-minute, original documentary film was identified as the tentpole for the transmedia project. Second, students were told that they were required to engage the following stakeholders in brainstorming sessions and empathy research: First Point Volleyball Foundation leadership, members of the USA Men's National Volleyball team, and a handful of youth club and collegiate coaches around the country. After digesting this information, students quickly moved to the second phase of the project, which focused on forming a solid understanding of the primary and secondary audiences for their project.

Phase 2: Conduct Empathy Research

Henry Jenkins, a pioneer in theorizing and documenting the development of transmedia storytelling, defines "audience matters" as the links between transmedia storytelling and issues of audience engagement. He notes that in a convergence culture, it's not enough to simply attract an audience to a story. Rather, we must consider how fans might engage with the story by contributing to it and/or extending it beyond its original form. When it comes to journalism and strategic communication, we have seen a rise in citizen journalism (also referred to as "collaborative media," "participatory journalism," and "street journalism"), which allows members of the public to play "an active role in the process of collecting, reporting, analyzing, and disseminating news and information" (Bowman and Willis, 2003). Through this participatory culture, transmedia stories can provide a platform for the audience to have agency and voice and contribute meaningful content to the narrative at hand.

In the case of the *Match Point* project, students were challenged to form a thorough understanding of the audience segments associated with boys' and men's volleyball to build a storyworld that made room for their voices. Thus, the second phase of the project was driven by empathy research that included interviews with volleyball coaches and players, influencers within the sport, and fans. Coaches across the country were consulted to explore the barriers for starting new programs, recruitment strategies particularly related to athletes representing diverse demographics, and what about the game they would like people to know. Students interviewed volleyball players to understand perceptions of the sport and the opportunities volleyball provides. And students interviewed several influencers—including the executive director of the American Volleyball Coaches Association (AVCA), the founder and editor of a prominent volleyball media organization, and the chief executive officer (CEO) of First Point Volleyball Foundation—to understand the national status of the sport. In addition, an assessment of the media landscape associated with boys' and men's volleyball included careful analysis of the social media accounts associated with prominent sports organizations and influencers, as well as prominent media outlets that regularly cover the sport. Specifically, students examined social media brands that appeal to minority athletes, young male athletes, and their parents. Likewise, they explored social media activity around youth sports with similar levels of participation, like lacrosse, golf, and hockey. This work was done to identify and fully understand the target demographic for an original documentary and transmedia campaign.

Based on critical interviews and comparative studies, students identified five key motivations that characterize why audiences should want to engage with content developed for this campaign: (1) the thrill of competition, (2) participation in a team environment, (3) the diverse culture of growth in the sport, (4) opportunities to compete at the college level, and

(5) opportunities for colleges to increase men's enrollment and compete on a national stage in a rapidly growing sport. Knowing the target audiences' motivations helped illuminate the kinds of content to produce, as well as the specific types of engagement that audience members might enjoy. Students conducted audience research and analysis throughout the semester, but their most intense initial audience research activities began in the second week of the semester and continued through the end of week 4.

Phase 3: Engage in Creative Prototyping

Based on the findings from audience research, the students finalized the platforms that they would include in the transmedia campaign: (1) a thirty-minute, original documentary that serves as the tentpole for the transmedia story; (2) a website to serve as the hub for the storyworld, as well as a location to extend storytelling beyond the documentary; (3) a gaming app to leverage the spirit of competition and to increase visibility and interaction with the brand, provide accessibility for on-the-go users, and build a connection between users and its content; (4) a podcast to attract new audiences, featuring interviews with prominent figures in the boys' and men's volleyball world; and (5) a social media campaign designed to foster engagement with audiences and to support dialogue for fans, players, and others to consume, create, and share content.

During this time, the narrative arc for the documentary also began to take shape, as students interviewed a number of prominent figures in the sport for the story. Specifically, students on the documentary team worked to identify coaches and players instrumental in efforts to increase the number of minority athletes exposed to the sport. Interviews were filmed in several locations across the country, including Dallas, Chicago, St. Louis, and Anaheim, California. Student travel was funded by an internal grant program at BSU offered by the Office of the Provost.

During this phase of the project, the professor led discussions—both practical and theoretical in nature—about what might happen to the story as it crosses platforms. Students grappled with a number of important questions as they conceptualized more concretely how each media platform might fit into the larger transmedia ecosystem, including:

- What is the central narrative for this project?
- What are the secondary stories that emerge from the central narrative?

- What are the strengths and weaknesses of each platform chosen for the project?
- How can the individual strengths of each platform be leveraged to tell these stories?
- In what ways do you envision the audience engaging with and/or contributing to the story?

Students were also required to develop sketches, storyboards, and low-fidelity to mid-fidelity prototypes that visualized the ways in which the audience might experience the story. Finally, students were encouraged to be mindful of the audience-centered nature of the project. As such, they were required to engage in concept testing with potential audience members, including players, coaches, and other stakeholders. These activities continued through the eighth week of the semester.

Phase 4: Develop and Implement the Transmedia Campaign

Based on audience and stakeholder feedback, the graduate team spent the remaining eight weeks of the semester developing the content for the transmedia campaign, while the undergraduate team dove into the final editing for the documentary. *Match Point: The Rise of Boys' and Men's Volleyball* follows US Men's Volleyball National Team head coach John Speraw, collegiate coach Nickie Sanlin, youth club director Ed Wrather, and several others on a quest to showcase the sport in the US. The film also explores the challenges associated with attracting new athletes to the sport.

The documentary was designed to serve as the tentpole (the centerpiece of a storyworld) for the larger transmedia campaign. The term "tentpole" was first used in Hollywood to describe how popular movies are often promoted. For example, the Marvel superhero movies are often supported by companion websites, graphic novels, social media campaigns, and other platforms that allow the characters and storylines to extend beyond the movie screen, but the feature film is still the main hub or text, which all of the other elements support. Tentpole marketing also paves the way for fan fiction, conventions, games, and other participatory activities to emerge. As transmedia has come of age, the concept of tentpole marketing has become more visible in promotional campaigns for physical products, journalistic stories, and more. The *Match Point* documentary was launched in June 2020, but cultivating the audience for it began much sooner with the deployment of the companion website, gaming app, podcast, and social media campaign.

The website was developed as a hub to connect the various parts of the campaign. Regardless of how a user discovers the *Match Point* campaign, the website allows exploration and connection with all the storytelling elements, including movie trailers, photo galleries, and a blog that features ancillary stories about the growth of boys' and men's volleyball. The home page features a short teaser clip from the documentary trailer and provides viewers the option to watch the full trailer. The *Match Point* blog highlights stories that provide more depth about the growth of boys' and men's volleyball, as well as feature stories about prominent US players and teams. The blog is used to extend the storyworld beyond the documentary itself. The social media page contains a curated feed of all *Match Point* social media channels, allowing audiences to explore all social media posts in one place. Finally, links to download the competition app *Match Point: The Game* in the Google Play Store and Apple App Store raise audience awareness about the app. That section of the website also provides a brief description of the game and encourages audiences to visit these app stores to download it. The website launched in December 2019, six months prior to the release of the documentary, and was promoted on social media to grow and cultivate an audience.

Figure 10.1
The Matchpointmvb.com home page features a link to one of the documentary trailers, as well as original content and links to other *Match Point* platforms.

The ongoing social media campaign connects audiences and drives brand awareness to increase interest in the documentary and engagement in volleyball. Students developed and deployed strategies and content on several social media platforms to achieve those goals. Each social media platform catered to a distinct audience, and we took special care to be inclusive of various audiences by engaging with them on their preferred platforms with content that appealed to their unique/distinct engagement preferences. For example, the target audience for Facebook posts was defined as middle-aged adults, coaches, and parents. Targeted Instagram users were defined as middle school– and high school–aged athletes. This was determined through early empathy research, which indicated that approximately 72 percent of the *Match Point* Instagram audience would be younger than twenty-four, while only 15 percent of the Facebook audience would be younger than twenty-four.

The social campaign includes a variety of content and mediums. Short video clips tell the stories of members of the USA Men's National Volleyball Team, while photos show key people featured in the documentary. Graphics promote other channels of the transmedia story, such as the *Match Point* gaming app. The content on social media went beyond telling the

Figure 10.2
The *Match Point* social media campaign included Facebook, Instagram, and Twitter.

stories of individual people, expanding to feature stories about volleyball through sports trivia, facts, and history, and behind-the-scenes footage from the making of the documentary. The social media campaign launched in November 2019 and was maintained by a graduate assistant, who generated new posts through the spring of 2020.

Match Point: The Game is a twelve-week pick 'em confidence league app that allows users to become more immersed in the collegiate game by picking weekly winners in their National Collegiate Athletics Association (NCAA) conference of choice. Players could earn points and win prizes over the course of the 2020 men's collegiate volleyball season, which was scheduled to run from January to May. The app was also launched in December 2019 and promoted through social media in preparation for the Spring 2020 collegiate men's volleyball season. Although the app gained a strong following during the first half of the season, its applicability to the campaign ceased when the Spring 2020 collegiate sports season was cut short by the COVID-19 pandemic. Nonetheless, this experience was designed to be fun and competitive and to link a national audience of players and fans to one another and to the *Match Point* brand. The app provides a rich, interactive experience that leverages the competitive nature of the sport, its players, and its fans. To align with audience involvement, the students created posts on social media to remind audiences to pick their game choices each week, to highlight any game upsets, to announce weekly winners, and

Figure 10.3
The *Match Point: The Game* mobile app included (from left to right) an onboarding screen, leaderboard, results, and picks.

to tag users who won each conference during weekly challenges. The app also promotes the documentary, as players can earn points by watching the documentary trailers on the app.

Finally, *Match Point: Aces Only* is a podcast that features one-on-one interviews with prominent athletes, coaches, and sports influencers connected to boys' and men's volleyball. Each episode of the podcast highlights important initiatives and events in the volleyball world that would stimulate more elaborate discussion. Early *Match Point: Aces Only* guests included Speraw and two-time track-and-field Olympic gold medalist Edwin Moses, who was instrumental in helping start men's volleyball programs at several historically black colleges and universities in 2019. The first podcast aired in February 2020, after which six additional episodes aired through May 2020, prior to the release of the documentary.

Audience Engagement

By June 2020, exactly six months after the campaign launched, there was significant evidence that the transmedia approach to storytelling was an effective way to grow and engage audiences. On social media, the *Match Point* Instagram account accrued more than 2,000 followers, followed by Facebook with 725 followers, and Twitter with 617. In the lead-up to the release of the full documentary, three trailers were released on social media and viewed more than 150,000 times across all of the social media platforms we employed (Instagram, Facebook, Twitter, and YouTube). For content across all platforms, Twitter generated more than 650,000 impressions, Facebook generated more than 300,000 impressions, and Instagram generated more than 70,000 impressions. *Match Point: The Game* resulted in 193 app downloads, 189 on Apple iOS and 4 on Android, through the first half of the collegiate season. But the effect of the NCAA's cancellation of the remainder of all spring sports on March 12, 2020, due to the COVID-19 outbreak, left this aspect of the campaign incomplete. Finally, the podcast was downloaded by more than 500 unique users between February and June 2020.

Reflections on Teaching and Learning

All in all, these results are pretty impressive. In the first three weeks after it launched, the social media campaign reached roughly 338,000 people across all platforms, and more than 60,000 people viewed the first documentary trailer within forty-eight hours of its release. As of the summer of 2021, the documentary, which was released on the *Match Point* website, the USA Volleyball website, and the First Point Volleyball Foundation website, had been viewed more than 385,000 times. Likewise, in 2020, the documentary received a regional Emmy nomination for directing and an Award of Excellence in the Sports Documentary category of the Broadcast Education Association Festival of Media Arts. The transmedia campaign received a second-place award in the Interactive Multimedia and Emerging Technologies division of the Broadcast Education Association Festival of Media Arts; the website received a second-place award in the Best of the Web competition from the Association for Education in Journalism and Mass Communication (AEJMC); and the app received a first-place award in the Best of Digital competition from the AEJMC.

These statistics not only represent the success of this campaign; they also point to a meaningful learning process that allowed students to practice transmedia storytelling skills with a real story and a real audience. Parker Swartz, who led the graduate student team and was an executive producer and codirector of the documentary, says that learning to execute a transmedia campaign in an experiential learning format was critical to his ability to understand the complexities of transmedia storytelling and to execute a large-scale project. "Experiential learning provided us with the ability to work in a collaborative environment that is more like the real world," he said. "This is really important because it allowed us to actually apply our skills to a large campaign that made a real impact in the world. The result was more meaningful to us as students because we knew that a real audience would see it, as opposed to a traditional class where the professor is the only person who sees and evaluates your work" (personal correspondence, May 27, 2021).

Throughout the four phases of the *Match Point* project, students were provided readings relevant to transmedia strategy, audience research and analysis methods, and design and development for the platforms chosen for the campaign. Each week, students met with the instructor for scrum-like meetings, during which they offered a brief but polished presentation that provided an update on the project's status. The team was also required to submit, and update weekly, a document that chronicled all aspects of project design and development. Swartz says that the collaborative nature of the course design was a critical part of the experiential learning process. "I think collaborating with a group of students that is really diverse in terms of expertise was really impactful for me," he added. "I got to learn so much from the class itself, but also from my classmates. We got to build a more robust storyworld because we all brought different talents to the larger project" (personal correspondence, May 27, 2021).

The course design intentionally positioned the professor as a collaborator, team leader, editor, and consigliere. However, the professor stopped short of dictating the direction of the project. Unlike traditional classrooms, where the teacher is the authority and the dispenser of knowledge and students are passive recipients, this experiential project design fosters a relationship among teachers and students as collaborators and views learning as a process rather than an outcome. In this sense, the professor became more of a facilitator, and students were heavily engaged in the decision-making and problem-solving required for both the project and the learning process itself. "The lack of a super firm structure in the class was really great because students were able to make decisions about the direction of the project as they evolved," Swartz said. "With these projects—as is the case with the real world—there are unforeseen problems that you have to address, and learning to adapt to necessary changes is really useful when you're preparing for any kind of job, especially one in advertising, public relations, or journalism" (personal correspondence, May 27, 2021). In the end, project-based learning empowers students to be active participants in the learning process.

It's important to note, however, that giving students more agency to drive the creative direction of a complex transmedia project requires careful attention to the ethical considerations that must underpin a transmedia story that serves journalistic or strategic communication purposes. While entertainment franchises, alternate reality games, and other fictional transmedia properties are subject to fewer boundaries, journalists and strategic communication professionals must adhere to a code of ethics that requires special attention to unique concerns. For example, the ethics of journalism require that stories be truthful, accurate, objective, impartial, fair, and balanced. However, the distributed nature of a transmedia story may mean that segments of the audience see only some parts of a story, missing other parts. As a result, the perceived accuracy or balance of a story could be jeopardized. Likewise, while traditional transmedia stories often allow their audiences to interact with and even contribute content to the storyworld, any user-generated content in a journalistic story must be vetted for accuracy and objectivity. Finally, effective transmedia stories often suspend reality or seamlessly interweave reality and fiction to creatively engage audiences. However, transmedia journalism must never deceive audiences or otherwise hide the truth. Thus, transmedia projects like *Match Point* strive to take advantage of the rich storytelling potential of cross-platform narrative, while also upholding the standards of fair and honest reporting.

The *Match Point* team attempted to mitigate these concerns in a few important ways. First, each narrative platform—the website, the documentary, the competitive app, and others—made prominent reference to the cross-platform nature of the project. Although this would not guarantee that all viewers would find their way to all parts of the story, it ensured that the audience for any one platform at any moment in time would be aware that the others existed. In addition, each part of the transmedia story was designed to effectively stand alone as a complete, fair, balanced, and accurate representation of a segment of the larger narrative. In other words, nothing was left for the audience to discover elsewhere for an individual story to feel complete. Finally, although the team used fictional storytelling strategies—building a robust storyworld, creating an emotional journey for the audience, developing well-rounded documentary characters, and writing visually, to name a few—they did so with a consistent allegiance to truth.

Ultimately, experiential learning and transmedia storytelling represent separate disciplines that intersect to enhance a number of transferable skills that are critical to twenty-first-century learners. For example, the ability to think outside the box and display creativity is important in both professional and personal settings. Likewise, the ability to effectively collaborate and leverage the variety of strengths represented in an interdisciplinary team translates across an uncountable number of fields beyond journalism and strategic communication. And adaptability, responding quickly to changing ideas, and engaging in creative problem-solving are all critical to demonstrating flexibility and an eagerness to learn and grow.

Acknowledgments

Special thanks to EMDD graduate students Parker Swartz, Rachel Hayre-Edwards, Erin Drennen-Bonner, and Elijah Yarde for contributing visuals and narrative elements to the case study.

References

Beard, Colin. 2010. *The Experiential Learning Toolkit: Blending Practice with Concepts.* London: Kogan Page.

Bowman, Shayne, and Chris Willis. 2003. *We Media: How Audiences Are Shaping the Future of News and Information.* Reston, VA: The Media Center at the American Press Institute. https://www.hypergene.net/wemedia/download/we_media.pdf.

Caine, Geoffrey, and Renate Nummela Caine. 2006. "Meaningful Learning and the Executive Functions of the Brain. *New Directions for Adult and Continuing Education* 110: 53–61.

Experiential Learning Office, Ryerson University. 2009. "Critical reflection—An Integral Component to Experiential Learning." https://www.mcgill.ca/eln/files/eln /doc_ryerson_criticalreflection.pdf.

First Point Volleyball. 2021. http://firstpointvolleyball.com. Accessed December 6, 2021.

Jenkins, Henry. 2010. "Transmedia Storytelling and Entertainment: An Annotated Syllabus." *Continuum* 24, no. 6: 943–958.

Marton, Ference, and Roger Säljö. 1976. "On Qualitative Differences in Learning: I—Outcome and Process." *British Journal of Educational Psychology* 46, no. 1: 4–11.

Moloney, Kevin T. 2012. "Transmedia Journalism in 499 Words." *Transmedia Journalism*, November 6, 2012. https://transmediajournalism.org/2012/11/06/transmedia -journalism-in-499-words.

Moloney, Kevin T. 2015. "Future of Story: Transmedia Journalism and National Geographic's Future of Food Project." PhD dissertation, University of Colorado Boulder.

Moloney, Kevin T. 2020. "All the News That's Fit to Push: The New York Times Company and Transmedia Daily News." *International Journal of Communication* 14: 4683–4702.

Nel, Liezel. 2017. "Students as Collaborators in Creating Meaningful Learning Experiences in Technology-Enhanced Classrooms: An Engaged Scholarship Approach." *British Journal of Educational Technology* 48, no. 5: 1131–1142.

Silverstein, Jake. 2019. "Why We Published the 1619 Project." *New York Times*, December 20, 2019. https://www.nytimes.com/interactive/2019/12/20/magazine/1619-intro .html.

Transmedia Crosstalk: Lee Emrich and Jennifer Palilonis

Bob Beard: I'd like to start by asking you how you're both using the affordances of transmedia as a pedagogical strategy.

Lee Emrich: I wanted students to get to feel that they can be a part of the construction of both Shakespeare *and* his plays. Given the magnitude of Shakespeare's cultural place, I think students can often feel intimidated to speak back against his plays or critique them. By getting students to understand the "gaps" in the historical record regarding Shakespearean authorship, they can more easily see themselves as authors within the world of Shakespeare. So, my task was in part to work with this really powerful cultural figure, and reveal the transmedia constructions that have always been a part of his works and a part of the mythmaking surrounding him.

Jennifer Palilonis: In strategic communication, we often talk about how to attract and grow an audience. Transmedia affords us some interesting opportunities to explore how to do that beyond the more traditional marketing and promotional strategies. For example, we often include social media platforms in our transmedia projects and we talk a lot about how to engage the audience *in* the storytelling through those platforms. So, in that sense, social media not only becomes a platform for distributing and promoting a story; it also allows the audience to contribute to the story.

LE: Jenn, I feel like that speaks so well to how you approached transmedia teaching, if you will . . . getting the students to feel like they are active contributors not only in their project, but also as part of the course construction.

JP: Yes! Every transmedia project we do begins with a single sentence . . . a single "how might we" question. From there, the students are completely in command . . . they make all decisions about how to approach the story, what platforms to engage, who their audience is, and how to engage them. It's an incredibly exciting way to teach because not only is the story co-created, but so is the learning experience.

LE: Yes! Do you ever find the students nervous to have so much control in a classroom setting, or do they often embrace it easily?

JP: I work with both graduate students and undergrads in these types of settings. For the most part, they all embrace the opportunity to take an active role in determining the shape of their learning experiences.

What about you, Lee? Do you see hesitation from your students when using this approach?

LE: No, not really either, but I did get a lot of feedback about students not really ever questioning Shakespeare's place in our world before, and being told it's ok to think that Shakespeare's not ok was new for a lot of them!

JP: That's it! I am actively trying to work against what they have been trained to do in a classroom . . . sit back and listen . . . be taught . . . etc. My favorite thing to tell them on day one is: "My job is not to teach you. My job is to create an environment that fosters meaningful learning. We learn together." Including myself as "learner" is liberating for me and helps break down barriers for them. I think it helps create a safe space for experimentation.

BB: How do both of you manage this top-down, facilitated approach to transmedia? Part of the strength of transmedia storytelling as a medium is freedom and experimentation, but what sorts of boundaries or frameworks do you use to facilitate these as experiences with learning outcomes?

LE: I try to emphasize genre expectations as way to give them constraints. I also encourage my students to think—in as real-world a way as possible—about the media and genre for their final projects, and their desired audiences, as a way to ground and channel their creativity.

JP: I think that running your classroom this way is not easy . . . it's not for everyone . . . and it's not for the faint of heart. It can be really scary to give up control to the students. And it can be really scary for them to have so much freedom. They can't resist the urge to wonder if they're doing it "right." Like Lee, I often introduce "requirements" and/or "constraints" to help focus the project. We also do a *lot* of research at the start of a project. They have to immerse themselves in the subject matter, and learn as much as they can about their intended audience before they start shaping the story. So, I think Lee and I have a very similar mindset when it comes to how we guide these projects.

BB: What should others consider when taking a transmedia approach to teaching?

LE: A key conversation about any transmedia storytelling instance needs to be a discussion of power, financial or creative, over the narrative and the intentions surrounding the process. I think that a transmedia approach to Shakespeare opens up spaces to question and critique to whom Shakespeare "belongs" and helps students feel agency to speak back to the racism and misogyny in the plays themselves, and in those institutions that have used the plays to perpetuate and enact harm. So, for me, transmedia Shakespeare is deeply invested in thinking about ethics in the world of Shakespeare, and a transmedia approach should also include numerous opportunities for students to reflect on the power dynamics in classrooms or in narratives, as well as the opportunity to build, experience, or imagine new dynamics.

JP: Journalists are bound by a commitment to fairness, accuracy, and unbiased approaches to reporting. We are also bound by laws surrounding the First Amendment, copyright, libel, and related issues. So, when using transmedia strategies for journalistic purposes, careful attention must be paid to ensure that the story is not misrepresented and that the truth is not compromised.

11   Science Fiction, Simulation, Code: Transmedia and Translation in the *Foldit* Narrative Project

Katherine Buse and Ranjodh Singh Dhaliwal

Katherine Buse and Ranjodh Singh Dhaliwal's interdisciplinary chapter draws on perspectives from media theory, critical software studies, and the history of science to explore the cultural work of the citizen science tool Foldit and its community. Because it is both an active research platform for combinatorial genetics and a public engagement vehicle for science, technology, engineering, and math (STEM) outreach, Foldit is a unique transmedia project that the authors interpret as a boundary object in the public performance and perception of science. Their analysis of how Foldit frames and invites user participation parallels Camillia Matuk's case study on speculative design as a teaching tool for inspiring positive connections to STEM for K–12 students (chapter 7). This modeling of a particular relationship to the culture of science, a structure of feeling based on expertise but also enthusiasm and participation, can also be read as a form of performance. The Foldit community performs a certain kind of citizen science work that parallels the hopefulness embedded in Matuk's pedagogy and the more explicitly theatrical transmedia project of UTOPIAN HOTLINE, as described by Kayla Asbell et al. in chapter 6. Ultimately, Buse and Dhaliwal relate how communities are informed by who shows up, who is counted as present, and who gets to tell the stories of what the community does. Both UTOPIAN HOTLINE and Foldit invite particular forms of collective storytelling and community-building, each with its own transmedia constraints. This close reading of Foldit goes on to address a deeper set of questions about the epistemological stakes of community authorship and communally generated knowledge. As Terra Gasque and Ioana Mischie argue in their contributions to the volume (chapters 15 and 16, respectively), the politics and material contexts of these imagined communities can have powerful impacts on knowledge production: Buse and Dhaliwal describe exchanges in which Foldit enthusiasts requested that they be included as coauthors on scientific papers published based on the platform's genetic discoveries. This chapter reminds us of the foundational questions about authenticity and identity at the heart of all storytelling—points articulated by Maureen McHugh Yeager, Dilman Dila, and Yomi Ayeni in their reflections on the practice of transmedia and the strategies and tactics required to cultivate communities with shared narratives (chapters 1, 4, and 5, respectively).

Paradigmatically, transmedia uses narrative across different media forms to generate coherent fictional universes, drawing on the unique affordances of different media to tell a richer and more participatory story than could be created using a single medium. In this chapter, we explore a depth model of transmediality by diving into the mutations across media of a citizen science video game, *Foldit: First Contact*. Through *Foldit*, we excavate notions of translation specificity, uncovering a history of multiply adapted and extended media forms within a seemingly singular scientific media object. Through the lens of translation specificity, we illuminate the transmediality that now characterizes cultures of scientific inquiry at large.

Foldit, our case study, is a citizen science video game that enables players to contribute to research on protein folding. Here, we describe the history of *Foldit*, our encounters with playing it, and our experiences designing a new iteration of the game. A transmedia lens is appropriate here: *Foldit* already exists as a "reskin" of the protein simulation program Rosetta, embedded within a video game that was an offshoot of a screensaver—a history detailed in the coming pages. Our addition to the game adds a new, comic book–influenced, graphical storyline to *Foldit*, but it also adds layers of code to a code base that has grown over the course of more than a decade. The design and implementation process for the *Foldit* narrative illuminates a key element of transmedia that requires further attention: transmedia's translation specificity, or the medium-specific effects of growing a transmedia project into new modalities.

Our goal in this chapter is to make a case for using media studies, particularly analytical approaches to transmedia, to understand how sciences of simulation work in the twenty-first century. We advance the idea of translation specificity as a concept that can capture the audience-oriented and artifactual effects of certain kinds of scientific knowledge production. In the first section, we use Rosetta—*Foldit*'s parent organization—to illustrate the broadly medial nature of a large simulation science collaboration, and its similarities to transmedia universes. In the second section, we trace the history of *Foldit* by considering how Rosetta came to be not just scientific software but a public-facing media object, and how the media specificities of games and gaming influenced the development of *Foldit*. In the third section, we sharpen our idea of translation specificity by analyzing the multilayered translation that we, as transmedia practitioners, had to undertake to make our objects "work" as negotiations between stories and simulations, as well as art, participatory media, and science.

Finally, inspired by the fact that our *Foldit* project was equal parts science and artistic design work, we reflect on these relationships as indicative of broader patterns of interaction in cultures of science. Just as graphic narrative, video game, simulation, and code cocontribute to *Foldit*'s epistemological and experiential impact, many cultures of science are characterized by knowledge that is reproduced polyvalently across media. Through this lens of media translation, we argue that scientific practice itself is already informed and animated by transmediality. In doing so, we invite transmedia designs and critiques of scientific processes as a means of improving our understanding of the cultural dimensions and impacts of science in the world.

To describe the *Foldit*/Rosetta universe as "transmedia" is to read traditional transmedia scholarship—first elaborated around Henry Jenkins's idea of "convergence culture"—somewhat against the grain (Jenkins, 2006).[1] Jenkins's focus, and that of the scholars who have continued this conversation, has traditionally been on storytelling. A traditional transmedia project/universe is unified, as it were, by narrative cohesion: a story unfolding across multiple platforms and formats, with a variegated audience that is drawn to the franchise by their attachment to the story.

A narrative-oriented analytic remains helpful when dealing with communication media such as film, television, radio, and video games, as Jenkins was originally doing in 2006, but contemporary media studies deals with a much more expansive definition of "media." Consider John Durham Peters's arguments about elemental media, which have encouraged a whole subdiscipline dealing with environmental media, seriously attending to ecological entities (e.g., clouds, soil, oceans, and atmosphere) as mediating our conditions of existence (Peters, 2015; see also Chang, 2019 and Jue, 2020). Or think about the recent interest in logistical and infrastructural media, where containers, assembly lines, addressing technologies, and undersea cables are shown to be mediating human networks, both communicative and economic, at scale (Hockenberry, 2021; Klose, 2015; Peters, 2013; Rossiter, 2016; Starosielski, 2015). Such an expanded notion of the term "media" takes seriously materialities, as well as all phenomena in the "middle" of life and experience, as starting nodes for media inquiry. With this idea of media in mind, the transmedia paradigm bears revisiting.

What is transmedia if mediation is a function not limited to communication forms? Transmedia is shaped by the technical and social contexts in which it emerges, but the technological artifacts—media technologies—that it relies on also have their own transmedialities. A new superhero spin-off is not merely an extension of a storyworld, but is itself composed of numerous media translations, new adjustments between audience, plot, motion-capture gear, computational rendering software, and camera technologies. What is at stake when we perceive not just narrative, but also technology, infrastructure, and materiality as sites of transmedia?

Longstanding conversations in the history of science also help to justify approaching *Foldit* as a simultaneously medial and scientific endeavor. Scholars such as Peter Galison (1997) and Hans-Jörg Rheinberger (1997) have shown that science itself is full of objects that can be better understood as media. The production of knowledge requires new ways of seeing, and new ways of seeing often amount to new media. The components of scientific apparatus—such as microscopes, test tubes, computers, and simulation software—quite literally mediate (i.e., stand in the middle of) scientific experiments. Scientific experiments can often be seen as relying upon experimental media: new ways of bridging a gap between human perceptions and the as-yet-unseen world of constructed, mediated, and therefore more "objective" knowledge (Daston and Galison, 2007, 17–53). Such an understanding of science and technology is exemplified by the media scholar Siegfried Zielinski, who insists that media technologies are best understood as generators of wonder and surprise. Zielinski's assessment is strikingly similar to Rheinberger's definition of laboratory apparatuses as experimental systems that are in the business of generating surprise and unpredictability (Rheinberger, 1994; Zielinski, 2019).[2]

This convergence of media/science studies thinking demonstrates a peculiar emphasis on ideas of surprise and speculation. Media technologies—and here, we are adhering to the expanded notion of media that is standard in critical scholarship today—thus play a role that is not only technically generative but also aesthetically provoking. Wonder and surprise are features, after all, not only of laboratory setups but also movie theaters, TV screens, and video game levels. We can further hone this understanding of science as an inescapably *mediated* enterprise by accounting for the fact that media technologies are cultural formations. A microscope may be a medium that requires some amount of aesthetic critique and attention to the cultures and norms that shape its use (see Daston and Galison, 2007, 115–190), but even more urgently, a video game that does science (such as *Foldit: First Contact*) is a medium that begs for sustained critical attention to its cultural and aesthetic dimensions.

Adopting a media/technological consideration of transmediality provides a way to critically comprehend these complex technological objects that already seem to belong to numerous media forms at once. *Foldit: First Contact* is many things: video game, science fiction, graphic novel, simulation, algorithm(s), software, platform, puzzle, and scientific tool. This transmedia palace was not built in a day, and we offer a brief, reflexive history in the next section.

Rosetta as Transmedia: Creating the *Foldit* Universe

In the beginning Rosetta was created from the Centroid and the Fragment.
And the Fullatom Pose was without Conformation, and Null; and darkness *was* upon the potential energy surface. And the Students of Baker moved upon the face of protein structure.
And Rosetta said, Let there be the Metropolis criterion: and there was convergence.
And Rosetta saw the folding funnel, and saw that it was good. Thus the Students of Baker divided the models from the decoys.
—Rosetta Commons, "The Rosetta Canon" (2021)

Foldit shares many of the features of a transmedia storyworld that would be difficult to identify and discuss without the analytical toolkit of transmedia. This includes, for example, how the Rosetta Commons (the parent organization that hosts *Foldit*) licenses, distributes, innovates upon, and remediates its products to provide numerous modes of interaction for audiences of scientists and gamers alike. Applying a transmedia lens reveals that questions and concerns around engagement, intellectual property (IP), and, a little perversely, even franchises animate the world of *Foldit* as much as they do more conventional transmedia projects.

Foldit's history, recounted for us as part of our initiation into the *Foldit* research community, goes like this: before there was *Foldit*, there was *Folding@home*, and before that was Rosetta. Rosetta is simulation software, made by and for biochemists. Originally created by members of the Baker Lab at the University of Washington, it predicts the three-dimensional (3D) structure of a protein by simulating the interactions among its amino acids. The need for such protein simulation software was dire: in late-twentieth-century biology, the Human Genome Project and related work revealed new deoxyribonucleic acid (DNA) sequences—and thus the chains of amino acids that would make up proteins—at an amazing rate. By contrast, the rate at which scientists could discover how proteins were shaped was barely a trickle: protein folding was complex and difficult to predict. The genome was commonly termed the "book of life," holding the information that drove biology. And yet, until the proteins could be decoded, the book of life could not be read: only understanding the 3D structure of a protein would give the "what" and "how" of its function—the grammar, as it were, of life.[3] Rosetta's creators believed that being able to predict the structures of proteins would allow them to finally interpret genomic information. For this reason, they named it after an icon of the power of translation: "we call our approach to *ab initio* structure prediction ROSETTA, after the stone that allowed the deciphering of Egyptian hieroglyphics" (Simons et al., 1999, 172).

Rosetta's development began in the mid-1990s, and within a few years, it had already taken multiple forms. While it began as a single, specialized software tool for rendering folded proteins, by the time of the first publications about the software in the late 1990s, Baker Lab graduate students were beginning to disperse to the winds, carrying their research to new faculty positions in universities around the US and the world. To allow these new faculty members to continue to work with Rosetta despite its institutional home in Baker's lab, the meaning of "Rosetta" needed to shift. In effect, Rosetta became an entity that mixed the qualities of franchise, brand, and platform. This new entity, the Rosetta Commons, has its own home-brewed approach to IP, as well as various customs for maintaining institutional culture and shared standards. Notably for our purposes, the Rosetta Commons has been known for its success at—and openness to—fostering spin-offs, ranging from new interfaces made by collaborators to biotech companies spawned after using Rosetta for drug discovery.[4]

For these reasons, it makes sense to see the Rosetta Commons—and *Foldit*, one of its still-attached spin-offs—as part of a transmedia universe. It has the same fuzzy boundaries between forms, formats, narratives, and fan/user allegiances prevalent in more traditional transmedia. Indeed, researchers using Rosetta as early as 2003 instituted a yearly event known as RosettaCon, established online wikis and other tools, and self-consciously declared themselves maintainers of "Rosetta Canon." Attendees of *Star Trek* conventions, editors of the *Memory Alpha* wiki, or fierce combatants in the "Kirk or Picard?" debate would find this form of collective organization familiar.

The explanation for these choices of nomenclature is probably not coincidence: the Rosetta Commons, as an innovative new approach to shared scientific research, likely reached for the familiar features of transmedia fandoms—the con, the wiki, and the canon—because of the form that its leaders wished (or perceived) their emerging organization to have. As we discuss in later sections of this chapter, scientists often borrow formal elements from popular culture to suit their needs. We suggest that drawing on transmedia franchises' modes of audience engagement was a way for Rosetta to create a nonhierarchical user/creator base, where participants could flexibly work at the intersections of consumer and producer. This allowed participation at multiple levels while still maintaining a centralized hub—Rosetta Commons—that refunneled engagement back toward the core rather than allowing it to disperse.

In the epigraph that began this section, we can see that members of the Rosetta Commons penned a creation story, which introduces the wiki page for the Rosetta Canon. The passage echoes the language and form of biblical Genesis, but with a twist that speaks to Rosetta's transformation from product to amorphous transmedial entity. It opens by saying that "Rosetta was created," and at first implies that Rosetta was authored by the "Students of Baker," who "moved upon the face of protein structure," just as God "moved upon the face of the waters" in the King James Bible. In this first part of the origin story, then, Rosetta exists as a piece of software, a product that has been created. But swiftly, by the end of this playful passage, we find that Rosetta has been slotted into the position of a God, not a creation: "And Rosetta said, Let there be the Metropolis criterion: and there was convergence. / And Rosetta saw the folding funnel, and saw that it was good." No longer attributable to a single author, or even to multiple creators like the Students of Baker, Rosetta became a locus of creation unto itself, "and saw that it was good." Rosetta, a scientific project, emerges as a transmedia franchise—like Marvel, Star Wars, or The Matrix—that supersedes any individual authorship as the self-authorizing wellspring of its own universe. And this is precisely why we, in this chapter, treat it as such.

Media Forms Multiplied: Rosetta Meets Its Public

As it evolved, Rosetta underwent several medial translations at the material and infrastructural levels. Most immediately, its entire code base was translated multiple times: originally written in FORTRAN, it was first translated into C++ in the mid-2000s, as the scholars using it began to look for applications that could not be supported by the original language. At first, it was an automatic translation, but this code was soon abandoned in favor of a second, hand-coded translation into C++, this time with an eye to taking better advantage of object-oriented programming.[5]

Alongside (but not always in parallel with) these back-end redesigns of Rosetta came a series of remediations, which allowed it to bring the public into the world of protein folding for the first time. The first of these was the development of *Rosetta@home*, a citizen-science screensaver that allowed volunteers to devote unused central processing unit (CPU) time on their home computers to calculating protein-folding iterations. The benefit of this for researchers was that they were finally able to test a computationally intensive approach for protein structure prediction, using "aggressive sampling and all-atom refinement . . . for the majority of targets" (Das et al., 2007, 118).

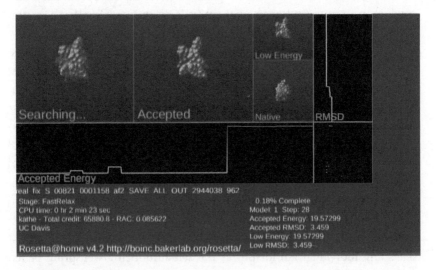

Figure 11.1
Screenshot of *Rosetta@home* taken by the authors.

In this transformation, a visual, graphic media genre was born. In exchange for the computing power that they donated, volunteers were given two rewards: first, the satisfaction of contributing to "real science," and second, 3D renderings of the proteins that they were helping to fold. In these early public-facing forms, Rosetta was still ultimately a tool for researchers. But for the *Rosetta@home* volunteers, it was something else: a rendering, an aesthetic experience, and a marker of identity that symbolized the consumer's support for science, much as *SETI@home* (which was operated through the same middleware infrastructure at the Berkeley Open Infrastructure for Network Computing) did for space enthusiasts helping to search for signs of extraterrestrial intelligence.

This new media format allowed a new fan base for the software to emerge. David Baker describes how this visual rendering led to a new paradigm for Rosetta: "Several [*Rosetta@home*] volunteers wrote in a few years ago saying that, after watching Rosetta fold proteins up on their screensavers, they thought that it was in some cases inefficient and they could do better if there was some way for them to guide the protein as it folded." In response to this user interest in having more control, the Baker Lab "teamed up with the University of Washington computer science department, and developed an online multiplayer computer game called Foldit which provides an interactive game interface to the Rosetta optimization algorithms and energy function" (Baker, 2014, 228). In Baker's narrative, which matches the explanations given to us conversations with *Foldit* collaborators at the University of California, Davis, and in Baker's lab, *Foldit* was a natural spin-off or outgrowth of *Rosetta@home*, and particularly of the new fan base's demand for more access to the simulations that they were receiving as screensavers. Although these motivations seem natural enough, the apparent seamlessness of the transition from *Rosetta@home* to *Foldit* ought to be investigated. Baker makes it sound as if accessing the "Rosetta optimization algorithms and energy function" through "an interactive game interface" was a simple matter, but it has fascinating implications. After all, a game is a medium that has certain specific features. If Baker's claim is true, then Rosetta was itself already structured like a game. If it is false, what kinds of translation need to take place to release an algorithm for predicting protein folding *as if* it were a game?[6]

Consider the philosopher Bernard Suits's definition of a game, still much-cited, as "a voluntary attempt to overcome unnecessary obstacles" (2005,

10). The goal of basketball is, when oversimplified, to put a melon-sized ball into a specific melon-sized net more times than the opposing team puts the ball into a melon-sized net at the opposite side of the court. However, one can neither simply carry the ball to the opponent's net and drop it through repeatedly, nor run around the bleachers and hide in nearby brush cover to prevent one's opponent from scoring. To play the game is to consent to unnecessary obstacles in achieving the goal, such as neither carrying nor kicking the ball, observing the spatial boundaries of the court, and consenting to a "reset" whenever one team scores. Video game scholars like Chris DeLeon (2014) and Stephanie Boluk and Patrick LeMieux (2017) have built on Suits's definition to show that while most games have obstacles that we call "rules," digital games have mechanics. If rules in basketball or a board game are like the laws of human society—one must learn and follow the rules—then rules in a video game are more like laws of nature: you cannot "break the rules" of *Tetris* any more than you can "break the rules" of reality itself. In this sense, video games are more like natural environments—spaces in which players are free to use any means they choose to accomplish their goals, rather than adhering to specific rules. As we will discuss later in this chapter, this makes them particularly promising for remediating the kinds of complex systems that are described by the social and natural sciences, as exemplified by *SimCity*'s famous playable representation of sociological theories about urban life (Wardrip-Fruin, 2009, 299–352). In this sense, Rosetta's algorithms and energy function are a set of "natural laws" coded into a computer, already much like a video game.

If the existence of these "natural laws" generally differentiates video games from analog games, the ways that each produces a different world or space of play are similar. Games have often been described in terms of players entering the game's "magic circle," a way of denoting the game's separateness from normal reality (Salen Tekinbaş and Zimmerman, 2003). Games traditionally involve a sense of separation; does this same fact not also apply to somewhat surreal simulations of protein folding? The magical space of the games in question, separate from reality, is ensured both by the simulation's own separateness from the "world," and by the graphical user interface that allows the *Foldit* player to enter into that world.

The characteristics of video games lead directly to the question of experimentation, which recent scholarship has started exploring in detail. In *Mondo Nano*, Colin Milburn (2015) analyzes the playful, digital nature of nanotechnology, which both operates in video games by way of citizen science (*Foldit* is a case study) and cultivates a ludic sensibility in its practitioners. In *Respawn*, Milburn (2018) argues that "the logic of experimentation is inherent to video games at every level," including "procedures of exploration, testing the capacities of the game, [and] discovering its laws and limitations, even if trying to break them." And while Patrick Jagoda (2020) discusses how games today offer an "unprecedented cultural means" for experimentation, Alenda Chang (2019) considers games' capacity to reflect the natural world by rendering mechanisms and theories from ecology as playable mechanics or representations.

Considering all these gamic features—remediation of experience, separation of reality, and proclivity toward experimentation—together with Rosetta leads us to conclude that it is partly true and partly false that Rosetta could be directly translated into game form. It is more precise to say that Rosetta became a base upon which the medial qualities of a game were layered. The basic simulation algorithm had always relied on sampling a search space and calculating the energy of different configurations for a protein. In this sense, Rosetta had always been a kind of idle game, a game being played with and by itself.[7] The video game format for *Foldit* was both a departure from and a translation of this preexisting Rosetta prediction methodology (Cooper et al., 2010). The goal of the methodology has always been to discover the lowest-energy form of a protein. However, arriving at this form often requires passing through energetically unfavorable states as different atoms within the protein try to attract or repel one another. Rosetta uses automatic processes, both random and strategic, to get to formerly unnoticed corners of the free energy landscape for a given protein. *Foldit* was to replace those random processes with human interventions while "retaining the deterministic Rosetta algorithms as user tools" (Cooper et al., 2010, 756).

This meant, among other things, that the game version of Rosetta needed to communicate with an expanded user base—with people who could not be expected to have a basic understanding of protein biochemistry. From the perspective of consumers and markets, producing Rosetta as *Foldit*, a game that could be played by the public, did require dramatic reconfigurations, and the Rosetta Canon had to be expanded to accommodate this new part of the Rosetta universe. A mass of new modes of interaction emerged with *Foldit*, including a new wiki (now hosted on fandom.com), online forums and competitions accessible within the game itself and on the *Foldit* website, and new categories of creator/consumers, such as Twitch streamers, power users, and attendees at live launch events. Unlike Rosetta, *Foldit* is a game because of the ways that it engages competitive and collaborative interactions among players, as well as how it offers rewards in the form of points and leaderboards. The game reframes badly folded protein conformations as "puzzles," which are released during a specific time frame as challenges for *Foldit*'s citizen-scientist player base to see who can create the lowest-energy fold (which means having the highest point value), both individually and in teams.

Rosetta adapted to the new video game format by translating what had once been data about a given "fold" into a set of abstractly semiotic indicators, while renaming existing functions with "terms in more common usage" (Cooper et al., 2010). Using color, strategic simplification of visual rendering, and visual cues, the protein hovered before the eyes of the player and indicated its needs. For example, areas of the protein's "backbone" that were red (looking like nothing so much as representations of pain in a Motrin commercial) spoke to "energetically frustrated areas of the protein where the player can probably improve the structure," while shapes in the space around the protein would attest to the presence of "hydrophobicity ('exposed hydrophobics'), interatomic repulsion ('clashes') and cavities ('voids')" (Cooper et al., 2010, 756). The interface was far more "intuitive" than Rosetta, allowing the player to click and drag the protein to manipulate it, as well as use a number of ready-made tools such as "rubber bands," which coaxed the protein to compress in a specific direction in the most energetically favorable way.

Like many other transmedia projects, *Foldit* blurred the creator-consumer boundary in new ways. As the researchers wrote of the game in a *Nature* article about the potential of crowdsourcing protein folding, they took "approaches from players who did well and [made] them accessible to all players. Most of the tools available to players today are a product of this refinement" (Cooper et al., 2010, 759), meaning that player strategies became canonical and were adopted as tools that could automatically be used by future players. Although it was created to bring a new audience to the practice of protein biochemistry, *Foldit*'s relatively intuitive and tactile way of rendering proteins was useful enough to protein scientists that *Foldit Standalone* was released, offering a degamified version of the *Foldit* game that could be used for pure protein manipulation by scientists.

As a scientific-simulation-turned-game, *Foldit* exhibits a self-conscious tension among its various layers of remediation. On the one hand, it must be accurate to the science, but on the other hand, it must be playable as a game by amateurs. This has led *Foldit*'s developers to be anxious that the game does not alienate players by being too technical or suggesting that knowledge of biochemistry is necessary. For example, any success had by protein researchers engaging with *Foldit* has been downplayed, and players are often lauded for their superiority over the career-scientist community, as when a developer announced on the *Foldit* wiki ("Updates" 2019), "Once again, Foldit players beat actual scientists" in reference to a specific, recently published paper.

For *Foldit* players, multiple layers of media, from the original Rosetta simulation, the screensaver, the player-produced tools and recipes, the wiki articles, and gamified elements (points, teams, leaderboards, and others) are entangled with one another—never fully dissociable and yet often contending for primacy. Several top *Foldit* players noted in an appendix to the original *Nature* article about the game that they were primarily motivated by competitive and team-based impulses, while *Foldit*'s own tagline instead enjoins "solving puzzles for science," indicating a kind of volunteerism as the heart of the game, which in turn harkens to the days of *Rosetta@home*, where donated CPU time was the altruistic mode of user engagement. Meanwhile, *Foldit* players are occasionally given author credit in major articles published by the game's developers. An exchange in the December 2019 developer chat suggests that this is another motivation for players: when one player asked, "is it correct for us to claim we are co-authors of a Nature paper?" the developer replied, "yes indeed . . . !" ("Foldit Developer Chat," 2019). This seems to have sparked a conversation about how some *Foldit* players would like their work with the game to translate into job opportunities, and players passed around information about where jobs are being listed. As multiple media forms, from software simulation to citizen-science screensaver to participatory puzzle game, provoke new kinds of engagements, there remains a kind of fluidity to *Foldit* as a transmedia entity: not only does the distinction between players and scientists seem to fade away, but the line between game and scientific simulation becomes blurry and complicated. This game-science hybrid incorporates numerous media specificities that are the result of media translation.

Foldit in Translation

In this section, we will elaborate on the most recent layer of media specificities to emerge as the *Foldit* universe expanded to add a new narrative version of the game's tutorial levels. As members of the narrative design team,
we had privileged access to the processes of media translation that were
needed to make this additional fold in the *Foldit* universe. Responding to
the desire to further widen the game's user base, perhaps to include players
who are motivated by narrative for entertainment, the redesign of the tutorial levels of *Foldit* by our group—ModLab, a digital humanities laboratory
at the University of California, Davis—beginning in 2016 is the latest transformation, a layer of new genre and of new medial qualities accreting atop
an already multilayered transmedia object.

Our team modeled the storyline of *Foldit: First Contact* on the format of a
graphic novel, owing to translation specificities that offered both opportunities and barriers. The first such barrier was practical in nature: the original
2008 version of *Foldit* was designed as a wraparound for Rosetta's preexisting visualization software, rather than in a game engine or design environment like Unity or Unreal Engine. Without rebuilding *Foldit* with a new
game engine, 3D or even two-dimensional interactive graphics were out of
the question.[8] Aiming for maximum entertainment value without adding
interactive graphics, we chose the graphic novel format—a visual medium
that tells a linear story and recalls a tradition of paper-based arts that may
at first seem at odds with a simulation-based game.

But perhaps it would be more accurate to say that many layers of mediation, from the mundanely suggestive to the deeply media-archaeological,
were swirling together in our design practice. In the deep end of this pool
of mediation, we might observe the history of protein visualization and
the pivotal role played by the biochemist Jane Richardson in the 1970s
and 1980s. Richardson created the first "ribbon diagrams" of proteins, long
before computer graphics could do the same, using ink and colored pencils
to represent the most important elements of protein structure while leaving
it clean and easily legible to the eye (Key, 2018). It is perhaps because of this
origin that, in addition to being called "ribbon diagrams" and "Richardson
diagrams," these renderings are sometimes referred to as "cartoons" (Edelsbrunner and Koehl, 2017).

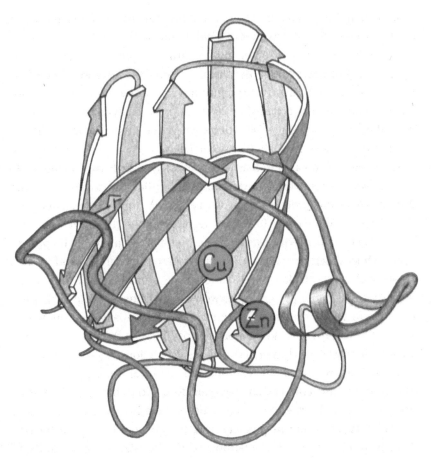

Figure 11.2
Jane Richardson's 1981 rendering of a part of a protein, in ink and colored pencil. *Source*: WikiMedia Commons.

What better accompaniment to a game about the generation and perfection of cartoon diagrams of proteins than a graphic narrative? Even *Foldit* developer posts about the aesthetics of protein folding—calling on players to observe the protein's "pose" and evaluate its shapeliness and color—gesture to this odd, skeumorphic relationship between protein science and visual art, and particularly (yet counterintuitively) the relationship between protein science and hand illustration (AGCohn821, 2021). Indeed, while it was composed primarily in Adobe Photoshop, our storyline draws heavily from the hand-illustrated tradition, using brushes and other techniques to create the characteristic textures of a hand-drawn aesthetic.

Our science fiction storyline opens with news of a fictional, worldwide ecological crisis caused by misfolded proteins. An entity known as the World Science Council is trying to determine the causes of the crisis, but the proteins that are misfolding need to be analyzed to understand what their shapes ought to be. This is where the player comes in: a new organization called F.O.L.D. (Forces of Lifeform Defense) is established. F.O.L.D. has been created to harness potential synergy between worldwide citizen science volunteers and AMINA, a new artificial intelligence (AI) that can quickly predict protein folding with assistance from a human operator. The player is Octavia, the first "new recruit" among this citizen-scientist team, who is charged with learning about protein folding while helping to debug AMINA's self-designed training tutorial so the operation can go live.

Many of the particulars of our narrative are a direct echo of the context for *Foldit* as a game. For example, we were at pains to avoid a "heroic" narrative in which the player is supposed to individually save the world, so that the narrative would be more compatible with the values of citizen science. Similarly, we chose to create a science fiction story—drawing on a genre with a long history of scientific and technical explanations, as well as reflections on science and society, embedded within fictional plots—that centrally featured protein folding as a topic. We hoped that our science fiction storyline would not merely offer players an escape or distraction from frustration or waning attention spans, but also an opportunity to reflect and build on their understanding of protein folding, its promises, its social context, and (some of) its technical background. For us, Rosetta's many forms are not an example of design evolving from one media format to another; instead, they embody the accrual of, and translation among, multiple layers of medial functions. The simulation algorithm, distributed infrastructures, gamic functions, and narrative wrapper all represent just some of the medial entanglements nested within what comes across as a single product, *Foldit: First Contact*, to the end consumer.

As we touched on earlier, we were also guided by the medium specificity of *Foldit* as a game. *Foldit* was built on top of Rosetta, and in this case "on top of" is more literal than metaphorical: from a coding perspective, the entire game is built up of layers of graphical user interface (GUI) placed on top of a 3D protein-folding simulation. In a small example of the

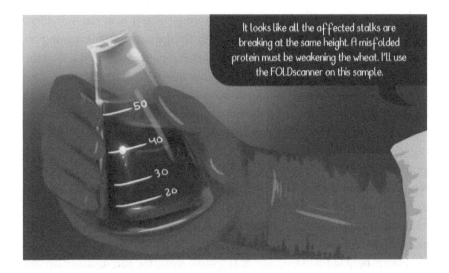

Figure 11.3
Snapshots from the *Foldit: First Contact* narrative.

architectural affordances of a stack,[9] the formal centrality of the individual protein simulation is so deeply built into the game that even adding an image or some text requires one to attach that image or text to the load file for a specific protein puzzle. As Rosetta became *Foldit* became *Foldit: First Contact*, the foundations laid down by the original platform continued to dramatically shape what could be built on top of and around them.

In this sense, probably the most influential single element in our narrative design was something deceptively simple from the original *Foldit* game: a pop-up, looking much like a speech bubble, which would emerge repeatedly from the protein itself during the tutorial levels' folding simulations. As we will unpack here, this element required extraordinary levels of thought and effort regarding translation specificity. Specifically, every graphic element we added to the game had to be shaped out of this pop-up speech bubble function, and at the same time, we had to maintain the original use of the function even while a narrative framework began to reshape its meaning.

The speech bubble has always been a mundane but key element of the *Foldit* game's tutorial: it introduces the player to new tools and how to use them. It also inserts commentary on the history of the game and of protein

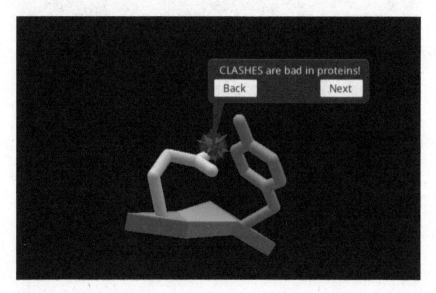

Figure 11.4
Foldit's speech bubble feature.

science more broadly and adds reminders and encouragement at places where players have become stuck in the past. This feature, the primary "interactive" element of the previous version of *Foldit*'s tutorial, became one of the most significant shapers of our design.

While the form of the speech bubble may have helped to suggest the graphic narrative format to us, the specific language used within the speech bubbles offered us a challenge, sliding as it were from a mode wherein "the simulation speaks" to a mode wherein "the developers speak about the history of science," as well as many things in between. Because we wanted to enable a side-by-side test of "original *Foldit*" and "narrative *Foldit*"—owing to the funding structures and scientific aims of the game's development context—we wanted to change as little of the original game's tutorial as possible, adding a layer of narrative without removing elements. And yet the speech bubbles coming from the protein seemed broadly incompatible with a fictional narrative, emerging as they did out of various histories of mediation, from tutorial redesigns for player engagement to prompts intended to help them along. Whose voice was this bubble expressing?

Out of this compromise was born *Foldit: First Contact*'s central character, AMINA. Like the speech bubbles, AMINA was there to guide the player. In fact, although our game was but another layer superimposed on the medial strata of *Foldit*, we encourage the player to interpret the extant speech bubbles as AMINA's utterances. For example, we strategically echo specific bubbles in the graphic narrative's dialogue—making it seem as if AMINA speaking to Octavia is picking right up from the speech bubble speaking to the player directly. This helps the game acquire a sense of immediacy, rather than the hypermediacy (i.e., the many levels of layering calling attention to themselves) that is the truth of the back end of *Foldit*. We prevented potential disasters resulting from the speech bubbles' occasional references to things like "the Baker Lab," the source of *Foldit* but not the source of the fictional AMINA, by removing the problematic bubble. But other times, we could not remove the element that seemed inappropriate, as with the ubiquitous appearance of firework-like confetti to celebrate successful level completion. Surely this is not the GUI choice that a specialized citizen science "special ops" team would choose during an unprecedented global disaster! Problems like this one led to still more design choices: we framed AMINA as having "designed her own tutorial," and we gave her a character arc, where she began as a "buggy AI" that might indeed have read the literature on gamification and ended up applying it inappropriately during dark times.

After incorporating an AI character to account for the translation specificities of our transmedia project, we discovered other affordances the character had, including ways to comment on some of the difficult elements of *Foldit* gameplay. For example, when we first played the game, we struggled to succeed because we wanted to use the "intuitive" aspects of the interface too much. While clicking and dragging the protein is possible in *Foldit*, it is the *correct* choice relatively infrequently. Ultimately, it is the human user's job to explore the search space and use large-scale pattern recognition, but Rosetta knows the mysteries (so to speak) of the energy function and can usually manipulate the protein and avoid accidentally mangling it far better than a human.

Our scientist collaborators explained that it is this unique nexus of human-computer interaction that was the core of *Foldit*'s advancement of protein folding. For this to work, both humans and computers need to concede the parts of the task at which they don't excel to one another. AMINA became our way of refocusing on human-computer interaction and using elements of humor, affect, and personality to help the game build a relationship with the player. Our hope was that players could come to personify *Foldit* by personifying AMINA, thus learning to trust the strengths of the algorithm and to think about their work as a collaboration, rather than as them using a tool. This, too, was a result of the medial history of Rosetta and *Foldit*. As players, and even as designers, we've found that layers of media history entangle—solving puzzles "for" real-life science, reaping the rewards of being a coauthor in *Nature*, competing for your team and against other players in the leaderboards, contributing to the wiki, and the intrinsic aesthetic pleasure of the screensaver-like cartoons are all present at different moments in different ways. Through and during *Foldit*'s many redesigns, new forms open up. The pop-up function, a call-out coincidentally shaped like a cartoon speech bubble, inspired a version of *Foldit* in which linguistic meaning (in the form of narrative) is layered on top of it, finally giving truth to the speech bubble's appearance, and lending the protein simulation algorithms a personified character for the first time.

Will *Foldit: First Contact* ever become canon, as *Foldit* became part of the Rosetta Canon? Only time will tell.

Translations in/of Science

At stake in this narrative of the Rosetta multiples—precisely the many his-tories, technicalities, uses, and affordances of Rosetta and its outgrowths that we have been documenting in this chapter—is an understanding of a certain kind of scientific enterprise, not just *through*, but also *as* transme-dia. While most transmedia scholarship attends to narratives or storyworlds that move through objects of various media forms (films, books, TV series, figurines, games, and so forth), our claim extends that transmedial impulse, both in critique and design, to identify its operation *within* media objects. One part of the "trans" of "transmedia," we posit, must pertain to the work of translation among the layers of a single media object. If web pages, as Grusin and Bolter (2000) tell us, often remediate older forms of media (such as graphics, animation, and video), then the aforementioned narratives should exhort us to see how, for a project such as *Foldit* to work, it also must reconcile with (or translate among) its own media forms actively.

Such translation work is dynamic: it operates both during and after the design of the objects in question. The medial layers (and their genealogies) are primordially entangled with each other; the graphic novel form in *Foldit: First Contact* had to adapt its shape and scale to a screen background that was itself limited to being a precursor to the protein-simulation view (or if you prefer a different model of agency, we designers had to do it). Our approach, incorporating this new narrative between the layers and structures of what came before, is common, especially in large, collaborative, and research-driven contexts. The addition of new content and new features usually only happens (for logistical, infrastructural, institutional, and social reasons) atop extant media forms. This dynamic translation work stays active even when the player interacts with the game: players navigate and negotiate the links between the layers of media involved in real time through the gamic sys-tem. They can, after all, actually see the simulation layer appearing in front of them as the graphic novel layer peels off when they click "Next Puzzle." Likewise, even in the 2008 version of *Foldit*, players had to negotiate between the mild fictionality of the protein having pop-up speech bubbles telling the history of the game (or offering a fun fact) with the scientific simulation of a protein that would otherwise not be a bad fit inside a laboratory.

But such an account only begins to scratch the surface of the relation-ships between the many media forms at hand. In reconciling content (and form) between multiple media forms within the same object, *Foldit: First Contact* indicates broader patterns of interaction in cultures of science. To identify these patterns, we must first ask, where exactly does an object like *Foldit*, a scientific simulation/game/community, lie on the chart of science and media cultures?

To begin with, it is important to establish that objects such as *Foldit* perform many roles at once. Given that one of the utilities of this project is that it produces data for "actual" science, *Foldit: First Contact* is both a media-cultural artifact and a scientific one. And it is clearly not the only scientific media object, as evidenced by other citizen science games and projects, from *EyeWire* to *SETI@Home*. Similarly, as we have discussed here, many scientific devices can also be seen as media technologies in the expanded sense of media that we began this chapter by invoking. If scientific projects are contiguous with media in terms of both media technologies and (less commonly but still frequently enough) entertainment and communication technologies, it is no longer possible to assume a history of science without a concomitant theory of mediation.

Furthermore, the story of *Foldit: First Contact* allows us to glimpse another connection between science and media that has been well explored by scholars: the shared projects of narrativity, genre, emplotment, and reception that often animate scientific cultures at large. While many scholars have observed that narratives and storytelling are central to scientific practice and scientific communities,[10] others have identified cultures of technoscientific speculation that flow bidirectionally between fictional narratives in popular (or high-artistic) media and scientific media. For example, Donna Haraway (2016), N. Katherine Hayles (2008), Colin Milburn (2010), Katherine Buse (2020), Sherryl Vint (2021), and Paweł Frelik (2011) all discuss, in different ways, not just how science fictional cultures affect science (and vice versa) but also how the science fictional valences frequently present *within* science itself. For example, Colin Milburn (2008) has studied, in detail, the science fictional elements present in the whole discipline and practice of nanotechnology—fictionalities that suture the science fiction world and the scientific world in general. In this sense, the science fiction storyline of *Foldit: First Contact* was less a choice among equivalent options than a choice to let germinate the seed of science fictionality that is so often latent beneath cultures of science.

Finally, considering this merger of science and media in historical context leads us to reflect upon an epistemic shift in recent decades. While science has always been medial, and our media always technoscientific, historiography and philosophy of science and technology show a qualitative change in the scientific cultures of the twentieth century. As Peter Galison shows, computational mediations in the mid-twentieth century started to replace mechanical parts of the experimental apparatus, but also to "stand in a novel epistemic position within the gathering of knowledge" (1997, xix). The rise of Monte Carlo simulations made science a practice of media technologies as much as the biological, chemical, or physical "stuff" of science (Winsberg, 2010). Modeling as a practice became prevalent, and models, as mediating instruments, started reshaping scientific and even sociocultural inquiry at large (De Chadarevian and Hopwood, 2004; MacKenzie, 2008; Morgan and Morrison, 1999; Weisberg, 2013). Today, we learn about proteins through models of proteins, as *Foldit* does—or to frame it as a general condition, we learn about the world and life from models (often software models) of the world and life. The interrelations of these considerations of cultures of media and science suggest a mediatic construction of science and, more important, a thorough co-relation between our media and science.

In fact, the translation specificity of transmedia outlined in this chapter reflects the movements of these very notions of science and media. Considering the media of science as cultural entities leads us to interrogate the long histories of remediation ensconced in each scientific-media object in question: graphic novels, slideshows, video games, computer graphics, and simulations swirl together in *Foldit: First Contact*, while visual windows and gamic histories linger in the Monte Carlo simulations used in physics laboratories (Galison, 1997). Similarly, considering the epistemic trends in cultural (and often fictional) constructions of science necessitates a transmedial view of scientific cultures. In thinking about science transmedially, we suggest that not only are media technological artifacts such as *Foldit: First Contact* products of transmedial translations themselves, but they also show how scientific culture produces itself through transmediality. Therefore, scientific processes show themselves to be dependent on, and coproductive of, the cultures surrounding long-mediated (and -remediated) histories of photography, illustration, cinema, animation, science fiction novels, video games, and simulation technologies, to name a few media forms implicated in these webs (Blackman, 2019; Jasanoff, 2004; Lenoir, 1997). In these webs, science and media formations become one single hybrid—scientific transmedia—joined at the hip; apart from *Foldit*, one can think of the role of games and virtual reality in psychology research, or the incredibly dense popular-scientific-medial nexus of space science. Just as graphic narrative, video game, simulation, and code cocontribute to *Foldit*'s epistemological and experiential impact, many cultures of science are characterized by knowledge that exists polyvalently across media. We can even identify scientific transmediality as a kind of historical practice, a cultural technique[11] that always keeps media as a central object of its scientific consideration, whether it is played out in a video game or a laboratory console (Siegert and Winthrop-Young, 2015; Winthrop-Young, Iurascu, and Parikka, 2013). Our media situation is increasingly transmedial, and our scientific condition increasingly medial.

Even as science becomes more and more central to—and even necessary for the perpetuation of—human life (epidemiology and climate science being two very apropos cases in point), the public's ability to participate in the same media forms—from simulations to stories to wikis—that buttress and constitute science has never been greater. We now study simulations of simulations and build models upon models, as with *Foldit* and Rosetta. If one were uncharitably reductive, one could argue that everyone in this part of the universe is playing a simulation game titled "science"—it's just that some people (e.g., scientists, especially those who are well funded) have more sophisticated models (whether conceptual, physical, or technological) and consoles (instruments, machines, and infrastructures) than others. In some respects, the two cultures have become integrated, if not indistinguishable, and knowledge production (as with consumption and critique) has become intertwined in transmedial layers of culturo-scientific artifacts that speak in many tongues. Translating between these tongues and calibrating these layers are tasks that call upon transmedia scholars to lend their expertise to this collaborative enterprise of scientific transmedia.

What would seem to be necessary, then, is the ethical consideration of these transmedial technoscientific histories, the past-laden medial "back ends" that underlie all knowledge production in the way that Rosetta underlies *Foldit*. Instead of considering science as a practice that requires "science communication" ex post facto, can we more thoroughly examine how technologies of experimentation themselves communicate in certain, delimited ways? Instead of teaching "media literacy" as a module disjointed from scientific education at large, might we learn to develop pedagogies and literacies that are scientifically transmedial in nature?

If the transmedial nature of a scientific project constrains what that project can say to, and/or include in, the (story)worlds of fact, fiction, and public discourse, then how might that space of possible utterances be expanded using the affordances of transmedia? When the protein speaks, what stories do we want it to be able to tell?

Acknowledgments

The authors would like to express their gratitude to Colin Milburn, Melissa Wills, Raida Aldosari, Patrick Camarador, Justin Siegel, Joshua Miller, Seth Cooper, and other members of ModLab (University of California, Davis) and the Siegel and Cooper Labs at the University of California, Davis, and Northeastern University, respectively. The research for this article was partly supported by NSF grant 1627539. Finally, we would also like to thank the Center for Science and the Imagination at Arizona State University, including the editors Ed Finn, Ruth Wylie, Joey Eschrich, and Bob Beard, as well as our review partner, Lee Emrich, for their many astute comments and suggestions. All errors, of course, are our own.

Notes

1. See also Ryan (2004, 2017) for a similar treatment of transmedia.

2. For a similar claim regarding artistic practices at large, see Schwab (2013).

3. The sense that decoding the structure of proteins would allow scientists to "speak the language" of biology has been explicitly articulated to us by our collaborators in the Siegel lab at the University of California, Davis. In making this claim, our collaborators draw on a well-documented analogy: see Kay (2000).

4. For more about this institutional culture and Rosetta Commons as a franchise/platform/brand, see Abbass and Nebel (2020) and Leman et al. (2020).

5. As we've been analyzing the intersections between media and history of science, it is worth noting here that this issue of compatibility and translation specificity is common in large scientific projects. For example, many climate models were originally written (and parts still appear) in FORTRAN, and numerous health-care and insurance systems are still running on MUMPS, COBOL, and FORTRAN (Hicks, 2020).

6. For other work on translation and transmedia, see Saldre and Torop (2012); Gambarato (2013); Malenova (2018). See also Harvey (2015).

7. Idle games, sometimes called "clicker games," are a genre of games where minimal player interaction is required to make the game progress. Much game time is spent waiting, often as resources accumulate or processes complete.

8. As we will discuss later in this chapter, this is a result of both the experimental design of our task—the need to be able to publish on our A/B tested release—and the institutional residues of Rosetta and *Foldit* as vast conglomerations with far too many stakeholders to allow a single group to do a full-scale rewrite of the game for any reason.

9. For more on how coding stacks formalize at scale, see Bratton (2015).

10. On the uptake of popular narratives in the practice of science, see Wald (2007). On the way that narratives operate on a discursive level to structure the culture of science, see Traweek (1988) and Haraway (1989).

11. Theories of "cultural techniques," or *Kulturtechniken*, provide a conceptual framework for reflecting on the historical and cultural valences of techniques (or habits) and technologies (or machines) altogether.

References

Abbass, Jad, and Jean-Christophe Nebel. 2020. "Rosetta and the Journey to Predict Proteins' Structures, 20 Years On." *Current Bioinformatics* 15, no. 6, 611–628. https://doi.org/10.2174/1574893615999200504103643.

AGCohn821. 2021. "How to Foldit, Part 2: An Eye for Beauty." *Foldit*, January 5, 2021. https://fold.it/portal/node/2010984#comment-43814.

Baker, David. 2014. "Protein Folding, Structure Prediction and Design." *Biochemical Society Transactions* 42, no. 2: 225–229. https://doi.org/10.1042/BST20130055.

Blackman, Lisa. 2019. *Haunted Data: Affect, Transmedia, Weird Science*. London: Bloomsbury.

Bolter, Jay David, and Richard A. Grusin. 2000. *Remediation: Understanding New Media*. Cambridge, MA: MIT Press.

Boluk, Stephanie, and Patrick LeMieux. 2017. *Metagaming: Playing, Competing, Spectating, Cheating, Trading, Making, and Breaking Videogames*. Minneapolis: University of Minnesota Press.

Bratton, Benjamin. 2015. *The Stack: On Software and Sovereignty*. Cambridge, MA: MIT Press.

Buse, Katherine. 2020. "The Working Planetologist: Speculative Worlds and the Practice of Climate Science." In *Practices of Speculation: Modeling, Embodiment,*

Figuration, edited by Jeanne Cortiel, Christine Hanke, Jan Hutta, and Colin Milburn, 7–30. Bielefeld, Germany: Transcript Verlag.

Chang, Alenda Y. 2019. *Playing Nature: Ecology in Video Games*. Minneapolis: University of Minnesota Press.

Cooper, Seth, Firas Khatib, Adrien Treuille, et al. 2010. "Predicting Protein Structures with a Multiplayer Online Game." *Nature* 466, no. 7307: 756–760. https://doi.org/10.1038/nature09304.

Das, Rhiju, Bin Qian, Srivatsan Raman, et al. 2007. "Structure Prediction for CASP7 Targets Using Extensive All-Atom Refinement with Rosetta@home." *Proteins: Structure, Function and Genetics* 69, no. 8: 118–128. https://doi.org/10.1002/prot.21636.

Daston, Lorraine, and Peter Galison. 2007. *Objectivity*. New York: Zone Books.

De Chadarevian, Soraya, and Nick Hopwood, eds. 2004. *Models: The Third Dimension of Science*. Stanford, CA: Stanford University Press.

DeLeon, Chris. 2014. "Rules in Computer Games Compared to Rules in Traditional Games." *DiGRA '13—Proceedings of the 2013 DiGRA International Conference: DeFragging Game Studies* 7 (August). http://www.digra.org/wp-content/uploads/digital-library/paper_477.pdf.

Edelsbrunner, Herbert, and Patrice Koehl. 2017. "Computational Topology for Structural Molecular Biology." In *Handbook of Discrete and Computational Geometry*, 3rd ed., edited by Jacob E. Goodman, Joseph O'Rourke, and Csaba D. Tóth, 1709–1735. London: Chapman and Hall.

"Foldit Developer Chat." 2019. *Foldit*, December. https://fold.it/portal/node/2008363.

Frelik, Paweł. 2011. "Of Slipstream and Others: SF and Genre Boundary Discourses." *Science Fiction Studies* 38, no. 1, 20–45.

Galison, Peter. 1997. *Image and Logic: A Material Culture of Microphysics*. Chicago: University of Chicago Press.

Gambarato, Renira Rampazzo. 2013. "Transmedia Project Design: Theoretical and Analytical Considerations." *Baltic Screen Media Review* 1, no. 1, 80–100.

Haraway, Donna J. 1989. *Primate Visions: Gender, Race, and Nature in the World of Modern Science*. New York: Routledge.

Haraway, Donna J. 2016. *Manifestly Haraway*. Minneapolis: University of Minnesota Press.

Harvey, Colin B. 2015. "Fantastic Transmedia." In *Fantastic Transmedia: Narrative, Play and Memory Across Science Fiction and Fantasy Storyworlds*, 12–39. London: Palgrave Macmillan.

Hayles, N. Katherine. 2008. *How We Became Posthuman: Virtual Bodies in Cybernetics, Literature, and Informatics*. Chicago: University of Chicago Press.

Hicks, Mar. 2020. "Built to Last," *Logic Magazine*, August 31, 2020. https://logicmag .io/care/built-to-last.

Hockenberry, Matthew. 2021. *Assembly Codes: The Logistics of Media*. Durham, NC: Duke University Press.

Jagoda, Patrick. 2020. *Experimental Games: Critique, Play, and Design in the Age of Gamification*. Chicago: University of Chicago Press.

Jasanoff, Sheila, ed. 2004. *States of Knowledge: The Co-production of Science and the Social Order*. New York: Routledge.

Jenkins, Henry. 2006. *Convergence Culture: Where Old and New Media Collide*. New York: New York University Press.

Jue, Melody. 2020. *Wild Blue Media: Thinking through Seawater*. Durham, NC: Duke University Press.

Kay, Lily E. 2000. *Who Wrote the Book of Life? A History of the Genetic Code*. Stanford, CA: Stanford University Press.

Key, Lindsay. 2018. "Science's 'Mother of Ribbon Diagrams' celebrates 50 years at Duke." *DukeStories*, October 19, 2018. https://stories.duke.edu/sciences-mother-of -ribbon-diagrams-celebrates-50-years-at-duke.

Klose, Alexander. 2015. *The Container Principle: How a Box Changes the Way We Think*. Cambridge, MA: MIT Press.

Leman, Julia Koehler, Brian D. Weitzner, P. Douglas Renfrew, et al. 2020. "Better Together: Elements of Successful Scientific Software Development in a Distributed Collaborative Community." *PLoS Computational Biology* 16, no. 5. https://doi.org/10 .1371/journal.pcbi.1007507.

Lenoir, Timothy. 1997. *Instituting Science: The Cultural Production of Scientific Disciplines*. Stanford, CA: Stanford University Press.

MacKenzie, Donald. 2008. *An Engine, Not a Camera: How Financial Models Shape Markets*. Cambridge, MA: MIT Press.

Malenova, Evgeniya D. 2018. "Creative Practices in Translation of Transmedia Projects." *Humanities & Social Sciences* 5, no. 11: 775–786.

Milburn, Colin. 2008. *Nanovision: Engineering the Future*. Durham, NC: Duke University Press.

Milburn, Colin. 2010. "Modifiable Futures: Science Fiction at the Bench." *Isis* 101, no. 3: 560–569.

Milburn, Colin. 2015. *Mondo Nano: Fun and Games in the World of Digital Matter.* Durham, NC: Duke University Press.

Milburn, Colin. 2018. *Respawn: Games, Hackers, and Technogenic Life.* Durham, NC: Duke University Press.

Morgan, Mary S., and Margaret Morrison, eds. 1999. *Models as Mediators: Perspectives on Natural and Social Science.* Cambridge: Cambridge University Press.

Peters, John Durham. 2013. "Calendar, Clock, Tower." In *Deus in Machina: Religion, Technology, and the Things in Between,* edited by Jeremy Stolow, 25–42. New York: Fordham University Press.

Peters, John Durham. 2015. *The Marvelous Clouds: Toward a Philosophy of Elemental Media.* Chicago: University of Chicago Press.

Rheinberger, Hans-Jörg. 1994. "Experimental Systems: Historiality, Narration, and Deconstruction." *Science in Context* 7, no. 1: 65–81.

Rheinberger, Hans-Jörg. 1997. *Toward a History of Epistemic Things: Synthesizing Proteins in the Test Tube.* Stanford, CA: Stanford University Press.

"The Rosetta Canon." 2021. *Rosetta Commons,* March 31, 2021. http://new .rosettacommons.org/docs/latest/getting_started/Rosetta-canon.

Rossiter, Ned. 2016. *Software, Infrastructure, Labor: A Media Theory of Logistical Nightmares.* New York: Routledge.

Ryan, Marie-Laure. 2004. *Narrative across Media: The Languages of Storytelling.* Lincoln: University of Nebraska Press.

Ryan, Marie-Laure. 2017. "Transmedia Storytelling as Narrative Practice." In *Oxford Handbook of Adaptation Studies,* edited by Thomas Leitch, 527–541. Oxford: Oxford University Press.

Saldre, Maarja, and Peeter Torop. 2012. "Transmedia Space." In *Crossmedia Innovations: Texts, Markets, Institutions,* edited by Indrek Ibrus and Carlos A. Scolari, 25–44. Bern, Switzerland: Peter Lang.

Salen Tekinbaş, Katie, and Eric Zimmerman. 2003. "The Magic Circle." In *Rules of Play: Game Design Fundamentals,* 92–99. Cambridge, MA: MIT Press.

Schwab, Michael, ed. 2013. *Experimental Systems: Future Knowledge in Artistic Research.* Leuven, Belgium: Leuven University Press.

Siegert, Bernhard. 2015. *Cultural Techniques: Grids, Filters, Doors, and Other Articulations of the Real.* Translated by Geoffrey Winthrop-Young. New York: Fordham University Press.

Simons, Kim T., Rich Bonneau, Ingo Ruczinski, and David Baker. 1999. "Ab Initio Protein Structure Prediction of CASP III Targets Using ROSETTA." *Proteins* 37 (Suppl. 3):

171–176. https://doi.org/10.1002/(SICI)1097-0134(1999)37:3+%3C171::AID-PROT21 %3E3.0.CO;2-Z.

Starosielski, Nicole. 2015. *The Undersea Network*. Durham, NC: Duke University Press.

Suits, B. 2005. *The Grasshopper: Games, Life and Utopia*. Peterborough, Canada: Broadview Press. Originally published in 1978.

Traweek, Sharon. 1988. "Pilgrim's Progress: Male Tales Told during Life in Physics." In *Beamtimes and Lifetimes: The World of High Energy Physicists*, 74–105. Cambridge, MA: Harvard University Press.

"Updates." 2019. *Foldit* Wiki, November 11, 2019. https://foldit.fandom.com/wiki /Foldit_Wiki.

Vint, Sherryl. 2021. *Science Fiction*. Cambridge, MA: MIT Press.

Wald, Priscilla. 2007. *Contagious: Cultures, Carriers, and the Outbreak Narrative*. Durham, NC: Duke University Press.

Wardrip-Fruin, Noah. 2009. *Expressive Processing: Digital Fictions, Computer Games, and Software Studies*. Cambridge, MA: MIT Press.

Weisberg, Michael. 2013. *Simulation and Similarity: Using Models to Understand the World*. Oxford: Oxford University Press.

Winsberg, Eric. 2010. *Science in the Age of Computer Simulation*. Chicago: University of Chicago Press.

Winthrop-Young, Geoffrey, Ilinca Iurascu, and Jussi Parikka. 2013. "Cultural Techniques." Special Issue, *Theory, Culture, and Society* 30, no. 6 (November).

Zielinski, Siegfried. 2019. *Variations on Media Thinking*. Minneapolis: University of Minnesota Press.

12   Frankenmedia: Using Narrative and Play in Informal Transmedia Learning Environments

Ruth Wylie, Areej Mawasi, Joey Eschrich, Peter Nagy, Bob Beard, and Ed Finn

Throughout this volume, the contributors demonstrate how transmedia projects can facilitate connective action based on personal perspectives and acts of self-expression. As in previous chapters from Maureen McHugh Yeager, Caitlin Burns, Yomi Ayeni, and Kayla Asbell et al. (chapters 1, 2, 5, and 6, respectively), as well as later in the book, significant work is required to establish the cognitive and distributive infrastructures to enable intertextual exchanges and meaning-making among participants. In this chapter, Wylie et al. demonstrate the effectiveness of using a well-known, preexisting text as a foundation for an accessible, audience-driven learning experience. The authors describe their findings in creating an informal science, technology, engineering, and math (STEM) learning project based on Frankenstein—both the original 1818 novel by Mary Wollstonecraft Shelley and the story's legacy of adaptation, translation, and remixing across decades. As in Lee Emrich's discussion of transmedia Shakespeare in the classroom (chapter 9), employing a culturally resonant and ubiquitous narrative hook provided participants a ready-made grammar and familiar set of associations with which to engage the themes and iconography of the experience in ways that were personally meaningful and supportive of collaborative learning. The same challenge of co-creating spaces for shared learning is taken up by Camillia Matuk in chapter 7, on speculative design methods in the K–12 classroom. Wylie and her coauthors highlight the effectiveness of transmedia experiences in informal learning environments, where participants can freely explore multiple related concepts and increase their "time on task"—a strong predictor of learning through concentrated engagement. Whereas commercial transmedia productions are often assessed according to the narrow logics of multimedia platforms and audience retention across them, educators interested in utilizing transmedia environments will be heartened by these authors' assertion that any activity that invites communal engagement and reflection on a narrative experience can itself be classified as transmedia learning.

Introduction

When Mary Shelley began writing *Frankenstein; or, the Modern Prometheus* in 1816, she likely did not imagine that the vision that she was committing to paper would grow into one of the most powerful myths of modernity. Today the *Frankenstein* story is told and remade through thousands of adaptations and homages in every possible medium, from popular films and television shows to video games, comic books, and novelty foods. Indeed, *Frankenstein* is so pervasive that it has created its own grammatical trope: we can prepend "franken-" to any word to signal an uncanny or taboo juxtaposition, a sign of the natural order run amok, like "frankenfood" or "frankenfish." Many of these retellings explore that traditional view of the novel as a cautionary tale, a narrative of transgression and the inevitable punishment that follows. But this simplification of the story does not explain its enduring cultural resonance.

Our commitment to *Frankenstein*, the reason we keep returning to this story, is attributable not to its singular moral clarity but rather to its swirling ambiguities. Like all great works of literature, Shelley's novel poses great questions rather than presenting easy answers. She invented the character of Victor Frankenstein roughly a decade before the word "scientist" was first coined in English, and the shadow of Victor's flawed curiosity has haunted public perceptions of the scientific endeavor ever since. This is a story of transgression, to be sure, of a Promethean figure unlocking the mysteries of the gods to create life artificially. But the moral weight of the novel rests on the consequences rather than the transgression itself: the choices Victor and his creation face as they navigate their responsibilities to one another and to society once they find themselves tied together as creator and creature. And while the novel adopts the formal conservatism of a tragic play, the duo's deaths do little to resolve its profound unanswered questions: what is the nature of scientific creativity, and what are our responsibilities to our creations?

These questions inspired our group of collaborators at Arizona State University to pursue a new kind of academic project on the eve of *Frankenstein*'s bicentennial. Recognizing the novel's role as a pervasive myth, a techno-social referent that informs public perceptions of science in many ways, we sought to frame this anniversary of Shelley's seminal novel not as a commemoration but as an opportunity for prospection: an examination of science in society today and in the future. To this end, we pursued a range of activities, including publishing a new, annotated version of the original text (Finn and Guston, 2017); screening the classic 1931 monster movie *Frankenstein* while a local chamber orchestra performed the score live; and curating a set of *Frankenstein*-themed activities at a local arts-science festival. One activity, and the focus of this chapter, was the development of a set of transmedia learning activities that used the *Frankenstein* narrative as a way to engage young people in conversations about scientific ethics and responsibility. As we see in the other chapters in this collection, the term "transmedia" has numerous definitions, and its meaning often shifts depending on context and audience. When we first began our educational transmedia project, we operationalized the term as a multimodal, multimedia set of activities connected through a single story universe. We were particularly interested in how learners might benefit from switching between different types of activities, spanning the physical and the digital, each contributing to the story in different ways.

In designing our transmedia activities, we drew upon educational theory and hypothesized that transmedia learning could present a number of benefits to learners. For example, multiple activities would allow various "on-ramps," or points of entry, for people with different interests to learn about our transmedia experience and become engaged. In addition, by developing a suite of activities, we could better align educational goals with the particular affordances of each activity type (see Mawasi et al., 2022). Our Frankenstein transmedia experience, *Frankenstein200*, consisted of a set of hands-on tabletop activities that were distributed to informal learning spaces like children's museums and science museums around the US, as well as an online interactive experience where participants joined the fictional Laboratory for Innovation and Fantastical Exploration (L.I.F.E.), became lab assistants to a descendant of Victor Frankenstein, and faced ethical decisions that would determine the fate of the lab. Both the hands-on activities and the digital experience introduced concepts around scientific ethics and responsibility; we provide further details about *Frankenstein200* in later sections of this chapter.

Through this work, we sought to better understand the effects of using transmedia activities in informal learning environments. Informal learning environments (e.g., museums, after-school clubs, and self-study through reading or watching videos) are quite diverse, encompassing all learning activities that fall outside of formal schooling (Schugurensky, 2000). While formal schooling usually starts around age five and ends in early adulthood (with possible returns later in life for retraining, work toward additional degrees, or other purposes), informal learning experiences engage us throughout our lives. Even when enrolled in formal schooling, weekends and after-school time present many opportunities to engage in informal learning experiences. For children, these experiences allow for playful exploration and foster connections between everyday life and formal schooling (e.g., a student learning about friction in her science class may experiment with the different rates at which objects move down a slide at a playground). It is through these various forms of informal learning that we continue to grow and develop our knowledge and understanding throughout life.

Using Transmedia for Learning

We opted to create a transmedia experience, rather than a single-media narrative learning intervention, because of transmedia's capacity both to educate and to entertain (Fleming, 2013). Transmedia environments engage audiences within and across various formats and media; when these techniques are combined with the pull of a popular narrative frame to create a *transmedia storytelling* environment, it is possible to encourage learners to engage deeply with learning materials. Transmedia storytelling also presents an opportunity as a novel research environment. Prior work indicates that transmedia learning experiences can be effective educational tools, both in promoting collaboration among learners and in increasing skills and competencies (e.g., Fleming, 2013; Scolari et al., 2019).

We intentionally designed a transmedia experience that engages learners with a variety of modalities to test the affordances of different activities and their effects on science self-efficacy and perceptions of science and scientists. Self-efficacy is the belief that one can successfully complete a task or perform a behavior (Bandura, 1994) and has been shown to successfully predict academic achievement (Britner and Pajares, 2006). Science self-efficacy, therefore, is one's belief in the ability to successfully complete science-related tasks. Those with low science self-efficacy may avoid pursuing science-related careers or engaging in public conversation around scientific issues. A core belief of our project is that by improving people's science self-efficacy, we can engage broader and more diverse audiences in public conversations around science and responsibility.

The social-cognitive psychologist Albert Bandura (1994) identified four ways to increase self-efficacy: mastery experiences, vicarious experiences, social persuasion, and addressing physical states. Mastery experiences, the focus of our current work, are the most effective means of developing self-efficacy, and they occur when people successfully complete a task. Guided by this insight, our transmedia experience included a number of hands-on activities that learners could engage in, so that they could have the experience of successfully completing a science or engineering activity. We intended for these activities to be facilitated to prevent learners from getting lost or frustrated. Similarly, one way for learners to change their perceptions of science is to become more immersed or to try on different scientific roles. To achieve this goal, we created an online narrative-based experience in which learners adopt the role of a research assistant and collaborate with other (nonplayer) characters to tackle scientific and ethical questions. We hypothesized that the different affordances of the digital and physical activities, integrated by a common narrative, would lead to learners who participated in both types of activities showing greater self-efficacy improvements compared to those who participated in only one type of activity.

Creating *Frankenstein200*

One advantage of working within the *Frankenstein* story to create a transmedia experience is its cultural ubiquity. Even if people have never read Mary Shelley's original novel or seen any of the numerous *Frankenstein* adaptations, they are still familiar with the rudiments of the story. Despite being over 200 years old, Shelley's tale about Victor Frankenstein, a scientist who fails to take responsibility for his creation, unleashing catastrophic effects, continues to resonate today, and be adapted, alluded to, and integrated into a variety of cultural texts and experiences, from novels, comics, and film to Halloween costumes, TV series, and even breakfast cereal. To create our transmedia experience, we selected and designed activities that fit within the cultural space of *Frankenstein* narratives and aligned with our learning goals of increasing science and creative self-efficacy, supporting ethics literacy and public engagement in science, and creating an informal learning environment that bridges education and entertainment.

The *Frankenstein200* transmedia experience combines a set of hands-on activities (titled, collectively, "Frankenstein's Footlocker") and an online narrative game focused on scientific issues like ethics and responsibility. Frankenstein's Footlocker was designed to be implemented in informal learning environments, specifically children's museums and science museums. Activities (described in more detail next) were designed to appeal to a broad range of ages, and to involve light facilitation by museum staff or volunteers. In the narrative game experience, developed in collaboration with the multiplatform entertainment company No Mimes Media, players assume the role of a lab assistant at L.I.F.E.

Founded and led by Dr. Tori Frankenstein, a distant descendant of Victor Frankenstein, L.I.F.E. is at the forefront of research on genetics and artificial intelligence (AI). Players interact with two other lab assistants, Mya and Xavier, and help to solve a wide range of problems and puzzles. Throughout the ten-episode experience, players investigate the L.I.F.E. archives and get a close-up look at the radical ideas and sticky dilemmas that scientists face (e.g., Can a robot be creative? Should genetic engineering be used to revive the woolly mammoth?). As learners progress through the game, these ideas are revealed to be more than just hypothetical, as the character Mya uncovers something mysterious about her own origins. Players work alongside Mya, Xavier, and other characters in the lab to unravel the secrets at the heart of Tori's experiments.

We designed Frankenstein's Footlocker and the related resources to complement the online narrative game. In creating this kit, we looked for existing, established science and technology learning activities that could be reworked to integrate the themes of *Frankenstein*. For each hands-on activity, we developed a set of questions to encourage learners to reflect on the scientific products that they were creating and manipulating by exploring their own moral and ethical values and beliefs. For example, one activity, Scribble Bot (Lande, 2016), invites people to create a drawing machine by attaching markers to a twelve-inch section of a foam pool noodle, decorating it to give it a face, and then using an electronic toothbrush motor to "give it life" and enable it to make drawings (figures 12.1 and 12.2). After creating their scribble bot, we ask the learners four questions:

1. Is your scribble bot alive?

2. Who is the artist of the drawing? You, or your scribble bot?

3. If someone wants to buy the drawing, who should receive the money?

4. If your scribble bot scribbled on your family's couch, who should be responsible?

Each activity was designed to be playful and engaging while also raising questions around scientific ethics and responsibility. (For a complete description of the activities included in the kit, see https://www.nisenet.org /frankensteinkit.)

The kits were developed using the iterative process of the National Informal STEM Education Network (NISE Network), which included peer review by educators, scientific review by subject-matter experts, visitor testing in informal education settings, and feedback from partner organizations (Ostman, 2016). Since the primary goal of *Frankenstein200* was to work in informal learning spaces like children's museums and science museums, we were particularly interested in identifying hands-on activities that were designed for young people ages five to ten, and we selected activities that could be completed with common household items and/or items that were inexpensive to acquire (e.g., craft supplies, rubber bands, and pool noodles), to maximize accessibility. In focusing on activities that prioritized *doing* or *making*, we differentiated our work from other transmedia experiences. While many transmedia projects focus on consuming, interpreting, and drawing connections among different types of media, *Frankenstein200* invited learners to produce physical objects with a connection to the story-world and its themes. Even when learners encountered *Frankenstein200* via the online experience rather than at a museum or science center, they were encouraged to complete the hands-on activities at home and upload photos of their products as evidence of completion.

Both the online and hands-on experiences aligned with three key themes from the Frankenstein myth: unexpected consequences of innovation, taking responsibility for our creations, and ethical decisions around invention and creating. Since the hands-on activity kits were deployed at fifty-one children's museums and science museums around the US, the activities were designed to appeal to a variety of ages, including young children as well as teens and adults. The online narrative, however, was more focused on reaching older children, as the Children's Online Privacy Protection Rule (COPPA) in the US imposes limits and constraints on collecting information from children under the age of thirteen. In addition to these legal

Figure 12.1
A scribble bot is assembled using a cut pool noodle and crafting supplies.

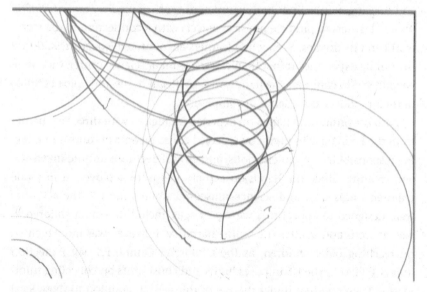

Figure 12.2
Example of scribble bot art.

and logistical considerations, creating multiple types of activities let us test our hypothesis that learners would benefit more from the combination of online experiences, which encourage them to adopt different roles and identities, and hands-on activities, which build self-efficacy through mastery experiences, than they would from completing either the online or hands-on activities alone.

Evaluating *Frankenstein200*

We collected data in a number of ways. We visited thirteen museums (approximately 25 percent of the total museums that received an activity kit) and collected observation notes while visitors engaged in each activity. We also interviewed adults and children at each museum and asked them to complete surveys. To understand the effects of the online narrative experience, a presurvey and postsurvey were embedded into the game mechanics, and we invited participants to complete an additional reflection questionnaire after completing the experience. The results were useful for understanding how the activities were being used across a variety of settings and with different age groups, as well as in determining the effectiveness of the online experience. However, since we could not connect participant data between museum experiences and online activities, we needed to employ a different methodology to test our hypothesis of the benefits of hands-on plus online over hands-on or online activities alone. To this end, we collaborated with elementary and middle schools in the Phoenix, Arizona, metropolitan area to work with their science classes over a one-week period. We randomly assigned one class to complete the hands-on activities only, one class to complete the online experience only, and one class to the transmedia condition, where students completed both the hands-on activities and online experience. Due to the nature of school schedules, each condition had students working with the *Frankenstein200* materials for approximately the same amount of time. As a result, while students in the transmedia condition completed a greater number of different activities, students in the other two conditions had more time to focus on the activities that they did complete, and often more time for discussion and reflection as well. While more details regarding methodology and results can be found in other publications by members of our team (e.g., Nagy et al., 2022; Ostman et al., 2022; Nagy, Mawasi, and Wylie, 2020; Mawasi et al., 2021), here we summarize our findings and reflect on how these results have shaped our understanding of transmedia approaches for informal learning spaces.

We used the data collected at our museum site visits to see if the hands-on activities succeeded in engaging audiences. Informal learning spaces like children's museums and science museums are filled with activities to engage their audiences, so one question was whether children and their families would choose to spend time with activities that focused on topics like science ethics and responsibility. Our observation notes reveal that the activities were very successful in engaging a variety of museum visitors (Ostman et al., 2022). Activities were often facilitated by museum staff or volunteers, and there were several examples of museum personnel using people's awareness of and cultural associations with *Frankenstein* as a way to invite visitors to engage in the activity. For example, rather than simply asking people if they would like to build a scribble bot, a staff member facilitating the activity might ask a family if they had ever heard of Frankenstein and whether they would like to build their own creature. Some museums, especially around Halloween, embraced the story's spooky associations, with facilitators dressing up like Victor Frankenstein or the creature. These observations highlight one advantage of presenting our activities through the lens of *Frankenstein*: audiences are curious to learn and explore when the activity is connected to a familiar narrative. In this way, these activities and facilitation could be generative for intergenerational learning, where a variety of participants build connections through familiar narratives as they learn together.

Our classroom findings were similar to the observations in museums. We found *Frankenstein* to be an effective hook for bringing students into conversations. Students were excited to complete the activities, which also were effective in setting the foundation for class discussions about ethics and scientific responsibility. Our quantitative results showed that overall, students had significantly higher science self-efficacy scores on the postsurvey than the presurvey, but contrary to what we had hypothesized, we saw no difference among the conditions (Nagy et al., 2022). Students increased their science self-efficacy over the course of the week of engaging with our activities, but we did not see additional benefits for students who had a transmedia experience, completing both the hands-on activities and online narrative. Similarly, when we interviewed learners following the weeklong experience, we found that both the hands-on and digital experiences provided a useful foundation for conceptualizing scientific ethics. The characters in the online activities provided moral exemplars, which enabled learners to see examples of different types of behaviors, and the interactive elements of the story allowed learners to wrestle with making ethical decisions of their own. The hands-on activities served as productive scaffolds for ethical conversations about unintended consequences and scientific responsibility (Mawasi et al., 2021).

While we expected to see compounded benefits for engaging in multiple types of activities, a closer look at our methodological decisions suggests that our findings can be explained with theoretical perspectives from the learning sciences. Much work (see Karweit, 1984) suggests that one of the most powerful predictors of learning is "time on task": the amount of time spent learning about a given construct, whether that is drawing pictures to illustrate a student's thinking, conducting a lab experiment, or learning via an educational video game. In this light, we would expect to see conditions performing equally well, since we kept the time on task consistent across conditions to align with school schedules.

This insight has implications for other transmedia projects, and it highlights a limitation of attempting to evaluate informal learning environments in a formal school setting. Although our study controlled for time on task, so it was equal for all participants, transmedia or otherwise, the importance of time on task is one of the reasons why transmedia environments can be effective in informal learning spaces. A transmedia environment, which presents multiple opportunities to learn about a given construct, can encourage greater levels of engagement and thus increase time on task. Informal learning, unlike formal learning, is not constrained by an external time schedule; learners can explore new paths, make discoveries, and test their own hypotheses for as much or as little time as they want. This can have benefits for learning, as one can become immersed in the space and thus immersed in the material itself. One challenge, however, is to develop an informal transmedia learning environment that can successfully compete against all the other activities that people could be engaging with during that same time. Anecdotally, we noticed that museum visitors spent less time at one of our *Frankenstein200* activities when it was situated next to a seventy-foot indoor climbing structure than when it was placed elsewhere in the same museum.

Redefining Transmedia

Our results also encouraged us to reexamine our definition of "transmedia." We had originally defined it as engaging with a single story across multiple modalities, and operationalized it to mean completing both hands-on and digital activities, since they span media types. A closer examination of the *Frankenstein* narrative, however, suggests that any activity that invites learners to engage with and reflect on the themes of this narrative is itself a transmedia learning activity. The themes of *Frankenstein* transcend boundaries, and the narrative can be used to engage audiences across multiple discourses (Saggini and Soccio, 2018); thus *Frankenstein* is, at this point in the sprawling cultural iteration and speciation of the narrative, always inescapably a transmedia entity. As a novel that is over two centuries old, *Frankenstein* has evolved from a single story to a set of cultural referents or myths (Hitchcock, 2007; Perkowitz and Von Mueller, 2018; Turney, 1998). Its central dyad of Victor and his monster, creator and creature, has become embedded in collective cultural memory in ways that transcend Shelley's original narrative. Typically, when people think about the novel, they think about these characters, not the scenes in the Arctic Ocean or the lengthy descriptions of traveling across Europe. With this focus on the novel's central dyad, and the reduced emphasis on its many literary particularities, the story can be endlessly retold, adapted, and reworked in new contexts and media forms.

Because of its age, Shelley's *Frankenstein* is also in the public domain, though many of its modern retellings are commercial properties and Universal Pictures still retains a trademark on the iconic Boris Karloff interpretation of the creature. The shared mythos and public ownership of *Frankenstein* grant us important freedom in how to retell that story, and also invite participatory collaboration from other artists and publics who might want to remake the story for themselves. Unlike the Marvel Cinematic Universe, Harry Potter, or Star Wars, there is no officially sanctioned *Frankenstein* canon, and thus no one to police whether we are accurately telling the story. This freedom also sidesteps challenges of inconsistencies or devotion to a particular canonical text: every adaptation of *Frankenstein* already reinterprets and revises fundamental aspects of the narrative and marries it to different genres and contexts.

Viewed in this light, each set of activities and accompanying learning experiences (in our project, the hands-on activities alone or the online activities alone) is always part of a broad, ongoing transmedia experience. The key shift is this: we came to realize that we were not creating a transmedia *Frankenstein*, but rather contributing to a Frankenstein mythos that has been a form of transmedia narrative for two centuries. In other words, we didn't need to integrate hands-on with online activities and broker frequent shifting between the two activity sets to create a transmedia experience within the *Frankenstein* universe. Our revised operationalization of transmedia focuses on how the activities engage with the story rather than on the requirement for multiple media types to be present.

Framing *Frankenstein* as a transmedia experience provides additional insights into how it can be used in educational settings. By providing multiple on-ramps through both the online and hands-on activities, we can encourage learners to explore the themes of the narrative from multiple angles. Furthermore, the various on-ramps are likely to engage learners with different interests and prior knowledge. For example, a child who likes to build may be initially drawn to one of the hands-on activities, whereas another who prefers playing video games may first engage with the online narrative experience. Once learners are engaged, they may be enticed to explore other aspects, thereby increasing their overall time on task and gaining exposure to new experiences.

Lessons Learned

Reflecting on our data, as well as the larger structure and expectations built into our project, enables us to identify a number of components that contributed to its success. Given our learning aims and audiences, *Frankenstein* was a good choice for our transmedia project for a number of reasons. The story's themes strongly aligned with our learning goals. As mentioned previously, despite being over 200 years old, the themes from the novel surrounding scientific responsibility and ethics still resonate today. These connections allowed us to use the *Frankenstein* story as the initial hook and then draw learners into more contemporary conversations: who is at fault when an automated vehicle causes a traffic accident, or whether it would be responsible to bring back extinct animals like the wooly mammoth.

Frankenstein's age, and particularly the fact that 2018 was the bicentennial of its initial publication, gave us the opportunity to contribute to an existing public conversation around the narrative. Through this alignment, we were able to pique the interest of museum collaborators and capture media attention to promote our work to larger audiences (e.g., Blakemore, 2018), both of which otherwise would have proved more challenging. Another advantage of working with a classic text and a ubiquitous story is the role that it plays in our culture. Since the basic story is so well known, visitors already possessed sufficient knowledge to participate without us having to provide a primer on the story, and they were intrigued to learn more. This was true even for those who had never read the novel or seen the iconic Universal Studios film and its sequels. *Frankenstein* served as a helpful and inviting frame to discuss challenging concepts around ethics and scientific responsibility.

Our project and data collection efforts helped us realize that more media options, within a set amount of time, does not necessarily mean better learning outcomes. When time on task was held constant, learners who completed both sets of activities (hands-on and online) benefited just as much as students who completed one set or the other. While our studies found that shuttling back and forth between media types wasn't critical to learning success, there are likely motivational benefits to creating multiple on-ramps to an experience, taking advantage of the affordances of different media forms, both for individual learners as well as partner institutions. We also observed much support for the power of story in attracting participants into the experience. For example, the Halloween costumes worn by museum staff and the introduction of the activities through the lens of *Frankenstein* were successful tools for beginning a deeper engagement. Topics like ethics and scientific responsibility may be intimidating to some audiences or seem too complex for younger children. By framing these conversations with a familiar narrative, we were able to overcome these perceived barriers and engage audiences of all ages to think deeply about these topics. It was particularly satisfying to witness intergenerational conversations, when parents or grandparents would begin to discuss one of our prompts for reflection with their children or grandchildren. These conversations often highlighted that questions around ethics and responsibility do not have easy or obvious answers, and thereby encouraged audiences to engage more deeply with the material, bringing out nuances and evoking connections to their own lived experiences. Despite, or perhaps because of, its age, *Frankenstein* and its many retellings continue to influence public perceptions of science ethics and responsibility, and serve as an excellent foundation for engaging transmedia experiences.

The benefits of using culturally ubiquitous texts extend beyond the Frankenstein narrative. New transmedia stories are frequently emerging or expanding to keep pace with technological developments such as virtual reality (VR) or augmented reality (AR), to align with consumer expectations, and to garner dedicated multiplatform audiences and fan communities; we can see this process unfold from the Alien franchise to Star Wars, and in the expansion of video game and toy properties like *Minecraft*, *Halo*, and *League of Legends* to feature films, streaming television, books, and other media. It is no longer sufficient to tell a good story; to capture attention, the story must have the facility for adaptation and movement across media forms, from pages to screens to action figures. This trend, as our *Frankenstein200* project shows, presents tremendous opportunities for educators, specifically when we can use these narratives to engage learners and enhance learning.

References

Bandura, Albert. 1994. "Self-efficacy." In *Encyclopedia of Human Behavior*, vol. 4, edited by V. S. Ramachandran, 71–81. New York: Academic Press.

Blakemore, Erin. 2018. "Frankenstein Game Teaches Kids about Science." *Washington Post*, January 28, 2018. https://www.washingtonpost.com/national/health-science/frankenstein-game-teaches-kids-about-science/2018/01/26/7fecf478-010e-11e8-bb03-722769454f82_story.html.

Britner, Shari L., and Frank Pajares. 2006. "Sources of Science Self-Efficacy Beliefs of Middle School Students." *Journal of Research in Science Teaching* 43, no. 5: 485–499.

Finn, Ed, and David H. Guston. 2017. *Frankenstein: Annotated for Scientists, Engineers, and Creators of All Kinds*. Cambridge, MA: MIT Press.

Fleming, Laura. 2013. "Expanding Learning Opportunities with Transmedia Practices: Inanimate Alice as an Exemplar." *Journal of Media Literacy Education* 5, no. 2: 370–377.

Hitchcock, Susan Tyler. 2007. *Frankenstein: A Cultural History*. New York: W.W. Norton & Company.

Karweit, Nancy. 1984. "Time-on-Task Reconsidered: Synthesis of Research on Time and Learning." *Educational Leadership* 41, no. 8: 32–35.

Lande, Micah. 2016. "MAKER: It's Alive! Super Low-Cost Hands-On Activities for Public Engineering Outreach to Build STEM Literacy. *2016 ASEE Annual Conference & Exposition*. https://peer.asee.org/maker-it-s-alive-super-low-cost-hands-on-activities-for-public-engineering-outreach-to-build-stem-literacy.pdf.

Mawasi, Areej, Peter Nagy, Ed Finn, and Ruth Wylie. 2021. "Using Frankenstein-Themed Science Activities for Science Ethics Education: An Exploratory Study." *Journal of Moral Education*, 1–17. https://doi.org/10.1080/03057240.2020.1865140.

Mawasi, Areej, Peter Nagy, Ed Finn, and Ruth Wylie. 2022. "Narrative-Based Learning Activities for Science Ethics Education: An Affordance Perspective." *Journal of Science Education and Technology* 31: 16–26.

Nagy, Peter, Areej Mawasi, Ed Finn, and Ruth Wylie. 2022. "Increasing Learners' Self-Efficacy Beliefs and Curiosity through a Frankenstein-themed Transmedia Storytelling Experience." *British Journal of Educational Technology* 53, no. 6: 1626–1644. https://doi.org/10.1111/bjet.13202.

Nagy, Peter, Areej Mawasi, and Ruth Wylie. 2020. "Fostering Science Identity Through Transmedia Storytelling: A Mixed-Methods Approach." In *The Interdisciplinarity of the Learning Sciences, 14th International Conference of the Learning Sciences (ICLS) 2020*, vol. 2, edited by Melissa Gresalfi and Ilana Seidel Horn, 873–874. Nashville: International Society of the Learning Sciences.

Ostman, Rae. 2016. "Program Development: A NISE Network Guide to Creating Effective Learning Experiences for Public Audiences." *NISE Network*. https://www.nisenet.org/catalog/nise-network-program-development-guide.

Ostman, Rae, Peter Nagy, Areej Mawasi, Ed Finn, and Ruth Wylie. 2022. "Exploring Responsible Research and Innovation in Museums through Hands-on Activities." *Curator: The Museum Journal* 66, no. 1: 29–57. https://doi.org/10.1111/cura.12530.

Perkowitz, Sidney, and Eddy von Mueller. 2018. *Frankenstein: How a Monster Became an Icon: The Science and Enduring Allure of Mary Shelley's Creation*. New York: Pegasus Books.

Saggini, Francesca, and Anna Enrichetta Soccio, eds. 2018. *Transmedia Creatures: Frankenstein's Afterlives*. New Brunswick, NJ: Rutgers University Press.

Schugurensky, Daniel. 2000. "The Forms of Informal Learning: Towards a Conceptualization of the Field." Centre for the Study of Education and Work, Ontario Institute for Studies in Education, University of Toronto. https://tspace.library.utoronto.ca/handle/1807/2733.

Scolari, C. A., M. J. Masanet, M. D. M. Guerrero Pico, and M. J. Establés. 2019. "Transmedia Literacy in the New Media Ecology: An Internacional Map of Teens' Transmedia Skills." In *Proceedings of the 2018 Connected Learning Summit;* August 1–3; Cambridge, MA, edited by J. H. Kalir, 244–253. Pittsburgh: Carnegie Mellon University.

Turney, Jon. 1998. *Frankenstein's Footsteps: Science, Genetics, and Popular Culture*. New Haven, CT: Yale University Press.

Transmedia Crosstalk: Katherine Buse, Ranjodh Singh Dhaliwal, and Ruth Wylie

Bob Beard: There are a lot of great connections between these pieces; both of these projects position the audience/player as a research assistant or new recruit, and use science fiction storytelling as a frame for science learning and exploration. Let's dig into some of that.

Ruth Wylie: I agree. I also thought it was interesting to look at who the players/participants for each our experiences were. Ranjodh and Katherine, do you know what motivates people to engage with *Foldit*?

Ranjodh Singh Dhaliwal: The demographic varies widely. There are teenagers and retirees who want to contribute to science, and we get a bunch of US-based players but also from around the globe. Some hardcore gamers, some only doing this because they like the idea of contributing to science.

RW: I can imagine that when people bring different motivations it also changes their expectations for the experience. Someone doing it for the science or in hopes of contributing to a *Nature* article may care less about the game mechanics.

Katherine Buse: Absolutely, and might not feel hailed by a narrative either. However, it also seems as if players switch between these different motivations, based on my reading of how they interact on forums, etc.

RW: It's interesting to think about how people switch roles throughout a transmedia experience. Our experience was designed in accordance with literature that suggests that online experiences can help people—especially young people—test out different roles, so even though our data didn't address that specifically, I think the experience still served as a useful tool for thinking about scientists and scientific practices.

I think asking learners to be a character in this science fiction story also allows them to explore perspectives and ideas in interesting ways.

RSD: That's interesting. For us, the role playing was in some ways a symbolic move, re-presenting the citizen science aspect of *Foldit* (everyone can participate), but also a way of actually incorporating and justifying the very act of playing this game narratively. As a participant, you are playing with all these molecules because you *are* playing a scientist.

KB: Science fiction helped us play with the multiple scales of engagement. We were presenting a vision of fictional science to people who are already doing real science. But we also used it, like you, as a way of presenting the ethical, social, and educational aspects of the project to *Foldit* players. Science fiction is good at laminating these kinds of overlapping issues into a frame.

RW: Our initial idea was to make the online experience collaborative and something you would do with a cohort of players, but we got concerned about how to create a safe online environment for young people that we could effectively moderate. To build in the collaboration elements we were aiming for, we had players do activities where they interacted with other characters in the story via a chat feature, using very simple speech algorithms to interact.

KB: That is fascinating, Ruth! The way you're phrasing it almost sounds as if story can stand in for multiplayer engagement.

RW: Definitely! We used simple keyword matching and scripting to enable interactions between players and characters, but I think it felt more real since it was done in the context of the story.

KB: So you have a science activity, and integrating it with story does what? Does it make it more "science-y" for the player? Reinforcing their relationship to the history of science, or making it more universal?

RW: For our project, I think the role of story was an invitation. I don't think people typically jump at opportunities to talk about science ethics, but they were excited to do Frankenstein activities and a Frankenstein online experience.

What about you? What do you think integrating story with science does for the players, the material, or even the story itself?

KB: We wanted it to broaden the context of the tutorial so that the player saw herself as part of the project of protein biochemistry, rather than merely a puzzle-solver.

So there's an entry into the world and a suspension of disbelief in which she has agency in protein biochemistry, in service of providing a richer context off the bat for why protein folding (1) makes sense, (2) is useful, and (3) needs her participation.

RW: I also think the narrative you developed aligns well with the overall goals of the larger *Foldit* project. In other words, I think citizen science activities can be a successful on-ramp for scientific careers or future science exploration, so giving the player the role of a scientist makes sense here.

RSD: It does! Plus, as we hint at the end of our piece, the making things (scientific data or physical things) is also deeply tied to the meaning-making. This project with *Foldit* was a rich space for this: doing science through science fiction.

KB: There's also an interesting notion in all of this of how storyworlds are carried along with the scientific projects, or issues they get bound up with. Transmedia logics allow us to see how Frankenstein is as much a part of the history of the life sciences as is CRISPR. It's exciting to think about what these projects offer us when thinking about the role of stories, and of genre, in constructing scientific literacies.

III   The Future of Transmedia

13   Medical Transmedia

Kirsten Ostherr

In this chapter, Kirsten Ostherr draws on arguments about the endless expansion and speciation of transmedia experiences and logics across media environments made throughout part I of this book by Maureen McHugh Yeager, Paweł Frelik, and Dilman Dila (chapters 1, 3, and 4, respectively), and extends them to an unexpected and complex arena: the medical system, with its vast archives of electronic medical records and the fraught intensities of the doctor-patient relationship. Ostherr explores the useful potential of transmedia medical records and the failures of the current system. Patient medical records are increasingly digitized, shared, and layered across multiple specialties and providers over the course of a patient's life, comprising a sort of multifaceted media narrative. However, the current structure of these electronic records reflects a limited, flat, anachronistic data model that decontextualizes the patient's experiences, objectifies the patient, and fails to capture psychological, affective, and social aspects of wellness and illness. However, a holistic "whole patient" approach that is transparent and open to patient review and input, and which makes space for a broader range of mediated content—not just test results and providers' session notes but also videos and photos, patients' social-media posts, and more—is possible, and patient advocates are already designing and piloting such systems. Like other chapters throughout this volume, including chapters 5 and 14 by Yomi Ayeni and Zoyander Street, respectively, Ostherr's discussion considers transmedia ethics in terms of the politics of representation, with members of marginalized groups (in this case, patients with chronic conditions in an increasingly depersonalized health-care system) seeking to use transmedia texts to stake out more nuanced and culturally grounded representations, in the face of media paradigms that render their experiences in meager or distorted ways. Like many chapters in this collection, in settings ranging from big-budget media to education and citizen science, this chapter locates transmedia dynamics playing out in a high-stakes context and considers how critical interrogation of transmedia affordances can materially change people's experiences for the better.

Sara Riggare is a Swedish engineer and medical informatics researcher who was diagnosed at age thirty-two with Parkinson's disease. She gained international recognition for her work in patient advocacy and design, and her story starts with a simple but powerful observation:

> I see my neurologist twice a year, about half an hour every time. That's one hour per year in healthcare for my Parkinson's disease. During the same year I spend 8,765 hours in selfcare, applying my knowledge and experience together with what I get from my neurologist to manage a difficult condition as best I can. . . . And it's also during this one hour that my condition is evaluated by my neurologist and my treatment is prescribed. But it's during the 8,765 hours of selfcare that I put my treatment into action. I take 6 prescription drugs, 6 times a day, in 5 different combinations, with 6 different time intervals. Because let's face it, my doctor doesn't even know if I take my medications or not. (2014)

Recognizing that she needed a better way to document her experiences "in the wild"—that is, beyond what was captured in her medical record

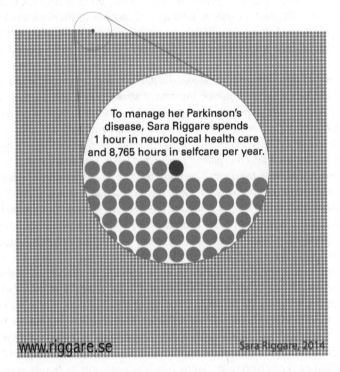

Figure 13.1
Sara Riggare's infographic visualizes the contrast between the 1 hour of clinical time she spends each year with her neurologist and the 8,765 hours she spends in self-care. Sara Riggare, "1 vs 8,765" infographic (2014). https://www.riggare.se/1-vs-8765.

twice a year—Riggare designed and developed systems for documenting and analyzing her own health data, building on existing consumer-oriented technologies. Inspired by the user-friendliness and appeal of platforms like Google and Facebook and wearables like Fitbit and Jawbone, Riggare and her community of "Parkies" constructed richer, more detailed and comprehensive narratives that were full of evidence and personal perspective (Palfreman, 2014). But these patient-led innovations were not incorporated into the traditional practices of clinical documentation; their electronic health records (EHRs) still only contained those notes and test results from the two half-hour-long appointments per year that Riggare described in her blog post. As Riggare ruefully observed, "patients are using the internet and other technologies as well as fellow patients to diagnose their own problems, find the best treatment, continually optimise their treatments, and even fund and conduct research. *They are doing this not thanks to, but despite, healthcare*" (Riggare, 2018; emphasis added).

Riggare's frustrations have been echoed by patients all over the world; indeed, instances of truly patient-centered care remain aspirational in most contexts (Collado, 2019). Yet the particular challenges faced by patients vary widely depending on the cultural and health-policy contexts in which they seek care (Tikkanen and Abrams, 2020). For that reason, the discussion that follows should be understood as deriving from research grounded primarily in the US, though the findings may be generalizable to other settings where patients are pursuing new strategies for integrating their own narratives and health data into formal clinical documentation systems. For nearly half of the adults in the US, documentation of their illness data and experiences is a critically important and ever-present part of daily life, and their identities as patients, or as people with Parkinson's disease, diabetes, heart disease, cancer, depression, or other conditions, are interwoven with their identities as parents, workers, community members, and so forth. This means that to document a complete picture of a person's health-relevant experiences, the representation and mediation of that person's daily life through social sites such as Instagram, TikTok, Facebook, YouTube, blogs, and other venues should be interwoven with the representation and mediation of a person's illness experiences.

Elsewhere, I have described these unofficial sites of health-data creation as "metaclinical" sites because they exist outside traditional, formal settings where health care takes place, such as hospitals, doctors' offices, or pharmacies. Metaclinical data sources may allow for more creative forms of expression, but they also raise new concerns about data mining, privacy, and vulnerability (Ostherr, 2020). Moreover, although metaclinical social media platforms are full of patient communities featuring personal narratives and data, these detailed accounts of daily life are consistently separated out from biomedical documentation of a patient's disease history. In the absence of metaclinical documentation, patient health profiles are comprised entirely of data drawn from their infrequent encounters with clinicians who focus on traditional biomedical registers of documentation. These isolated snapshots leave out most of the details of the patient's life, yet they are the basis for life-and-death treatment decisions. It is this gap between lived experiences and data documentation that the medical transmedia discussed in this chapter aims to address.

Drawing on years of work in diverse health-care fields with a broad range of collaborators, I have come to see transmedia storytelling as a rich method for linking patient narratives and data and for addressing the existing gaps in health-care information and communication exchange, especially as a vehicle for presenting the patient's perspective. Contemporary health-care systems in the US are inundated with devices and screens, but also are plagued by fragmented narratives and poor usability. Stitching together what is and what could be, this chapter will argue that transmedia systems could help patients to capture and share a more accurate version of their experiences than is currently available through clinical media or consumer-facing media alone. This new form of medical documentation, representation, and communication could convey the patient's perspective to health-care providers through visual, audio, and textual forms that link diverse realms of experience and data to provide a more holistic picture of a person's health and illness. This approach also enables a new role for health-care practitioners as co-creators of the patient's narrative. A practice of co-creation or conarration is consistent with "shared decision-making" (Légaré et al., 2018), a model of patient-centered care that is endorsed as the standard of care by numerous medical associations, which could be radically extended through participatory transmedia practices.

I have used the concept of transmedia to help medical doctors and health technology developers think about the fact that their users—patients—live in a world of digital tech, and whatever they might design for health-care application must smoothly and engagingly interface with other apps (like

YouTube, Instagram, or TikTok) if they want patients to actually use their products more than once. In the end, this approach also becomes a use case for why a humanities-based approach to technology development, grounded in media and social justice theory, is an essential (though often missing) component of software design and development. I have also used transmedia to teach my premedical students in a human-centered-design course where they work collaboratively with clinicians to solve real-world medical visualization and communication problems. On the basis of those collaborations, I have seen that my medical partners come to value humanities expertise because it helps them to think about the role of technology in "care" in nuanced and complex ways.

This chapter will briefly explain the role of patient narratives in health care, how patient narratives are currently documented in EHR systems, the consequences of the failure to fully capture patient narratives in health care, and the alternative options offered by consumer-oriented social media platforms. I will draw from existing examples of components of a transmedia ecosystem (i.e., real-world examples of creative uses of technologies that patients have adopted or developed to better capture their experiences), and build on those through speculative design work that imagines how those components could become a flourishing, cohesive transmedia feedback loop that integrates with clinical infrastructures. The goal of this approach is to facilitate patient self-representation that embraces complexity and multidimensional, multimedia narratives, in contrast to the distortion and flattening of narratives that all too often occurs through EHRs.

Why Patient Narratives Matter in Health Care

Patients' personal narratives bring value to their health-care experiences and outcomes when those narratives are genuinely incorporated into clinical care (Greenfield, Kaplan, and Ware, 1985; Kaplan, Greenfield, and Ware, 1989). Patients have always known that they are not reducible to a set of symptoms or pathologies; as one study participant with a chronic illness observed, "For me those are two different things: how I am as a person, my personality, and how my body works and the limitations my disease brings. They are not one and the same" (Duncan et al., 2019). Scholars in medical humanities have also long recognized the value of personal narratives as sources of perspective on patients' lives (Banks and Pollard,

1982). Practitioners of narrative medicine have argued that patient stories are essential to a complete medical record (Charon, 2008), arguing that efforts should be made to include them and to resist their replacement by generic drop-down menu selections. However, since the passage of the federal HITECH Act of 2009, which encouraged health-care providers to adopt EHRs, the increased use of systems designed around drop-down menus at the expense of narrative text in the US has posed a significant challenge to advocates of narrative medicine (Varpio et al., 2015).

Studies of patient narratives in health care have shown that they provide qualitative data that serve a function distinct from physiological measurements such as heart rate and blood pressure. Patient narratives illuminate the concerns, values, and attitudes that contribute to health outcomes but are often invisible or ignored in patient care (Couser, 1991; Frank, 1995; Hawkins, 1999; Kleinman, 1988). For example, financial strain, the inability to pay one's medical bills, is rarely documented in the EHR, but is strongly associated with poor health outcomes in cardiovascular disease, primarily due to "medication nonadherence": failure to take medications as prescribed, often because they are too expensive (Osborn et al., 2017). Chronic stress is often invisible in the patient record (Rod et al., 2009), yet the stress-inducing effects of structural racism, for example, have been linked to a wide range of negative health outcomes (Paradies et al., 2015).

When we consider the sheer number of people who have a vested interest in keeping track of their own health information, the importance of making that undertaking as effortless as possible becomes evident. The Pew Research Center found in 2010 that approximately 70 percent of Americans engage in some form of self-tracking for health purposes, with 34 percent doing so with a simple pen and paper, 49 percent tracking "in their heads," and 21 percent using digital technologies (Fox, 2013). A more recent Gallup poll indicated that 34 percent of Americans had tried a fitness tracker or wearable, and 20 percent regularly used a digital health-tracking device (McCarthy, 2019). Many self-tracking apps for mobile phones and wearable devices have emerged in the past decade, but most of those tools are incapable of integrating their data with a patient's EHR (Dinh-Le et al., 2019). These shortcomings and gaps in current documentation technologies, especially in light of their growing ubiquity, point to a need for an approach that harmonizes patients' attempts to self-document and craft their own narratives with more official EHR systems.

What Happens to Patient Narratives in Electronic Health Records

How are patient experiences presently captured and represented to clinicians, family members, other caregivers, and to patients themselves? And how might transmedia logics help to better capture these experiences? To understand the potential impact of a transmedia approach to patient narratives, it is important to understand the current form in which patient narratives are captured for clinical documentation, as well as the role of media technologies in this process. In an influential early study of patient narratives in EHRs, Patel, Arocha, and Kushniruk demonstrated the transformation of a clinical narrative into EHR format. The original clinical note is narrative and chronological in form but includes minimal information about the patient's perspective:

> Patient is 47 years old and is known to be a diabetic for one year, but possibly for longer. He has fatigue, drowsiness, polyuria and nycturia. He was discovered to have diabetes and has been treated by Glucophage and Diabeta since that time. He had an ophthalmologic evaluation but no renal examination. In 1973 he stepped on a nail, and since that time had 30 operations for repeated infection. (Patel et al., 2002, 13)

The authors contrast this summary to the fragmented style of the EHR, where the same patient history would be documented as (Patel et al., 2002, 13):

CHIEF COMPLAINT: Type II diabetes mellitus

PERSONAL HISTORY

SURGICAL: cholecystectomy: Age 50 years old

MEDICAL: hyperthyroidism: asymptomatic since 25 years

LIFESTYLE

MEDICATION

DIABETA (Tab 2.5 MG)

Sig: 1 tab(s) Oral before breakfast

Contemporary EHRs are similar in function to the EHR analyzed in Patel et al.'s study, quantifying disease through biomedical data points such as blood pressure, weight, height, pulse, temperature, oxygen saturation, respiratory rate, pain level, medications, and procedures (Zhou et al., 2016). Research on EHRs has shown that patient perspectives are absent by design: "For a long time, patients have been deliberately excluded from access to the medical records that contain clinical information about their health problems, resulting in an enforced health illiteracy supported by medical professionals" (Agency for Healthcare Research and Quality, 2017).

The nonpatient-centered medical record has direct consequences for how disease is understood, leading to the reinforcement of divergent perspectives between physicians and patients: "Physicians explained the patient problems in terms of causal pathophysiological knowledge underlying the disease (disease model), whereas patients explained them in terms of narrative structures of illness (illness model). . . . Use of [EHRs] was found to influence the way patient data were gathered, resulting in information loss and disruption of temporal sequence of events in assessing patient problem" (Patel et al., 2002, 8). Moreover, patients whose physicians allow the technological frame of the EHR to guide their interview may be less likely to trust or follow through on treatment plans recommended by those clinicians (Patel et al., 2002). For example, a patient in the study explained that she felt that her physician did not understand the real cause of her malady because she had not been able to fully narrate her illness experience to the doctor. As a result, the doctor's approach to diagnosis seemed, to the patient, to be based on an incomplete and inaccurate assessment of the problem, and the patient therefore considered the treatment to be inappropriate as well.

Increased use of EHRs has led to more frequent complaints about the role of these interfaces in dehumanizing the clinical encounter for both doctors and patients (Hsiao and Hing, 2012; Shanafelt et al., 2016). As discussed previously, EHRs are not designed to capture experiential and affective dimensions of patient narratives; consequently, they undermine the practice of narrative medicine, which emphasizes the inclusion of the patient's perspective to ensure a complete and accurate clinical picture, and improved health outcomes as a desired result. While many patients share their illness narratives freely online, the clinical repositories for these narratives are becoming more constrained and restrictive. What we need is an expansion, but also a radical reimagining, of the media that make up EHRs.

What Are the Consequences for Patients When Their Narratives Are Invisible?

Improved access to patient narratives within and beyond clinical settings would be of particular benefit to patients with complex conditions, as well as those seeking to maintain health and prevent the onset of disease. The scale of the need is enormous. In the US, six in ten adults have at least one chronic disease, and four in ten have two or more chronic diseases (National Center for Chronic Disease Prevention and Health Promotion, 2021). By focusing on the need to document, store, and transmit patient narratives, we can see that managing these complex conditions is as much a media problem as it is a medical problem. As the central node in a communication system that includes numerous health-care providers and other caregivers, patients must manage vast amounts of both structured and unstructured information. Because that information changes form—from observation to narrative, from image to data, from data to narrative—through space and over time, and because that information must be capable of adapting to respond to the shifting perspectives of the different human and technological entities that interact with the patient, the problem is not just a media problem but a transmedia problem.

While the suffering of these millions of people with chronic disease is widely distributed, it is not distributed evenly, and racial health disparities are particularly stark, especially for African American, Latinx, and Native American communities, as well as members of communities that are marginalized on the basis of social class, gender, and sexuality (Baah, Teitelman, and Riegel, 2019; Havranek et al., 2015; Quiñones et al., 2019). This means that any discussion of how best to capture and mediate patient experiences must include attention to the ways that illness is experienced and represented differently in different groups; culture and aesthetics are important dimensions of clinical documentation, and while they have received little attention in the medical research literature, they are often explored in health humanities scholarship (Benjamin, 2019).

In the US alone, there are vast numbers of people who see multiple types of health-care specialists on a regular basis to manage their intersecting, complex conditions. These people need to maintain a centralized repository of their medical information, including prescription drugs, pathology reports, imaging studies, narratives of disease progression, and records of hospitalizations, and this information should take a form that is usable both by the patient and by many different types of clinicians (Tinetti, Fried, and Boyd, 2012). This documentation must be data-rich but also narratively coherent, and it must be accessible and usable for the patient in between their encounters with the health-care system—that is, in daily life. Finally, this documentation must be capable of cultural adaptation in terms of race, ethnicity, gender, sexuality, religion, and a range of other dimensions. This is a demanding set of expectations, and in the present system, these processes of documentation and collation are typically the patient's responsibility, if they happen at all. Considering the burden of disease described in this chapter, this kind of personal medical record-keeping may not be feasible for many, especially for those who are in acute phases of disease and treatment.

As two participants in a study of patient innovation without adequate clinical support described:

> I have a great need for an easy method to keep track of side effects. If I had the strength and the energy to do it, I would have created an app for it . . . [FI2]
>
> There are many things to remember since the last encounter, and that is completely hopeless for many people. It's impossible . . . I have an idea of using activity trackers for people with mental health issues, to register important aspects of the disease automatically, as an objective measurement . . . [MI1] (Duncan et al., 2019)

These patients express the need for easier methods of documenting side effects and other aspects of disease management, and they find themselves struggling to pull the disparate pieces together, particularly in their low-energy state of illness.

As I have discussed, the most acute need for more robust and inclusive patient narratives is inspired by the prevalence and particular needs of patients with chronic conditions, yet the transmedia approach could also be used to capture patient histories (including family information, life experiences, and other details) that could help guide preventative care. The privacy-protecting transmedia ecosystem that I will describe next might even develop risk assessments to screen for family history of cancer, heart disease, rare inheritable conditions, or deleterious environmental exposure in the home or neighborhood. Patients are part of communities who are often aware of their own unique vulnerabilities; a medical transmedia ecosystem could surface and value those situated knowledges (Haraway, 1988) to enhance patients' autonomy.

What about Nonclinical Media as an Alternative to the Existing (Inadequate) Form of the Electronic Health Record? (aka Beware of Evil Transmedia)

Health care is not usually considered to be an enjoyable part of life—but imagine if it were. What if we engaged with health-care media with the same fervor with which we refresh our social media apps every waking hour of the day? Excess screen-time critiques notwithstanding, there is a real case to be made for the need to bring more usable media into health care, especially media that could help bridge the documentation of the day-to-day experiences that make up our lives with the much-less-frequent moments of clinical documentation that make up our encounters with the health-care system. This is where the big technology companies that excel in user engagement enter the discussion.

The increasing involvement of big tech companies (e.g., Google, Facebook, Apple, and Amazon) in the health-care sector already shows that they see their media ecosystems as traversing the popular and clinical realms. I would argue that these companies are attempting to develop "transmedia health care," and they aim to capitalize on their strength in managing user data and media to take over chunks of the health-care ecosystem. From this vantage point, "transmedia" could also be seen as an analytic, a diagnostic tool that allows a researcher to essentially follow the money across various platforms to understand the (often indirect) health relevance of what we do online. For example, one's shopping history on Amazon might lead to recommendations for products such as Alexa that can be placed in the home to listen to and interpret the user's purchase and search history and subsequently recommend pharmaceutical or pseudopharmaceutical interventions that could be purchased and delivered to the home through Amazon's subsidiaries, such as PillPack. The signal traffic between the Amazon website, the Alexa device, and the pills in the mailbox could be understood as a form of transmediality—the same basic, binary signals of sick and well, normal and pathological, and the commercial ventures surrounding and maintaining those categories traverse the platforms to ultimately deliver a cohesive transmedia experience that a user never has to leave.

These might be considered "evil transmedia" practices that presently threaten to harm rather than help patients. Digital surveillance and profiling based on social scraping and other forms of targeting produce "risk profiles" by using patients' online narratives against them to raise insurance premiums, selectively offer or withhold health-care resources, engage in predatory marketing of pharmaceuticals, or simply sell the data to third-party data brokers (Price and Cohen, 2019). All these potential harms are further compounded by the likelihood that these practices will discriminate against patients on the basis of race, class, gender, and/or sexual identity

(Kleinberg, Mullainathan, and Raghavan, 2016). The social, affective, and practical value of sharing personal health data was clear to early adopters in online patient communities. Since then, the monetary value of this data has also become evident to pharmaceutical companies, insurance underwriters, artificial-intelligence developers, and others (Eubanks, 2018; Tanner, 2017). For one group, the value of connecting online lay in the exchange of personal narratives; for the other, it lay in data-mining opportunities. Issues of privacy and health equity have emerged as central challenges to unregulated social-data scraping (Hargittai and Sandvig, 2015), increasing the pressure on policymakers and technologists to foreground transparency and social accountability in digital ecosystems. Meanwhile, patients are left wondering whom they can trust with their data. Any practitioner who embraces the idea of transmedia storytelling for patients must be aware of the potential for exploitation and the need to establish strong bonds of trust. The opt-in, patient-owned, and privacy-protecting affordances of the transmedia ecosystem that I envision at the end of this chapter aim to address some of these threats.

Many of the ideas about transmedia logics for health care expressed here have drawn from the ways that patient groups have self-organized on platforms not designed for their purposes, like Facebook and Twitter, as well as the interfaces created by self-tracking companies like Fitbit that capture data and re-present it to tell a story about a user's "progress" over time. As in the case of Sara Riggare, the aesthetics of these interfaces have inspired patients to imagine how they would like to see their own health narratives displayed visually, in data, and in text—in ways that go well beyond the existing data-visualization possibilities in EHRs (Diamond, 2019). As I have discussed, the benefits and harms of participating in these sites are not evenly distributed. Members of groups who have historically experienced exclusion from or unethical treatment by medical establishments, including African American, Indigenous, Latinx, LGBTQIA+, and people with disabilities are likely to find their vulnerability as patients compounded by their experiences as members of marginalized communities (Havranek et al., 2015). These legacies highlight once again the importance of considering intersectional dimensions to transmedia logics (Crenshaw, 1991; Egede and Walker, 2020).

How Might a Transmedia Approach to Health Records Improve Patients' Health Outcomes?

A patient-led transmedia approach to health data and narratives is aligned with existing efforts to redesign the system in a way that better suits patients' needs and expresses their perspectives (Duncan et al., 2019). A recent collaborative effort between patients, physicians, designers, and technology developers concluded, "Patients and the public should be involved in EHR interface design if these systems are to be suitable for use by patient-users" (Warren et al., 2019). Building on the Quantified Self and e-patient movements, engaged patients take an active stance toward curating their own stories and health data (Ferguson, 2007). This approach transforms the process of health datafication into a process of health "data-making" (Nafus and Sherman, 2014; Pybus, Coté, and Blanke, 2015) that aims to benefit the people whose bodies generate the data rather than those who manufacture their devices or act as data brokers (Van Dijck and Poell, 2016).

Further efforts have taken place under the rubric of the OpenNotes movement (Bell, Delbanco, and Walker, 2017; Fossa, Bell, and DesRoches, 2018), which enables patients to see their clinicians' notes. This simple shift in transparency demonstrates how clinical free-text notes, when written with patient participation in mind, can foster shared decision-making, increased trust and engagement, and patient-centered care. A medical transmedia ecosystem would compound these benefits by shifting the patient's role from that of passive subject to that of author, producer, and co-creator.

In line with an expansion of OpenNotes called "Our Notes," which allows patients to contribute directly to their medical records (Mafi et al., 2017), elements of medical transmedia already exist in creative uses of technologies that patients have adopted or developed to better capture their experiences. The designer and patient Katie McCurdy uses images, narratives, and hand-drawn flowcharts to create what she calls "visual histories" for patients and health-care providers to personalize the experience of care (McCurdy, 2018). Patient advocate Liz Salmi of "The Liz Army" (Salmi, 2008) shares multimedia representations of her experiences by posting brain cancer images in her blog and depicting her efforts to co-create better health-care experiences for herself through clever posts on LinkedIn and Craigslist with the subject line, "Rock star patient seeks primary care physician to form all-star super group" (Salmi, 2017). Some patients have produced medical transmedia through biomedical device–hacking collectives, such as the Do-It-Yourself-Pancreas-System (also known as continuous glucose monitoring in the cloud or CGM in the Cloud) created by the group Nightscout (2014), which takes ownership of medical-device creation and openly disseminates their blueprints for hacking proprietary devices to better serve patient needs. These disparate examples, if linked through a cohesive transmedia ecosystem, would produce a rich, multidimensional, patient-centered, and useful representation of the illness experiences of these patients, providing a fresh perspective for health-care collaborators and valuable documentation for patients and their care teams.

Medical Transmedia Dreaming

I'd like to end this chapter by imagining what the affordances of a medical transmedia ecosystem might look like. Pursuing this approach to speculative design, I draw on the work of Ruha Benjamin, who observed, "Fictions, in this sense, are not falsehoods but refashionings through which analysts experiment with different scenarios, trajectories, and reversals, elaborating new values and testing different possibilities for creating more just and equitable societies. Such fictions are not meant to convince others of *what is*, but to expand our own visions of what is *possible*" (Benjamin, 2016, 2, emphasis added). What follows is a preliminary sketch of the design specifications for a medical transmedia ecosystem.

Drawing further inspiration from the work of Sara Riggare that opens this chapter, we'll imagine a patient with Parkinson's disease who is able to draw upon a wide range of media resources to document, share, comment on, and enjoy representations of various aspects of their life. These media forms would be private and inaccessible to third parties by default, so that their owner—the patient and/or their intimate caregivers—would explicitly consent, or opt in, to the recordings and to allow others to access the data. This would enable a multimedia universe to exist for the sole purpose of supporting the patient's needs, whether for self-care, social interaction, creative expression, self-tracking and data-mining, or communication with friends, family, or health-care professionals. The patient could choose to share part or all of the transmedia universe with specific health-care professionals, to help facilitate communication and understanding of the patient's priorities and values as they relate to aspects of their care (Warren et al., 2019).

The media would be shareable, portable, and interconnected (in health information technology terms, the media would be "interoperable"), so that they could be created and accessed seamlessly across platforms and devices. All recordings would be transparent in their metadata, so that date, time stamp, geolocation, and other important contextual dimensions of the recording would enable a verifiable and chronological construction of the patient's story. This feature would enable diverse media forms to be interwoven based on when and where they were created; for example, the patient with Parkinson's disease might photograph a delicious meal that they enjoy, while a caregiver might record a video of the patient eating. Both could provide important data about quality of life and health status by documenting social and emotional well-being, nutrition, manual dexterity, tremor, mobility, postural sway, voice tone and speech patterns, and other aspects of both daily life and disease monitoring. In addition, the inclusion of a chronological perspective or a time line would shift the perspective toward the patient's experience over time and support the documentation of potentially subtle changes that might otherwise go unnoticed, while shifting away from a clinician-centered model based on organ systems or disease classifications (Kleinman, Eisenberg, and Good, 1978; Warren et al., 2019).

Finally, patients could further choose to monetize their transmedia universe by selling their data to third parties if they wish. Perhaps the vendors of EHRs would pay a licensing fee, based on how much and what kinds of data they are permitted to integrate into the patient's EHR, if the patient consents for those data to be repurposed for clinical or operations research. This model might help move the patient away from the hazards of "evil" medical transmedia, and toward a more open-source yet transactional model of health-data ownership and exchange.

This speculative design leaves myriad practical issues to be addressed, including the challenge of synthesizing multiple complex storylines that appear across a range of media platforms, as well as the related challenge of extracting clinically actionable data. In other words, because this alternative EHR has been imagined from the perspective of the patient and with patients' needs at the forefront, the question of how to ensure that this model can be useful for physicians remains to be fully addressed. This is an intriguing design challenge in itself, as the usability of this counter-EHR is premised on the idea that the normative assumptions about clinically relevant data themselves must be expanded and redefined. This speculative model of a medical transmedia ecosystem is an opening gesture toward that paradigm shift.

References

Agency for Healthcare Research and Quality. 2017. "Strategy 6C: OpenNotes." http://www.ahrq.gov/cahps/quality-improvement/improvement-guide/6-strategies-for-improving/access/strategy6c-opennotes.html.

Baah, Foster Osei, Anne M. Teitelman, and Barbara Riegel. 2019. "Marginalization: Conceptualizing Patient Vulnerabilities in the Framework of Social Determinants of Health—an Integrative Review." *Nursing Inquiry* 26, no. 1: e12268. https://doi.org/10.1111/nin.12268.

Banks, Joanne Trautmann, and Carol Pollard. 1982. *Literature and Medicine: An Annotated Bibliography*. Pittsburgh: University of Pittsburgh Press.

Bell, Sigall K., Tom Delbanco, and Jan Walker. 2017. "OpenNotes: How the Power of Knowing Can Change Health Care." *NEJM Catalyst*. https://catalyst.nejm.org/doi/full/10.1056/CAT.17.0372.

Benjamin, Ruha. 2016. "Racial Fictions, Biological Facts: Expanding the Sociological Imagination through Speculative Methods." *Catalyst: Feminism, Theory, Technoscience* 2, no. 2: 1–28. https://doi.org/10.28968/cftt.v2i2.28798.

Benjamin, Ruha. 2019. *Race after Technology: Abolitionist Tools for the New Jim Code*. Cambridge, UK: Polity.

Charon, Rita. 2008. *Narrative Medicine: Honoring the Stories of Illness*. Oxford: Oxford University Press.

Collado, Megan. 2019. "Just Putting Patients at the Center of Health Care Is Not Enough to Improve Care." *Health Affairs*, October 3, 2019. https://www.healthaffairs.org/do/10.1377/hblog20191002.127318/full.

Couser, G. Thomas. 1991. "Autopathography: Women, Illness, and Lifewriting." *a/b: Auto/Biography Studies* 6, no. 1: 65–75. https://doi.org/10.1080/08989575.1991.10814989.

Crenshaw, Kimberle. 1991. "Mapping the Margins: Intersectionality, Identity Politics, and Violence against Women of Color." *Stanford Law Review* 43, no. 6: 1241–1299. https://doi.org/10.2307/1229039.

Diamond, Sara. 2019. "Addressing the Imagination Gap through STEAMM+D and Indigenous Knowledge." *Proceedings of the National Academy of Sciences* 116, no. 6: 1851–1856. https://doi.org/10.1073/pnas.1808679115.

Dinh-Le, Catherine, Rachel Chuang, Sara Chokshi, and Devin Mann. 2019. "Wearable Health Technology and Electronic Health Record Integration: Scoping Review and Future Directions." *JMIR MHealth and UHealth* 7, no. 9: e12861. https://doi.org/10.2196/12861.

Duncan, Therese Scott, Sara Riggare, Sabine Koch, Lena Sharp, and Maria Hägglund. 2019. "From Information Seekers to Innovators: Qualitative Analysis Describing Experiences of the Second Generation of E-Patients." *Journal of Medical Internet Research* 21, no. 8: e13022. https://doi.org/10.2196/13022.

Egede, Leonard E., and Rebekah J. Walker. 2020. "Structural Racism, Social Risk Factors, and Covid-19—a Dangerous Convergence for Black Americans." *New England Journal of Medicine* 383, no. 12: e77. https://doi.org/10.1056/NEJMp2023616.

Eubanks, Virginia. 2018. *Automating Enequality: How High-Tech Tools Profile, Police, and Punish the Poor.* New York: St. Martin's.

Ferguson, Tom. 2007. *E-patients: How They Can Help Us Heal Health Care.* Nutting Lake, MA: Society for Participatory Medicine. https://participatorymedicine.org/e-Patient_White_Paper_with_Afterword.pdf.

Fossa, Alan J., Sigall K. Bell, and Catherine DesRoches. 2018. "OpenNotes and Shared Decision Making: A Growing Practice in Clinical Transparency and How It Can Support Patient-Centered Care." *Journal of the American Medical Informatics Association* 25, no. 9: 1153–1159. https://doi.org/10.1093/jamia/ocy083.

Fox, Susannah. 2013. "The Self-Tracking Data Explosion." Pew Research Center, June 4, 2013. https://www.pewresearch.org/internet/2013/06/04/the-self-tracking-data-explosion.

Frank, Arthur W. 1995. *The Wounded Storyteller: Body, Illness, and Ethics.* Chicago: University of Chicago Press.

Greenfield, Sheldon, Sherrie Kaplan, and John E. Ware. 1985. "Expanding Patient Involvement in Care: Effects on Patient Outcomes." *Annals of Internal Medicine* 102, no. 4: 520–528. https://doi.org/10.7326/0003-4819-102-4-520.

Haraway, Donna. 1988. "Situated Knowledges: The Science Question in Feminism and the Privilege of Partial Perspective." *Feminist Studies* 14, no. 3: 575–599. https://doi.org/10.2307/3178066.

Hargittai, Eszster, and Christian Sandvig. 2015. *Digital Research Confidential: The Secrets of Studying Behavior Online.* Cambridge, MA: MIT Press.

Havranek, Edward P., Mahasin S. Mujahid, Donald A. Barr, et al. 2015. "Social Determinants of Risk and Outcomes for Cardiovascular Disease: A Scientific Statement from the American Heart Association." *Circulation* 132, no. 9, 873–898. https://doi.org/10.1161/CIR.0000000000000228.

Hawkins, Anne Hunsaker. 1999. "Pathography: Patient Narratives of Illness." *Western Journal of Medicine* 171, no. 2: 127–129.

Hsiao, Chun-Ju., and Esther Hing. 2012. Use and Characteristics of Electronic Health Record Systems among Office-Based Physician Practices: United States, 2001–2012." *NCHS Data Brief* 111: 1–8.

Kaplan, Sherrie H., Sheldon Greenfield, and John E. Ware. 1989. "Assessing the Effects of Physician-Patient Interactions on the Outcomes of Chronic Disease." *Medical Care* 27 (3 Suppl): S110–S127. https://doi.org/10.1097/00005650-198903001-00010.

Kleinberg, Jon, Sendhil Mullainathan, and Manish Raghavan. 2016. "Inherent Trade-Offs in the Fair Determination of Risk Scores." *ArXiv:1609.05807 [Cs, Stat].* http://arxiv.org/abs/1609.05807.

Kleinman, Arthur. 1988. *The Illness Narratives: Suffering, Healing, and the Human Condition.* New York: Basic Books.

Kleinman, Arthur, Leon Eisenberg, and Byron Good. 1978. "Culture, Illness, and Care." *Annals of Internal Medicine* 88, no. 2: 251–258. https://doi.org/10.7326/0003-4819-88-2-251.

Légaré, France, Rhéda Adekpedjou, Dawn Stacey, et al. 2018. "Interventions for Increasing the Use of Shared Decision Making by Healthcare Professionals." *Cochrane Database of Systematic Reviews* 7: CD006732. https://doi.org/10.1002/14651858 .CD006732.pub4.

Mafi, John N., Macda Gerard, Hannah Chimowitz, Melissa Anselmo, Tom Delbanco, and Jan Walker. 2017. "Patients Contributing to Their Doctors' Notes: Insights From Expert Interviews." *Annals of Internal Medicine* 168, no. 4: 302–305. https://doi.org /10.7326/M17-0583.

McCarthy, Justin. 2019. "One in Five U.S. Adults Use Health Apps, Wearable Trackers." *Gallup News*, December 11, 2019. https://news.gallup.com/poll/269096/one -five-adults-health-apps-wearable-trackers.aspx.

McCurdy, Katie. 2018. "Blood and Barbed Wire." *Pictal Health*, March 5, 2018. https://medium.com/pictal-health/blood-barbed-wire-cfef600bfdd4.

Nafus, Dawn, and Jamie Sherman. 2014. "Big Data, Big Questions | This One Does Not Go Up to 11: The Quantified Self Movement as an Alternative Big Data Practice." *International Journal of Communication* 8: 1784–1794.

National Center for Chronic Disease Prevention and Health Promotion. 2021. "Chronic Diseases in America." Last reviewed January 12, 2021. https://www.cdc .gov/chronicdisease/resources/infographic/chronic-diseases.htm.

Nightscout. 2014. "Welcome to Nightscout." http://www.nightscout.info.

Osborn, Chandra Y., Sunil Kripalani, Kathryn M. Goggins, and Kenneth A. Wallston. 2017. "Financial Strain Is Associated with Medication Nonadherence and Worse Self-Rated Health among Cardiovascular Patients." *Journal of Health Care for the Poor and Underserved* 28, no. 1: 499–513. https://doi.org/10.1353/hpu.2017.0036.

Ostherr, Kirsten. 2020. "Risk Media in Medicine: The Rise of the Metaclinical Health App Ecosystem." In *Routledge Companion to Media and Risk*, edited by Bishnupriya Ghosh and Bhaskar Sarkar, 107–117. New York: Routledge. https://doi.org/10.4324/9781315637501-6.

Palfreman, Jon. 2014. "Profile: Sara Riggare." *Journal of Parkinson's Disease*, March 20, 2014. https://www.journalofparkinsonsdisease.com/blog/patient_perspective/profile-sara-riggare.

Paradies, Yin, Jehonathan Ben, Nida Denson, et al. 2015. "Racism as a Determinant of Health: A Systematic Review and Meta-Analysis." *PloS One* 10, no. 9: e0138511. https://doi.org/10.1371/journal.pone.0138511.

Patel, Vimla L., José F. Arocha, and André W. Kushniruk. 2002. "Patients' and Physicians' Understanding of Health and Biomedical Concepts: Relationship to the Design of EMR Systems." *Journal of Biomedical Informatics* 35, no. 1: 8–16. https://doi.org/10.1016/S1532-0464(02)00002-3.

Price, W. Nicholson, II, and I. Glenn Cohen. 2019. "Privacy in the Age of Medical Big Data." *Nature Medicine* 25, no. 1: 37–43. https://doi.org/10.1038/s41591-018-0272-7.

Pybus, Jennifer, Mark Coté, and Tobias Blanke. 2015. "Hacking the Social Life of Big Data." *Big Data & Society* 2, no. 2. https://doi.org/10.1177/2053951715616649.

Quiñones, Ana R., Anda Botoseneanu, Sheila Markwardt, et al. 2019. "Racial/Ethnic Differences in Multimorbidity Development and Chronic Disease Accumulation for Middle-Aged Adults." *PLoS ONE* 14, no. 6: e0218462. https://doi.org/10.1371/journal.pone.0218462.

Riggare, Sara. 2014. "1 vs 8,765." *Sara Riggare: Not Patient but Im-Patient*, April 25, 2014. https://www.riggare.se/1-vs-8765.

Riggare, Sara. 2018. "E-Patients Hold Key to the Future of Healthcare." *BMJ* 360: k846. https://doi.org/10.1136/bmj.k846.

Rod, Naja Hulvej, M. Grønbaek, P. Schnohr, E. Prescott, and T.S. Kristensen. 2009. "Perceived Stress as a Risk Factor for Changes in Health Behaviour and Cardiac Risk Profile: A Longitudinal Study." *Journal of Internal Medicine* 266, no. 5: 467–475. https://doi.org/10.1111/j.1365-2796.2009.02124.x.

Salmi, Liz. 2008. *The Liz Army: Brain Cancer Patient Blog*. https://www.thelizarmy.com/blog.

Salmi, Liz. 2017. "Rock Star Patient Seeks Primary Care Physician to Form All-Star Super Group." *The Liz Army: Brain Cancer Patient Blog*, January 16, 2017. https:// www.thelizarmy.com/blog/2017/01/rock-star-patient-seeks-primary-care-physician -to-form-all-star-super-group.

Shanafelt, Tait D., Lotte N. Dyrbye, Christine Sinsky, et al. 2016. "Relationship between Clerical Burden and Characteristics of the Electronic Environment with Physician Burnout and Professional Satisfaction." *Mayo Clinic Proceedings* 91, no. 7: 836–848. https://doi.org/10.1016/j.mayocp.2016.05.007.

Tanner, Adam. 2017. *Our Bodies, Our Data: How Companies Make Billions Selling Our Medical Records*. Boston: Beacon Press.

Tikkanen, Roosa, and Melinda K. Abrams. 2020. "U.S. Health Care from a Global Perspective, 2019: Higher Spending, Worse Outcomes?" *The Commonwealth Fund*, January 30, 2020. https://doi.org/10.26099/7avy-fc29.

Tinetti, Mary E., Terri R. Fried, and Cynthia M. Boyd. 2012. Designing Health Care for the Most Common Chronic Condition—Multimorbidity." *JAMA* 307, no. 23: 2493–2494. https://doi.org/10.1001/jama.2012.5265.

Van Dijck, José, and Thomas Poell. 2016. "Understanding the Promises and Premises of Online Health Platforms." *Big Data & Society* 3, no. 1. https://doi.org/10.1177 /2053951716654173.

Varpio, Lara, Judy Rashotte, Kathy Day, James King, Craig Kuziemsky, and Avi Parush. 2015. "The EHR and Building the Patient's Story: A Qualitative Investigation of How EHR Use Obstructs a Vital Clinical Activity." *International Journal of Medical Informatics* 84, no. 12: 1019–1028. https://doi.org/10.1016/j.ijmedinf.2015.09.004.

Warren, Leigh R., Matthew Harrison, Sonal Arora, and Ara Darzi. 2019. "Working with Patients and the Public to Design an Electronic Health Record Interface: A Qualitative Mixed-Methods Study." *BMC Medical Informatics and Decision Making* 19. https://doi.org/10.1186/s12911-019-0993-7.

Zhou, Li, Sarah Collins, Stephen J. Morgan, et al. 2016. "A Decade of Experience in Creating and Maintaining Data Elements for Structured Clinical Documentation in EHRs." *AMIA Annual Symposium* Proceedings (February 2017): 1293–1302.

14   *Cis Penance*: Transmedia Database Narratives

Zoyander Street

In this chapter, Zoyander Street explores artistic, political, and theoretical tensions around creating a transmedia installation that bridges the digital and the tactile within a museum space. In their work, Street encourages audience members to engage with artifacts—specifically, interactive virtual portraits representing transgender people, based on interviews that Street has conducted—as glimpses of a larger world, engaging their transmedia literacies to "read up" and imaginatively construct their own sense of a more expansive narrative. As Kirsten Ostherr does in chapter 13, Street's work with transgender people intervenes directly in a politics of representation, challenging audience members who encounter their work to eschew self-serving, touristic reactions of empathy and to instead consider relationships of power and oppression, centrality and marginalization, and the material consequences of people's actions. Connecting to chapters 4 and 5 by Dilman Dila and Yomi Ayeni (as well as the one by Ostherr), this chapter examines how transmedia narratives can reveal, through their process-oriented modes of interpretation across multiple textual sites, the complex social processes that underlie the production of identities and communities. Like Dila's work on transmedia stories and folklore in Uganda, Street's chapter draws attention to the framework stories that define reality—stories of national identity and reactions to the collective trauma of war in Dila's case, and of the brutalizing power of cisnormative ideas about gender in Street's. The main theoretical point of reference for Street is Hiroki Azuma's "database narratives," which they use to consider how transmedia texts are built from the bottom up, presenting many compelling fragments that audience members connect in a cohesive whole. This notion of transmedia narratives generating immersive worlds that we enjoy fabricating and inhabiting is reflected in Ioana Mischie's discussion in chapter 16, later in this book, which discusses a project in which youth create virtual reality (VR) cities of the future; as well as in Ayeni's chapter, about a participatory steampunk narrative built up through audience contributions; and, more darkly, in chapter 1, which considers the appeal of QAnon and other conspiracy theories as compelling, aestheticized narrative spaces constructed from fragments into a rich whole through acts of interpretation and media literacy.

In this chapter, I discuss a transmedia reading and writing technique by reflecting on *Cis Penance*, a project that I have not yet completed at the time of writing. By writing about this unfinished project, I aim to surface tensions and gaps, understanding the affordances of interactive media and tactile museum installation through an account of unexpected outcomes and messy unknowns. Rather than presenting this project as a solution to a problem, I aim to take stock of my increasing familiarity with the tangle of unstable connections in which I work.

When I primarily produced work in writing, I grew tired of people expecting me to tell them facts. I don't live in a world of facts, but of processes and ideas. As a neurodivergent, queer person, I don't fit into the world that is narrated to me every day. The storying of my life has been an ongoing, collective process of narrating the world otherwise, from the margins rather than the center. I'm drawn to a way of thinking about transmedia that sees it as a practice of navigating ambiguity. I want to create things that allow people to understand something about the world differently by moving through the tangled connections that tie things together.

Linear writing suits a normative way of thinking about time and space; to make sense, I have to discard multiplicities in order to uncover one singular argument, and I have to decide the one correct order in which you will encounter each of the things I have to say (even if you, like me, tend to jump around a text and read it backward to better understand it, you probably assume that you're not reading it the way that the author intended). Nonlinear media such as video games excite me because they open up different possibilities for how we connect cause and effect, beginning and end, up and down. In my training in history and culture studies, I learned to do research primarily using written materials such as source documents from archives. The outcome would primarily be another kind of written material, such as an essay. But as I've followed my own interests and instincts, I've ended up with a transmedia art-research practice, taking materials such as oral interviews and physical objects and interpreting them through film and interactive media such as video games, as well as in writing beyond the narrow form of the academic essay.

I view transmedia as a democratizing reading technique. For creators, the process of transmedia storytelling conceives of any individual work (e.g., a comic book, a gaming experience, a piece of short fiction, or a film) as showing only part of a larger world; for readers, transmedia ways of engaging with texts involve "reading up" from the partial elements they have encountered, and constructing their own subjective image of the whole. As other writers in this book have shown, developing a sense of media literacy in this kind of environment is key to navigating the political challenges of our time. If anybody can construct their own subjective view of reality from the pieces they've encountered, how can we agree collectively on what is correct and true? My stance is that we can't, and we never have; our job is not to recapture a lost sense of stability, but to learn how to move more skillfully through ever-shifting terrain.

My project *Cis Penance* uses a transmedia technique of reading and authoring to bring audiences into the process of coming to a new understanding of gender, time, and the relationship between the individual and the state. When experiencing *Cis Penance*, visitors/players come into dialogue with interactive portraits—virtual characters representing transgender people I have interviewed in real life—and are given simple choices between dialogue options that put them in control of the direction of conversation. They only ever get a partial view of each individual's testimony, and each character presents a singular perspective on the vast systemic and cultural problems that transgender people face in the UK.

This reflects how reading up has been a liberating practice for marginalized people whose reality is not narrated directly by centralized histories or official, overarching descriptions of the human condition. To make sense of your experience and the world around you from a marginalized perspective requires building solidarity through listening to others like you, consciousness-raising by finding stories about the world that actually include your people, and from these various fragmentary sources, piecing together a narrative universe. In this chapter, I describe this process using Hiroki Azuma's notion of "database narratives" (2009).

However, the liberatory worldbuilding project at work in this kind of storytelling has often been missed in favor of narratives that focus on normative affective goals such as "empathy." Empathy narratives foreground the self-other relationship between author and reader, ignoring the self-world relationship that is at the heart of database narratives. I therefore also touch on the context of the queer games movement, a growth of creative activity in indie game development that I feel has been misread, in part because of an unreadiness among critics to understand media texts as database narratives.

I will begin by describing the social conditions that *Cis Penance* aims to portray, and the role of the idea of database narratives in how I have envisaged this project. I will then contextualize the project in a recent history of games made by LGBTQ+ people in order to narrate our own experiences of the world—and the faulty analytical framings that have been used to understand these games from the emotional perspective of an assumed heterosexual, cisgender player.

Trans Issues in the UK: *Cis Penance*

My projects have materialized both as fully digital online experiences and as hybrid pieces involving handmade custom hardware installed in gallery spaces and at festivals. In designing this custom hardware, I hope to shape the relationship between visitors and the characters being depicted to engender a sense of care. One project, based on a set of twelve interviews with trans people in Japan, involved a rudimentary simulation of body language and emotional responses tied to the content of what the character is saying, to give a clear sense that there are consequences to the visitor or player's actions when they choose questions to ask.

My current work in progress, *Cis Penance*, is based on forty-five interviews. *Cis Penance* is named after an essay by trans writer Patience Newbury, "Maybe You Should Never Transition" (2012), which argues that to deny trans people the right to transition when they decide to do so "serves positively no benefit to a trans person. It merely impresses a cis person's own denial of a trans person onto that trans person, forcing the latter to serve a cissexist penance." In this project, trans people talk about their experiences of time, many describing the cissexist penance that they have paid to bureaucratic and cultural gatekeepers in the UK.

I have interviewed transgender and nonbinary individuals from around the UK, and highlighted material about temporality, to draw attention to the Sisyphean bureaucratic processes imposed on transgender people in a country growing increasingly hostile to trans civil rights. *Cis Penance* portrays characters as though they were standing in line, queueing for something. Through the image of the queue, I hope to make visible the "waiting lists" that put UK trans people's lives on hold for years—you never see these lists, it is rare to even be informed of your position on any such list, and getting to the top of a list is only the beginning of yet another waiting period.

In addition to bureaucratic waiting, the process of physical change after starting hormones is itself unavoidably slow. Despite this arduous process of waiting that almost every trans person in the UK experiences, transphobic narratives widely disseminated in the media and discussed openly in Parliament still describe transition as though it were an alarmingly rapid process, a dangerous and irreversible decision that could transform a person's body and identity overnight. Unfortunately, these alarmist narratives by uninformed cisgender people continue to take precedence over the lived experiences of transgender people, in a manner not unlike the media campaigns against gay people when I was growing up in the 1990s.

Cis Penance opens on an image of these many characters all lined up horizontally, as though they were waiting in line for something, or as though the current historical moment were being portrayed on an artifact like the Bayeux Tapestry, which shows the passage of events in the form of sideways movement. Users can click on any character and begin an interactive dialogue with them. Text taken verbatim from the interview is shown at the top of the screen, and dialogue options are shown at the bottom. There should always be two options to choose from (at the time of writing, there are still parts where only one option is shown, but I hope to amend that). Most of the time, the choice of option changes which branch of dialogue the user sees next, but sometimes both options lead to the same outcome. My aim as the designer is to give the user a sense of responsibility for their choices, while also sometimes putting them in the uncomfortable position of having to choose between two options when neither feels like a good fit.

In portraying a large number of characters, I aim to give people the sense that they have met a large number of trans people; in my experience, when you've only met one or two trans people, cisnormative ideas about gender mostly remain intact, and you just make an exception for the people you know whose gender does not match the one they were assigned at birth. But once you know a lot of trans people, and you hear all their diverse yet unified stories about self-understanding beyond the sex one has been assigned at birth, the whole conceptual system of gender shifts; gender is no longer a natural fact, but, in the words of Leslie Feinberg, "the poetry each of us makes out of the language we are taught" (1998, 10). This familiarity with gender as a complexly layered language, rather than a simple binary fact, is the product of a kind of cultural immersion, a similar cognitive shift to those I have experienced when doing ethnographic fieldwork.

The goal of my practice as a whole is, eventually, to use interactive media to scale up the direct experience of ambiguity that normally an ethnographer can report on only afterward in writing. I use Azuma's notion of database narratives to explain this immersive experience that comes from meeting a large number of people—the sense that the people you have met constitute a larger context or world rather than simply sharing a condition that deviates from the norm (thereby reinforcing its normativity).

Database Narratives

Azuma's arguments come from the specific conditions of otaku culture that developed around anime, video games, and comics in 1990s Japan, but he uses that lens to broadly describe postmodernity as a historical condition. Within the context of otaku culture, "What consumers truly value and buy are the settings and the worldview. Yet in reality, it is difficult to sell settings and worldviews themselves as works" (Azuma, 2009, 31). The word translated as "worldview" here is *sekaikan* in the original Japanese. In addition to referring to the notion of *Weltanschauung*, which encompasses ideological, moral, and philosophical positions about our own world, *sekaikan* points to the aesthetic goals of a writer, manga artist, or video game developer when they try to realize their own vision of a fictional world. To say that consumers are attracted to the *sekaikan* of a piece of media does not necessarily mean that they share its views on the world as a whole, but more that they enjoy the fictional world that it portrays. Azuma's database narrative theory describes how enjoying individual works contributes to the consumption of a *sekaikan*. The purpose of this is to answer a more general question about how meaning and identity function in postmodernity.

Many theories of postmodernity have observed that while modernity is associated with all-encompassing grand narratives such as progress or evolution, postmodernity is associated with the loss of such unified narratives. Theorists have conceived of multiple spatial metaphors to try to explain what has taken the place of grand narratives. Many of them involve things that are tangled up, nonlinear, and multidirectional. Deleuze and Guattari's Capitalism and Schizophrenia project ([1980]1987) proposed the image of the rhizome, which allows multiplicities and nonhierarchical conceptual structures, in contrast to modernity's tree structures, which have a clear hierarchy between the central stem and peripheral branches. Donna Haraway (2016) has more recently extended these tangled-up metaphors with her notion of string figures, which suggests not only nonlinear and nonhierarchical bundles of connections, but also an interactive process of moving and reconfiguring these structures with human and nonhuman others.

Azuma sees the database as an alternative to the rhizome that is easier to understand for his purposes, focusing on references to the database and additions to it rather than to the decentralized interconnections of the rhizome—fundamentally, these two ideas are reflections of one another, and Azuma draws a similar contrast between tree narratives and database narratives. The rhizome gives us access to a liveliness of natural systems, a theme that has found a resurgence in recent years as mycological metaphors proliferate in postmodern more-than-human feminist writing and in conceptual art. While the rhizomes and databases of the 1990s were structures observed in the making, the mycelial nets of the late 2010s and early 2020s are unknowable, living bundles of potentiality lying deep under the earth. Whereas modern scholarship aimed to surface the underlying root of things, postmodernism showed that there was no longer a root and stem, only an interconnected root system—and contemporary scholarship goes further, shifting the relationship from a surfacing and disentangling of roots to the arts of noticing, watching for the fruiting bodies of meaning to arise (Lowenhaupt Tsing, 2015).

Azuma's own description of the relationship between the reader and this narrative structure is "reading up": a process of extrapolating from individual media works to construct a picture of the overall database narrative. Each individual work adds to the database, and none has a totalizing claim to reality. To take a non-Japanese example, when I watch *Star Trek: Enterprise* and learn that the culture of the Denobulans is polyamorous, I add these specific conditions for polyamory into my picture of the database of Star Trek's worldview. Of course, nowadays there is also a literal database online where fans have transcribed these narrative details, so I am able to search a narrative database to check my own reading up against that of other viewers. Azuma views reading-up practices in transmedia franchises of the 1990s as a way that otaku read *sekaikan* directly through their consumerist engagement with database narratives. For Azuma, there is a great political cost to this narrative shift, which places otaku in a passive position, having to construct an identity out of their engagement with the products of capitalism.

It is possible that this notion of passivity has been made a little more complicated by the rise of social media and user-generated content in the twenty-plus years that have passed since Azuma wrote his book. These developments in capitalism's capture of ever more aspects of our lives and identities have shifted the assumption that the consumer is a passive reader, while also centralizing the most lucrative intellectual property (IP) into the hands of a shrinking pool of media conglomerates (including the Star Trek universe, owned by the conglomerate ViacomCBS). This leads to the parallel construction of multiple database narratives concerning the same narrative universes—canon narratives, and shared understandings within specialist fan communities. To take the Star Trek example again, a romance between Elim Garak and Julian Bashir on *Star Trek: Deep Space Nine* is well documented in fan communities, but it is not a part of the canon. What emerges is neither a passively determinist state of affairs where fans are forced to accept whatever bits and pieces are given to them by capitalist media corporations, nor a totally liberated and decentralized free-for-all where users simply create content for each other and ignore capitalist media commodities; instead, there is an interplay and exchange between multiple database narratives that readers both consume and alter. This reading method, which has developed in the context of fictional media properties, could also apply to the ideological "canon" narratives of hegemonic cisheteropatriarchy.

In the current context of shifting political and social ideas about how subjectivity and power are to be arranged, I see potential in reading up through the database narrative of social media: a decentralized idea of what it is to be a person emerges through exposure to multiple personal narratives. This played a significant role in my transition, and that of many of the characters in *Cis Penance*. We came to understand ourselves outside of the dominant cisheteronormative narrative because we were able to read up on a different database narrative through our encounters with trans, nonbinary, and other queer people online in blogs, social media, and user-generated video. This process is a significant part of what I aim to simulate for people who experience *Cis Penance*, by creating work based on a large number of interviews rather than focusing on one or just a few protagonists—whereas traditional documentary might tell a compelling story about one character, I aim to create a shift in perspective by experiencing simulated dialogues with a large number of characters, all of which contribute to a broader database narrative in the visitor's mind.

The database narrative of the online trans world is always changing, and there is a constant tension between establishing and maintaining stable narrative concepts that help us to make sense of ourselves and each other ("Trans men are men"), and pushing to expand and deconstruct those concepts to facilitate more liberation and movement ("Trans men can have a complicated relationship with 'man,' and might also identify as lesbians"). It is not only trans people who have created such an online narrative universe: I have seen similar movements arise among autistic people creating language for each other that differs from or extends the medical model of autism, people with dissociative conditions who affirm all their multiple personalities as valid individuals sharing one system, and people guiding each other through methods of reflective inquiry that expand the very experience of selfhood itself. This is a disturbing time in many ways, as emerging database narratives developed through online movements advocating for marginalized subject positions upend ideas such as the singularity of self-identity, binary gender, and neurotypical assumptions about the nature of time, space, and phenomenological perception. But it is possible that decentralized database narratives offer a malleable, open space of ambiguous reality that allows us to challenge, or at least create alternatives to, dominant narratives about how to be a person. And though that ambiguity is challenging, we learn to navigate it through transmedia reading techniques.

Queer Games: Empathy

Projects that take nonfiction material and present them in other media forms, such as video games, virtual reality (VR), or immersive theater, are often understood through a framing of "empathy" that is defined as "walking in someone else's shoes," experiencing a simulation of the life of an other.

In this framing, emotions evoked in the viewer or user are imagined as a result of the perceived affordances of digital media, as interfaces that address the body in ways that many other media do not. A story initially captured in one medium, such as interviews or archival research, can be remediated as text (essays), oral performance (lectures), or film (documentaries), and each medium is believed to bring with it a different set of affordances and strengths—some pedagogical theories, such as the National Training Laboratories diagram of the Learning Pyramid, suggest that people retain different proportions of the information conveyed to them depending on the medium of expression (e.g., 30 percent of the information from a demonstration, and only 5 percent of the information from a lecture); as pointed out by Kare Letrud (2012), this idea is not supported by any empirical evidence. As advocates of "games for change" and prosocial uses of VR explore medium-specific benefits to other ways of transmediating nonfiction material, "empathy" has come to the fore.

Scholars in queer games studies have critiqued this framing for the limited scope of prosocial affects it imagines, and for positioning the subject of such pieces as the "other," rather than imagining collective subject positions whereby the player and the characters share a common experience and can exist in solidarity (Pozo, 2018; Ruberg, 2019). Many of the games by queer creators that these critics study were in fact created with an audience of other queer people in mind—the point is to share stories with each other in order to make sense of our own experiences and collectively imagine a world that centers our lived realities, not to educate cisgender heterosexuals about our lives. Yet the critical discourse about these works contorts them to make them about feeling empathy for the other, and this takes the work out of the hands of the community and strips it of its meaning.

To put it in the words of Wendy H. K. Chun, quoted by the queer game developer Robert Yang (2017): "if you 'walk in someone else's shoes then you've taken their shoes.'" A critique of exploitative shoe-swapping empathy narratives has an established history in critical race studies; for example, bell hooks and Ron Scaap have argued that "this act of redescription IS still an attempt to appropriate others" (hooks, 2014, 13). The received narrative about "empathy" assumes that if a piece of media portrays a marginalized identity, then its intended audience must be people who belong to the dominant identity, and this assumption itself centers the gaze of the dominant class. The empathy framing centers the moral feelings of the privileged and pays little attention to the material consequences of people's actions or to the realities of the systems that harm marginalized people in the first place. It doesn't envisage systemic change, but instead imagines that the consumer experiences of relatively privileged individuals can themselves be an intrinsic moral good—in doing so, it commodifies the stories of marginalized people, turning labor that was intended for uplifting a community into a service for tragedy tourists.

Instead of this dualistic approach to empathy, I pursue a sense of "response-ability," a term from Donna Haraway (2008, 2016) that refers to being responsible for how your actions affect others in a connected system. It is not enough to know how someone else feels—what matters is our own flexibility to undergo change in recognition of the fact that we do not exist in an isolated way, but as part of interdependent systems. When someone experiences *Cis Penance*, I don't want them to feel sad and then move on with their lives, satisfied that they had an appropriate moral emotion—I want their worldview to change a little bit, even if that is uncomfortable, and even if it suggests that they might have to do things differently in their own lives in the future. In another project, I used software design that blends role-playing game design with virtual pets, and custom hardware involving warm textiles rather than cold plastic, to explore possibilities for engendering care and response-ability. In *Cis Penance*, by collecting large numbers of interviews and representing them as characters filling an environment, I create a database narrative that avoids the focus on singular protagonists in traditional documentary, with the aim of creating a sense of cultural immersion in a social context outside of normativity.

Beyond the field of queer games studies, the feminist anthropologist of technoscience Lucy Suchman (2006, 2007, 2011) has pointed out that designers' and users' understanding of emotion is based on animated software exhibiting an appropriate visual response to stimuli that are assumed to have affective power. Examining projects from the early 2000s such as Joseph Bates's *Edge of Intention* and Steve Grand's *Creatures*, she points out that "what 'emotions' become in this system are a series of emotional/ behavioral attributions mapped to visual features of the figures" (2006, 211). While a mystified narrative about such projects states that these software agents have been programmed to "have emotions," and that the visual change in body language reflects this appropriate development of an affective system coded into the agent itself, Suchman argues that the success of such an agent relies upon "the artful synthesis of cartoonists' design work and viewers' readings" (2006, 212).

According to Suchman, what motivates the mystification of such design work into a myth about the creation of artificial life itself is a worry about the separation between humans and the technological artifacts that we have created: that they are too complex for us to be able to comprehend directly, so we must render them into a form of life that resembles ourselves closely enough that they could explain themselves to us in terms that we understand (2006, 213–214). One of the motivations behind Suchman's work is to break down these kinds of mystifications, creating space for computers and robots to simply be different from us and examining the agencies of nonhumans as they are, rather than rendering them into something more like us.

For me, this worry about the distance caused by difference echoes the politics of assimilation versus separatism in theories of LGBTQ+ liberation. Do trans people have to prove that we are "just like everyone else" to be accepted, and is that even an effective rhetorical move when a significant motivating factor in our lives is to be more true to ourselves and less alienated by the work of fitting into cisnormativity? A great many trans people are left behind by the politics of sameness: nonbinary people, gender-nonconforming trans people, trans people in poverty, disabled trans people, autistic trans people, kinky trans people, trans sex workers, and many other intersecting marginalizations that make up a disproportionate number within the trans community. Meanwhile, others in the community worry that if trans people on the whole are perceived through the media gaze as strange and different, our position in society will never improve. One of the motivations behind my work is to create space for trans people to be who we are, even if that means exploring ways of being that haven't been narrated before, rather than rendering ourselves into model citizens, "just like you."

The interactive portraits that I create in *Cis Penance* and other projects speak to another imaginary that Suchman describes: they could be a proxy for emotional labor that would have otherwise been coercively extracted from a human worker. Ironically, when showing my previous project in public, I've often had to be that worker, as people see that I'm presenting work about trans issues and decide to ask me invasive questions about surgery and mental health. I have to navigate in the moment how much vulnerability to share in order to help the other person understand without harming myself. I am relatively privileged in this situation, because I get to decide what the desired outcome from such an encounter should be—my friends who have to advocate for their own inclusion in the workplace or in their places of worship do not get to choose to simply walk away from a discussion when it is taking a serious toll on their mental health. It might therefore be tempting to imagine that the characters in *Cis Penance* can do the work of narrating trans experiences without experiencing the negative effects that real humans suffer as a result. Suchman highlights the theorist, poet, and fiction author Alexandra Chasin's work on the gendered imaginary of technological agents as "servants," and Marvin Minsky's statements as an engineer of robotic agents, which bring up troubling historical examples of coerced labor such as slavery and domestic services provided by displaced workers vulnerable to exploitation (2006, 220). Technological agents fulfill a desire for workers that are intelligent enough to understand context, but not willful enough to want to change it.

Storying the World Otherwise

I try to create work that does not appear high-tech enough to provoke this fantasy—I want users to see the rough edges of the work and imagine how it was made, so that the human agency behind its creation remains visible. But what often happens is that people treat the interactive portrait as an opportunity to extract emotional labor from a trans person without facing the real-world consequences of doing so. I hear comments like, "It's great, you get to ask questions that you don't want to ask in real life," and although this is intended as a compliment, I am deeply troubled by this extractive relationship the user has taken with the piece.

Similarly, I am troubled by reports that while I am not around, users are having long interactions with these portraits, trying to find every possible variation of how the conversations can go. I am relieved when my work breaks because it almost feels like it is exerting its own agency, refusing to be compliant in the hands of a demanding audience. Part of my responsibility in future will be to create interfaces that resist extractive and exploitative interaction by the user.

What I have observed from watching and talking with visitors is complex, and brings to light the extent to which social and physical context shapes the experience; it is not all a matter of design, but it is also about how I show up as the transgender artist behind the work, the role the installation plays in the social lives of visitors, and the experiences, assumptions, and flexibility of visitors themselves. For example, someone engaged in an interactive dialogue online through their computer during COVID-19 lockdown can comfortably take a completionist approach, redoing the same conversation over and over again to get all the information they can. Someone experiencing the piece in a social space, narrating their actions to another person, is more likely to experience a need to perform the right kinds of affects in their dialogue choices—and a time pressure, as their companion might not appreciate their dawdling in the gallery for twenty minutes to explore the whole possibility space. What's at stake is as much about the visitor's performance as it is about the content of the work itself.

I often feel more comfortable about audience engagement with my work when I am present to act as a mediator. Part of this is because I want to encourage people to adopt a particular affect when engaging physically with the interfaces that I have built—left to their own devices, people will physically contact as little of an artwork as possible, since the social contract of an art gallery usually involves no touch whatsoever, but in the past I've designed installations that involve a total embrace of the artwork, with a cushion nestled in the user's lap and their hands cradling a custom-built portable console. It is difficult to persuade people to use the work this way unless someone acts as a concierge, welcoming them into a cozy space and inviting them to take a seat before handing them a cushion.

From the point of the view that the connection between thing A and thing B requires interface layers that render different things into something vaguely similar to one another, it is reassuring to imagine the other as somewhat similar to ourselves because the (threatening) alternative is to be forced to reimagine ourselves as somewhat similar to the other. If we let go of the obligation to reassure users—if we assume the right to disrupt and discomfit, perhaps by using the label "artist" rather than "designer"—then this alternative path starts to open up. What if we imagine ourselves as in some sense database-like? What if we imagine gender as infinitely multiple and mysterious, rather than as a knowable, binary way of classifying people as "like me" (homo) and "not like me" (hetero)?

These two provocations have a point of connection because databases hold such a large number of entities. As Azuma understands database narratives, every story adds to or modifies a shared database, and no one database has a totalizing claim to reality. If our database narratives are contingent and participatory, then no one person's identity implies anything about another's. Rather than understanding one documentary subject as emblematic of the trans experience as a whole, I aim to create work that suggests a vast array of gendered experiences, and positions the player—whether cis or trans—within a world where multiplicity is assumed. I want to invite people to imagine themselves as part of database narratives, rather than modernist grand narratives.

When you encounter one person who is different from you, your effort to understand is directed outward, as they become an object of interest. When you enter a space where *everybody* is different from you, your effort to understand is turned inward—there is something that everybody else understands that I don't, and I will have to undergo a change in myself in order to make sense of it.

References

Azuma, Hiroki. 2009. *Otaku: Japan's Database Animals*. Translated by Jonathan E. Abel and Shion Kono. Minneapolis: University of Minnesota Press. Originally published in 2001.

Deleuze, Gilles, and Félix Guattari. 1987. *A Thousand Plateaus: Capitalism and Schizophrenia*. Translated by Brian Massumi. Minneapolis: University of Minnesota Press. Originally published in 1980.

Feinberg, Leslie. 1998. *Trans Liberation: Beyond Pink or Blue*. Boston: Beacon Press.

Haraway, Donna. 2008. *When Species Meet*. Minneapolis: University of Minnesota Press.

Haraway, Donna. 2016. *Staying with the Trouble: Making Kin in the Chthulucene*. Durham, NC: Duke University Press.

hooks, bell. 2014. *Black Looks: Race and Representation*. 2nd ed. New York: Routledge.

Letrud, Kare. 2012. "A Rebuttal of NTL Institute's Learning Pyramid." *Education* 133, no. 1 (Fall): 117–124.

Lowenhaupt Tsing, Anna. 2015. *The Mushroom at the End of the World: On the Possibility of Life in Capitalist Ruins*. Princeton, NJ: Princeton University Press.

Newbury, Patience. 2012. "'Maybe You Should Never Transition': On the Four Cisnormative Corridors of Denial Trans People Face When Readiness to Transition Is Voiced." Cisnormativity (blog). https://cisnormativity.wordpress.com/2012/01/15/maybe-you-should-never-transition.

Pozo, Teddy. 2018. "Queer Games after Empathy: Feminism and Haptic Game Design Aesthetics from Consent to Cuteness to the Radically Soft." *Game Studies* 18, no. 3. http://gamestudies.org/1803/articles/pozo

Ruberg, Bo. 2019. *Video Games Have Always Been Queer*. New York: New York University Press.

Suchman, Lucy. 2006. *Human-Machine Reconfigurations: Plans and Situated Actions*. Cambridge: Cambridge University Press.

Suchman, Lucy. 2007. "Feminist STS and the Sciences of the Artificial." In *The Handbook of Science and Technology Studies*, 3rd ed., edited by Edward J. Hackett, Olga Amsterdamska, Michael Lynch, and Judy Wajcman, 139–164. Cambridge, MA: MIT Press.

Suchman, Lucy. 2011. "Subject Objects. *Feminist Theory* 12, no. 2: 119–145.

Yang, Robert. 2017. "If You Walk in Someone Else's Shoes, Then You've Taken Their Shoes": Empathy Machines as Appropriation Machines." Radiator (blog). https://www.blog.radiator.debacle.us/2017/04/if-you-walk-in-someone-elses-shoes-then.html.

Transmedia Crosstalk: Kirsten Ostherr and Zoyander Street

Bob Beard: This volume reckons with different definitions of transmedia, and ways that these logics can be operationalized. Traditionally, this is about centering the audience's experience—turning them from spectators to coproducers—but your two pieces alter that paradigm a bit. Can you talk about that?

Kirsten Ostherr: I think that both of our pieces look at the liberatory, or at least improved, narrative capabilities that transmedia has to offer, if used to center the perspectives of people whose stories are not often told, or whose stories are subsumed within other narratives about them.

Zoyander Street: Yes. There is a common cause around self-definition and struggles in medicalised contexts, where the voices of people with authority have more weight (of course, that's how authority works) than the voices of people whose experiences are being described. And then there's this contextual shift between the conversations that we have with each other about our experiences and the conversations that other people have about us. And whether transmedia's capability (or provocation) to shift between contexts and means of articulation might offer new ways of translating and speaking "up."

KO: Yes, I think what Zoyander says about the conversations that other people have about us is so key. The description Zoyander offers of what happens with the artworks when they are not in the room, as they've been told, and how that raises all kinds of ethical concerns, made me think about how doctors and other health-care professionals talk about patients when they are not in the room, and the problems that arise in those gaps. To me, transmedia is a space where there is a multiplicity of conversations, such that the binary of doctor-patient—and the hierarchy that goes with that—might be displaced.

ZS: Something that stood out to me in your chapter is the different modes through which transmedia logics can be enacted—e.g., transmedia logics of capture as well as transmedia logics of reading. That relates strongly to the kind of thing I'm struggling with in my practice, around whether my work is read as a means of capture or a provocation/opportunity for engaged reading/listening. And I wonder how far this is about patients producing an account of their own lives, and how far it is about doctors/clinicians learning transmedia reading techniques that facilitate a greater degree of nonhierarchical communication?

KO: I think both are needed, and I also think that transmedia reading techniques are a lot more fun than the kind of reading clinicians are accustomed to doing. So there could be a pleasure in the communication process that might be capable of really shifting the affect around these encounters. But your question also makes me wonder, how do you enlist the visitors to your art shows as a certain kind of participant who is willing to engage in trans-media logics of reading? I suppose maybe that needs to be part of the artwork itself, but you can't control who walks in the door . . .

ZS: Yeah, I'm still trying to figure this out. Or more, how do I respond to the multiple reading techniques that people bring to something like this? I don't want to be the kind of creator who tries to control what people do with their work, but I also feel responsible for how people treat these characters. I guess a major thing is that sense of multiplicity that I'm trying to communicate by having a large number of characters—I'm trying to break people out of the narrative assumptions that we associate with a single protagonist's journey, and prompt an approach that considers multiple perspectives and world-level narrative.

BB: It's interesting how both of your examples also do something unexpected with the traditional momentum of transmedia. Participation and collabora-tion is less about gathering information and assembling the pieces to unlock a story or solve a problem, and more concerned with serving the population through more complex and careful storytelling.

ZS: I suppose I'm trying to relocate the problem. In the introduction to Shon Faye's *The Transgender Issue: An Argument for Justice*, she explains what she's doing in the title of the book—redirecting a fetishizing and objectifying fram-ing of trans people as a "social issue" into a discussion about the social and systemic issues faced by trans people. And I imagine a similar thing in more strictly medical contexts—being made into a patient is being made into a problem to be dealt with by doctors, where a good outcome for them is you getting discharged, your care coming to an end! Instead the problem could exist between us.

KO: Well said! I guess I'll add that there are so many problems to solve, but for me, if a person could capture and communicate their experiences with health and illness through transmedia logics, then the rigid boundary between being a person and being made into a patient might start to dissolve a bit, and that would be an improvement.

ZS: There is also a piece here about the design of systems of communication and interaction (human-device and human-human)—Kirsten, you mention in your chapter that "patient perspectives are absent by design" from con-ventional medical systems, suggesting that what's needed is a redesign that addresses this absence. There's a specificity to this that I really appreciate—it's not that there's a technology that itself is capable of saving the world or whatever, but that there is a collective human process of designing systems that we can do differently, and transmedia engages affordances that are avail-able to us in our present context. I want to ask you how we remain critical of the extractive design of many transmedia technologies, while also trying to do liberatory things with what we've learned from using them (I think you achieve this in the chapter but wanted to highlight it as it seems important).

KO: Zoyander, this is such an important and difficult question. There is always the risk of objectification and exploitation, in the contexts we describe in both of our chapters. I think that some ground rules can be put in place, but they will never be capable of outpacing the new ways of mining and repurposing data, at least not if the financial logics are on the other side of things, so to speak. So, who benefits from a transmedia logic of capture in health care? In trans representation? Is it possible to ensure that only the patients and the trans community benefit? Is that even the goal? Not if the communication needs to go beyond those groups, but then how to ensure that we, in a way, "protect" those whose data are circulating through these new pathways? I don't have one single answer, but I do think that these questions always have to be asked alongside any creative venture these days.

ZS: For sure, and I guess I just hope for some kind of generative dialectic about the ethics of what I'm doing, because I don't anticipate being able to follow a certain set of standards and thereby entirely avoid harm (I hope that doesn't sound defeatist or avoidant—I do of course also think about how best to achieve a good outcome for everyone). I expect a work in progress—one of the things I long for is some kind of established relationship with an intermediary that one of the people I've interviewed can work with if I've hurt them, because it seems difficult for them if their only option is bringing things up with me directly. And of course, it's even harder to seek redress from a large platform corporation when they've done something that hurts us, or when the systems they've designed are unable to protect us.

BB: One more question: What is one skill that a would-be transmedia producer needs for doing this type of work—applying transmedia logics in their field?

KO: The ability to listen without interrupting. And the ability to sit with non-linear storylines (that may be a given for many in transmedia, but not in health care!).

ZS: I'd like to challenge people not to assume that what they're making has to try super hard to please the user—this kind of work isn't game design or UX [user experience] in the same way that you'd see in a commercial context, and it's okay when dealing with serious subject matter to have to sit with some discomfort.

15   Emergent Transmedia

Terra Gasque

This chapter invites us to reflect on concepts that cut across the entirety of this volume: it considers how tabletop role-playing games (TTRPGs) provide a model for how players can use the tabletop form and various digital extensions (e.g., podcasts, interactive livestreams, and other media) to create compelling storyworlds; remediate existing fictional worlds with new themes, identities, and tensions; and democratize access to acts of imaginative worldbuilding, by linking physical play with easy-to-use tools for digital production. Using the theorist adrienne maree brown's Emergent Strategy as a guide, Gasque opens up conversations about who holds power in the corporate-funded worlds discussed by Maureen McHugh Yeager and Caitlin Burns in chapters 1 and 2, respectively, and also considers how TTRPGs can be an accessible entry point for engaging in the kinds of transmedia experiences described by Dilman Dila and Yomi Ayeni (chapters 4 and 5, respectively), which span the physical and the virtual. Like Kayla Asbell et al.'s discussion of their UTOPIAN HOTLINE project in chapter 6, Gasque frames transmedia stories and the communities that gather around them as sources of succor in the face of the traumas inflicted by unjust social systems. Like the chapters in this volume that deal with bigger-budget experiences, Gasque insists on the importance of co-creation and a communal energy to transmedia as an art form and a mode of critical inquiry—the challenge is, of course, to develop structures whereby transmedia creators aren't constrained by the threat of takedowns or legal action by intellectual property (IP) owners. In this way, Gasque presents a counternarrative to many of our other chapters, which present constructive guides and positive examples of best practices for building and managing transmedia experiences. Gasque's perspective is shaped by their experiences with transmedia as a more conflictual space, in which enthusiastic fan-creators are frequently stymied by corporate owners who strictly regulate the repurposing of their beloved characters, settings, and lore. This represents a failure state for a vision of transmedia as open, dialogic, and welcoming to fan-made texts that deepen and extend existing narratives. Like earlier contributions by Ruth Wylie et al. (chapter 12) and Francis Quek et al. (chapter 8), Gasque finds hope in the power of play and experimentation with storytelling. Examining TTRPG mechanics that support collaborative imagination and nonhierarchical narrative generation, they envision transmedia worlds as spaces for exploration rather than tools for capital accumulation.

In his lecture "Why Our Future Depends on Libraries, Reading and Daydreaming," Neil Gaiman (2013) expounded on the necessity of fiction in our lives:

> Fiction can show you a different world. It can take you somewhere you've never been. Once you've visited other worlds, like those who ate fairy fruit, you can never be entirely content with the world that you grew up in. Discontent is a good thing: discontented people can modify and improve their worlds, leave them better, leave them different. (para. 21)

As an avid explorer of these far-flung worlds of fiction, I harbor many discontents with the reality that I grew up in. And while the power of fiction itself certainly is not in danger, I feel a growing discontent with the direction in which transmedia has moved in recent years—particularly with the encroachment on, and growing control of, transmedia worlds and the engagement of their fans by corporate and capitalistic systems. If left unchecked, this corporate oversight threatens to create an oligarchy of powerful entities that control which creative visions are allowed to be experienced, to rigidly define what can and cannot exist in these fairy-fruit fictional storyworlds. The corporate owners and stewards of transmedia worlds achieve this control by cutting fan interactivity off at the knees and, more impactfully, by undermining and silencing the voices of marginalized individuals. I wish to challenge this shift in power and ownership within popular culture and the limited, mass-produced commodification of transmedia that these structures sell to their customers. In this chapter, I turn to the assistance of adrienne maree brown's book *Emergent Strategy: Shaping Change, Changing Worlds* (2017).

Part self-help book, part community-organization guide, part primer on resistance against systemic oppression, *Emergent Strategy* provides seeds of solutions to globe-spanning societal issues, small at first appearance but massive in their fully realized state. Here, brown's approach provides what might seem like overly simple solutions that gradually reveal themselves to possess the unadorned precision of a sharp knife. For example, brown takes the complex topic of living in a capitalist society that constantly demands time, energy, and effort from the individual with little to no emotional support or recompense offered in return, and compares it to living in a toxic relationship. Through this comparison, brown is able to make the brutality of our social system visible, and therefore open to challenge, to rethinking, to alternatives. In so doing, brown cuts complex topics into manageable chunks, bringing to light unseen aspects of our lived experiences and enabling us to consider how we might reconfigure our understanding and then rebuild something better.

But when it comes to the contemporary transmedia landscape, where should we use this knife? What limitations and abuses are we blind to? Once we can recognize them, what should we build in their place? How will we differentiate the bad from the good? Using the tabletop role-playing game (TTRPG) *Little Fears* (Blair, 2001, 2009), which likewise centers on concepts of belief and discontent, brown (2017) can help us chart a course through the profit-focused, controlled experiences of modern transmedia and rediscover the vibrant, messy wilds of the living collaborative experience.

Transmedia experiences are intended to embrace audience participation, using the collective creativity of fans and participants to expand and enrich narrative universes built from a wide range of media texts, from movies and books to games, comics, websites, and more. The corporate clampdown on audience involvement and creativity threatens these affordances of transmedia as a medium for telling stories and building worlds. TTRPGs like *Little Fears* are designed for collaborative, participatory, improvisational storytelling, worldbuilding, and problem-solving. On a small scale, at their best, TTRPGs can capture the vibrancy and collaborative energy of transmedia storytelling. And this is more true today than ever, as the experience of playing TTRPGs and participating in the communities around them becomes transmediated through livestreams, podcasts, fan art, and more.

Methodological Foundation

Transmedia storytelling, while drawing its roots from fandoms, was first described in the terms used today by Henry Jenkins's *Convergence Culture* (2006). His book delved into how new technologies like cell phones could be combined with media creation to form three new aspects of cultural production, consumption, and interaction: collective intelligence, transmedia storytelling, and participatory culture (2006, 3–4). Jenkins saw television shows like *American Idol*, which paired big-budget presentation with opportunities for consequential audience engagement through voting, as an example of convergence culture, where audience members could exert influence on the shape of media texts outside of the traditional one-way transmission process that characterized older forms of media like film and radio (2006, 61–62).

In Jenkins's formulation, *collective intelligence* involves the way that technologies, as well as multiplatform forms of media production and consumption, hail users to solve problems, interpret texts, and construct new meanings collectively, drawing on different specialties and bodies of knowledge. Working together allows people to solve problems faster and stitch together diverse points of view, as well as providing new opportunities for building relationships and social bonds around shared media experiences.

Transmedia storytelling characterizes how audiences actively participate in both creating and experiencing stories that unfold across multiple types of media. A narrative experience may flow from a video game, to a social media platform, to a TV episode at the whim of its creators, and sometimes at the whims of its audience co-creators, who may fashion their own texts, rework existing texts, or create paratextual materials like fan art.

Participatory culture captures how new technologies encourage a shift among audience members from passive consumers to active participants. In Jenkins's thinking on convergence culture, fans interact with content dynamically, remixing and remaking it for their own use and layering on new meanings.

Across these three aspects of emergent cultural production and consumption, Jenkins recognized that technological change created opportunities for creative works to become deeper, more complex experiences, with creators and fans working together in a push-pull of collectively intelligent meaning-making, multimedia story creation, and a remix culture wherein content could be shaped to fit the unique needs, desires, and preoccupations of individuals and communities.

Since the publication of *Convergence Culture*, a power imbalance that Jenkins notes in the book has intensified: corporate creators and owners of transmedia universes have exerted greater levels of control over the creation process to the detriment of fans, who enjoy ever-smaller spaces for genuine acts of co-creation and suffer from a diminished ability to shape the media experiences in which they are invested. Modern transmedia is becoming a structure centered on unrelenting capitalistic consumption, stifling the creative possibilities in its users because of the perceived danger that audience creations pose to the potential profitability of the transmedia universe. A Star Wars fan might be inspired to make a provocative piece of art centered around the conflicted emotions of the character Kylo Ren during the time just after Luke Skywalker tries to kill him. However, in doing research and exploring ideas, the fan may come across a number of cautionary anecdotes from other community members telling how Disney has sent threatening cease-and-desist orders to fan creators, prompting hesitancy in the would-be artist. These limitations are further compounded by the 2014 removal of all Star Wars material from the official canon except the original three films, the *Clone Wars* television series and film, and any new material made from that date forward by Disney (Star Wars, 2014). Although any material deemed worthy from the old canon (now called *Star Wars Legends*) is available for inclusion in the new canon as references, this act removed the vast collective history of Star Wars and created a sort of quantum state where nothing made between 1983 and 2014 officially exists in the franchise's lore, but still remains available for corporate plundering for future materials should it be deemed shiny enough to attract customers. This act delegitimized fan creativity around a huge catalogue of well-loved texts, from novels to video games and much more.

While the pruning of an overgrown franchise is not in and of itself a bad thing, Disney's use of scorched-earth tactics with regard to their beloved legacy media pieces, in conjunction with the cherry-picking of characters and settings to resell to fans outside their original context purely because they are recognizable and marketable, creates an inherently tenuous relationship among the corporation, the fans, and the media. This, combined with Disney's notorious litigiousness (e.g., its suits against day-care centers for having images of Mickey Mouse, Minnie Mouse, and Goofy on their walls as described in Mikkelson, 1996) and dogged attempts to keep their works from entering the public domain (Lee, 2013), creates a specter of possible legal action that discourages even the most casual participants from contributing in any way that isn't officially sanctioned or approved.

This nebulous yet ever-present threat of being accused of copyright infringement instills anxiety in many creators, to the point that sharing personal creations with others no longer seems worth the risk. Many fan creators resign themselves to just consuming the media presented to them rather than risk falling victim to legal action as a result of their work. In the early 2000s, a series of similarly aggressive litigious actions by the author Anne Rice nearly killed the highly creative fandom around her *Vampire*

Chronicles series (Jackson, 2018), scaring off scores of enthusiastic fanfiction authors and leading to the takedown of numerous creative works using Rice's charismatic modern-day vampire characters and the mythos surrounding them.

How do we decouple transmedia from the gated, stifling experience that corporations have grafted onto it in recent years? According to the science writer Pagan Kennedy, "Nature uses multiple strategies rather than a monoculture to solve problems. . . . Nature's research and development is based on billions of experiments. It is a resilient, decentralized, and wildly diverse scheme" (2016, 222). Undoing the corporate takeover of transmedia and restoring the culture's more participatory, democratic, and organic character is a complex and multifaceted challenge, and will require a multitude of perspectives: expertise in intellectual property (IP) law, concepts of media literacy, sociological insights on fan culture, and more. Viewing transmedia creation through the lens of the collectivist and anticapitalist structure of brown's *Emergent Strategy* (2017) provides a helpful guide for understanding the dynamics of power and hegemony, as well as for harmonizing these diverse perspectives. Here, brown's methodology provides a revealing vantage from which to consider the medium of TTRPGs and its extended culture. TTRPGs, and the acts of participatory co-creation that they invite, provide a model for creating transmedia projects divorced from the profit-driven imperatives that constrain the most popular and mainstream experiences. Through this combination of transmedia studies and TTRPGs, we can begin to formulate principles for compelling experiences that are more fundamentally open and collaborative than what corporate-dominated spaces currently sanction, while also serving as a means of resistance against corporate encroachment into creative spaces.

Inspired by readings and investigation into the novels of the late, legendary science fiction author Octavia E. Butler, particularly the *Parable of the Sower* (1993) and *Parable of the Talents* (1998), brown takes Butler's key themes, provocations, and morals and translates them for real-world use in social justice movements and what brown calls "societal-help." Building on science fiction, a genre that was founded on and flourishes through its intrinsic ties to fandom, brown takes what the literary theorist Istvan Csicsery-Ronay, Jr. (2008) terms the *Technologiade* of Butler's worlds and, in a transmediation of her own, adapts them into political actions. The three systems of oppression that brown focuses on are capitalism, supremacy, and false peace:

Capitalism: We are taught that love is about belonging to one person or community, and we must contort in order to ensure continued belonging. We are taught that our value is in what we can produce, and emotions impede production.

[On supremacy:] We are taught, that if we are not white, male, straight, able, wealthy, adult, etc., our truths don't matter. This starts very early, we are taught that our feelings and thoughts as children are unimportant, that we are to "be seen and not heard."

The Oppression of false peace: We are taught that out truths are disruptive, and that disruption is a negative act. This one is particularly insidious, and ties back to capitalism—only those moving towards profit can and should create disruption, everyone else should be complacent consumers. (2017, 142)

Throughout *Emergent Strategy*, brown spotlights issues of oppression that fans and critics of the corporate domination of transmedia are introducing into the cultural conversation around these spaces. These properties, especially capital-intensive universes like Star Wars, increasingly eschew narrative and psychological complexity, and any whiff of contentious social issues, in an effort to reach the broadest possible global audience and to avoid alienating paying customers across the political spectrum. brown emphasizes threats to our creative fulfillment and unfettered participation in using our imagination, telling stories, co-creating meaning, and participating in rich transmedia worlds: capitalism, the inability to be accepted if we aren't productive; supremacy, being viewed as too unimportant to be involved in discussions; and false peace, the notion that we shouldn't be disruptive in the face of oppression, as those disruptions might lead to the destruction of our communities. The TTRPG medium, and especially the *Little Fears* system, provides ways to ameliorate these threats by embracing a foundationally collaborative ethos and insisting upon our ability to work through trauma and oppression in ways that are honest, affirming, and cooperative.

Medium of Investigation

TTRPGs combine improv theater, creative writing, and visual art, centered on the principle of collaborative storytelling. As the medium has gained cultural ground, participants have begun to branch out, drawing other media into the experience: adding music compositions and soundscapes to enhance ambience and feeling during a gameplay session; editing recordings of the TTRPG experience into audio dramas or podcasts; and creating extensive writings that further fill in the story or setting outside of the gameplay experience. This *transmediation*—the translation of the content of one medium to another (McLuhan, 1994)—allows individuals to more deeply explore various aspects of the TTRPG experience and personalize it into something more meaningful.

Working in conjunction with transmediation is the concept of *remediation*, the idea that "new media" always reconfigures older media while actively suppressing previous forms (Bolter and Grusin, 2000). Thus, a Netflix series is a remediation on the concept of a television series or season, itself a remediation of theater, which is also a remediation of written texts, folklore, and oral traditions, and so forth and so on. For example, Bram Stoker's novel *Dracula* (1897) remediated the figure of the vampire, codifying a mass of folkloric stories into a single narrative and establishing a set of tropes and aesthetic cues. The novel was then remediated by theatrical adaptations and radio that occluded and transformed the text, building on its success and resonance but standing in for it in the cultural imaginary. Film and television followed, suppressing and transforming the meanings of the earlier mediations.

In *Narrative across Media: The Languages of Storytelling* (2004), the literary scholar Marie-Laure Ryan puts remediation into a less conflictual frame. For Ryan, transmediation involves the translation of content between media (e.g., faithfully adapting a book to film), while remediation is concerned with cherry-picking the best elements of a medium and applying them to something new without adding to the original source (e.g., taking classic painting styles and transforming them using digital photo filters). Ryan approaches transmediation and remediation as conversations between texts and media forms. Transmediation can be adaptive and playful (e.g., Jane Austen's 1815 novel *Emma* becomes the 1995 cult-classic comedy film *Clueless*), while remediation can involve the mutual exchange of ideas and innovations across media (e.g., Charles Yu's 2020 novel *Interior Chinatown* uses the format of a screenplay to critique the racial politics of crime dramas and martial arts films), rather than a composting process that consumes and detracts from older forms.

Little Fears (Blair, 2001, 2009) embraces this perspective on remediation, providing openings for participants and audiences to capitalize on the affordances of other media, to restage emotionally resonant narratives from elsewhere in popular culture, and to integrate their own life experiences to enhance the experience of play. In contrast to corporate-controlled transmedia experiences, *Little Fears* and other TTRPGs use cross-media shifts, references, and adaptations to create exciting and unplanned experiences, to shatter the myth of a solitary creator masterminding a bounded story, and to generate opportunities for social critique and personal reflection. These systems also model how we might unsettle power imbalances between creators/owners and audiences/fans by framing audience-generated contributions like fan art, fan fiction, and other adaptations as part of a dialogue, opening up new avenues for storytelling and community building.

Little Fears

In *Little Fears* (2001), designed by Jason L Blair, players take on the role of children fending off incursions by terrifying creatures from Closetland. To combat these entities, players have access to Belief, a magical ability that can turn imagination into reality. However, the presence of magic doesn't mean that the original edition of *Little Fears* was a happy game; in fact, the original system's bleak setting often required pyrrhic victories if the player-characters wished to escape alive. The game saw significant praise upon its initial release and was nominated for the Origins Award for Best RPG and Game of the Year, and it won the Most Disturbing/Controversial Game Book award from RPGnet in 2001 in recognition of its divisively dark themes. In response, the second edition of the game, *Little Fears: Nightmare Edition* (*LFNE*; Blair, 2009), softened some of the more upsetting aspects of the original setting.

In addition to the gameplay rules and suggested narrative, Blair's source book for *Little Fears* provides an internally consistent speculative fiction setting that capitalizes on the adaptable nature of TTRPGs, inviting players to continue and remediate their previous cultural experiences in an interactive environment. Want to play as a child learning to use their force powers in the Star Wars universe? Want to explore what it's like to be a child in Derry, Maine, from Stephen King's killer-clown novel *It* (1986)? Want to see what happened to Closetland after the edition change of *Little Fears*? *Little Fears* encourages these acts of remediation, taking beloved, nostalgia-evoking texts from a variety of media and exploring, and expanding, their themes through interactive, co-creative play.

Elements of *Emergent Strategy* in TTRPGs

Traditionally, a TTRPG is a collaborative narrative led by an individual called the game master (GM) and shared with other people, often in groups of one to six players. The GM is in charge of adjudicating the rules of the specific instance of the game that the group is playing, as well as the over-arching guidelines provided by the TTRPG system (whether it's the legendary *Dungeons & Dragons*, *Little Fears*, or something else). They also design and oversee the narrative framework that is presented to the players. The GM provides a setting for the players to interact within and reacts on the fly—in an enabling and supportive way—to the other players' choices. The action moves forward through improvisation within the boundaries of a prees-tablished set of rules, constraints, and narrative laws, with certain actions being decided or influenced by randomization mechanics such as dice rolls. Imagine that a player needs to get away from a zombie chasing them. The player, responding in the narrative world of the game, says that their char-acter will attempt to vault a headstone. The GM gives them a target number to roll dice against; for instance, the player might have to roll a 10 or higher on a twenty-sided die. Depending on the roll, the efficacy of the player's desired action is decided: roll a high enough number, and the character swiftly vaults the headstone. Roll too low, and the character trips and falls. Unlike the average TTRPG system, *Little Fears* is focused on the "theater of the mind"; there is no board or map to play with, and no tokens or artifacts aside from dice. This lack of physical objects divorces the gameplay of *Little Fears* from the physical limitations often placed on creativity and helps players achieve the imaginative feats necessary to overcome the daunting situations presented by the game.

Just as *Little Fears* and *LFNE* invite players to remediate existing cultural texts as interactive, co-created role-playing experiences, these systems, in combination with concepts from brown's *Emergent Strategy*, can help us both to understand the inequitable dynamics of mainstream, corporate-controlled transmedia worlds, and to imagine how to revivify transmedia as a participatory space for collaborative exploration.

Resilience and Transformative Justice: How We Recover and Transform

One of the trickiest concepts that adrienne maree brown details in *Emergent Strategy* is transformative justice—not because the concept itself is difficult to grasp, but because the scale of the task is overwhelming. Transformative justice seeks to transform the root causes of injustices and requires shifts in societal issues that are often masked as personal failings. According to brown, transformative justice requires four things: acknowledgment of the reality of state harm; alternative methods to address/interrupt harm that do not rely on the state; reliance on strategies that are community-created and community-sustained; and transformation of the root causes of violence (2017, 135). Instead of sending someone to jail for stealing food, give them access to a food pantry or other long-term means of meeting their needs, be it food, money, or shelter. The monumental nature of this task is why brown introduces it with the concept of resilience, as defined in the *Merriam-Webster Dictionary*: "the ability to become strong, healthy or successful again after something bad happens. The ability of something to return to its original shape after it has been pulled, stretched, bent, etc. an ability to recover from or adjust easily to misfortune or change" (123).

Transformative justice requires resilience because the task of creating this form of justice is never-ending. Thinking that a single solution will solve all problems only leads to further injustices; as such, all solutions need to be investigated to find a variety of better ways to transform the lives of those involved. This constant struggle to discover, test, and create a just situation is exemplified in *Little Fears* by how players interact and attempt to deal with the game's horrific monsters.

Playing *Little Fears* requires great resilience. The game is about resisting terrifying, seemingly insurmountable events. Typically, these events are triggered by a monster that needs to be defeated. However, the classic method of depleting a monster's Health to zero will only cause it to disappear for a short time; it will inevitably return again, possibly in the next session or maybe even in the next scene. There are other ways to drive off monsters; in addition to removing a monster's Health, players can give a monster a Weakness in the form of a narrative and/or mechanical limitation (e.g., a vampire being repelled by a religious symbol, garlic, or running water), or perform a Ritual, a more powerful and esoteric action that bends the reality of the narrative, but often at a steep price (e.g., a player can create a ring of salt to contain a ghost, but someone must always be touching the salt to keep it powered). The problem, however, is that all these methods merely kick the metaphorical can down the road for another time, when you or someone else will, hopefully, be better prepared to deal with the monster's Terror and permanently destroy it.

The Terror that sustains monsters across multiple encounters is a perversion of the Belief powers wielded by the players. It represents the fear the entity imposes upon both the characters and the setting, draining the characters' ability to believe in themselves and their hope of overcoming their nightmares. Terror also serves as a mechanical representation of how powerful a monster is: example monsters from the game's source book range from the weakest Terror rating of 6 for a generic Zombie to a rating of 10 for the folkloric Baba Yaga (Blair, 2001, 152). Regardless of the rating, arduous effort is required to remove a monster's Terror completely, and this necessitates resilience from all participants in a game. This is because, to attack a monster's Terror, players much first destroy all of the monster's Stuff, their supernatural parallel of Kid's Stuff: items such as a favorite pillow or a beloved teddy bear that house Belief and empower the players to do strange and wonderful things.

This utter destruction, however, is not transformative justice. In fact, acts of violence are pretty much the opposite of transformative. Thankfully, *LFNE* rewards players for dealing with monsters through appeasement. All monsters have a desire; sometimes these are horrific and sometimes silly, but if the monster achieves its desire, it stops being antagonistic to the players. Imagine a Zombie with a stitched-up mouth that wants to "have the last word." If the players cut the stitching, it would allow the Zombie to finally speak its piece and stop being aggressive. It might even turn its ire toward Baba Yaga, the entity responsible for creating the Zombie, and assist the players in fighting her. With this simple thought experiment, we've re-created an element of the 1990s cult classic comedy-horror Disney film *Hocus Pocus* (1993) in a TTRPG scenario!

What if, when the final traces of Terror empowering a monster are eliminated, the original entity underneath the warping effects of fear reveals itself rather than disappearing? One example of this would be a re-creation of another cult classic, the coming-of-age sports comedy *The Sandlot* (1993): after a series of misadventures, the players finally stand up to a terrifying beast that's been chasing them relentlessly, only to encounter a large, shaggy Saint Bernard standing where the beast once was. In this context, the players' and surrounding community's Belief actually changed a local pet into a monster, and the players' removal of that warped perception freed the animal to return to its original form. Rather than accidentally harming an innocent animal, the players can, by confronting and understanding their fears, defuse the conflict.

In a scenario from the original *Little Fears* system (Blair, 2001, 112–116), a spirit is terrorizing the player characters' town, kidnapping people and feeding them into a haunted car crusher. It is eventually revealed that the events taking place are related to the unsolved murder of a mother and child that has been mythologized within the community. The Terror driving the spirit is a combination of individual and societal belief: communal fear at the unsolved murder, the intermingled guilt and fear of discovery and punishment felt by the surviving perpetrator, the player characters' belief that there is no clean solution to the unravelling events, and the murdered child fueling the mythologized spirit. In this case, the monster acts as a manifestation of a societal ghost that haunts the town and the individuals involved. However, unlike the monster-dog example, when the community belief is removed, the ghost loses agency and once again becomes the memory of a murdered child, so while the physical threat is removed, its social impact remains.

The resilience and transformative justice that brown writes about requires dogged persistence, with the goal of changing the conditions that made injustice possible in the first place (2017, 126). TTRPGs make room for players to unearth issues of trauma and injustice, and to work through them creatively and collaboratively. They also provide a seed bed for forming communities, both virtually and in person, where participants can further address issues that emerge during play. This is particularly evident in a system like *Little Fears*, with its focus on realistic childhood horrors like abuse and neglect, and especially with the second edition's emphasis on finding labor-intensive, nondestructive solutions that capture brown's notion of transformative justice. This kind of reckoning with achingly personal and disturbing issues that join individual experience and social structures of injustice is harder to pursue for participants in more mainstream transmedia experiences, which undergo so much edge-smoothing and focus-testing to ensure that they appeal to the broadest possible audience.

Interdependence and Decentralization: Who We Are and How We Share

According to brown, interdependence is iterative, requiring repetitive actions that might start small but lead gradually to larger steps. brown enumerates four steps of personal interdependence: "be seen; be wrong; accept my inner multitudes; and ask for, and receive, what I need" (2017, 93–95). This act of putting yourself out there, being wrong, learning how to be wrong, and being able to both ask and receive support, only to repeat the cycle ever outward to accomplish larger and larger steps, mirrors the movements of the creative process and the process of how communities thrive.

This is why it is so vital to understand and tap into the iterative pattern of interdependence in TTRPGs and transmedia experiences alike.

TTRPGs exemplify this cycle of doing, failing, and learning in the experience of play, in the nature of GMing and in how the larger TTRPG community so rapidly changes and builds new experiences, including transmedia experiences ranging from podcasts and music to fan art and bespoke, customized rule sets for familiar game systems. Decentralization of creative authority is necessary to foster such interdependence. Prolonged centralizing and prioritizing of one voice above the rest often create an overreliance upon a "correct" or "canonical" interpretation of a piece of media, which in turn discourages free-form, participatory creation and privileges the voices of creators and owners/managers of media over those of fans and community participants. This breeds a sense of dependency upon authorial intent as dogma, which corporate transmedia owners take advantage of and weaponize to put themselves into a controlling position over media they view solely as property, rather than as a co-created communal experience.

This tendency is illustrated within the TTRPG community through the concept of "railroading." Often considered a marker of poor management or authorial inflexibility, railroading is when a GM forces their players into a predefined series of narrative beats or actions so that their intended story is perfectly acted out, allowing little or no meaningful input, creative engagement, or narrative divergence from the players. In contrast, *Little Fears* offers a vision of how we might foster brown's interdependent, decentralized process in a setting where the author/manager—the GM—would seem to wield significant power to direct and constrain creativity. In *Little Fears*, the GM ideally works in conversation and collaboration with players, in the service of making their experience rewarding and self-determined.

Especially in *LFNE*, the game's second edition, there are no leaders or formal organizations, only characters. *LFNE*'s harrowing standard setting requires both independent action and teamwork in times of great physical danger or emotional distress, reflecting the lack of central governance, hierarchical organization, and proscribed mechanisms in most TTRPGs. Sure, the companies that create these systems send updates and publish new material, and there are organizations that give awards to various TTRPG media, but ultimately each play group determines its own rules and culture. The lack of powerful institutions and rigid structures allows for the constant mulching, turnover, and creation of new stories that might otherwise be overlooked and excluded by the creators of popular TTRPG systems, as well as other media texts. The whole of the TTRPG hobby then takes new creations, and through Marie-Laure Ryan's mode of remediation, introduces them back into the medium to see what conversations they spark and how they might expand the medium further. A new character might create a narrative situation that necessitates the group to create a new rule, which inspires a new setting, which then goes on to inspire a totally new game system to combine the new rules, settings, and character interactions more cohesively.

This decentralized, interdependent character of transmedia experiences and engaged fan-participant communities, as we see in the TTRPG scene, is precisely what the current corporate approach to controlling and deriving profit from transmedia universes seeks to curtail. Gatekeeping material within a small, controlled environment means that instead of the wild growth of possibilities and chaotic creative processes that might lead to failure, corporate creators can carefully sculpt both the experience and user interactions to optimize for profit. If Henry Jenkins's original notion of transmedia involves a convergence of fan and author as equal partners, modern corporate transmedia dresses itself up in equality while maintaining authorial supremacy over everyone else. For example, Disney's approach to fanworks is to allow unlicensed merchandise, videos, and fan creations as a form of free word-of-mouth marketing for their franchises (George-Parkin, 2017), but they will use copyright claims both to suppress content that they deem objectionable, and to claim ownership over any fan-created content that they find particularly marketable. Communities involved with the experience pay for access to these walled gardens, but members are never completely free to create.

However, there is a challenging mismatch in contrasting the TTRPG medium as a method of shared freedom and interdependent co-creation with the more controlling aspects of corporate transmedia management: the GM. Traditionally, the GM is viewed as the leader of a TTRPG experience. Does the collaborative promise of TTRPGs fail in the face of the GM's central role?

The prevailing wisdom of the role of the GM in a TTRPG experience is summed up in the writings of *Dungeons & Dragons* co-creator Gary Gygax (Gygax, 1987, 1989; Gygax and Arneson, 1974), who situates the GM at the center of the experience. The game, both system and genre, control the player's ability to interact with the world and, since the GM is the person controlling the experience, it is the job of the players to assist the GM in their act of creation—thus, any collaboration is in service of the GM's vision. This view mirrors the current mode of creative control in corporate transmedia: all entities involved are subservient to the officially sanctioned experience first and then, should they prove useful or disruptive, are sent to face the entity controlling the experience. Useful creators are brought into corporate spaces to make more product (e.g., Sega hiring fan programmers to create official *Sonic the Hedgehog* games), while disruptive creators are threatened (e.g., Nintendo threatening lawsuits against programmers creating edgier fan games or modifying existing Nintendo games not currently available for purchase) (Pot, 2016).

Note that brown's framework allows us to shift our perspective on the GM from that of an unquestionable, godlike leader to something more akin to a moderator or facilitator—an observation that Jason L Blair also suggests within *LFNE*'s "Some GM Advice" section: "Your job as the game moderator is to draft setups and have an overall story goal and structure in mind. But this is a shared narrative, collaborative storytelling, and the players have a say in what happens" (2009, 100–101). Managing this collaborative process is easier said than done, and the TTRPG community often falls short. But there are strategies circulating in the community to decenter the GM and increase the agency of all players. One popular way to ensure that all individuals at the table stand on equal footing is to use the "rotating GM" structure, where players share the responsibility of GMing. Instead of a world created by an individual GM and populated by the players exploring the limits of the play space, the experience of a rotating GM game is populated by unknowns for both the GMs and players to explore, making space for greater depth and complexity in the setting and storytelling.

The rotating GM structure challenges the inherent oppression of superiority, as brown describes, which is baked into the fundamental structure of TTRPGs. As brown writes, "If the vision is only clear to one person, that person ends up trying to drive everyone towards their vision, or at minimum control how everyone gets to the vision" (2017, 70). In calling for a redistribution of power in the TTRPG experience, the GM is longer a "master," but rather a person occupying one role, temporarily, to assist in a co-collaborative experience. While this does require players increase their workload and take on aspects of GMing that not everyone will feel comfortable doing or want to do, this approach helps to refocus the experience on the core goal of both TTPRGs and transmedia: the act of collaborative creation. This co-created vitality is under threat in the world of mainstream transmedia experiences, but both brown's thinking on interdependence and decentralization, and the opportunities afforded by *Little Fears* and other TTRPGs to build genuinely dialogic, democratic, co-constituted spaces for creative exploration, point to principles which ought to be at the heart of future transmedia projects.

Adaptation: How We Change

Within TTRPG culture, one major contributor to the view of the GM as an absolute authority is the perception of GMing as a daunting task, prone to catastrophic failure should the GM lose control over the experience. According to this way of thinking, the overwhelming pressure to create, maintain, and explain the experience lies squarely on the GM's shoulders. The storyworld, the lives of the player-characters, and the environments that they interact with depend on the GM's ability to craft and anticipate, in the moment, an inherently unpredictable and partially randomized experience using only the materials that they've prepared ahead of time. The rigidity and fear of the unknown that are implicit in this narrative about GMing mirror the impulse to stifle fan/audience creativity in contemporary transmedia. Unfettered free play and narrative murkiness challenge the corporation's control of its IP. To retain control of the IP, a corporation must successfully maintain a predictable image that they can iterate across a broad range of media and merchandise—a goal threatened by the inherently chaotic nature of fan creation. Disney, for instance, might hypothetically take legal action against a punk-rock rendering of Minnie Mouse in fan art since that aesthetic is perceived to threaten the apolitical, virginal vision of the character that Disney is engaged in selling to nostalgic fans, concerned parents, and merchandisers.

Contrary to this narrative that emphasizes the need for control and predictability, brown offers another perspective through which to consider the act of GMing: instead of working with a pure, unfiltered translation of the story that they intend to tell, individuals should instead work through intentionally cultivated and guided adaptation by focusing on the "process of changing while staying in touch with our deeper purpose and longing" (2017, 70). This represents a shift in emphasis away from the particular sequence of story beats, characters, and twists that the GM wants to unfold, toward a focus on the themes, motifs, and resonances that make the experience emotionally resonant and creatively enriching. For example, a pure, unfiltered translation of J. R. R. Tolkien's novel *The Fellowship of the Ring* (1954) would include all the narration, the internal thoughts of characters, the poetry, and the genealogy from the book within a new medium, like a film or TV series. In contrast, Peter Jackson's film *The Lord of the Rings: The Fellowship of the Ring* (2001) is a guided adaptation, with considerations for time, pacing, and the unique creative affordances and limitations of the cinematic medium.

There's more to TTRPGs than the performance-heavy task of running the game and, much like the design of a transmedia experience, an individual might enter the GM role by focusing on more abstract and adaptive elements. A GM might decide to let the game experience run a little looser, giving the players more agency to determine the action, and take notes, provide art, or help establish the experience across multiple formats or mediums with music, illustrations, and other enhancements. This kind of GM expands the experience of play rather than managing with a focus on adherence to a narrative devised in advance, while sticking with areas of creativity or genres of storytelling in which they feel confident. *Little Fears*, which encourages players to allude to and adapt beloved stories from other corners of popular culture, is especially apt for this looser game structure since players have pre-existing knowledge of the themes, ethical quandaries, and narrative dynamics of the story. Let's imagine that the previous two transmediated examples of *Hocus Pocus* and *The Sandlot* were brought into the same narrative world, each introduced by different GMs in a rotating game. When a third member of the group takes their turn GMing, they could design a new scenario that merges these separate narratives into something new and more complex than the sum of its parts—perhaps long ago, the witchy sisters of *Hocus Pocus* fabricated the pernicious legend of the killer dog that menaces the young people in *The Sandlot*—allowing the themes and narratives of these two cinematic worlds to blur and feed into one another. This rewards players involved in both scenarios and encourages additional group theory-crafting outside of play sessions as they merge these adapted narratives together. This, in turn, could snowball into the contributors creating an expansive and personalized extended transmedia universe.

Remediation as an adaptive method showcases how individuals coming from a wide variety of backgrounds and skill sets can add to a singular shared experience through the various mediums in which they are most comfortable and passionate. Through the use of focused adaptation and guided creation centered around a dedicated purpose or longing, the energy of chaotic independent creation is refined and put toward a more harmonious purpose, which both drives the original source material forward and readapts it into something new.

Going Nonlinear and Iterative: The Pace and Pathway of Change

TTRPGs have grown in a nonlinear way, as a medium. David M. Ewalt's book *Of Dice and Men* (2013), through a focus on the history of *Dungeons & Dragons*, reveals how much time the medium has had to evolve, and the cultural upheavals that it has survived. From TTRPGs' humble beginnings as war games before transitioning into children's suburban kitchen table playthings, to riding out the demonization of the Satanic Panic period (Ewalt, 2013, 155–160) and rising to a position of unexpected popularity, they have morphed into different forms and pathways over time, rather that following a steady upward arc. The current cultural vibrancy of TTRPGs isn't due to any one technological advancement—there's no technodeterminism here, just decades of iterative adaptation punctuated by random spurts of growth. As brown writes, on the topic of transformation:

> Transformation doesn't happen in a linear way. . . . It happens in cycles, convergences, explosions. If we release the framework of failure, we can realize that we are in iterative cycles, and we can keep asking ourselves—how do we learn from this? (2017, 105)

TTRPG's herky-jerky stop-and-go creation permeates the medium, and one of its most recent growth spurts occurred through adaptations on podcasts such as Loading Ready Run's *Dice Friends* (2020) or *Roleplaying Public Radio* (2020). By packaging a TTRPG session into a recorded and shareable format, the adaptive and invitational aspects of rotating GMs and co-collaborative design expand to an even wider audience, pulling in the opinions, ideas, suggestions, and feedback of an invisible audience, distributed over time and geography, which the players and GM can then work into subsequent sessions and scenarios.

Podcasts allow producers to incorporate art, music, writing, and other media into the presentation of a game, emanating from both the physical play group and the digital fan community that forms around the recordings. Fans value these TTRPG podcasts both for the excitement of

the actual play and for the communal story that emerges from the experience. Thus, a rotating-GM podcast that includes our *Hocus Pocus*, *Sandlot*,
and cross-over experience might be presented as a group trying to explore
nostalgia via a "more realistic" retelling of the experience of their favorite
1990s media. Transmediation can expand the experience for both the audience and the players. Removing out-of-character conversations, reactions,
and other player improv mistakes from the main recording and releasing
an additional "B-roll" or "blooper reel" recording, for example, allows the
performance group to highlight the emotionally impactful moments and
maintain tonal consistency without sacrificing otherwise-welcome levity
and silliness.

   If in TTRPGs the process of play is just as fulfilling as the completion of a
story, then podcasts allow for iterative change, both good and bad, to these
experiences. Fan responses provide an external barometer of what works,
what fails, and what might need improvement in the experience. This
allows for creators to iterate on their creations and co-collaborative techniques and demonstrate an understanding and acceptance of the modes of
failure that Gary Gygax's model of the almighty GM is so haunted by.

Prototyping a New Model for Transmedia Co-Creation

TTRPGs showcase how we might reconfigure our understanding of transmedia across a variety of dimensions. The combination of TTRPGs and
technology has created a means for near-instant feedback from those participating in the experience, alongside the core group of players.

   The rise of digital livestreaming, with audio and video, allows individuals not interested in directly playing a TTRPG (or who aren't able to find a
group, or can't find time for regularly scheduled play sessions) a means of
interacting with and being a part of a community. This mode of community participation is exemplified by RevScarecrow's TTRPG-inspired experience *The Town of Nowhere* (2020), which actively engages the audience
as creative collaborators, shaping the experience through the chat features
of the popular livestreaming platform Twitch. *The Town of Nowhere* suggests modes of interaction, improvisation, and communal storytelling that
could emerge if new innovations in streaming technology continue to be
integrated into TTRPGs and transmedia experiences. RevScarecrow tasked

his Twitch chat with collectively piloting and directing the actions of the player character through a voting and suggestion system. While he provided a basic motivation, goal, and loose time limit, he otherwise allowed chat participants to determine all other nonessential facts about their character to whatever granularity they desired, from selecting their name to deciding their go-to coffee order. This was achieved by RevScarecrow generating polls from "pushed" messages that members of the chat paid artificial currency to include, and the rest of the participants were then invited to vote on. RevScarecrow would then typically choose the top two or three nonconflicting actions to have the player character perform in the way that he felt best represented the intent and mood of the live chat.

In addition, he uploaded recordings of these game sessions onto YouTube for people to watch asynchronously, much like listening to a prerecorded podcast. This choice culminated in an excellent marriage of passive participation by those who have no desire to play in the game directly but wish to experience the story, and active participation by those inclined and able to join the prescheduled game sessions. Best of all, this method allowed both passive and active participants to come together on forums, message boards, chat clients, and comment threads to collectively theorize and figure out the game's mystery, and come up with community strategies that the active participants could enact in the next scheduled play session.

How could we incorporate these more cutting-edge transmedia and participatory elements into our 1990s-nostalgia TTRPG game and podcast? Perhaps a GM might draw inspiration from another 1990s video-store hit, *The Truman Show* (1998), and use its framework of a tightly controlled world that is influenced by the whims of an unseen outside force. Players could communicate with the chatting audience using *LFNE*'s Stuff, via an object such as a Magic Eight Ball, Ouija board, or a sibling's cell phone. Another angle of attack could be to place the GM in a position similar to the all-powerful director played by the actor Ed Harris in *The Truman Show*, who must appeal to the mercurial desires of the audience that is empowered to deliver both favorable boons and disastrous outcomes to the players via online subscriptions, digital polls, or other intervention mechanics. This kind of structure would place adaptability, change, and openness to the collective creativity of the audience at the center of a compelling narrative that draws on, and remediates, existing IP.

Conclusion

Modern transmedia is dominated by corporate entities that curtail and control the voices and creative agency of individuals within these potentially very interactive worlds, motivated by profits and the imperative of drawing in the broadest possible audience. This betrays the original concept of transmedia as an expansive social space where no singular person's experience has priority over another's—one which fosters a vibrant realm for participants, writers, fans, and onlookers to engage freely without judgment, and free from the obligation to honor limiting notions of authorial intent or adherence to canonical source texts (Jenkins, 2014). Without interventions to push transmedia experiences back toward their more open, participatory, dialogic, and democratic roots, corporate rigidity and strategies that reclassify transmedia audiences as consumers rather than co-creators will continue to stifle new and future contributors, warping the medium beyond recognition. Through adrienne maree brown's guidance in *Emergent Strategy* on how to recognize and resist oppressive systems, we can learn ways to identify and work to unmake societal ills. However, without specific examples of how to resist, especially within socially and technologically complex arenas like transmedia, brown's program for liberation can be tricky to enact.

The empathetic, collaborative methods presented in *Little Fears* to contextualize trauma, taken in conjunction with brown's methods, allow us to see how we might resist the current shift in transmedia and return to experiences that are more open and welcoming to all kinds of participation. Combining brown's resistance to capitalism with *LFNE*'s approach to combating Terror (via slowly working away at difficult tasks to reach the heart of the problem) helps instill resilience in individuals to stand firm against the incursions of corporate, profit-driven mindsets into transmedia's ethos of collaborative creation. Likewise, brown's defiance of supremacy, as mirrored in *Little Fears*' affordances for a rotating GM structure that invites all players to contribute equitably to managing the game and introducing narrative complications and twists, illuminates a way to return to the past of the medium of transmedia while addressing previously unobserved issues. Finally, by combining brown's discontent with false peace and the acceptance of both the limitations and integrative possibilities of TTRPGs, equity and inclusiveness in co-collaboration can return to the center of conversations about transmedia.

In this spirit of equitable collaboration, how should we continue this work? How can we build on our hopes and beliefs to expand this creative realm so it continues to thrive? While the current, popularly understood view of transmedia is that of a gated, walled garden that requires entry fees, is limited in its scope of interaction, and takes constantly from users while giving little back in exchange, brown's insights and the living example of *Little Fears* help us reorient our thinking about transmedia, celebrating its core value of convergence between creators and fans in spaces designed to facilitate a mutual exchange of stories, ideas, and mediated experiences.

References

Blair, Jason L. 2001. *Little Fears: The Role-Playing Game of Childhood Terror*. Oakland, CA: Wizard's Attic.

Blair, Jason L. 2009. *Little Fears Nightmare Edition: The Game of Childhood Terror*. Fun Sized Games.

Bolter, J. David, and Richard A. Grusin. 2000. *Remediation: Understanding New Media*. Cambridge, MA: MIT Press.

brown, adrienne maree. 2017. *Emergent Strategy: Shaping Change, Changing Worlds*. Chico, CA: AK Press.

Butler, Octavia E. 1993. *Parable of the Sower*. New York: Four Walls Eight Windows.

Butler, Octavia E. 1998. *Parable of the Talents*. New York: Seven Stories Press.

Csicsery-Ronay, Istvan. 2008. *The Seven Beauties of Science Fiction*. Middletown, CT: Wesleyan University Press.

Ewalt, David M. 2013. *Of Dice and Men: The Story of Dungeons & Dragons and The People Who Play It*. New York: Scribner.

Gaiman, Neil. 2013. "Why Our Future Depends on Libraries, Reading and Daydreaming." *The Guardian*, October 15, 2013. https://www.theguardian.com/books/2013/oct/15/neil-gaiman-future-libraries-reading-daydreaming.

George-Parkin, Hilary. 2017. "Why Notoriously Litigious Disney Is Letting Fan Stores Thrive." *Racked*, September 5, 2017. https://www.racked.com/2017/9/5/16192874/disney-fan-stores-instagram.

Gygax, Gary. 1987. *Role-Playing Mastery*. New York: Perigee Books.

Gygax, Gary. 1989. *Master of the Game*. New York: Perigee Books.

Gygax, Gary, and Arneson, Dave. 1974. *Dungeons & Dragons*. Lake Geneva, WI: Tactical Studies Rules.

Jackson, Gita. 2018. "It Used to Be Perilous to Write Fanfiction." *Kotaku*, May 16, 2018. https://kotaku.com/it-used-to-be-perilous-to-write-fanfiction-1826083509.

Jenkins, Henry. 2006. *Convergence Culture: Where Old and New Media Collide*. New York: New York University Press.

Jenkins, Henry. 2014. "Rethinking 'Rethinking Convergence/Culture.'" *Cultural Studies* 28, no. 2: 267–297.

Kennedy, Pagan. 2016. *Inventology: How We Dream up Things That Change the World*. Boston: Houghton Mifflin Harcourt.

Lee, Timothy E. 2013. "15 years ago, Congress Kept Mickey Mouse Out of the Public Domain. Will They Do It Again?" *Washington Post*, October 25, 2013. https://www.washingtonpost.com/news/the-switch/wp/2013/10/25/15-years-ago-congress-kept-mickey-mouse-out-of-the-public-domain-will-they-do-it-again.

McLuhan, Marshall. 1994. *Understanding Media: The Extensions of Man*. Cambridge, MA: MIT Press. Originally published in 1964.

Mikkelson, David. 1996. "Did Disney Demand the Removal of Cartoon Murals from Daycare Center Walls?" *Snopes*, December 29, 1996. https://www.snopes.com/fact-check/daycare-center-murals.

Pot, Justin. 2016. "Nintendo Threatens Diehard Fans; Sega Hires Them." *TNW*, September 14, 2016. https://thenextweb.com/news/nintendo-threatens-diehard-fans-sega-hires.

Ryan, Marie-Laure. 2004. *Narrative across Media: The Languages of Storytelling*. Lincoln: University of Nebraska Press.

Star Wars. 2014. "The Legendary Star Wars Expanded Universe Turns a New Page." *Star Wars News + Blog*, April 25, 2014. https://www.starwars.com/news/the-legendary-star-wars-expanded-universe-turns-a-new-page.

16   *Tangible Utopias*: Omni-Transmedia and Civic Imagination

Ioana Mischie

In this chapter, Ioana Mischie, a transmedia artist, media scholar, and documentary filmmaker, extends themes that run throughout this volume: the politics of media production and co-creation, civil society, and how transmedia stories open up or reshape public discourse. She pursues this space of imagination and social change through the case study of Tangible Utopias, a virtual reality (VR) experiment in collective design that brings together young people in her native Romania and elsewhere with production designers, graphic artists, architects, musicians, and other professionals to envision and build immersive, wildly experimental cities of the future. Like Camillia Matuk's discussion of transmedia storytelling, speculative design, and education in chapter 7, and building on Terra Gasque's exploration of the liberatory nature of co-creation in tabletop role-playing in chapter 15, Mischie positions transmedia as a set of emancipatory practices that can help us not only imagine hopeful visions of our shared future, but build the social infrastructure and marshal the resources needed to bring that future into being. Tangible Utopias is an experience explicitly designed to give young people a voice in shaping the future that they will inhabit through direct connections with policymakers, bridging virtual experiences with in-person conversations and forums. Mischie captures the potential power of transmedia through a term she coins, "omni-transmedia," which "levels up" transmedia from a storytelling form or content-management strategy to a thoroughgoing program for nonhierarchical, interdisciplinary practice. Through omni-transmedia, Mischie positions political activism as an act of play and takes seriously the notion that stories, art, and speculative design can set actionable templates for real-world change. Following on our editors' introduction to this collection, Mischie emphasizes the stakes of transmedia creativity. In the introduction, we described how digital capitalism has used transmedia interfaces and tools to rebuild, and extract profits from, our cultural infrastructure, while Mischie argues that collaboratively crafted transmedia experiences can help us imagine our infrastructure differently, rebuilt to better match our shared values and hopes for a more equitable and verdant future. Critically, Mischie centers her work on the imaginative capacities of young people, and like Quek et al. in chapter 8, on imaginative play and transmedia visualization, her Tangible Utopias project relies on young people's as-yet-untrammeled ability to spin tales and envision reality otherwise.

Every human construct surrounding us began as a glimpse of imagination. Although we celebrate childhood as a time of vivid imagination, in practice we privilege the imaginative production of adults, made manifest in the form of policy proposals, laws, design interventions, technological innovations, and other work products. Decision-makers have often considered themselves the only legitimate wielders of imagination, dictating the look and function of the physical constructs that define modern human habitats. As we've populated our planet with agglomerations of buildings, cars, streets, and factories, we've found ourselves confronted with a seemingly irresolvable set of crises: escalating climate chaos, a global health crisis, cyclical economic catastrophes, the moral tragedy of widening inequality, and a deep crisis in selfhood and identity as ever more people feel displaced in our communities and social systems. If noninclusive, anthropocentric modes of defining and using imagination are a constitutive factor in these overlapping crises, could collaborative, inclusive imaginative modes be a solution? Although media scholars Henry Jenkins, Gabriel Peters-Lazaro, and Sangita Shresthova contend that "Imagining is a process, not a panacea" (2020, 38), I believe that imagination can be a powerful force for healing, and even for remaking our societies, if it's channeled wisely.

As the novelist Mohsin Hamid has observed, "Everywhere around the world, people are having difficulty imagining a future" (2017). This "failure of imagination," in Hamid's words, emerges from our failure to train our imaginations—to build the collective capacity to envision our societies differently, organized around different values and priorities. Our urgent mission as transmedia artists should be to revive meaningful collaborative imagination in aid of changing actual societal outcomes. Participatory transmedia experiences can hone people's imaginative capacity, helping them to articulate the characteristics of better societies for the long term. Once activated in a strategic and dialogic manner, this practice of civic co-imagination enables us to question the world at an unprecedented level, to alter our taken-for-granted perspectives, to heal inequitable systems, and to generate new societal forms toward which we can strive.

Transmedia experiences, which interconnect multiple media platforms in an intricate manner, building a story or experience through connections rather than closed, singular texts, has been a subject of fascination for decades in entertainment, education, and even activism. But the medium is still rarely seen as an engine that can transform our experience of time, space, and spirit beyond mere escapism, marketized consumerism, or even organizing and raising consciousness around political issues. Transmedia methodologies can open up fundamentally new ways to understand humanity, society, and culture, focusing on interconnection. Transmedia can be a tool for getting us more in harmony with the natural world, other species, and other layers of our ever-expanding universe. Using transmedia methodologies, we can interconnect not only media platforms, but the imaginations of individuals and communities, in order to prototype new existential and societal models.

What if we could use the best practices of transmedia to make our world more inclusive, equitable, connected, and responsive? What if, instead of just immersing ourselves in ever-more-expansive fictional universes, we could try to solve real-world puzzles as playful citizens?

In this chapter, I will argue that we can use transmedia methodologies to foster civic imagination and to work toward holistic solutions for societal and planetary evolution. I will begin by exploring the historical importance of civic imagination and futurescaping, while highlighting how transmedia could advance collaborative civic imagination. I will illustrate the potential of collaborative transmedia approaches through a practical example, *Tangible Utopias*, a virtual reality (VR) franchise that brings to life futures inspired by the imaginations of children worldwide, working in collaboration with a transdisciplinary group of professionals. Taking this immersive project as a prototype for a wider transmedia-powered movement with social impact, I will propose a new, radical model for *omni-transmedia*, and discuss its power to form holistic practices and solutions for the long-term future. By blending best practices from artistic worlds and social research, omni-transmedia promises to frame an interconnected system of systems and provide a new lens on our world: from the tyranny of the *monologue*, to the playfulness of *infinite-logue*. If transmedia is designed to work as a stand-alone experience, drawing on but not integrated with larger social reality, omni-transmedia has the mission to facilitate a long-term process bridging imagination and direct social impact.

From Civic Imagination and Futurescaping to Societal Change

As the journalist and storyteller Pagan Kennedy asks in *Inventology*, "What kind of imagination is required to predict the future?" (2016, xvii). To get away from the quandary of predicting the future and focus instead on our agency to bring our preferred futures into being, I would revise the question: what kind of imaginations are required to co-create the futures that we want to build together?

Numerous theorists, pioneers, and artists have advocated for the importance of civic imagination and its potential to contribute to tangible societal improvement. The media theorists Jenkins, Peters-Lazaro, and Shresthova interpret civic imagination as "the capacity to imagine alternatives to current cultural, social, political, or economic conditions." They argue that "one cannot change the world without imagining what a better world might look like" (2020, 9). Sharing the spirit, the renowned author and storyteller Neil Gaiman has also praised the courage of imagining alternatives: "Political movements, personal movements, all begin with people imagining another way of existing" (2013, 8, 14–15). Similarly, the poet and digital media scholar Nick Montfort has argued, "One way to chart a future is to describe a society that doesn't exist, perhaps as a beacon toward which our present society might steer" (2017, 34).

All these complementary lines of thought highlight an urgent need: imagining a better future world is a sine qua non of inhabiting more meaningful, equitable, thriving societies, today and tomorrow. But how can we imagine vivid future worlds, and the pathways to bring them into being, when most of our education and daily routines exclude, or are even hostile to, this practice? How can we heal and accelerate our imaginative capacity, individually and collectively? How can we create transmedia bridges between our current knowledge and what is yet to be learned?

Civic imagination, like any human skill or tendency of mind, will require training and regular rehearsals. How should we foster it, and how can we connect imaginative processes to actual real-world change? The designers and ethnographers Anthony Dunne and Fiona Raby propose that "to achieve change it is necessary to unlock people's imagination and apply it to all areas of life at a microscale" (2013, 44). Transmedia artists can give people opportunities to hone their civic imagination skills by exploring urgent societal challenges and providing opportunities for participants to tackle those challenges and generate possible solutions.

Although our approach in envisioning better futures is often to marshal creativity and imagination to repair the imperfections of the past and present, the architect Cedric Price has argued that design "must move from the curative to the preventive" with respect to social ills (1984, 92–93). Preventative forms of imagination could offer us more freedom in creating new systems from scratch rather than premising our thinking on diagnosing and remediating flaws in existing systems. Instead of using a problem-to-solution mechanic in our imaginative projects about the future, we can use an ideal-case-scenario mechanic and focus our energy on devising strategies to transform idealism into realism.

Civic Imagination Prototyping: Archiving Futures

There are several stages involved in generating and acting on visions of desirable futures: imagining, prototyping, designing, debating, curating, implementing, and revising them continuously. A variety of inspirational existing methodologies, from curatorial approaches to worldbuilding, speculative design, design fiction, and futures thinking, provide practices for achieving each of these steps, and can serve as a basis for transmedia work on futures and collaborative civic imagination.

Decades ago, Nikola Tesla aimed to invent a camera that would take pictures of the world inside our imagination: "I expect to photograph thoughts" (quoted in Kennedy, 2016, 128). Today's technologies offer us multiple options to virtually preserve works and emanations of civic imagination, to make the imaginative process more tangible, more exploratory, more easily shared, and more impactful.

In the 1960s, the engineer and inventor Genrich Altshuller advocated for designing a "registry of science fiction ideas," a central clearinghouse for visionary solutions, technologies, and future systems (Kennedy, 2016, 142). In addition to archiving ideas from professional science fiction authors, what if we could explore ideas from anyone who has the desire to contribute? If we cannot compile a registry of this magnitude with ease, perhaps we could centralize microregistries from distinct categories through smaller projects (like *Tangible Utopias*, discussed later in this chapter) and then analyze them comparatively. These smaller collections could over time be brought together into a centralized civic-imagination registry for social improvement.

Whether centered on civic imagination or other modalities, numerous methodologies have aimed to democratize the process of designing future visions, making it more inclusive and efficient. The production designer Alex McDowell initiated the World Building Institute at the University of

Southern California, where he uses the "world building" technique as a storytelling tool, inviting practitioners and students to codesign possible futures—to imagine and develop a variety of new societal systems, with their biological, economic, and cultural layers. This method often involves projecting into the future a specific place in the short or medium term, producing as a preliminary result an artistic prototype (e.g., a vision of the city of Detroit in 2050). The process is founded on three key principles: "that storytelling is the most powerful system for the advancement of human capability due to its ability to allow the human imagination to precede the realization of thought; that all stories emerge logically and intuitively from the worlds that create them; and that new technologies powerfully enable us to sculpt the imagination into existence" (McDowell, 2008). Although innovative as a storytelling methodology, the process of worldbuilding does not imply real-world change; it focuses more on technologies that allow us to realize higher-fidelity visions of the future than on enacting the imagined futures into real-world policy and infrastructure.

Similarly, Anthony Dunne and Fiona Raby (2013) at the Royal College of Art in London propose "speculative design" to reinforce how design has the power to shape not only tools, but also ideas for desirable future scenarios. The outcomes often consist in outstanding design artifacts; however, these remain disparate initiatives, unable to foster a "whole better than the sum of the parts," which would be in any case a holistic real-world social movement.

In 2005, the science fiction author Bruce Sterling coined, in his book *Shaping Things*, the term "design fiction" to name a process of imagining concrete objects and services prototyped through writing, video, do-it-yourself making, and other methods (2005, 16). Brian David Johnson, formerly the futurist for Intel Corporation, now the director of the Threatcasting Lab at Arizona State University, believes in experimenting with written narratives, films, and cartoons to envision future scenarios through a technique called "science-fiction prototyping," which helps in portraying our imagined futures and exploring the social consequences of technological change (Johnson, 2011). For both approaches, art forms serve as prototyping tools for meaningful futures, perhaps as a starting point to accelerate real change.

The designer and engineer Carlo Ratti and the designer/urban planner Matthew Claudel have designed a method called "futurecraft," wherein participants "posit future scenarios (typically phrased as What If? Questions), entertain their consequences and exigencies, and share the resulting ideas widely, to enable public conversations and debate" (Ratti and Claudel, 2016, 5). This pairing of scenario development with a larger societal dialogue is perhaps the closest these existing methods come to facilitating real-world action.

Some of the methods are focused on devising imaginative solutions for social challenges, while others focus on creating engaging and thought-provoking artifacts of the future. However, they rarely combine both pathways and even more rarely advocate for a hands-on societal follow-up. So, how can we take the next step, and bridge the gap between shaping ideas and shaping societies? Advanced transmedia can unify the imaginative with the actual, building a pathway where design artifacts and collaborative-imagination processes are linked with actual changes in civic institutions and the built environment. Our goal is, therefore, to draw together lessons and best practices from these existing approaches, and also to bring them together in a holistic omni-transmedia practice.

Expanded Civic Art Forms: From Visionary Thinking to Visionary Making

The transmedia intervention that I will describe in this chapter, *Tangible Utopias*, takes the city as a site for imagining changes to our social and built environments, with a focus on the intersection of public policy, technology, infrastructure, and the relationship between humans and nature. Imagining the long-term future of urban development is not a new endeavor. In an article for the *Boston Globe* in 1900, Thomas F. Anderson imagined what the city of Boston might look like in the upcoming millennium. His speculations, informed by conversations with educators, health-care professionals, and even the city's postmaster, envisioned an urban habitat with moving sidewalks, airships, and pneumatic-tube delivery of every product (Ratti and Claudel, 2016, 3). Even now, 120 years later, much of Anderson's vision still seems closer to a fictional projection than to a plausible urban environment.

Entire cycles of science fiction media production, from books and film to video games and comics, imagine futuristic cities and societies that inspire and resonate with audiences, but fail to materialize into real-world changes in our societies and built environments. Ratti and Claudel call these "paleofutures": visions of the future that never come to pass and quickly show their age, existing more as relics of a cultural zeitgeist than starting points for tangible change—think of the hyperdense, neon-overloaded, vertically oriented, flying car–studded cities of the 1970s and 1980s cyberpunk imaginary. Therefore, the key questions are: How can we measure the impact of an imaginative proposal for a future society or social form? And how can we keep those visions of the future open, so they can be enriched gradually rather than becoming obsolete?

Recent new media arts projects, which integrate interactivity into their designs, come closer to interconnectedness between the imaginary and real-world civic and social impact. Many of these exhibit transmedia features and build on the documentary form; instead of imagining pure fictions, they start from reality and layer on possible paths into the future.

Fort McMoney (Dufresne, 2013), a documentary designed as a video game, tells the story of a Canadian city, Fort McMurray, and its relationship to heavily polluting oil sands. Canada's oil sands are the world's third-largest proven oil reserve, so the nation is caught between the economic activity generated by the oil industry and the values of environmental stewardship and safeguarding human health promulgated by climate activists. Players of *Fort McMoney* are invited to balance the pros and cons of maintaining the oil industry. They may vote or act on crucial aspects of the alternative digital city to improve the quality of life of the residents. For example, they can manage a hypothetical multibillion-dollar fund to be directed toward oil investment or toward other purposes. By addressing the mayor of the digital city, players could send their policy proposals to the mayor of the actual city of Fort McMurray during the release period of the experience. This method is a wonderfully crafted bridge between the artistic and the social. Although *Fort McMoney* didn't lead to actual policy changes—the oil industry in the real-world city continues to thrive—the project did help to prototype an innovative pathway toward not just civic awareness, but actual engagement and interaction.

Another example of an expanded civic imagination path is *Hollow* (McMillion Sheldon, 2013), an interactive documentary depicting the phenomenon of population decline in McDowell County, a rural region of West Virginia, in the US. The stories of the remaining residents are archived in a manner that succeeded in gathering an entire community to deliberate about depopulation, as well as prospects and strategies to retain the existing population, and even to repopulate. Debates catalyzed by *Hollow* led to small-scale political actions aimed at the betterment of the region.

The Australian interactive documentary *My Grandmother's Lingo* (Joshua, 2016) succeeded in igniting interest among a worldwide audience for Marra, a nearly extinct Aboriginal language. The web-documentary activates the microphone at key moments to allow players to practice speaking Marra words. Once the player pronounces a word correctly, they unlock a new chapter of the experience and are thereby invited to discover the personal stories intertwined with this rare cultural heritage. Thousands of people from around the globe have engaged with the project, learning Marra words and helping to keep the language alive in the global consciousness.

These interactive works use the affordances of transmedia storytelling, drawing their power by blending formal elements from film, video games, novels, and learning media and connecting them to real-world conversations and gatherings. More recently, video games and VR projects have emerged as sites for transmedia creativity and social impact. Initiatives like Games for Change, VR for Good, and Unity for Humanity support works that have civic engagement as a core goal.

While all these works strive for social impact, build a limited extension for real-world impact into the project, or engage audiences with real-world gatherings outside the media text, my ideal is to build experiences in which civic imagination, as well as connections between imaginary designs for future societies and real-world change, are central to the process of creating the work and the mechanics of interacting with it. In my own work, I seek to increase the social-impact potential of an artistic piece not only around the time of the artwork's release, but over the long term. Transmedia approaches to civic imagination and civic action, especially ones that can be built upon and continued by the participants and players, provide a way to achieve this longer-term engagement and cross the bridge from learning, engagement, and entertainment to real-world impact.

Tangible Utopias: Envisioning Future Habitats in Virtual Reality and Beyond

Tangible Utopias (2020), a transmedia world that I wrote and directed, is a visionary VR experience that immerses players via a first-person perspective into potential future human habitats. The design of these habitats is

Figure 16.1
Tangible Utopias: Urban Futurism poster.

inspired by the ideas of children ages seven-to-twelve years, and is brought to life in virtual form by a transdisciplinary team of professionals (art directors, architects, graphic designers, landscape designers, musicians, anthropologists, sociologists, and psychologists).

The project is part of a transmedia universe that unites numerous platforms: workshops with children; transdisciplinary debates around their visions; film, VR, and web extensions; and forums with decision-makers, real-world policy debates, and direct civic action. It is the continuation of *Government of Children* (2019)—a civic imagination three-dimensional (3D) film and web playground that aims to encourage children from all over the world to see themselves as leaders and to design future societies, engaging themes of education, justice, transportation, architecture, and more (Mischie, 2019a).

In creating *Tangible Utopias*, my team gathered more than 100 visions of the future from children, out of which approximately 10 key visions were prioritized to serve as the foundation for an interactive VR world. The children we interviewed are from Romania, though in the prototyping phase we also hosted focus groups in the US and France. At the moment, we're partnering with organizations in several continents to expand the project. While many entries featured dystopian or highly fantastical elements, we opted to adapt visions of the future that were visionary, but also gestured toward feasibility.

We first conceptualized the project in 2017, and production unfolded during the pandemic year of 2020. Despite production difficulties related to the pandemic, we were inspired by the need to achieve, at least virtually, more hopeful, collaborative, equitable visions of urban futures to inspire real-world transformation. Philosophically, *Tangible Utopias* is rooted in questions and ideals around the improvement of contemporary cities. We approach cities not only as practical habitats, but as mirrors of the advanced human mind. As the urban researcher and economist Edward Glaeser has argued, "The city is humanity's laboratory, where people flock to dream, create, build, and rebuild" (quoted in Ratti and Claudel, 2016, 25). As such, we perceive urban imagination as a space for interrogating and better understanding the values of different human communities. The project builds a transgenerational conversation, synthesizing the visions of children, transdisciplinary artists, and technologists. A key part of the project design from the outset was to offer *Tangible Utopias* as a case study for civic imagination and urban design to parliaments and other governing bodies, decision-making forums, and institutions concerned with societal design.

We consciously designed *Tangible Utopias* as a VR-native world to foster full immersion into the visionary architecture of the imagined cities, but also to offer agency to users in customizing the virtual spaces. Our goal was to make these collectively produced imaginative visions into tangible spaces, bridging the expansiveness and creative energy of the imagination with the solidity of a navigable environment. VR was the ideal choice to materialize the future habitats inspired by children's ideas: a highly spatial form of mediation, with the ability to integrate interactive elements.

Methodologically, we employed a transdisciplinary and transgenerational approach. After numerous trials, we developed a strategy that would elevate not only the potential of the children's ideas but also the creativity of the transdisciplinary professionals. At first, we started to develop futuristic cities based on drawings made by the children, but we soon realized that this overfaithful approach is more utopian than tangible. The resulting cities wouldn't be organized enough, and wouldn't be feasible as actual urban environments, because the children didn't have specialized training in design, urbanism, or architecture. Instead, we opted to interview the children in an audio-video setup. Then, we curated the children's ideas for future cities, combined the compatible ones into cohesive scripts, and then invited architects, landscapists, and urbanists to expand on them visually. These ideas were open enough—"a city made of sphere-shaped buildings," "a place where humans, plants and animals can live together equally"—to leave significant space for our designers and artists to engage with them creatively. As we advanced, it became harder to separate the contributions of children providing the initial ideas and the work of adults fleshing those ideas out; the result is a set of organic, immersive worlds fueled by both age cohorts and their respective creative processes. Rather than viewing the exchange of ideas from children to adults as a challenge, we came to view it as a valuable aspect of the process: a negotiation between multiple imaginaries, bringing together contributions from a diverse range of creators, as well as users who are given the opportunity to customize the cities. In this way, the entire project becomes a palimpsest, reflecting layers of creative engagement and meaning-making across various stages of production and consumption.

Interactive Gameplay: Balancing Technology and Nature

Over the course of hundreds of interviews with children, we found that many of their ideas about future cities are complementary, but we noticed one pronounced split: a contrast between technology lovers and nature lovers. Some children prioritized living in equality and harmony with wild animals and surrounding greenery, while others focused on humans achieving a similarly harmonious bond with technology through robots, teleportation, and flying homes. In interpreting these children's visions of the future, we wondered how we could balance these differing points of emphasis and create immersive habitats that treat humans and nature equally but also integrate technological advancements.

These observations guided our design for the gameplay. We opted to give each VR player agency to choose how technologically dense or environmentally integrated these future cities will be. Using a controller, each user can access from a menu a highly technologized version of the city, a highly natural version, or a balanced version. The users can compare and contrast the three layers at any time, making their own judgments on the ideal habitat. Also, using an extensive menu of options, the users can customize the colors of the buildings or change the time of the experience (morning, afternoon, sunset, night), seeing the cities in a more sober or more playful light. In future iterations of the VR experience, users will be able to place technological or natural objects in the virtual space, and thereby customize it to a much greater degree.

This strong participatory component aims to transform players into change-makers. Users are initially invited to explore a balanced version of each city that harmonizes tech and nature, but they can also steer it at any point toward a hypertech version or a nature-filled version, exercising their choices and redesigning the virtual world in the hopes that this prepares them for greater awareness of their agency as decision-makers in the real world.

In future iterations of *Tangible Utopias*, we are considering ways to add increased interactivity and causality to the choices: for example, if the player chooses to narrow the roads to make room for more trees, the number of polluting vehicles will decrease. In this way, the VR experience could turn into an educational journey, demonstrating to children and adults the consequences of their choices and advocating for balanced, systemic thinking.

Tangible Utopias users engage with the VR environments, and beyond, in a variety of ways. They first observe the five cities from afar before selecting one to explore in depth, then traverse that city up close, walking down designated "golden paths." They then visit indoor spaces and have the option to customize the environment by reorienting it more toward technological development or natural spaces. At the end of the experience, users can export a postcard from the city of their choice and receive it by email, both as a souvenir from the experience and as an awareness tool for practicing civic imagination further. After the VR experience, we have piloted a social media extension, which puts users into a group of fellow Tangible Utopists who can propose measures to improve actual societies, and discuss ways to enact their visions. Later in this chapter, I will discuss additional ways that we bridged the VR experience with real-world change through direct dialogue with policymakers and interactions in other venues for social transformation.

Exploring the Transformative Habitats

The first *Tangible Utopias* module presents five futuristic human habitats fully adapted in VR. Each depiction of an urban space provides a deep dive into a potential society of the future. Most of them combine rural and urban patterns into settings that aim to encompass both ecological and technological advancements. The virtual world is designed as a long-term process through which we intend to expand and enrich the initial set of five cities, to add new visions of urban futures, and to facilitate connections with the physical world.

The collaborative methodology for *Tangible Utopias* was designed in three stages: ideas offered by children were continued by adults, and then customized in VR by players of all ages, genders, and cultural backgrounds. I will introduce three examples of cities developed through this process and then discuss our process for connecting the experience to policy deliberations and real-world governance, insights and lessons from the project thus far, and next steps.

Spheres City: A Floating Lifestyle

Spheres City was the first futuristic world that we brought to life in VR. The rounded buildings at the heart of this design were inspired by the vision of a nine-year-old Romanian girl. In her view, the architectural spheres would blend better with the surrounding natural environment and the shape of clouds. After identifying the key aspect of her vision to expand on, we added layers collected from other children, such as the idea of mobile habitats, transforming the spheres into floating homes. The floating buildings, which resemble hot-air balloons, add a meditative, ethereal feeling to the experience of navigating the city. Overall, Spheres City suggests a calming lifestyle with both nature-driven explorations and cutting-edge technologies.

Triangle City: Modular Living

Triangle City emerged from the visions of multiple children who pleaded for flying homes, modular habitats, and colorful cityscapes. Each triangular module can be static or endlessly moving and roving, depending on the personality of its inhabitants. Residencies and modes of transportation have merged in this world, and every triangular module can easily move elsewhere. This is one of the most bohemian and playful habitats, as players have the ability to customize the colors of the buildings, steering the color palette of the city toward blues, violets, and yellows. Relying mostly on slow and silent aerial transportation opens up space on the ground for nature and wild animals to thrive. In the high-tech version of Triangle City, there are further enhancements to mobility, while in the nature-driven version, the ground level hosts deer, wild squirrels, and a more walkable, strolling-through-autumn quality.

Figure 16.2
Spheres City in two versions (tech-driven, nature-driven), with buildings designed by the architect Alexandru Pop.

Figure 16.3
Preliminary three-dimensional (3D) models of Triangle City, designed by Alexandru Pop.

Tube City: An Adaptive Natural Home

Inspired by the stunning slides and tubes in amusement parks as proposed by Julia, a Romanian child, Tube City is a state-of-the-art nexus of architecture and nature. The habitat is surrounded by nature externally, and its interiors are also filled with natural life. Water powers the slides, transforming them into transportation infrastructure for the playful residents. The compact city leaves the surrounding environment free from human development, while beneath the construct, there is an entire ocean where life emerges and thrives. Although with the magnitude of a city, Tube City has the look and feel of one organic building that is networked and cohesive, as if the entire community shares one home.

The goal of Tube City is not only to be innovative, but also to be adaptive to its surroundings; residents are able to alter the transparency of the city's walls to facilitate communion with the external world. As Ratti and Claudel write, "Architecture must do more than just look like a living organism: it should perform as a living system" (2016, 77).

From Artistic Impact to Social Impact

Although its development has been hosted by several international markets,[1] *Tangible Utopias* has not yet been launched for a mass audience; it is

Figure 16.4
Preliminary 3D models of Tube City, designed by architect Alexandru Pop.

still being expanded and refined, and so far users have interacted with it through focus groups of early testers. Even at this early stage, we can begin to distill lessons about how a transmedia approach with VR at its center can move users from virtual immersion to critical thinking and advocacy for real-world change.

Within the media industry, the release of the first futuristic city, Spheres, was perceived as a pioneering step, receiving the Open Frame Award for VR at the GoEast Festival—the first international award for a Romanian VR experience. The jury praised "the long term ambition of this meaningful project that will develop and grow over the coming years, giving a voice to children in such a creative way, embracing and celebrating them as our true hope for our global future" (Storyscapes, 2021). The project's success contributed to the development of an evolving artistic trend, as multiple brands (Orange, Siemens, Shell), entities (World Building Institute, Unity for Humanity, Going Green), and international artists (Denis Semionov, Alex Pearson) are now investing in envisaging positive future cities. Over time, this trend may develop into a movement that interrupts the chain of dystopian visions of the future of urban life that are created by the news and entertainment media.

Young people described the exploratory project as "hopeful," "empowering," and "beautiful" in the focus groups that we have led. One of our user-testing sessions invited ten children with various attention disorders to experience the virtual worlds. All ten participants stayed joyfully focused for unusually long periods of time. For most, it was their first VR experience. One young woman who did not talk at all during the preliminary sessions, in part because of a speech disorder, felt elevated by the VR journey and after taking the headset off, talked ceaselessly about it. There was a feeling of enchantment and empowerment experienced by this young person, as if she were not aware previously that imagination could be used in this tangible and constructive manner. Many of the players reported that the project helped them to feel that their visions of the future do matter, in both virtual and real worlds.

The social extensions of the transmedia project took numerous shapes, including transdisciplinary debates, panels, and roundtables with children. One of the debates invited an educator, an anthropologist, and a sociologist to explore how virtual worlds can be integrated into their daily work and become active tools for shaping contemporary learning. Another event invited five of the children who had contributed to the project to talk with business leaders about how they would reshape society. One event focusing on the theme of digital heritage, addressed to architecture students, included a *Tangible Utopias* presentation and explored crucial questions such as: How might we combine futuristic cities with existing cultural heritage? How much novelty should we integrate into a city to make it innovative, and how much heritage should we conserve so as not to lose our identity? Global Shapers Bucharest Hub, a Romanian nongovernmental organization focusing on social innovation, invited some of the children to discussion sessions on shaping medium-term futures for the country. Preliminary roundtables with children led to brainstorming sessions on how to implement some of the futuristic ideas prototyped in *Tangible Utopias* into our current habitats. Our in-progress goal for the ongoing project is to have a European Parliament discussion-debate session in which children and decision-makers prioritize measures to execute societal changes for the next ten years.

Forward-looking participants in the process proposed ways to continue the project. Julia Marcan, one of the young participants, argued that imagining advanced beautiful habitats is necessary but insufficient, and perhaps a more important step in the long run would be to imagine the evolution of human relationships. In her view, it is our inner selves that we need to reimagine and change first, even if the future spaces look exactly like today's.

Her proposal was to continue the expansion of the current single-player worlds with more human presence, social interaction, and civic rituals, as these could lead to transformative changes in behavior. We noted the proposals for further iterations of the piece.

In addition, we have monitored actions emerging from the groups of children and adults involved in either creating or testing the project. Martha Buia, one of the young participants that went through the civic imagination process, began to gradually lead her own workshops to help children with autism become more involved in society. Her initiatives were true proof that change needs to start within each of us. One of the collaborating anthropologists, inspired by the visionary cities, decided to create a short-term policy brief for the improvement of real cities such as Cluj-Napoca, Romania, and Nantes, France, and proposed the strategy to local authorities. The same anthropologist initiated a cross-cultural project with the goal of creating closer relationships between Romanian and French cities through the sharing of constructive urban-design practices.

The continuation of the project has an extensive potential for social impact. All the cities in *Tangible Utopias* may serve as architectural visualizations to imagine how buildings could look in the future. The group of Tangible Utopists may coprototype legal proposals for achieving more ethical cities in the short and medium term. Live events that we host may bring together children and decision-makers to accelerate change.

While navigating the process, we understand that obtaining tangible and lasting forms of social impact isn't easy or quick; it requires many transmedia iterations, extensions, and training over a long time span. Besides, civic imagination needs to be joined by civic (self-)trust and action. Some of the VR explorers, especially those who had experienced extreme poverty, felt less trusting that better, richer, more equitable futures could truly emerge from our imaginations. This reminded us of Stephen Duncombe's notion of the "tyranny of the possible": the widespread belief that as individuals, we cannot change the external world with ease (Duncombe and Peters, 2012). Perhaps inhabiting the material world and its repetitive challenges for too long might hinder our engagement in a visionary realm. So, how can we achieve the embodiment of civic imagination in such a grim context? How can we grow not only our imaginative power, but also our trust that imagination can be a part of meaningful real-world change? Moreover, once we succeed in envisaging preferred future worlds, are we ready to advocate for them? The technology critic and legal expert Jamie Susskind has argued, "We are not yet ready—intellectually, philosophically or morally—for the world we are creating" (2018, 1). As we train our imagination through creative prompts, we need to also train our readiness levels through microactions, without exclusively waiting for existing authorities to make the first move in enacting real-world change.

Therefore, *Tangible Utopias* is the beginning of a continuous endeavor to inspire societal change. Its goal is to gradually become a centralized archive of long-term futures, but also an inspiration for immediate civic actions. As Italo Calvino observed in 1968, describing the libraries, museums, and newspapers that power the intellectual life of contemporary cities, "What we are planning to build is a centralized archive of humankind" (1995, 135). However, unlike many static archives, this one is interactive, immersive, adaptive, and regenerative.

Now that we've begun to construct an archive of futures fueled by civic imagination, the next step is to bring these visionary proposals into our society in the future. One preliminary answer would be through constant holistic work: educational, artistic, political, and economic. It's not enough to have transmedia, transdisciplinary, and transgenerational policies in the production of a project; these structures must carry on to future iterations and activations to become a habitual doing, not merely a novel experience or one-off proof of concept.

The shape and governance of our cities are often the result of decisions made by small groups of leaders and political representatives who don't always consult residents. Collaborative artworks can help us hone our collective skill to generate a plurality of visions for preferred urban futures—even when the initial urban imaginaries are extravagantly visionary, as in *Tangible Utopias*, they capture the values and priorities of a broader range of participants. As Pagan Kennedy argues, one hope is to "reinvent invention itself and put the designed environment in the hands of the many rather than the few" (2016, 222). Through *Tangible Utopias*, we have created a more inclusive realm for future codesign; however, there are still limitations that can be overcome only if we continue to develop and broaden the project. For example, we hope to incorporate contributions from children from a broader range of cultural backgrounds as we grow the project.

Combining civic imagination with VR is impactful because it not only familiarizes us with potential better worlds, but also teleports us inside these visions, allowing us to take on roles as explorers, discoverers, leaders, and shapers. In his book *Virtual Reality*, the technology writer Samuel Greengard poses the question, "How will immersive virtual experiences affect the way we view other societies, religions, and people?" (2019, 209). For me, that question also extends into the built environment, and it also flows in the other direction, from the physical world back into the virtual, in a feedback loop. How will immersive worlds revolutionize the physical world, and vice versa?

Through processes for civic imagination, transmedia methodologies, and plans for iterative development going forward, *Tangible Utopias* offers a set of practices to achieve progressive social impact, both by changing the attitudes of city residents and by facilitating the actual emergence of visionary urban designs. It is a prototype for a new, radical manner of thinking that borrows best practices from arts, education, politics, architecture, and social sciences: *omni-transmedia*. By bringing imagination into virtual forms that serve as a prototype for future physical habitats, an omni-transmedia approach generates a long-term pipeline that promises to achieve not only artistic, but also societal advancement.

Omni-Transmedia: The Evolution of a Transmedia Societal Concept

The field of transmedia has constantly evolved on a theoretical and practical level over the past decade. The term "transmedia storytelling" was defined by the media scholar Henry Jenkins as a narrative that "unfolds across multiple media platforms, with each new text making a distinctive and valuable contribution to the whole" (2006, 97), and this approach has become the cornerstone of franchised entertainment, from the Marvel Cinematic Universe to Disney's princesses. As the term has matured and technological change has made deploying and participating in transmedia stories easier than ever, we need to expand its meaning beyond entertainment. The intersection of transmedia with civic imagination suggests a more multilayered approach that bridges virtual spaces and fictional stories with transformations in society, policy, and infrastructure in the physical world.

I propose the term *omni-transmedia* to address the long-term evolution of this field. Omni-transmedia links transmedia systems into an ongoing universe of narrative and meaning-making that unfolds across multiple disciplines and initiatives: technologies, arts, sciences, human communities, and social institutions, all leading to holistic civic and social engagement, social change, and social empowerment (Mischie, 2019b). If edutainment was coined to name efforts to make education more fun, perhaps we could coin *civictainment* as a way to make our social and political actions more playful and purposeful simultaneously, and *omnitainment* as a way to use transmedia experiences to foster thinking for the long term, not only the "now." Omni-transmedia experiences afford users opportunities to practice civic imagination, building skills and confidence in our ability to change our societies for the better.

Omni-Transmedia Principles

An omni-transmedia approach suggests a series of principles or guidelines that might help communities or artists to increase the complexity of their works, as well as bolster their long-term impact in the physical world and actual communities and societies. Based on my experiences with *Tangible Utopias* and other media projects aimed at social impact, here I propose a preliminary set of practices that can be considered, adopted, and iterated on by people seeking to design omni-transmedia projects that blend the immersive thrill of transmedia storytelling with efforts to foster civic imagination and catalyze real social change.

The infinite transmedia principle: Holistic projects ought to include scalable, loopable methodologies and technologies to iterate on and continue developing a concept in the long term. A continuously developing prototype city might integrate fiction stories and speculative essays, VR to illustrate and explore architecture and urban form, and participatory engagements like alternate-reality games and live-action role-playing to consider social relations, governance, and culture.

The transgenerational principle: Putting multiple generations in dialogue can create a truly holistic outcome. In an omni-transmedia project, an adult creator like an artist or producer would not be enshrined as the all-seeing author of an experience, but rather as a facilitator who guides a network of collaborators across age cohorts. This enables fresh perspectives and different ways of evaluating feasibility—for example, elders can bring historical perspectives from their lived experiences to bear on new ideas. In *Tangible Utopias*, we hope that children involved in this initial stage of the project will become trainers for future groups of young participants.

The transdisciplinary principle: Complex omni-transmedia works require blending expertise and perspectives from a variety of disciplines. We invited architects, graphic designers, anthropologists, sociologists, psychologists, and landscape designers to contribute to the *Tangible Utopias* project. Many acted as consultants, while a few took hands-on, creative roles in coprototyping future cities. In the future, we hope to achieve greater global participation, and to include the voices of Indigenous people and communities in order to add more diversity to our conceptualization and design processes.

The transreal principle: In omni-transmedia, we have the ability to navigate consciously through multiple realities: material, spiritual, and virtual (Mischie, 2019b). An omni-transmedia work aims to combine virtual worlds with real-world debates and actions, and with ethical and moral contemplation. Even if we can't physically realize our visionary cities in the short term, specific elements, such as "floating homes," might inspire real-world innovation and implementation. Even if we might not live in Spheres City anytime soon, we could see concepts like floating spheres in the real world as part of reimagining public transit systems.

The transtemporal principle: Omni-transmedia works are continuous in time. The archive of civic imagination that we seek to construct is not a static repository, but rather an ongoing process. In *Tangible Utopias*, transtemporal thinking might help us track how participants' ideas, values, and aspirations change over time. For example, we could reinterview the same children every five years to see how their visions change, and enrich the project's prototype cities with more elements and customization tools depending on the findings.

The transspatial principle: Omni-transmedia projects should expand continuously in space and geography. Omni-transmedia projects blend local and global elements, reflecting how cities can be networked globally while still retaining their unique character.

The transmeaning principle: Projects should be constantly analyzed, gauging their impact across criteria drawn from artistic fields, technology, and social science. Constant evaluation is part of an active omni-transmedia work: Is this initiative enriching the human spirit? How can we map its role in real-world transformations over the short, medium, and long term?

Together, these principles are meant to provide a set of starting points, to give practitioners a foundation of interconnection and border crossing as they design transmedia experiences. Already, we see examples of artworks that imaginatively bridge the virtual and the actual, paving the way for a larger movement: murals that also purify urban air, geolocative mobile games inviting residents to walk instead of riding in cars, VR simulations that encourage explorers to undertake meaningful real-world actions to unlock further installments. Omni-transmedia can seem hopelessly utopian, but it builds on the success of initiatives worldwide that use integrated media experiences to catalyze critical thinking, spark new ways of imagining our communities and built environments, and motivate real-world transformation.

Resolutions

As transmedia proved to be an effective approach for fostering civic imagination, it opened up a new set of horizons, paving the way for more multi-layered thinking systems such as the omni-transmedia concept that I have introduced here.

In the short term, immersive projects such as *Tangible Utopias* suggest the shape of this omni-transmedia future by connecting immersive and participatory media experiences with real-world debates and artifacts, by integrating extensive connections to education and civic engagement, and by drawing together fields like architecture, psychology, art, and technology. Over time, projects like this serve as prototypes for the future of our societies, as well as prototypes for new systems through which we might think individually and collectively about societal change.

Transmedia and omni-transmedia practices have the power to reshape the attitudes of individuals, communities, and even perhaps entire societies through activating collaborative civic imagination, distributed across a multitude of mechanisms, from immersive media and social technologies to in-person gatherings and forums. This methodology needs refinement through practice and experimentation.

Omni-transmedia suggests that to create engaging media and motivate social change, we must borrow practices from multiple systems, technologies, and platforms and interlink them into cohesive and visionary forms of thinking. What if imagining futures could become a field in itself—not confined to niche academic circles and corporate-futurist consultancies, but explored in schools, debated in parliaments, discussed over family dinners, and brainstormed in workplaces? This could bring us closer to turning the ideas at the heart of *Tangible Utopias* into social action and institutional change. Still, a number of questions remain open: How can we introduce complex omni-transmedia principles in the fast-everything world that we inhabit? Once we have long-term visions for the future of our cities and communities, what are the intermediary steps to actually building them? Should we hack our current cities? Elevate them gradually? Build new ones? How do we build consensus for enormous changes in people's lived realities, no matter how vivid our imaginative projections might be?

Despite its imperfections, the exercise of codesigning meaningful futures is worthwhile. As Jamie Susskind warns, "The biggest risk would be not to try to anticipate the future at all" (2018, 5). It's equally important to develop new approaches for storytelling and collaborative worldbuilding; our current expressive and creative tools may not be sufficient to grapple with the complexities of global, transformational change.

Finally, omni-transmedia approaches should work to preserve a sense of idealism and possibility. As the sociologist Peter Frase has written, "It's up to us to build the collective power to fight for the futures we want" (2016, 150). Transmedia experiences have the power to help us visualize, create, and imaginatively inhabit those preferred futures, and thereby galvanize us to work to bring them into being.

Note

1. During its development phase, the project was supported by and showcased in a variety of international venues, including the Cannes XR Development Showcase, Venice Gap Financing Market, VR Days Immersive Funding Market, and the Web Summit 2020. (The latter two events were hosted digitally as a result of the COVID-19 pandemic.)

References

Anderson, Thomas F. 1900. "Boston at the End of the 20th Century: A Glimpse into the Distant Future," *Boston Globe*, December 24, 1900.

Calvino, Italo. 1995. "World Memory." In *Numbers in the Dark and Other Stories*, translated by Tim Parks, 79–89. Boston: Mariner Books.

Dufresne, David. 2013. *Fort McMoney*. Interactive documentary. Produced by the National Film Board of Canada and ARTE. https://www.arte.tv/digitalproductions /en/fort-mcmoney.

Duncombe, Stephen, and Sarah Peters. 2012. "Utopia Is No Place." *Primer*, Walker Art Center, Minneapolis, August 27, 2012. https://walkerart.org/magazine/stephen -duncombe-utopia-open-field.

Dunne, Anthony, and Raby, Fiona. 2013. *Speculative Everything: Design, Fiction, and Social Dreaming*. Cambridge, MA: MIT Press.

Frase, Peter. 2016. *Four Futures: Life after Capitalism*. New York: Verso.

Gaiman, Neil. 2013. "Why Our Future Depends on Libraries, Reading and Day-dreaming." *The Guardian*, October 15, 2013. https://www.theguardian.com/books /2013/oct/15/neil-gaiman-future-libraries-reading-daydreaming.

Greengard, Samuel. 2019. *Virtual Reality*. Cambridge, MA: MIT Press.

Hamid, Mohsin. 2017. "Magical Novel "Exit West" Explores What Makes Refugees Leave Home," *PBS NewsHour*, March 16, 2017. https://www.pbs.org/newshour/show /magical-novel-exit-west-explores-makes-refugees-leave-home.

Jenkins, Henry. 2006. *Convergence Culture: Where Old and New Media Collide*. New York: New York University Press.

Jenkins, Henry, Gabriel Peters-Lazaro, and Sangita Shresthova, eds. 2020. *Popular Culture and the Civic Imagination: Case Studies of Creative Social Change*. New York: New York University Press.

Johnson, Brian David. 2011. *Science Fiction Prototyping: Designing the Future with Science Fiction*. San Rafael, CA: Morgan & Claypool.

Joshua, Angelina. 2016. *My Grandmother's Lingo*. Interactive documentary. Produced by SBS (Special Broadcasting Service, Australia). https://www.sbs.com.au /mygrandmotherslingo.

Kennedy, Pagan. 2016. *Inventology: How We Dream up Things That Change the World*. Boston: Houghton Mifflin Harcourt.

McDowell, Alex. 2008. "What Is the World Building Institute?" World Building Institute, University of Southern California, Los Angeles. Accessed August 1, 2021. https://worldbuilding.institute/about.

McMillion Sheldon, Elaine. 2013. *Hollow*. Interactive documentary. http://hollow documentary.com.

Mischie, Ioana. 2019a. "How a Society Envisaged by Children Would Look Like." Filmed December 2019 at TEDxBucharestWomen. Video, 15:56. https://www.ted .com/talks/ioana_mischie_how_a_society_envisaged_by_children_would_look_like.

Mischie, Ioana. 2019b. "The Impact of Transmedia on Cinema: A New Contemporary Immersive Avant-Garde." PhD dissertation, Caragiale National University of Theatre and Film, Bucharest.

Montfort, Nick. 2017. *The Future*. Cambridge, MA: MIT Press.

Ratti, Carlo, and Matthew Claudel. 2016. *The City of Tomorrow: Sensors, Networks, Hackers, and the Future of Urban Life*. New Haven, CT: Yale University Press.

Price, Cedric. 1984. *Cedric Price Works II*. London: The Architectural Association.

Sterling, Bruce. 2005. *Shaping Things*. Cambridge, MA: MIT Press.

Storyscapes. 2021. "The Sphere City×Tangible Utopias, the Visionary VR Franchise Directed by Ioana Mischie, Wins the Prestigious Open Frame Award at goEast Film Festival 2021." *feeder.ro*, May 11, 2021. https://www.feeder.ro/2021/05/11/the-spheres-city-x-tangible-utopias.

Susskind, Jamie. 2018. *Future Politics: Living Together in a World Transformed by Tech*. Oxford: Oxford University Press.

Transmedia Crosstalk: Terra Gasque and Ioana Mischie

Bob Beard: What comes through in both of your essays, I think, is a moral argument to liberate transmedia. Can you talk about that?

Ioana Mischie: I feel transmedia is an ever-growing path; it liberates us as we liberate it. We are often biased by seeing it from capitalistic, profit-focused perspectives, rather than thinking of it as a larger connective tissue, as a playground for social impact. But if we look around at how water circles in nature through multiple platforms, that is a model for transmedia I'd be inspired by. If we look deep down into our genes, into the way DNA travels from generation to generation, this is transmedia too. So, once we acknowledge its potential for liberation, how can we use it creatively? How can we use it to advance the world, rather than to disrupt it?

It is also interesting to talk about transmedia in the emerging context of the metaverse. In the past, transmedia was fragmented, was "spreadable." Now it seems to search for its essence, to be more cohesive, to be more unified, digitalized, global.

Terra Gasque: *(Gazes into the distance like Roy Batty)* I come from a time where the internet was young and wild. I've seen mash-ups and remixes of dead worlds, and forgotten stories. I've watched as the digital has become picked over and separated for capital gains. . . .

I think about transmedia in two ways. First, I think my desire for liberation is ultimately a desire for access. Take, for example, my latest delve into my past: *Digimon* [a multiplatform media franchise originating in the late 1990s]. It is one of the few fond memories I have of my childhood, and now I wish to reexperience it, flaws and all—but access to all of the parts of the *Digimon* universe is separated across multiple dead media platforms, distribution rights, and paid services. I want people to access these crazy niche experiences—to see the stories of the world grow.

Second, as Ioana says, I see transmedia liberating us as we liberate it. It's like queer theory: an anti-structural argument that we use to challenge ourselves with, and then we use the results of that challenge to interrogate our new understanding, iteratively on and on. It's a cycle of interactions and learning and challenges that keeps the introspection up and the consumption down.

IM: *(Gazes into the distance like Terra)* Perhaps transmedia is an angle from which we can perceive the world—practicing a reverse-engineering worldbuilding technique with our own world.

BB: I wonder if we can go back to your comment on the metaverse, Ioana. Can you expand on that?

IM: There is now this ever-evolving trend to unify all the digital worlds into a cohesive metaverse where users would be embodied by avatars and access information in a sensorial manner, not in the "antique" World Wide Web style that imitates the linear navigation of a library, and is mostly textual, image, or audio-driven. The metaverse promises immersive presence. It could be seen as a collection of transmedia worlds. Or a transmedia galaxy in itself.

Now, how can we relate to it, so we make sure it does not turn into a dystopia, alienating everyone? How can we make sure we connect the metaverse with the real-verse? How can we design mechanisms to have a metaverse that does not disillusion its residents, as the World Wide Web ended up doing with fake news, an excess of sponsored posts, and unethical data use? How are we going to navigate through multiple transmedia worlds at times, without losing our groundedness?

If we could borrow the methodology of the metaverse, but fill it with forms of constructive social impact and co-creation, perhaps we could have a transformative step towards a better future.

The nice part is: a shift like this happens probably once a century, so if there is a moment to shape the metaverse for the good, perhaps this is the ideal time and space to debate it.

BB: So, liberatory transmedia, including your projects for young people and Terra's examples in tabletop role-playing games, are like the training wheels for how to demand and live in a better, more equitable metaverse?

IM: Yes, but also in a better, more equitable real world. Ideally, we should interconnect the metaverse and the real world, so that it does not become only an escapist tool.

TG: I'm with Ioana—not just the metaverse, but the world we live in. Thinking only about the future leaves the terms of the present to be dictated by those in power. Without addressing the current issues, the future we're all try to "fix" is still being controlled by those with power today. And unless that power is wrested from them, or they opt to share in that power, all this planning for the future won't do much.

IM: It would be a disappointment to have a cruel reality and to step into fiction to forget about it! Instead, we could tackle the real-world problems through metaverse actions, perhaps, and see a constructive change in both interconnected realms.

This would mean connecting the metaverse and the real-verse in a transmedia manner—only that it is not just a chain of two platforms, it is an ever-looping ping-pong between the two, transforming into an infinity of platforms.

This only makes sense if it is without a secret agenda and without a profit-driven goal, but then this cannot last long in capitalism. So, what system could host this? Perhaps a collection of systems called "transmedialism"—which would borrow best practices from all kinds of other systems and social structures.

BB: Much of this volume talks about the potential for transmedia logics in "nontraditional" spaces, outside of the entertainment sphere and into education, journalism, and even health care. And many of these applications are driven by the idea that transmedia is an ecosystem that we've all been raised in for the past twentysomething years, one in which we've developed certain kinds of familiarities and literacies. What other sectors would you like to see transmedia logics applied to?

IM: I would love to see transmedia applied in politics. We often create advanced projects in art, and education, but politics remains an ivory tower, the hardest to access and upgrade. Also, transmedia applied in psychology and noetic science—perceiving humans as platforms. I feel this could be the truly meaningful revolution of our times.

TG: Transmedia psychology is an interesting concept! Ideas and logics of transmedia can help make some of the perspectives of neurodivergent individuals easier to understand and conceptualize, for those who aren't aware of them.

I'd like to see transmedia logics applied to the ecological issues we are going to see more and more of as the effects of climate change intensify. Transmedia frameworks help to paint a more interconnected picture of these global systems and help us to see how the ripples of floodwaters in one area exist in relation with the drought in another region.

IM: I see potential for transmedia being applied in lifelong learning. How to interconnect new dots of knowledge and curiosity? How to do this at all ages? How to keep a mental space for transmedia thinking, perhaps ten minutes a day? Perhaps transmedia does not belong to the big studios, but to these small gestures, rituals, and routines.

Finally, my challenge now as I have a newly born baby is: How should I start presenting our world to him? With letters and numbers? With shapes? Or all these are perhaps not priorities? What is the essence to begin with, so we can understand the world in a multilayered manner from the beginning?

Coda: Last Words

What are the most important considerations or unexpected ethical challenges for transmedia projects in the future?

Yomi Ayeni: Creators forget that the audience is more than a metric. Participants connect with our stories for various reasons, they devote time to exploring our worlds, help move our stories forward through their interactions, and engage with each other because they trust us—the creators. We, as an industry, need to find new ways to reciprocate, beyond offering feedback that moves a narrative along to the next stage in a story.

The dilemma is usually a result of trying to appease a client funding the project who is interested in numbers, and not much else. Maybe it is time that creators offered a "value-added" component at no cost to the client, and build into the narrative a series of impactful rewards for participants, or for the target community.

Caitlin Burns: The biggest consideration for me is the human who is ultimately engaging with the experience you've built. The second is that the humans who create the work are working in sustainable and safe environments.

That audience member has to be taken care of (seriously, do no harm), but also presents the strangest wild cards, both creatively and practically as a creator who has a life in the real world. People have gotten vicious at me in the real world about things that occurred in storylines. One of the reasons I've often gravitated toward producer roles is that I end up becoming very protective of the teams I'm working with and want to have the authority and resourcing to make sure that everyone who is making a big project, and everyone who is engaging with that project, is going to have a productive experience that is in some way fostering growth and isn't traumatizing. There will always be audience members for whom moments of story will open something deeply personal, and it's impossible to predict who, why, or where. I remember the first time a college student in a lecture spoke to me about a scene in a kids' movie I wrote and their experience of that scene as a child . . . all media projects have the potential to influence people profoundly, and that responsibility is worth recognizing and bringing into the writers' room, and into the way a creative business is run.

Katherine Buse and Ranjodh Singh Dhaliwal: It is our contention that transmedia work, even when it is open and participatory, works best when it embraces formal and aesthetic ambivalence, especially with regard to the idea of worlds and the work of building them. A risk of transmedia is that it can *simulate* the properties of a world, including the pleasures of new discoveries and the sense of a shared reality, but still insulate that world from the very things that allow real discoveries and the very ethics that produce real, shared realities. The real world has ragged edges. The real world is contradictory, overlapping, glitchy, and mutable. The real world has to be constructed by its inhabitants and held in common between them. Transmedia should take care not to model smooth, closed worlds we can escape to, for they can make us believe that reality is an unbroken eggshell when it is really an ongoing explosion.

Denis Butkus: Inheritances. We will need to consider how we shed the cultural, institutional, and artistic inheritances that limit innovation in any field—and which, at their most injurious, debilitate the wholeness of a collaborative transmedia ethos among practitioners. We will need to recognize, assess, and dismantle these inheritances, not from a standpoint of reactive erasure, but rather thorough a lens of deep reflection, thoughtful consideration, and committed innovation.

Often the first examples of transmedia projects are large, well-funded commercial ventures: video games, The Matrix universe, etc. Perhaps the commodification of transmedia projects is a foregone conclusion, but it is important for artists and creatives to keep searching for new critical frameworks to engage with the practice of transmedia. Project scale and scope will be increasing challenges to consider as new transmedia projects are developed and released in the future. From an independent producing perspective, there is unlimited control within a finite amount of financial resources. As more corporate and commercial projects enter the marketplace, issues of authorship and ownership will arise as more capital is injected into the system, especially as virtual spaces become more of a player. This relates to the NFT-crypto-blockchain space, especially. The current "gold rush" mentality could wreak untold violence on BIPOC [Black, Indigenous, and People of Color] communities without innovative thought and proactive amplification of their transmedia projects and related intersections.

Ethically, access and equity will be central issues that institutions and organizations will need to address, as technology advances rapidly and costs become prohibitive for independent artists. Organizations will be where these artists will turn for support, training, and access to equipment and space to create their work. Without equitable strategies across funding and access to technology, any transmedia project of the future will be beholden to the White-supremacist-capitalist-competitive system unless radical thinking and challenges to the status quo can be maintained, while still providing livelihood opportunities to as-yet-unknown artists and makers.

Dilman Dila: I would put it in terms of money. Transmedia is being pushed for by corporations, and so their aim is to make as much money as possible from the audience for a story or universe, but at some point, perhaps, audiences get fatigued by all this. In the beginning, for example, there was only Netflix offering internet-based subscriptions, but now every major studio has their own version, and audiences are at a loss about which ones to subscribe to. Similarly, when there's a deluge, and an individual is invested in many different storyverses from many different studios, and they have to keep paying to consume all this, it strains the pocket.

Lee Emrich: Wow, this is a big question! I think a heavy focus on environmentalism would be really amazing to see, in addition to greater environmental accountability from large media companies. And of course, I'd like to see ever more promotion of, and support for, historically excluded content creators.

Paweł Frelik: I feel that an interesting ethical question here (although it engages a specific understanding of ethics) concerns the audience members' mental health, for the lack of a better word. For all its wonderful uses, the transmedia design logic, especially in the commercial transmedia sector, has been relentless in occupying the attention of transmedia audiences. But more is not always better, and there is a significant body of research concerning the cognitive costs of using digital media, the influence that heavy media use has on psychological and even somatic health, and the effects of media overload, even if there is not common agreement on how much screen time constitutes "overload." From this perspective, transmedia producers have, I feel, a degree of responsibility for their audiences' mental states.

Terra Gasque: I think the most important consideration is to notice who *isn't* in the conversation or experience. Those outside or incapable of engaging with the works often help identify who these worlds are built for.

Camillia Matuk: Given the widespread applications of transmedia storytelling, and the persuasiveness of stories in general, I think trust and reliability will be among the important considerations for transmedia projects in the future. Transmedia is now so pervasive in our movements through the web, and used for a variety of purposes, from selling products, to conveying political viewpoints, to communicating the news. I can see a renewed need for people to develop critical multimedia literacies, such that they can learn to distinguish between fact and fiction in transmedia, to interpret transmedia messages in light of their underlying intent, and to evaluate the soundness of arguments made in transmedia.

Another persistent consideration is to ensure that the tools and channels for transmedia creation and consumption are as accessible as possible, to as diverse a population as possible. There can be social equity consequences when some voices are privileged in speaking and being heard over others, especially in (trans)media, which has such power-wielding potential.

Ioana Mischie: In the course of working on my PhD, I coined the term "trans-ethics" to underline the need for balancing multiple platforms in a constructive manner. For example, an immersive extended reality (XR) platform, continued with a book and with an urban intervention, would perhaps dynamize the player in a healthier manner, whereas combining XR with multiplayer online role-playing games and hyperintrusive text messages might alienate the explorers. I believe balance is key in transmedia worlds—not only within the platforms, but especially when referring to their interconnectivity. Also, in my view, new jobs are needed in complex transmedia worlds, such as a director of ethics, similar to the director of photography, whose role is pivotal to any cinematic project. The addictiveness of digital platforms is a pressing problem, so finding ways to decrease or mitigate that tendency is necessary if we want to achieve complex, enjoyable, and ethical transmedia journeys.

Kirsten Ostherr: At their most radical, transmedia projects suggest the possibility of transcending the confines of ownership or authorship of narratives. Yet infrastructures that enable us to convey ideas from one setting to another are integral to the existence of transmedia, and it is very difficult to imagine a scenario where those pathways of communication are not owned, and where the owners do not exploit their access to the contributions of different media-makers. Is it possible to imagine open-source transmedia that also exist on an open internet, which somehow disallows aggregation and data mining?

Francis Quek, Niloofar Zarei, and Sharon Lynn Chu: The effectiveness of transmedia projects relies on the affordances of each medium that is involved. Media, however, are fluid and change as much with new technological developments as with evolving societal values. For example, the new wave of virtual reality devices has opened up a host of opportunities for transmedia projects, and yet it has also stirred new concerns over social isolation and health problems. Therefore, some of the most important considerations for future transmedia projects would be to critically analyze and understand the possible effects of each involved medium, and to account for these.

At the same time, future transmedia projects will suffer from the same challenges that current transmedia projects face. Media of all forms can be deceitful. While media may come across as innocuous in its presentation and use, it is able to produce deep and vast changes both for individuals and for the broader society. From transmedia games to transmedia documentaries and news, we have seen people change their personal habits and behaviors, and we have seen society turn in new directions. Creators of future transmedia projects need to be aware of, and ensure responsibility for, the powerful impact that they can produce.

Zoyander Street: I try to pay a lot of attention to the emotion stories that are being told about transmedia projects and stay critical of them. I think the narratives about the social good of particular emotions, such as "empathy" or "flow," can end up contributing to long-standing systemic harms rooted in the dominant medicalized paradigms of neurodiversity and trauma. The platforms that we use often come with a tacit demand that emotions themselves be turned into a resource that can be mined for capitalist extraction. We should be critical of the demand to turn something as private as a person's emotional response into something to be managed, quantified, and optimized for some imagined greater good.

Ruth Wylie and Ed Finn: One major ethical challenge we confronted in our *Frankenstein200* project was how to mark out the boundary between fact and fiction. By creating an alternate reality game (ARG), we immediately pushed the edge of reality, creating a pocket of fiction that purported to be "real" but invited our audience to play along with that fictive realness. This was especially difficult because we were also telling a story about scientific ethics: how could we portray our Dr. Frankenstein as a compelling and flawed villain without also telling a "science is bad" narrative? While some readers continue to interpret the Frankenstein myth solely as a cautionary tale, we believe it is a fundamentally optimistic story about the importance of care, responsibility, and sociality. To that end, our Dr. Frankenstein was buttressed by two younger, sympathetic scientists-in-training who offered a counterpoint on the theme of what it means to be a good scientist.

This challenge also played out in how we presented science, technology, engineering, and math (STEM) knowledge within our experience. Again, the blurred boundaries of fiction and reality in an ARG required us to pay close attention to the cues and rules of genre to clearly suggest what topics in our experience were fictional, and which were "real science" that had been imported into our storyworld.

This second challenge also played out in a more abstract way, in terms of epistemological frames. Transmedia as a process fundamentally leans on the apophenia of seeing every new medium and cultural object as part of the narrative web. Scientific inquiry, on the other hand, depends on observation that distinguishes evidence from noise, organizing and specifying knowledge. We fell back on the power of narrative to perform certain "structures of feeling" around science ethics and science identity, asking our participants to explore the moral and personal dimensions of what it might mean to act as a scientist, rather than asking them only to reproduce experiments or follow in the procedural footsteps of scientific inquiry.

Looking forward, we see many of the same challenges confronting transmedia projects operating at the intersection of fact and fiction. This is especially true when exploring the near future of science: several emerging technologies that were speculative fiction at the beginning of our project became fact by the end of it, such as CRISPR-based editing of humans.

Maureen McHugh Yeager: If transmedia is something that evolves pretty easily out of the way that the internet works, and I believe it is, then we're going to need to develop cultural norms around it. Right now, we have a naive audience—and transmedia allows people to feel empowered in a way that can blind them to false narratives. We like community, it's a pretty basic human need, and we are easily swayed by the beliefs of people we like. The way that transmedia creates community is different from the ways that we've built community in the past. It's easy to find a "tribe" online, and once I find them, it's easy to listen to them and ignore things that threaten that.

But every new advance in communication, be it writing (which reduced our reliance on memory, not an entirely good thing) or television, came with things that were more exciting and better. The people who recited Homeric ballads had enormous abilities to create sophisticated memory tools. It was amazing! But they also couldn't have as many stories at their fingertips as someone with a couple of dozen books has. Yes, there are also drawbacks to books. Books can have bad information in them, and because books can be disseminated, that means texts like *The Protocols of the Elders of Zion* can be disseminated widely and lead to harm. But the *New England Journal of Medicine* can also be disseminated widely and do a lot of good.

It's perhaps easier to think of worst-case scenarios in this industry, but can you envision a future project that uses the logics of transmedia for social good?

Yomi Ayeni: I would love to see a project that actively sets out to instigate positive impact and dedicates resources to documenting the process by using all the respective transmedia techniques and tools available. This would be the creation of a living success story that can be shared freely with the whole world. Wouldn't that be a great example?

Caitlin Burns: Transmedia is already used for social good and has been for decades! I love banging this drum. Some of the biggest influences on the way that I approach themes and messages come from purpose-oriented work, like the work done by PCI Media and other projects by UNICEF. PCI Media Impact has worked primarily on educational telenovelas and radio novellas, where public health messages or prosocial messages about how to apply for adult education are interwoven into storylines in classic media formats. They've had characters say lines like, "If you don't wash your hands before cooking, more than rice gets in your rice," and observed drops in infectious disease rates of up to 30 percent immediately following episodes' airings. Often, we trust characters differently than we trust the people around us—an interesting and somewhat troubling fact. Hearing a message from a familiar character, even if a family member says it all the time, has a different impact; it influences what we think people outside our direct circle think, and we change our behaviors according to that perceived social pressure.

Other programs, like UNICEF Kid to Kid Radio projects, teach kids all over the world the basics of project management, journalism, and leadership by funding radio shows written and presented by kids. One such show, on Radio Xai-Xai in Mozambique, is the only media in the Changana language, and the twelve-to-fourteen-year-old presenters report the news in Portuguese, Chopi, and Changaga languages each week. (You can stream shows from Radio Xai-Xai online.) There's not a huge difference, in my mind, creatively between developing intentionally helpful messages and developing powerful themes that underpin a major fictional storyline. The themes and character motivations that resonate are always ones that help the audience reach further, want to and believe that they can do more than before they engaged with the experience, and give the audience something substantial as a gift they can take away after they're through.

Katherine Buse and Ranjodh Singh Dhaliwal: The pleasure of transmedia is the process of making connections across media—realizing that a new way of seeing is actually a way of seeing something that you've seen before, but transformed. Audiences or participants feel a sense of ownership, insight, and meaning through the discovery of (even fictional) truths. In our chapter, we talked about how the history of science is riddled with discoveries made through new ways of seeing and mediating the world, meaning that science in some ways shares the structure of transmedia. However, in the real world, the process of discovery is not guaranteed, and worse yet, even after a discovery is made, a context to support and give meaning to that new way of seeing has to be built. In other words, knowledge production is more painful, boring, confusing, conflicting, and risky than most entertainment media can sustain. However: insofar as transmedia is able to train habits in its audiences and participants, it has the capacity to simulate, model, and therefore encourage real-world processes of discovery, and real-world practices of holding a reality in common, despite our differences. For this reason, we advocate for future transmedia projects that reward the patience, critical thinking, care, and epistemological honesty of their participants by refusing to create closed, comprehensible, or even *intact* worlds to be experienced. After all, the world itself is already broken, and art imitates life. So, as N. K. Jemisin writes in her novel *The Fifth Season*, "Let's start with the end of the world, why don't we? Get it over with and move on to more interesting things."

Denis Butkus: One of the primary actions of transmedia as a process of creation is disruption and interruption. It is a potent tool. It undoes the always asphyxiating frameworks of exclusive mastery, siloed artistic division, and exalted masterpiece benchmarking. In so doing it acknowledges plurality; it recognizes the migration of bodies, imaginations; and it celebrates the intermediacy of artistic form. It further reaffirms that the most potent artistic meeting of the moment is innovation—constant and committed innovation. And in so doing, it can continuously and methodically interrogate systems of power.

What we ask of our audience is to participate by being the continuity, by inventing the narrative. We use media as a bridge—it connects, it challenges, and it informs. It is our materiel, molded from a chorus of voices and perspectives. Transmedia projects have the unique ability to reach an exceptionally wide audience "where they're at," which is to say, a platform-agnostic message/project can be shared much wider when it exists in multiple media. Movies, TikTok, music, flyers, and mailers—all of these have specific audiences, and when we can engage with all platforms, independently and interdependently, within a single project, we can engage with a wider swath of the population, hopefully bringing people together and inspiring unity across platforms.

Dilman Dila: Transmedia has the potential to engage in diverse storytelling. The biggest criticism of mainstream media is their narrow focus on one set of people, but when you have transmedia projects, it is possible to have the same story told in multiple versions, with each version appealing to a particular category of people. Very much like in choose-your-own-adventure kind of games where the player decides the age, sex, gender, race, and all that, of the main character, transmedia has the potential to create stories that appeal to everyone and that everyone can easily relate to.

Lee Emrich: I think a lot of transmedia storytellers already create positive social change; what I'd like to see is more institutional investment in transmedia storytelling for pedagogical purposes. I felt a bit more on my own doing this sort of work, and I think a positive change, not necessarily using the logics of transmedia storytelling, but educating educators more about them, would be great! I would be interested in working on such a project.

Paweł Frelik: There is really no more pressing issue than the ongoing climate crisis, which spells the irrevocable end of the lifestyle that a portion of the global population has led for the last half a century. The current Anthropocenic condition has multiple and entangled consequences and complexities, but we do know that these consequences are not distributed evenly across the globe, or even within individual countries. A transmedia project that somehow directs attention to communities that have suffered the brunt of the ongoing changes but, at the same time, have remained invisible could, thanks to its multiplatform nature, help raise awareness of the plight of people already suffering from climate-related consequences. Needless to say, there is a certain irony in the fact that the ever-increasing use of energy-intensive media has centrally contributed to the Anthropocenic condition. Consequently, such a project could also, on a meta-level, serve as an example of responsible transmedia design that achieves its goals without multiplying media platforms and nodes for the sake of its mere spread.

Terra Gasque: I've mentioned transmedia for climate change and psychology before. I think for climate change, it would help show how the world's climate is changing in lots of small (and large) and deeply interconnected ways, and the effects that these changes are having on its inhabitants (human, animal, plant, etc.).

For psychology, transmedia can help show how we experience the world in ways that deviate from the broadly accepted norms. For example, a transmedia landscape of a posttraumatic stress case might be dominated by one single event or "experience."

Camillia Matuk: The fact that transmedia affords varied ways of communicating and engaging with content can itself be a way to serve a broader social good because it can include diverse perspectives on social issues, and so allow people to move forward on issues with empathy for others.

In terms of guiding learners to use transmedia for social good, I think it will be key to figure out how to dissuade creators from apocalyptic-oriented thinking, and instead use transmedia to uplift communities. For example, transmedia creators might reimagine social situations in light of assets, resources, and aspirations that exist in particular communities. I can see this being a challenge, but it may help to promote good examples of how to do this successfully. The apocalyptic examples just seem so much more common in popular culture.

Ioana Mischie: I feel our societies could be truly upgraded if they would embrace more transmedia methodologies, seeing each institution and discipline as a platform that can be interconnected instead of isolated. How would our schools look like if transmedialized? How would our hospitals look like if transmedialized? Perhaps art forms shouldn't be displayed only in museums, but also in institutions where they could become life-changing.

Before thinking of an entire society or set of institutions, let's start with each individual. Each of us, humans, is the result of millennia of existence. We can easily perceive one another as elevated transmedia biological platforms. Our great-great-grandparents lived to pass on their essence to us. The key question is: what legacy are we going to create for the next generation of humans?

Kirsten Ostherr: I hope that I described one such future project in my chapter. I believe that transmedia projects are necessary for a democratization of medicine, as a means of destabilizing paternalistic hierarchies. I think that the play, the joy, and the sense of experimentation that are possible in transmedia are vital to projects that seek to express new forms of hope for the future—in social movements, in political cultures, even in education. If we could reimagine our K–12 public schools as transmedia labs where kids learn through storytelling, that would give me hope for the future.

Zoyander Street: I hope my chapter describes the potential that I see in the logics of transmedia. I think these logics are becoming the dominant mode of reading all media in general, so working with them should allow us to tell persuasive stories in a way that is congruent with our current media landscape.

Ruth Wylie and Ed Finn: One arena where transmedia could have a significant positive impact is in mobilizing collective action around the climate crisis. Because climate change is so complex and broadly distributed, it can be difficult to capture in a single medium or narrative; transmedia offers a valuable toolkit for telling this sprawling, protean story across many different venues, formats, and audiences. This could be a powerful way to inspire local and community imagination around climate, inviting groups around the world to imagine their own positive climate futures, and also to include more diverse audiences by working with media that can reach many different populations with varying commitments, learning styles, and motivations to engage.

Maureen McHugh Yeager: Internet communities are already creating spaces where, for example, LGBTQIA+teens can find safe spaces to explore their identity and talk with peers. Transmedia is a new way of experiencing things, different from books and video in that it's interactive and community-based. But our lives are already interactive and social—transmedia is compelling because, more than most ways to deliver information, it reflects the way that we experience the world. We are social animals. We enjoy doing much more than we enjoy observing, and we learn better when we do rather than just observe. Transmedia has the potential to let us experience more, faster, and better. And at its best, it's really fun.

We are pretty adaptive animals, and it's natural for us to adopt and refine new behaviors. My belief is that we'll get less naive as we grow more accustomed to the internet, and we'll get better at deciding what is, for example, credible or moral, and what is not. There is a lot to be said for the singular experience of learning from a book, of feeling that I am receiving this information from a particular person, the author. But transmedia makes it possible to engage with the world in a group, with other people wrestling with and experiencing what I'm experiencing, and allowing me to have the same kind of engagement I have in the world, where I talk about things with the people I work with, study with, go to church with, and where part of the pleasure of the whole experience is the way it is broadened by social connection. At the end of the day, we are small-group primates who want to spend at least some of our time with others. Now we can reach across the world. My group of online friends includes people from Europe and South Asia, people in the Middle East, and of course, North America. When before in history was that possible?

Index